Practical Bootstrap

Learn to Develop Responsively with One of the Most Popular CSS Frameworks

Panos Matsinopoulos

Apress®

Practical Bootstrap: Learn to Develop Responsively with One of the Most Popular CSS Frameworks

Panos Matsinopoulos
KERATEA, Greece

ISBN-13 (pbk): 978-1-4842-6070-8   ISBN-13 (electronic): 978-1-4842-6071-5
https://doi.org/10.1007/978-1-4842-6071-5

Managing Director, Apress Media LLC: Welmoed Spahr
Acquisitions Editor: Louise Corrigan
Development Editor: James Markham
Coordinating Editor: Nancy Chen

Cover designed by eStudioCalamar

Cover image designed by Freepik (www.freepik.com)

Distributed to the book trade worldwide by Springer Science+Business Media New York, 1 New York Plaza, New York, NY 10004. Phone 1-800-SPRINGER, fax (201) 348-4505, e-mail orders-ny@springer-sbm.com, or visit www.springeronline.com. Apress Media, LLC is a California LLC and the sole member (owner) is Springer Science + Business Media Finance Inc (SSBM Finance Inc). SSBM Finance Inc is a **Delaware** corporation.

For information on translations, please e-mail booktranslations@springernature.com; for reprint, paperback, or audio rights, please e-mail bookpermissions@springernature.com.

Apress titles may be purchased in bulk for academic, corporate, or promotional use. eBook versions and licenses are also available for most titles. For more information, reference our Print and eBook Bulk Sales web page at http://www.apress.com/bulk-sales.

Any source code or other supplementary material referenced by the author in this book is available to readers on GitHub via the book's product page, located at www.apress.com/9781484260708. For more detailed information, please visit http://www.apress.com/source-code.

Printed on acid-free paper

Dedicated to my wife, Matina

Table of Contents

About the Author

Panos Matsinopoulos loves developing programs, both for web browsers and for mobile apps. He has been doing that for the last 25 years and has developed numerous applications. He also loves writing books, blogging, and teaching computer programming. He has organized a lot of programming classes for kids, adults, and elderly people. You can read more about him on his LinkedIn profile (www.linkedin.com/in/panayotismatsinopoulos) and find him on Twitter (@pmatsino).

About the Technical Reviewer

Alexander Chinedu Nnakwue has a background in mechanical engineering from the University of Ibadan, Nigeria, and has been a front-end developer for over 3 years working on both web and mobile technologies. He also has experience as a technical author, writer, and reviewer. He enjoys programming for the Web, and occasionally, you can also find him playing soccer. He was born in Benin City and is currently based in Lagos, Nigeria.

Introduction

Designing your website or web application to offer great experience for the user when they are on a mobile device is a very big challenge. Not only that, you want them to enjoy the same awesome experience no matter what is the size of the display they are using.

Don't worry! You are in good hands. Twitter Bootstrap has done the work for you. It is the CSS framework that gives you all the tools to develop an HTML page that works well on any display size—from iPhone 6 to iPhone X and to iPads and to large and extralarge displays. It has been engineered on top of the latest CSS tools and techniques, like flexbox, and works on the majority of the browsers on any device.

However, for those who haven't worked before with any CSS framework like this, their official documentation, which works more like a reference, might be intimidating, which leads you to this book here. You are going to learn Twitter Bootstrap using practical examples, instead of reading long reference pages with API details. Hence, you are going to be productive very quickly. You will get confidence, and you will apply it to your daily work and projects much sooner than just reading the official documentation. Official documentation is excellent reference, but this book here will put you up to speed much earlier.

Audience

This book is aimed at web developers in the front-end layer of the stack. It assumes that you have a good knowledge of HTML, CSS, and JavaScript. Also, you need to know jQuery, since it is the JavaScript library Twitter Bootstrap relies on.

Contents of This Book

- Chapter 1, "Getting Started": This chapter introduces you to Twitter Bootstrap and the grid system.

- Chapter 2, "Advanced Grid Techniques": This chapter brings you in contact with some more advanced features of the Bootstrap grid.

- Chapter 3, "Target Project 1": This chapter allows you to learn about navigation bars by building your first Twitter Bootstrap project.

- Chapter 4, "Theme Reference: Part 1": In this chapter, you build a long page with various Twitter Bootstrap components, like buttons, tables, and badges.

- Chapter 5, "Theme Reference: Part 2": This is the continuation of the previous chapter, with more Bootstrap components to build in the Theme Reference project.

- Chapter 6, "Cover Page Project": In this chapter, you implement a page which has a background image as cover and content centered in the middle.

- Chapter 7, "Admin Dashboard": In this chapter, you implement an administrator dashboard with left-side navigation bar, images, and tables.

- Chapter 8, "Forms": In this chapter, you implement a page with various Twitter Bootstrap forms.

- Chapter 9, "Modal Dialogs": In this chapter, you learn how to implement modal dialogs, a very popular UX component.

- Chapter 10, "ScrollSpy": In this chapter, you learn how to follow the user and highlight the correct menu item in the navigation bar, using ScrollSpy.

- Chapter 11, "Tooltips and Popovers": Finally, you learn about tooltips and popovers, which are very useful UX components in conveying extra information to the user.

Conventions Used in This Book

This book has the following typographical conventions:

`Constant width`

This is mainly used in code snippets and listings and to indicate variables, functions, types, parameters, objects, and other programming, coding-related constructs.

Constant width in Bold

It is used inside code snippets and listings to indicate the code parts that you need to pay more attention to.

$

The symbol $ is used to denote an Operating System shell prompt, that is, where you should type a command that will be executed by your Operating System. For example, if you work with a Mac OS, you can open a terminal and type the command that follows this symbol.

Using Code Listings

All the code listings of this book are available for download at `https://github.com/Apress/practical-bootstrap`.

CHAPTER 1

Getting Started

Creating responsive websites and applications is becoming a hard requirement now that many people have started using mobile phones and tablets. Twitter Bootstrap is here to give you all the necessary tools, so that the work you create is equally well viewed on various display sizes.

This chapter starts with the basics of Twitter Bootstrap, mainly its grid system.

You will learn about the 12-column grid system, so that you can divide your page in multiple rows and columns. Figure 1-1 shows an example of the Twitter Bootstrap grid system.

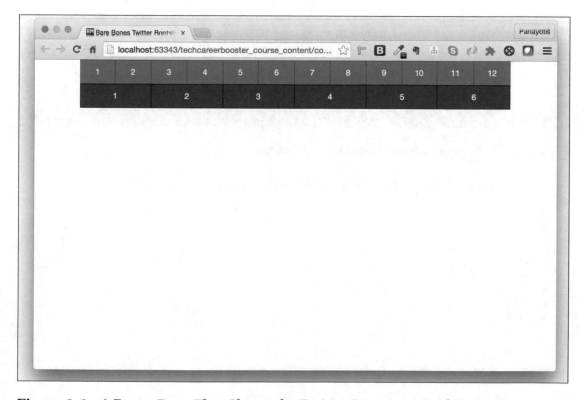

Figure 1-1. *A Demo Page That Shows the Twitter Bootstrap Grid System*

© Panos Matsinopoulos 2020
P. Matsinopoulos, *Practical Bootstrap*, https://doi.org/10.1007/978-1-4842-6071-5_1

You will make sure that you have a page as shown in Figure 1-2.

Figure 1-2. *Page as Viewed on Large Displays*

It can automatically be transformed to look like Figure 1-3 on smaller devices.

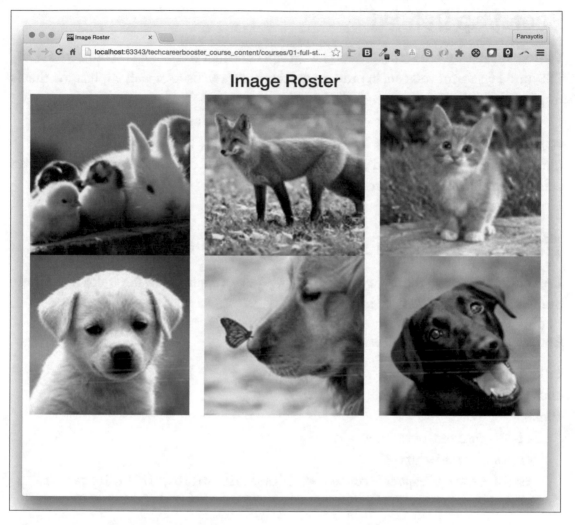

Figure 1-3. *Page Adapts Its Layout on Smaller Devices*

Learning Goals

1. Learn what Twitter Bootstrap is.

2. Learn how to include Twitter Bootstrap CSS and JavaScript libraries in your project.

3. Learn about the two main containers available and their differences.

4. Learn about how the grid system of Twitter Bootstrap can help you organize the content of your page and generate a responsive layout.

Bootstrap Defined

Twitter Bootstrap is a set of CSS and JavaScript code that you can base your own HTML, CSS, and JavaScript code on, in order to quickly have a website or web application that is responsive, with a mobile-first design approach.

In other words, it provides you with some CSS classes and JavaScript code that you can just go and use. You apply the classes, and you use the JavaScript modules and quickly have your website and your web application have features that would have taken you a lot of effort to develop from scratch.

The Bare-Bones Twitter Bootstrap Page

Let's start by creating the first Twitter Bootstrap page. Create a new file index.html and put the following content inside (Listing 1-1).

Listing 1-1. Bare-Bones Twitter Bootstrap Page

```
<!DOCTYPE html>
<html lang="en">
<head>
    <!-- Required meta tags -->
    <meta charset="utf-8">
    <meta name="viewport" content="width=device-width, initial-scale=1,
    shrink-to-fit=no">

    <!-- Bootstrap CSS -->
    <link rel="stylesheet" href="https://stackpath.bootstrapcdn.
    com/bootstrap/4.4.1/css/bootstrap.min.css" integrity="sha384-
    Vkoo8x4CGsO3+Hhxv8T/Q5PaXtkKtu6ug5TOeNV6gBiFeWPGFN9MuhOf23Q9Ifjh"
    crossorigin="anonymous">

    <title>Bare Bones Twitter Bootstrap Page</title>
</head>
<body>
    <!-- Optional JavaScript -->
    <!-- jQuery first, then Popper.js, then Bootstrap JS -->
```

```
<script src="https://code.jquery.com/jquery-3.4.1.slim.min.js"
integrity="sha384-J6qa4849blE2+poT4WnyKhv5vZF5SrPo0iEjwBvKU7imGFAVOwwj1
yYfoRSJoZ+n" crossorigin="anonymous"></script>
<script src="https://cdn.jsdelivr.net/npm/popper.js@1.16.0/dist/umd/
popper.min.js" integrity="sha384-Q6E9RHvbIyZFJoft+2mJbHaEWldlvI9IOYy5n3
zV9zzTtmI3UksdQRVvoxMfooAo" crossorigin="anonymous"></script>
<script src="https://stackpath.bootstrapcdn.com/bootstrap/4.4.1/js/
bootstrap.min.js" integrity="sha384-wfSDF2E50Y2D1uUdj0O3uMBJnjuUD4Ih7Yw
aYd1iqfktj0Uod8GCExl3Og8ifwB6" crossorigin="anonymous"></script>
</body>
</html>
```

This is a page that does not have any valuable content. Its body element is empty. However

1. It references the Bootstrap CSS library.

2. It references the jQuery library, which is a JavaScript library necessary for Twitter Bootstrap JavaScript modules.

3. It references the popper library. This is a JavaScript library that Bootstrap is using to position tooltips and popovers.

4. Finally, it references the Bootstrap JavaScript library too.

If you load the preceding page on your browser, you will see nothing. But all the Twitter Bootstrap features would be loaded.

Containers

When you start your page layout, you need to decide on the container style that would include your page content. There are three types of containers:

1. container, which sets a max-width at each responsive breakpoint.

2. container-fluid, which is width: 100% at all breakpoints.

3. container-{breakpoint}, which is width: 100% until the specified breakpoint. After the specified breakpoint (including), it uses the max-width as if it were a container.

Note   max-width defines the maximum width an element can have. This means that the element tries to occupy as much width as possible up to the max-width after which it expands its height in order to fit the content. This of course means that the actual width of the element cannot be more than max-width, even if the width property may have a larger value.

Tip   Twitter Bootstrap defines five breakpoints, that is, pixel widths, after which the grid layout changes. For example, a small breakpoint has the value 576px and is referring to displays with width between 576px and 767px. I will talk about breakpoints later on in this chapter.

You apply one of them by setting the corresponding div element (or equivalent block element) to have a class equal to the name of the container.

Enhance the content of your page so that it is like the following (in bold, you see the code that has been added - Listing 1-2).

Listing 1-2. Add Two Containers

```
<!DOCTYPE html>
<html lang="en">
<head>
    <!-- Required meta tags -->
    <meta charset="utf-8">
    <meta name="viewport" content="width=device-width, initial-scale=1,
    shrink-to-fit=no">

    <!-- Bootstrap CSS -->
    <link rel="stylesheet" href="https://stackpath.bootstrapcdn.
    com/bootstrap/4.4.1/css/bootstrap.min.css" integrity="sha384-
    Vkoo8x4CGsO3+Hhxv8T/Q5PaXtkKtu6ug5TOeNV6gBiFeWPGFN9MuhOf23Q9Ifjh"
    crossorigin="anonymous">
```

```
<!-- Custom CSS -->
<link rel="stylesheet" href="stylesheets/index.css" type="text/css">

<title>Bare Bones Twitter Bootstrap Page</title>
</head>
<body>
    <div class="container">
        This is a container
    </div>
    <div class="container-fluid">
        This is a container fluid
    </div>

    <!-- Optional JavaScript -->
    <!-- jQuery first, then Popper.js, then Bootstrap JS -->
    <script src="https://code.jquery.com/jquery-3.4.1.slim.min.js"
    integrity="sha384-J6qa4849blE2+poT4WnyKhv5vZF5SrPo0iEjwBvKU7imGFAVOwwj1
    yYfoRSJoZ+n" crossorigin="anonymous"></script>
    <script src="https://cdn.jsdelivr.net/npm/popper.js@1.16.0/dist/umd/
    popper.min.js" integrity="sha384-Q6E9RHvbIyZFJoft+2mJbHaEWldlvI9IOYy5n3
    zV9zzTtmI3UksdQRVvoxMfooAo" crossorigin="anonymous"></script>
    <script src="https://stackpath.bootstrapcdn.com/bootstrap/4.4.1/js/
    bootstrap.min.js" integrity="sha384-wfSDF2E50Y2D1uUdjOO3uMBJnjuUD4Ih7Yw
    aYd1iqfktjOUod8GCExl3Og8ifwB6" crossorigin="anonymous"></script>
</body>
</html>
```

1. I have added a reference to a local CSS file named `stylesheets/index.css`. I have put that exactly after the Twitter Bootstrap CSS reference. I will put inside this file the web page–specific CSS rules. This file needs to be after the Twitter Bootstrap CSS reference, because it will be relying on it.

2. I have created two `div`s that would function as the page containers. The first `div` is a `container`, whereas the second `div` is a `container-fluid`.

   Create the file `index.css` inside the folder `stylesheets` and add the following content (Listing 1-3).

Listing 1-3. CSS for the index.css File

```
.container {
    background-color: #8DC5CC;
}

.container-fluid {
    background-color: #aaad21;
}
```

Caution   Now that you are using Twitter Bootstrap, you will not need to write CSS reset rules like `* {box-sizing: border-box}`. This is because Twitter Bootstrap itself has a series of defaults that make very good sense, and they are aligned with the rest of the Twitter Bootstrap classes.

As you can imagine, this is used to apply specific, different colors to the two containers so that I can see how they are put on the page.

Save all files and load the `index.html` page on your browser. What you will see should be something like Figure 1-4.

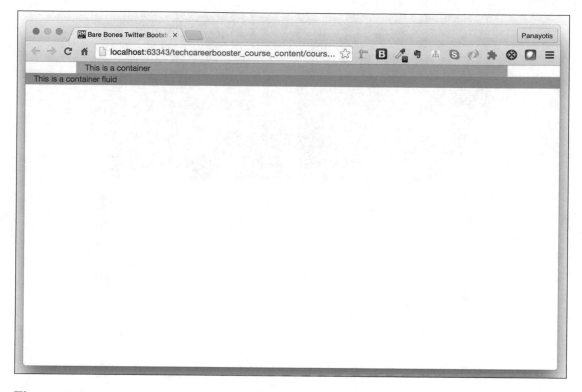

Figure 1-4. *container vs. container-fluid*

As you can see in Figure 1-4, the container has left and right margins, whereas the container-fluid does not have margins and covers the whole width of the page. container margins are not of fixed width. Their width changes depending on the viewport width.

On the other hand, both containers have left and right paddings, equal to 15px. You can see that the text "This is a container …" does not start at the edge of the left border, but it has some free blank space.

Note that even if you use a container, when you shrink the width of your browser window, so that it becomes less than 576px wide, the container loses its left and right margins and, essentially, behaves like the container-fluid. In other words, this page on an Apple iPhone X device would be displayed like what you see in Figure 1-5.

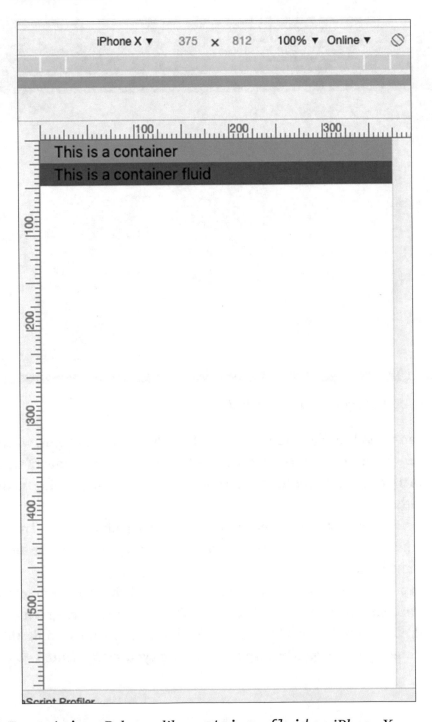

Figure 1-5. *container Behaves like* `container-fluid` *on iPhone X*

Hence, `container` and `container-fluid` in that case would be the same.

Grid System

The grid system, that is, dividing your layout into rows and columns, is a good practice to design the layout of your page. Twitter Bootstrap comes with handy classes that will allow you to scale your layout up to 12 columns, as the device or viewport size increases.

Hence, whenever you want to divide your page into a series of columns, you have to

1. Decide on the container type.

2. Inside the container, add a row class div.

3. Inside the row class div, add one or more col-* class div elements.

I will explain what a col-* class is using some examples.

Example: One Row with 12 Columns

Let's create a page with a one-row and 12-column layout as in Figure 1-6.

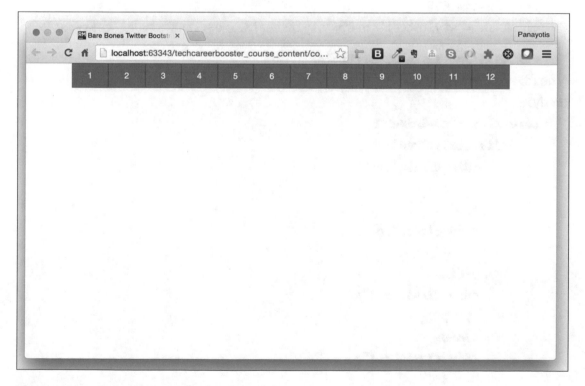

Figure 1-6. *One-Row 12-Column Grid*

One way you can create this page is shown in the following (Listing 1-4).

Listing 1-4. One-Row 12-Column Page

```
<!DOCTYPE html>
<html lang="en">
<head>
    <!-- Required meta tags -->
    <meta charset="utf-8">
    <meta name="viewport" content="width=device-width, initial-scale=1,
    shrink-to-fit=no">

    <!-- Bootstrap CSS -->
    <link rel="stylesheet" href="https://stackpath.bootstrapcdn.
    com/bootstrap/4.4.1/css/bootstrap.min.css" integrity="sha384-
    Vkoo8x4CGsO3+Hhxv8T/Q5PaXtkKtu6ug5TOeNV6gBiFeWPGFN9MuhOf23Q9Ifjh"
    crossorigin="anonymous">

    <!-- Custom CSS -->
    <link rel="stylesheet" href="stylesheets/index.css" type="text/css">

    <title>1 row 12 columns</title>
</head>
<body>
    <div class="container">
        <div class="row">
            <div class="col">
                1
            </div>
            <div class="col">
                2
            </div>
            <div class="col">
                3
            </div>
            <div class="col">
                4
            </div>
```

```
        <div class="col">
            5
        </div>
        <div class="col">
            6
        </div>
        <div class="col">
            7
        </div>
        <div class="col">
            8
        </div>
        <div class="col">
            9
        </div>
        <div class="col">
            10
        </div>
        <div class="col">
            11
        </div>
        <div class="col">
            12
        </div>
    </div>
</div>

<!-- Optional JavaScript -->
<!-- jQuery first, then Popper.js, then Bootstrap JS -->
<script src="https://code.jquery.com/jquery-3.4.1.slim.min.js"
integrity="sha384-J6qa4849blE2+poT4WnyKhv5vZF5SrPo0iEjwBvKU7imGFAVOwwj1
yYfoRSJoZ+n" crossorigin="anonymous"></script>
<script src="https://cdn.jsdelivr.net/npm/popper.js@1.16.0/dist/umd/
popper.min.js" integrity="sha384-Q6E9RHvbIyZFJoft+2mJbHaEWldlvI9IOYy5n3
zV9zzTtmI3UksdQRVvoxMfooAo" crossorigin="anonymous"></script>
```

```
<script src="https://stackpath.bootstrapcdn.com/bootstrap/4.4.1/js/
bootstrap.min.js" integrity="sha384-wfSDF2E50Y2D1uUdjOO3uMBJnjuUD4Ih7Yw
aYd1iqfktjOUod8GCExl3Og8ifwB6" crossorigin="anonymous"></script>
</body>
</html>
```

The CSS file (named `index.css`) is given in Listing 1-5.

Listing 1-5. CSS for the One-Row 12-Column Layout

```
.container {
    background-color: #8DC5CC;
}

.container .row div {
    background-color: #4e9013;
    padding: 10px 0;
    border: 1px solid green;
    color: white;
    text-align: center;
}
```

As you can see in the HTML file, `index.html`, I have used a `container` and inside it I have introduced a `row` class `div`. Then for each one of the 12 columns, I have used a `col` class `div`.

Again, I wanted 12 columns, and I added 12 `divs` with class `col`. All 12 `divs` have been added inside a single `row  div`. The `row  div` is used to lay out columns, and only columns can be immediate children of rows.

Example: Two-Row Grid, the Second with Six Columns

Let's add one more row to our grid page. But this time, let's assume that we want six columns on the second row, as in Figure 1-7.

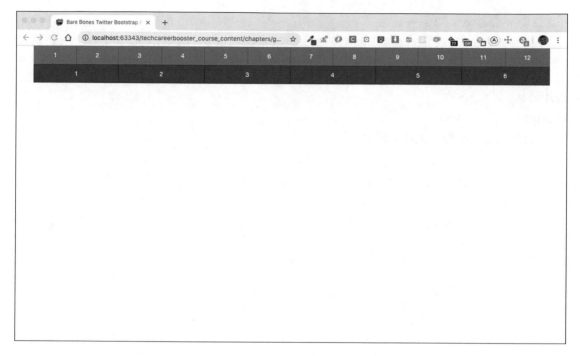

Figure 1-7. *Two Rows, the Second Row with Six Columns*

As you can see in Figure 1-7, each one of the columns of the second row occupies double the column width of the columns of the first row.

The full HTML code is in Listing 1-6.

Listing 1-6. Two Rows, the Second Row Having Six Columns, HTML Code

```
<!DOCTYPE html>
<html lang="en">
<head>
    <!-- Required meta tags -->
    <meta charset="utf-8">
    <meta name="viewport" content="width=device-width, initial-scale=1,
    shrink-to-fit=no">

    <!-- Bootstrap CSS -->
    <link rel="stylesheet" href="https://stackpath.bootstrapcdn.
    com/bootstrap/4.4.1/css/bootstrap.min.css" integrity="sha384-
    Vkoo8x4CGsO3+Hhxv8T/Q5PaXtkKtu6ug5TOeNV6gBiFeWPGFN9MuhOf23Q9Ifjh"
    crossorigin="anonymous">
```

```
    <!-- Custom CSS -->
    <link rel="stylesheet" href="stylesheets/index.css" type="text/css">

    <title>2 rows 2nd 6 columns</title>
</head>
<body>
    <div class="container">
        <div class="row">
            <div class="col">
                1
            </div>
            <div class="col">
                2
            </div>
            <div class="col">
                3
            </div>
            <div class="col">
                4
            </div>
            <div class="col">
                5
            </div>
            <div class="col">
                6
            </div>
            <div class="col">
                7
            </div>
            <div class="col">
                8
            </div>
            <div class="col">
                9
            </div>
            <div class="col">
```

```
                10
            </div>
            <div class="col">
                11
            </div>
            <div class="col">
                12
            </div>
        </div>
        <div class="row">
            <div class="col">
                1
            </div>
            <div class="col">
                2
            </div>
            <div class="col">
                3
            </div>
            <div class="col">
                4
            </div>
            <div class="col">
                5
            </div>
            <div class="col">
                6
            </div>
        </div>
</div>

<!-- Optional JavaScript -->
<!-- jQuery first, then Popper.js, then Bootstrap JS -->
<script src="https://code.jquery.com/jquery-3.4.1.slim.min.js"
integrity="sha384-J6qa4849blE2+poT4WnyKhv5vZF5SrPo0iEjwBvKU7imGFAVOwwj1
yYfoRSJoZ+n" crossorigin="anonymous"></script>
```

```
        <script src="https://cdn.jsdelivr.net/npm/popper.js@1.16.0/dist/umd/
        popper.min.js" integrity="sha384-Q6E9RHvbIyZFJoft+2mJbHaEWldlvI9IOYy5n3
        zV9zzTtmI3UksdQRVvoxMfooAo" crossorigin="anonymous"></script>
        <script src="https://stackpath.bootstrapcdn.com/bootstrap/4.4.1/js/
        bootstrap.min.js" integrity="sha384-wfSDF2E50Y2D1uUdjOO3uMBJnjuUD4Ih7Yw
        aYd1iqfktjOUod8GCExl3Og8ifwB6" crossorigin="anonymous"></script>
</body>
</html>
```

Listing 1-7 is the full CSS code (which is not critical to the creation of the grid, but it is only there to help me visualize the columns of the rows of the grid on my page).

Listing 1-7. CSS for the Page Having Two Rows, the Second Row Having Six Columns

```
.container {
    background-color: #8DC5CC;
}

.container .row:nth-of-type(1) div {
    background-color: #4e9013;
    padding: 10px 0;
    border: 1px solid green;
    color: white;
    text-align: center;
}

.container .row:nth-of-type(2) div {
    background-color: #902e07;
    padding: 10px 0;
    border: 1px solid #441180;
    color: white;
    text-align: center;
}
```

As you can see, it is very easy to have six columns by only having six divs with class col as children of the div with class row.

Example: Two-Row Grid, the Second with Five Columns

Let's say that you want one row to have five columns, instead of six, with the first column being double the size of the others. For example, see Figure 1-8.

Figure 1-8. *Second Row Having Five Columns, First Column Being Wider*

How would you do that? If you just changed your code to have five divs, inside the second `row div`, what would you get? You would get the page on Figure 1-9.

Figure 1-9. *Second Row Having Five Columns of Equal Size*

This is not exactly what you want. If you just put five divs, the columns generated have equal width. But what you want is the first column to be double the width of the others. Also, if you look more carefully, you will see that the first column occupies four out of the 12 available standard columns, whereas the other columns occupy two. Again, this is what you want to achieve (Figure 1-10).

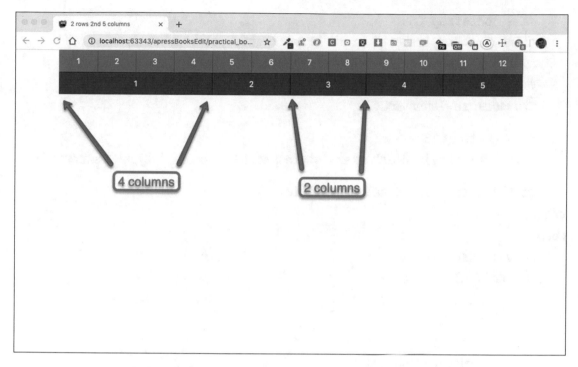

Figure 1-10. *What You Want to Achieve*

In order to do that, you have to be more precise on the class of each column div. You have to tell exactly how many standard columns each column should occupy.

Hence, for the first column, you have to use the class col-4, whereas for the other columns, you have to use the class col-2. The correct HTML code is in Listing 1-8.

Listing 1-8. Using col-4 for the First Column and col-2 for the Others

```
<!DOCTYPE html>
<html lang="en">
<head>
    <!-- Required meta tags -->
    <meta charset="utf-8">
    <meta name="viewport" content="width=device-width, initial-scale=1,
    shrink-to-fit=no">
```

```
<!-- Bootstrap CSS -->
<link rel="stylesheet" href="https://stackpath.bootstrapcdn.
com/bootstrap/4.4.1/css/bootstrap.min.css" integrity="sha384-
Vkoo8x4CGsO3+Hhxv8T/Q5PaXtkKtu6ug5TOeNV6gBiFeWPGFN9MuhOf23Q9Ifjh"
crossorigin="anonymous">

<!-- Custom CSS -->
<link rel="stylesheet" href="stylesheets/index.css" type="text/css">

<title>2 rows 2nd 5 columns</title>
</head>
<body>
    <div class="container">
        <div class="row">
            <div class="col">
                1
            </div>
            <div class="col">
                2
            </div>
            <div class="col">
                3
            </div>
            <div class="col">
                4
            </div>
            <div class="col">
                5
            </div>
            <div class="col">
                6
            </div>
            <div class="col">
                7
            </div>
            <div class="col">
                8
```

```
        </div>
        <div class="col">
            9
        </div>
        <div class="col">
            10
        </div>
        <div class="col">
            11
        </div>
        <div class="col">
            12
        </div>
    </div>
    <div class="row">
        <div class="col-4">
            1
        </div>
        <div class="col-2">
            2
        </div>
        <div class="col-2">
            3
        </div>
        <div class="col-2">
            4
        </div>
        <div class="col-2">
            5
        </div>
    </div>
</div>

<!-- Optional JavaScript -->
<!-- jQuery first, then Popper.js, then Bootstrap JS -->
```

```
<script src="https://code.jquery.com/jquery-3.4.1.slim.min.js"
integrity="sha384-J6qa4849blE2+poT4WnyKhv5vZF5SrPoOiEjwBvKU7imGFAVOwwj1
yYfoRSJoZ+n" crossorigin="anonymous"></script>
<script src="https://cdn.jsdelivr.net/npm/popper.js@1.16.0/dist/umd/
popper.min.js" integrity="sha384-Q6E9RHvbIyZFJoft+2mJbHaEWldlvI9IOYy5n3
zV9zzTtmI3UksdQRVvoxMfooAo" crossorigin="anonymous"></script>
<script src="https://stackpath.bootstrapcdn.com/bootstrap/4.4.1/js/
bootstrap.min.js" integrity="sha384-wfSDF2E50Y2D1uUdjOO3uMBJnjuUD4Ih7Yw
aYd1iqfktjOUod8GCExl3Og8ifwB6" crossorigin="anonymous"></script>
</body>
</html>
```

Another way you could divide your second row into five columns is shown in Listing 1-9.

Listing 1-9. Another Way to Divide into Five Columns

```
<!DOCTYPE html>
<html lang="en">
<head>
    <!-- Required meta tags -->
    <meta charset="utf-8">
    <meta name="viewport" content="width=device-width, initial-scale=1,
    shrink-to-fit=no">

    <!-- Bootstrap CSS -->
    <link rel="stylesheet" href="https://stackpath.bootstrapcdn.
    com/bootstrap/4.4.1/css/bootstrap.min.css" integrity="sha384-
    Vkoo8x4CGsO3+Hhxv8T/Q5PaXtkKtu6ug5TOeNV6gBiFeWPGFN9MuhOf23Q9Ifjh"
    crossorigin="anonymous">

    <!-- Custom CSS -->
    <link rel="stylesheet" href="stylesheets/index.css" type="text/css">

    <title>2 rows 2nd 5 columns</title>
</head>
```

```
<body>
    <div class="container">
        <div class="row">
            <div class="col">
                1
            </div>
            <div class="col">
                2
            </div>
            <div class="col">
                3
            </div>
            <div class="col">
                4
            </div>
            <div class="col">
                5
            </div>
            <div class="col">
                6
            </div>
            <div class="col">
                7
            </div>
            <div class="col">
                8
            </div>
            <div class="col">
                9
            </div>
            <div class="col">
                10
            </div>
            <div class="col">
                11
            </div>
```

```
                <div class="col">
                    12
                </div>
        </div>
        <div class="row">
            <div class="col-3">
                1
            </div>
            <div class="col-2">
                2
            </div>
            <div class="col-3">
                3
            </div>
            <div class="col-2">
                4
            </div>
            <div class="col-2">
                5
            </div>
        </div>
    </div>

    <!-- Optional JavaScript -->
    <!-- jQuery first, then Popper.js, then Bootstrap JS -->
    <script src="https://code.jquery.com/jquery-3.4.1.slim.min.js"
    integrity="sha384-J6qa4849blE2+poT4WnyKhv5vZF5SrPo0iEjwBvKU7imGFAVOwwj1
    yYfoRSJoZ+n" crossorigin="anonymous"></script>
    <script src="https://cdn.jsdelivr.net/npm/popper.js@1.16.0/dist/umd/
    popper.min.js" integrity="sha384-Q6E9RHvbIyZFJoft+2mJbHaEWldlvI9IOYy5n3
    zV9zzTtmI3UksdQRVvoxMfooAo" crossorigin="anonymous"></script>
    <script src="https://stackpath.bootstrapcdn.com/bootstrap/4.4.1/js/
    bootstrap.min.js" integrity="sha384-wfSDF2E50Y2D1uUdjOO3uMBJnjuUD4Ih7Yw
    aYd1iqfktjOUod8GCExl3Og8ifwB6" crossorigin="anonymous"></script>
</body>
</html>
```

If you save and load this page on your browser, you will see what is depicted in Figure 1-11.

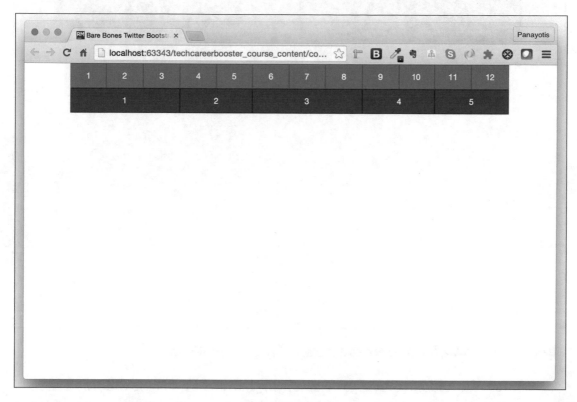

Figure 1-11. *Another Way to Divide into Five Columns*

As you can see in Figure 1-11, the second row is, again, with five columns, but with a different size for the first and third columns. These two are of size 3, whereas all the other columns are of size 2. However, even in this case, the total column sizes add up to 12: 3 + 2 + 3 + 2 + 2.

Example: Two-Row Grid, the Second Having Three Columns, with the Middle Wider

But you don't always have to be precise about the width of all the columns. Sometimes, you want to be specific only about the width of one column, and you want the others to have a width automatically calculated. See, for example, Figure 1-12.

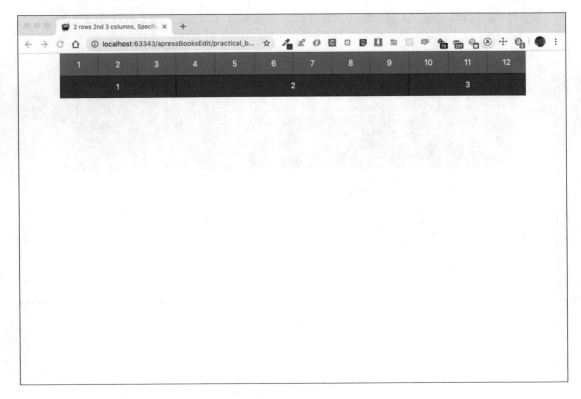

Figure 1-12. *Middle Column to Be Half of Available Width*

You want the middle column to be occupying half of the available width and leave the rest of the space shared between the first and third columns.

You could do that by giving col-3 to the first and third divs and col-6 to the second div, but it appears that you can do that by giving col to the first and third divs and col-6 to the second div, as in Listing 1-10.

Listing 1-10. Specifying the Width of the Middle Column Only

```
<!DOCTYPE html>
<html lang="en">
<head>
    <!-- Required meta tags -->
    <meta charset="utf-8">
    <meta name="viewport" content="width=device-width, initial-scale=1,
    shrink-to-fit=no">
```

```
<!-- Bootstrap CSS -->
<link rel="stylesheet" href="https://stackpath.bootstrapcdn.com/
bootstrap/4.4.1/css/bootstrap.min.css" integrity="sha384-
Vkoo8x4CGsO3+Hhxv8T/Q5PaXtkKtu6ug5TOeNV6gBiFeWPGFN9MuhOf23Q9Ifjh"
crossorigin="anonymous">

<!-- Custom CSS -->
<link rel="stylesheet" href="stylesheets/index.css" type="text/css">

<title>Specifying the width of the middle column only</title>
</head>
<body>
    <div class="container">
        <div class="row">
            <div class="col">
                1
            </div>
            <div class="col">
                2
            </div>
            <div class="col">
                3
            </div>
            <div class="col">
                4
            </div>
            <div class="col">
                5
            </div>
            <div class="col">
                6
            </div>
            <div class="col">
                7
            </div>
```

```
            <div class="col">
                8
            </div>
            <div class="col">
                9
            </div>
            <div class="col">
                10
            </div>
            <div class="col">
                11
            </div>
            <div class="col">
                12
            </div>
        </div>
        <div class="row">
            <div class="col">
                1
            </div>
            <div class="col-6">
                2
            </div>
            <div class="col">
                3
            </div>
        </div>
    </div>

<!-- Optional JavaScript -->
<!-- jQuery first, then Popper.js, then Bootstrap JS -->
<script src="https://code.jquery.com/jquery-3.4.1.slim.min.js"
integrity="sha384-J6qa4849blE2+poT4WnyKhv5vZF5SrPo0iEjwBvKU7imGFAVOwwj1
yYfoRSJoZ+n" crossorigin="anonymous"></script>
```

```
<script src="https://cdn.jsdelivr.net/npm/popper.js@1.16.0/dist/umd/
popper.min.js" integrity="sha384-Q6E9RHvbIyZFJoft+2mJbHaEWldlvI9IOYy5n3
zV9zzTtmI3UksdQRVvoxMfooAo" crossorigin="anonymous"></script>
<script src="https://stackpath.bootstrapcdn.com/bootstrap/4.4.1/js/
bootstrap.min.js" integrity="sha384-wfSDF2E50Y2D1uUdjOO3uMBJnjuUD4Ih7Yw
aYd1iqfktjOUod8GCExl3Og8ifwB6" crossorigin="anonymous"></script>
</body>
</html>
```

Different Display Widths

Twitter Bootstrap allows you to use different classes for your grid layout (and for other properties of your web page style), according to the different display widths that your web page will be displayed on. In particular, there are five key width breakpoints as listed in Table 1-1.

Table 1-1. *Twitter Bootstrap Responsive Breakpoints*

Name	Symbol	Display Width
Extrasmall	xs	<576px
Small	sm	>=576px
Medium	md	>=768px
Large	lg	>=992px
Extralarge	xl	>=1200px

You are referring to them by their corresponding symbol, as part of the class name that you are using.

So, if you are using, for example, the class col-lg-5, this means that this class refers to the breakpoint lg, for devices with width >=992px. However, further interpretation of each particular class depends on the class case itself. We will learn the most important classes in this section.

The Twitter Bootstrap grid classes that work based on the preceding five key breakpoints are

- `col-1`, `col-2`, and so on, up to `col-12`, for the extrasmall devices

- `col-sm-1`, `col-sm-2`, and so on, up to `col-sm-12`, for small devices

- `col-md-1`, `col-md-2`, and so on, up to `col-md-12`, for medium devices

- `col-lg-1`, `col-lg-2`, and so on, up to `col-lg-12`, for large devices

- `col-xl-1`, `col-xl-2`, and so on, up to `col-xl-12`, for extralarge devices

But what is the difference between `col-sm-2` and `col-md-2`, for example?

They both occupy two columns. `col-sm-2` will occupy two columns for any display area width that is >=576px, but `col-md-2` will occupy two columns only for display widths that are >= 768px. `col-md-2`, for display areas that are <768px, will not occupy two columns, but will stack one column above the other, as if they were two rows, essentially each column occupying the whole 12-column available width.

Let's see an example here. You are going to create a page with a row that has six columns, each one occupying two-column width. Write the following code into an HTML document (Listing 1-11).

Listing 1-11. Six Columns with the `sm` Breakpoint

```
<!DOCTYPE html>
<html lang="en">
<head>
    <!-- Required meta tags -->
    <meta charset="utf-8">
    <meta name="viewport" content="width=device-width, initial-scale=1,
    shrink-to-fit=no">

    <!-- Bootstrap CSS -->
    <link rel="stylesheet" href="https://stackpath.bootstrapcdn.
    com/bootstrap/4.4.1/css/bootstrap.min.css" integrity="sha384-
    Vkoo8x4CGsO3+Hhxv8T/Q5PaXtkKtu6ug5TOeNV6gBiFeWPGFN9MuhOf23Q9Ifjh"
    crossorigin="anonymous">
```

```
    <!-- Custom CSS -->
    <link rel="stylesheet" href="stylesheets/index.css" type="text/css">

    <title>Listing 1-11</title>
</head>
<body>
    <div class="container">
        <div class="row">
            <div class="col-sm-2">
                1
            </div>
            <div class="col-sm-2">
                2
            </div>
            <div class="col-sm-2">
                3
            </div>
            <div class="col-sm-2">
                4
            </div>
            <div class="col-sm-2">
                5
            </div>
            <div class="col-sm-2">
                6
            </div>
        </div>
    </div>

    <!-- Optional JavaScript -->
    <!-- jQuery first, then Popper.js, then Bootstrap JS -->
    <script src="https://code.jquery.com/jquery-3.4.1.slim.min.js"
    integrity="sha384-J6qa4849blE2+poT4WnyKhv5vZF5SrPo0iEjwBvKU7imGFAVOwwj1
    yYfoRSJoZ+n" crossorigin="anonymous"></script>
```

```
    <script src="https://cdn.jsdelivr.net/npm/popper.js@1.16.0/dist/umd/
    popper.min.js" integrity="sha384-Q6E9RHvbIyZFJoft+2mJbHaEWldlvI9IOYy5n3
    zV9zzTtmI3UksdQRVvoxMfooAo" crossorigin="anonymous"></script>
    <script src="https://stackpath.bootstrapcdn.com/bootstrap/4.4.1/js/
    bootstrap.min.js" integrity="sha384-wfSDF2E50Y2D1uUdjOO3uMBJnjuUD4Ih7Yw
    aYd1iqfktjOUod8GCExl3Og8ifwB6" crossorigin="anonymous"></script>
</body>
</html>
```

Write the following (Listing 1-12) CSS in the corresponding index.css file inside the stylesheets folder.

Listing 1-12. CSS for Listing 1-11

```css
.container {
    background-color: #8DC5CC;
}

.container .row:nth-of-type(1) div {
    background-color: #4e9013;
    padding: 10px 0;
    border: 1px solid green;
    color: white;
    text-align: center;
}
```

If you save the preceding code and then load the HTML page on your browser, you will see the following (Figure 1-13).

Figure 1-13. *One-Row Six-Column Layout—Each One Occupying Two Columns*

As you can see in the HTML code, I am using the breakpoint sm, and I instruct that each column occupies two of the available 12 columns. This will result in the row being divided into six columns, but only for display areas with width >=576px.

Enable the developer tools and shrink the browser window so that it has width exactly 576px. You will not see any significant difference on how your page is displayed. All six columns will be there, horizontally arranged (Figure 1-14).

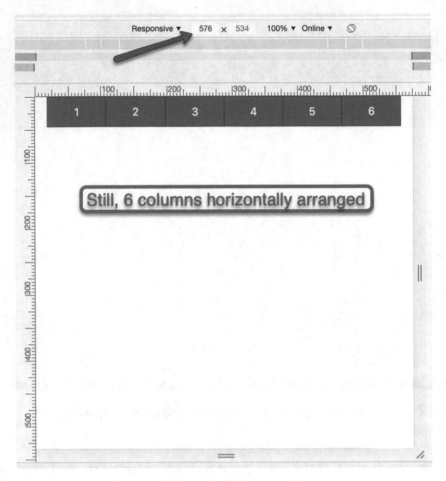

Figure 1-14. *Exactly 576px Width—Still Six Columns in Width*

Things will change when you shrink 1 pixel more, to 575px. You will see the following (Figure 1-15).

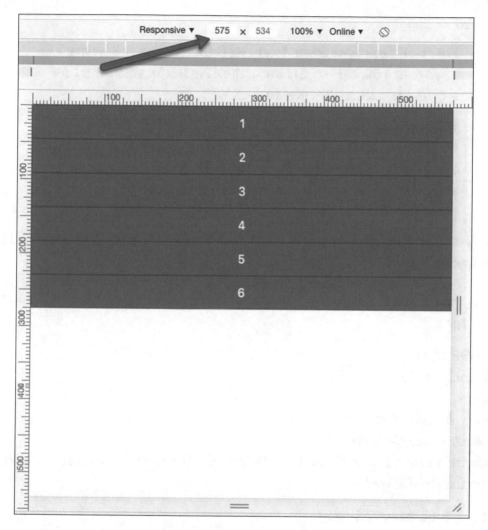

Figure 1-15. *Six Columns Stacked When Below the* sm *Breakpoint*

This happened because I have used the class col-sm-2. Again, this class stacks the columns one on top of the other for each display width less than 576px and keeps the columns horizontal for any width greater than or equal to 576px.

As you can see from the preceding picture, the initially two-column-wide columns are now 12-column-wide, occupying the whole row.

The nice thing with Bootstrap is that you can apply multiple classes of different breakpoints on the same div, in order to adapt the grid layout for different devices.

See the following example in order to understand what I mean. Let's suppose that I want, for small devices and above, to have six columns, but for smaller devices (less than 576px), I do not want one column per row, but two columns per row.

Hence

1. For small devices or larger, I want six columns. This means that I need to use the col-sm-2 class for the divs (sm for small and 2 for six columns, since 12/6 gives 2).

2. For extrasmall devices, I want two columns per row. Hence, I need to use the col-6 class for the divs (for extrasmall, I don't interpolate the symbol of the device width into the class name, since the default value is xs and 6 for two columns, since 12/2 gives 6).

Let's try that. Change the content of the preceding HTML page, in order to be like that in Listing 1-13.

Listing 1-13. Two Columns on Extrasmall Displays, but Six on Small Displays and Wider

```
<!DOCTYPE html>
<html lang="en">
<head>
    <!-- Required meta tags -->
    <meta charset="utf-8">
    <meta name="viewport" content="width=device-width, initial-scale=1,
    shrink-to-fit=no">

    <!-- Bootstrap CSS -->
    <link rel="stylesheet" href="https://stackpath.bootstrapcdn.
    com/bootstrap/4.4.1/css/bootstrap.min.css" integrity="sha384-
    Vkoo8x4CGsO3+Hhxv8T/Q5PaXtkKtu6ug5TOeNV6gBiFeWPGFN9MuhOf23Q9Ifjh"
    crossorigin="anonymous">

    <!-- Custom CSS -->
    <link rel="stylesheet" href="stylesheets/index.css" type="text/css">

    <title>Listing 1-12</title>
</head>
```

```
<body>
    <div class="container">
        <div class="row">
            <div class="col-6 col-sm-2">
                1
            </div>
            <div class="col-6 col-sm-2">
                2
            </div>
            <div class="col-6 col-sm-2">
                3
            </div>
            <div class="col-6 col-sm-2">
                4
            </div>
            <div class="col-6 col-sm-2">
                5
            </div>
            <div class="col-6 col-sm-2">
                6
            </div>
        </div>
    </div>

    <!-- Optional JavaScript -->
    <!-- jQuery first, then Popper.js, then Bootstrap JS -->
    <script src="https://code.jquery.com/jquery-3.4.1.slim.min.js"
    integrity="sha384-J6qa4849blE2+poT4WnyKhv5vZF5SrPo0iEjwBvKU7imGFAVOwwj1
    yYfoRSJoZ+n" crossorigin="anonymous"></script>
    <script src="https://cdn.jsdelivr.net/npm/popper.js@1.16.0/dist/umd/
    popper.min.js" integrity="sha384-Q6E9RHvbIyZFJoft+2mJbHaEWldlvI9IOYy5n3
    zV9zzTtmI3UksdQRVvoxMfooAo" crossorigin="anonymous"></script>
    <script src="https://stackpath.bootstrapcdn.com/bootstrap/4.4.1/js/
    bootstrap.min.js" integrity="sha384-wfSDF2E50Y2D1uUdj0O3uMBJnjuUD4Ih7Yw
    aYd1iqfktj0Uod8GCExl3Og8ifwB6" crossorigin="anonymous"></script>
</body>
</html>
```

If you save the preceding code and reload your page, while it is on 575px width (or smaller), you will see that, now, your page has two columns per row (Figure 1-16).

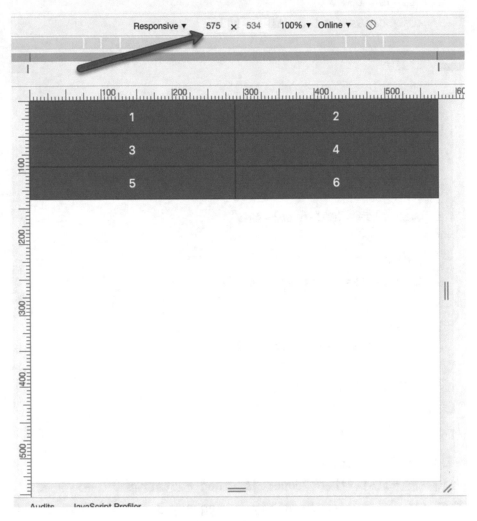

Figure 1-16. *Two Columns on Extrasmall Devices*

However, if you enlarge your display area to have a width greater than or equal to 576px, you will see that your page has six columns per row.

This is how the responsiveness of your grid is achieved.

Note   One might say, "Hold on! When on extrasmall devices, the columns inside the `div` have a number suffix (-6) that adds up to 36, not to 12." You need to know here that Twitter Bootstrap will automatically wrap the columns above the 12th to a new row.

The previous web page had one grid layout breakpoint actually—the 576px, whichever display width below 576px vs. whichever display width equal to or greater than 576px. You can apply the same concept to a second breakpoint in the same grid. For example, you may want the number of columns to be three for display areas greater than 576px (small) and six for display areas greater than or equal to 768px (medium or wider).

So what I want is the following:

a.   For extrasmall devices (<576px), two columns per row (hence, `col-6`)

b.   For small devices (>=576px, <768px), three columns per row (hence, `col-sm-4`)

c.   For medium or wider devices (>=768px), six columns per row (hence, `col-md-2`)

Now that I know what I want to achieve, it is pretty simple. I will apply the preceding classes to my column `div`s, and I am done (Listing 1-14).

Listing 1-14. Two for `xs`, Three for `sm`, and Six for Wider Displays

```
<!DOCTYPE html>
<html lang="en">
<head>
    <!-- Required meta tags -->
    <meta charset="utf-8">
    <meta name="viewport" content="width=device-width, initial-scale=1,
    shrink-to-fit=no">

    <!-- Bootstrap CSS -->
    <link rel="stylesheet" href="https://stackpath.bootstrapcdn.com/
    bootstrap/4.4.1/css/bootstrap.min.css" integrity="sha384-Vkoo8x4CGs
    O3+Hhxv8T/Q5PaXtkKtu6ug5TOeNV6gBiFeWPGFN9MuhOf23Q9Ifjh"
    crossorigin="anonymous">
```

```
    <!-- Custom CSS -->
    <link rel="stylesheet" href="stylesheets/index.css" type="text/css">

    <title>Listing 1-14</title>
</head>
<body>
    <div class="container">
        <div class="row">
            <div class="col-6 col-sm-4 col-md-2">
                1
            </div>
            <div class="col-6 col-sm-4 col-md-2">
                2
            </div>
            <div class="col-6 col-sm-4 col-md-2">
                3
            </div>
            <div class="col-6 col-sm-4 col-md-2">
                4
            </div>
            <div class="col-6 col-sm-4 col-md-2">
                5
            </div>
            <div class="col-6 col-sm-4 col-md-2">
                6
            </div>
        </div>
    </div>

    <!-- Optional JavaScript -->
    <!-- jQuery first, then Popper.js, then Bootstrap JS -->
    <script src="https://code.jquery.com/jquery-3.4.1.slim.min.js"
    integrity="sha384-J6qa4849blE2+poT4WnyKhv5vZF5SrPo0iEjwBvKU7imGFAVOwwj1
    yYfoRSJoZ+n" crossorigin="anonymous"></script>
```

```
<script src="https://cdn.jsdelivr.net/npm/popper.js@1.16.0/dist/umd/
popper.min.js" integrity="sha384-Q6E9RHvbIyZFJoft+2mJbHaEWldlvI9IOYy5n3
zV9zzTtmI3UksdQRVvoxMfooAo" crossorigin="anonymous"></script>
<script src="https://stackpath.bootstrapcdn.com/bootstrap/4.4.1/js/
bootstrap.min.js" integrity="sha384-wfSDF2E50Y2D1uUdjOO3uMBJnjuUD4Ih7Yw
aYd1iqfktjOUod8GCExl3Og8ifwB6" crossorigin="anonymous"></script>
</body>
</html>
```

Now, if you scale your browser width to be, for example, 760px, then you will see three columns on each row. See Figure 1-17.

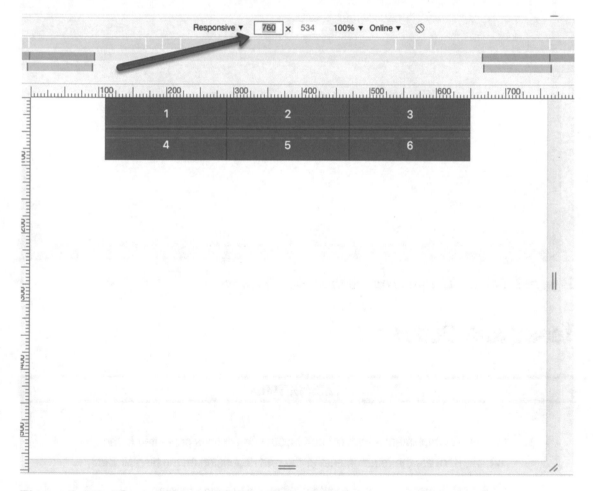

Figure 1-17. *Three Columns on Small-Size Displays*

But if you scale it even more, to be wider than 768px, it will display six columns per row (Figure 1-18).

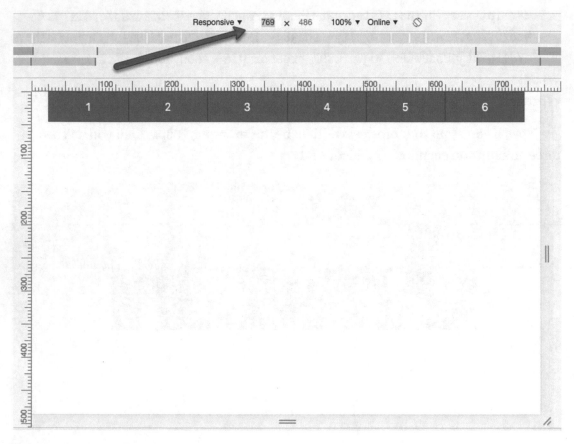

Figure 1-18. *Six Columns on Medium-Size Displays*

Tasks and Quizzes

TASK DETAILS

1. You need to implement a multicolumn layout like the ones presented in the chapter. Here are the requirements of the grid depending on the display width:

   1. For extrasmall displays, it should display one column per row.

   2. For small displays, it should display two columns per row.

3. For medium displays, it should display three columns per row.

4. For large displays, it should display four columns per row.

5. For extralarge displays, it should display six columns per row.

Good luck!

Key Takeaways

Congratulations! You have just finished the first chapter, and you already know so many things about how you make your web pages responsive. Here is a list of the key things you learned:

- The bare-minimum Twitter Bootstrap page and what it needs to include

- The containers

- The row divs

- The col divs as children of the row divs

- How to break the row into several columns of equal width or different widths

- The different Bootstrap breakpoints

- How to use different classes to define the layout of your page of different display widths

In the following chapter, you will use some more advanced techniques around the Twitter Bootstrap grid system.

CHAPTER 2

Advanced Grid Techniques

In the previous chapter, you started learning about the Twitter Bootstrap grid system. In this chapter, you will continue your work on the grid system, but you will use some different, more advanced techniques to do similar and other things.

Learning Goals

You will learn

1. How to use row columns

2. How to vertically align content

3. How to horizontally align

4. How to use less than the 12 available columns

5. How to nest content and a grid inside another

6. What the Twitter Bootstrap defaults are

Shortcuts on Rows: Row Columns

You are now going to explore one more set of alternatives in order to do all the things that you did in Chapter 1, "Getting Started." This is called *row columns*, and it is a set of classes that help you define the columns of a row but using them at the `row div`, not at the `col div`.

© Panos Matsinopoulos 2020
P. Matsinopoulos, *Practical Bootstrap*, https://doi.org/10.1007/978-1-4842-6071-5_2

Example: Six-Column Layout for All Devices

Let's suppose that I want to achieve a six-column layout that will be for all device widths. Listing 2-1 is my code.

Listing 2-1. Six-Column Layout Using Row Columns

```
<!DOCTYPE html>
<html lang="en">
<head>
    <!-- Required meta tags -->
    <meta charset="utf-8">
    <meta name="viewport" content="width=device-width, initial-scale=1,
    shrink-to-fit=no">

    <!-- Bootstrap CSS -->
    <link rel="stylesheet" href="https://stackpath.bootstrapcdn.
    com/bootstrap/4.4.1/css/bootstrap.min.css" integrity="sha384-
    Vkoo8x4CGsO3+Hhxv8T/Q5PaXtkKtu6ug5TOeNV6gBiFeWPGFN9MuhOf23Q9Ifjh"
    crossorigin="anonymous">

    <!-- Custom CSS -->
    <link rel="stylesheet" href="stylesheets/index.css" type="text/css">

    <title>Listing 2-1</title>
</head>
<body>
    <div class="container">
        <div class="row row-cols-6">
            <div class="col">
                1
            </div>
            <div class="col">
                2
            </div>
            <div class="col">
                3
            </div>
```

```
        <div class="col">
            4
        </div>
        <div class="col">
            5
        </div>
        <div class="col">
            6
        </div>
    </div>
</div>

<!-- Optional JavaScript -->
<!-- jQuery first, then Popper.js, then Bootstrap JS -->
<script src="https://code.jquery.com/jquery-3.4.1.slim.min.js"
integrity="sha384-J6qa4849blE2+poT4WnyKhv5vZF5SrPo0iEjwBvKU7imGFAVOwwj1
yYfoRSJoZ+n" crossorigin="anonymous"></script>
<script src="https://cdn.jsdelivr.net/npm/popper.js@1.16.0/dist/umd/
popper.min.js" integrity="sha384-Q6E9RHvbIyZFJoft+2mJbHaEWldlvI9IOYy5n3
zV9zzTtmI3UksdQRVvoxMfooAo" crossorigin="anonymous"></script>
<script src="https://stackpath.bootstrapcdn.com/bootstrap/4.4.1/js/
bootstrap.min.js" integrity="sha384-wfSDF2E50Y2D1uUdjOO3uMBJnjuUD4Ih7Yw
aYd1iqfktj0Uod8GCExl3Og8ifwB6" crossorigin="anonymous"></script>
</body>
</html>
```

If you save the preceding code into your index.html page and load on your browser, you will see something like that in Figure 2-1.

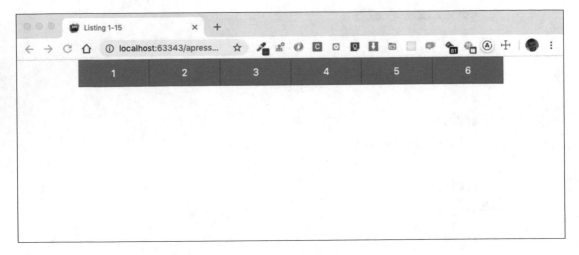

Figure 2-1. *Six Columns Using the row-cols-* Class*

This is exactly what I wanted. How was it created?

1. The row div was attributed with the class `row-cols-6`. The number 6 was exactly the number of the columns I wanted.

2. Then each column `div` only had the `col` class, since I wanted all the columns to have equal width.

Of course, I am now hearing you saying, "Hold on. The same would have been accomplished if I had used only the `row` class without the `row-cols-6` class." And you would have been right. The use of `row-cols-*` in the previous example didn't add too much value. But let's do another example in which the row column classes are much more valuable.

Example: Three Columns for Medium, Six Columns for Large

Now I want to create a responsive grid that would give me

- Three columns for all devices up to and including medium ones

- Six columns for all devices with large or wider displays

You already know how to do that with the `col-*` class at the column `div` level. Here, we are going to do it with `row-cols-*` classes at the row level. See Listing 2-2.

Listing 2-2. Responsive Breakpoints Using Row Columns

```
<!DOCTYPE html>
<html lang="en">
<head>
    <!-- Required meta tags -->
    <meta charset="utf-8">
    <meta name="viewport" content="width=device-width, initial-scale=1,
    shrink-to-fit=no">

    <!-- Bootstrap CSS -->
    <link rel="stylesheet" href="https://stackpath.bootstrapcdn.
    com/bootstrap/4.4.1/css/bootstrap.min.css" integrity="sha384-
    Vkoo8x4CGsO3+Hhxv8T/Q5PaXtkKtu6ug5TOeNV6gBiFeWPGFN9MuhOf23Q9Ifjh"
    crossorigin="anonymous">

    <!-- Custom CSS -->
    <link rel="stylesheet" href="stylesheets/index.css" type="text/css">

    <title>Listing 2-2</title>
</head>
<body>
    <div class="container">
        <div class="row row-cols-3 row-cols-lg-6">
            <div class="col">
                1
            </div>
            <div class="col">
                2
            </div>
            <div class="col">
                3
            </div>
            <div class="col">
                4
            </div>
```

```
            <div class="col">
                5
            </div>
            <div class="col">
                6
            </div>
        </div>
    </div>

    <!-- Optional JavaScript -->
    <!-- jQuery first, then Popper.js, then Bootstrap JS -->
    <script src="https://code.jquery.com/jquery-3.4.1.slim.min.js"
    integrity="sha384-J6qa4849blE2+poT4WnyKhv5vZF5SrPo0iEjwBvKU7imGFAVOwwj1
    yYfoRSJoZ+n" crossorigin="anonymous"></script>
    <script src="https://cdn.jsdelivr.net/npm/popper.js@1.16.0/dist/umd/
    popper.min.js" integrity="sha384-Q6E9RHvbIyZFJoft+2mJbHaEWldlvI9IOYy5n3
    zV9zzTtmI3UksdQRVvoxMfooAo" crossorigin="anonymous"></script>
    <script src="https://stackpath.bootstrapcdn.com/bootstrap/4.4.1/js/
    bootstrap.min.js" integrity="sha384-wfSDF2E50Y2D1uUdjOO3uMBJnjuUD4Ih7Yw
    aYd1iqfktjOUod8GCExl3Og8ifwB6" crossorigin="anonymous"></script>
</body>
</html>
```

Do you see how easy it is?

- I keep the column divs having only the col class.

- I use the two row column classes row-cols-3 and row-cols-lg-6 to tell how many columns I want according to the device width, in particular

  - row-cols-3 for all devices except the ones defined with the following class. Note the number 3 is the number of columns we want to occupy.

  - row-cols-lg-6 for all devices with large or wider displays, that is, >=992px.

If you save your page and reload on your browser, you will see the following for a page that has width 991px, for example (Figure 2-2).

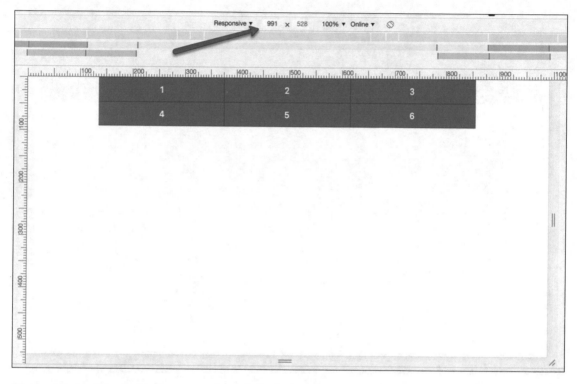

Figure 2-2. *Three Columns When Below 992px*

When you enlarge the width by 1 pixel more, to 992px, then you will immediately get six columns (Figure 2-3).

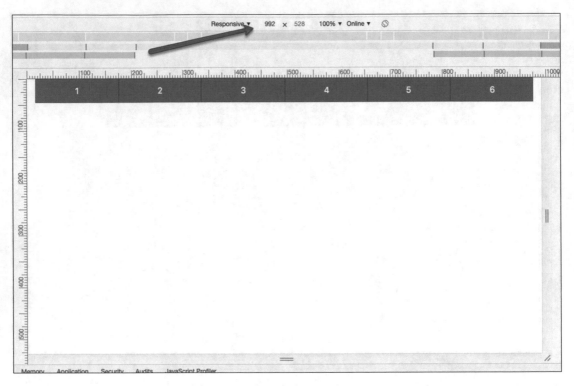

Figure 2-3. *Six Columns for 992px and Wider*

In Table 2-1, I compare the first solution with the col-* classes at the column level with the latest solution you just learned with the row-cols-* classes at the row level.

Table 2-1. *Compare Code Between* col-* *and* row-cols-*

col-* at Column Level	row-cols-* at Row Level
| ```
<div class="row">
 <div class="col-4 col-lg-2">
  1
 </div>
 <div class="col-4 col-lg-2">
  2
 </div>
 <div class="col-4 col-lg-2">
  3
 </div>
 <div class="col-4 col-lg-2">
  4
 </div>
 <div class="col-4 col-lg-2">
  5
 </div>
 <div class="col-4 col-lg-2">
  6
 </div>
</div>
``` | ```
<div class="row row-cols-3
 row-cols-lg-6">
 <div class="col">
 1
 </div>
 <div class="col">
 2
 </div>
 <div class="col">
 3
 </div>
 <div class="col">
 4
 </div>
 <div class="col">
 5
 </div>
 <div class="col">
 6
 </div>
</div>
``` |

I repeat so that it's crystal clear:

1. When I use classes to specify the column width at the column div level, I specify the number of columns (out of the 12) my column will occupy. For example, if I want my column to be three columns wide, I use col-3.

2. When I use classes at the row div level, I just specify the number of columns I want in the row. Then Bootstrap will automatically calculate the width of each column.

3. Obviously, when I use row classes, I set the width for all the columns of the row to an equal size. If I want to have columns with different widths within the same row, I have to use the column classes at the column-level `div`.

Vertical Alignment

You have learned how to lay out things using a 12-column-wide grid, but Bootstrap allows you to align things inside the row itself, in the vertical axis.

Middle Alignment

How would you put your content in the middle of a tall row like it is depicted in Figure 2-4?

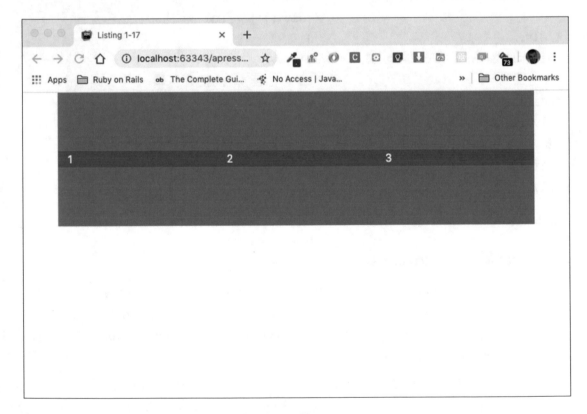

Figure 2-4. *Content in the Middle of a Tall Row*

In the preceding picture, you can see the content of the row, which, in fact, is composed of three columns, to be placed in the center of the vertical axis. In Listing 2-3, you can see how you can create this page.

Listing 2-3. Content in the Middle of a Tall Row

```
<!DOCTYPE html>
<html lang="en">
<head>
    <!-- Required meta tags -->
    <meta charset="utf-8">
    <meta name="viewport" content="width=device-width, initial-scale=1,
    shrink-to-fit=no">

    <!-- Bootstrap CSS -->
    <link rel="stylesheet" href="https://stackpath.bootstrapcdn.
    com/bootstrap/4.4.1/css/bootstrap.min.css" integrity="sha384-
    Vkoo8x4CGsO3+Hhxv8T/Q5PaXtkKtu6ug5TOeNV6gBiFeWPGFN9MuhOf23Q9Ifjh"
    crossorigin="anonymous">

    <!-- Custom CSS -->
    <link rel="stylesheet" href="stylesheets/index.css" type="text/css">

    <title>Listing 2-3</title>
</head>
<body>
    <div class="container">
        <div class="row align-items-center">
            <div class="col">
                1
            </div>
            <div class="col">
                2
            </div>
            <div class="col">
                3
            </div>
        </div>
    </div>
```

```
    <!-- Optional JavaScript -->
    <!-- jQuery first, then Popper.js, then Bootstrap JS -->
    <script src="https://code.jquery.com/jquery-3.4.1.slim.min.js"
    integrity="sha384-J6qa4849blE2+poT4WnyKhv5vZF5SrPo0iEjwBvKU7imGFAVOwwj1
    yYfoRSJoZ+n" crossorigin="anonymous"></script>
    <script src="https://cdn.jsdelivr.net/npm/popper.js@1.16.0/dist/umd/
    popper.min.js" integrity="sha384-Q6E9RHvbIyZFJoft+2mJbHaEWldlvI9IOYy5n3
    zV9zzTtmI3UksdQRVvoxMfooAo" crossorigin="anonymous"></script>
    <script src="https://stackpath.bootstrapcdn.com/bootstrap/4.4.1/js/
    bootstrap.min.js" integrity="sha384-wfSDF2E50Y2D1uUdjOO3uMBJnjuUD4Ih7Yw
    aYd1iqfktjOUod8GCExl3Og8ifwB6" crossorigin="anonymous"></script>
</body>
</html>
```

The difference is done by the class `align-items-center` at the `row` `div`. It instructs the browser to draw the columns that are children of this `div` at the center position of the row on the vertical axis.

Before you save and load this page on your browser though, you will have to give your row some minimum height; otherwise, you will not see any difference. Use Listing 2-4 for your `index.css` file.

Listing 2-4. CSS File That Gives the Row a Minimum Height

```
.row {
    background-color: #4e9013;
    color: white;
    min-height: 200px;
}

.col {
    background-color: #31907c;
}
```

The preceding CSS has the rule to apply `min-height` on the row `div`s. This will allow you to see the contents of the children `div`s in the center of the row on the vertical axis direction.

Top and Bottom Alignment

There are also two other classes that you can apply at the row `div` level and that have to do with vertical alignment: `align-items-start` and `align-items-end`. Let's use these to create the page depicted in Figure 2-5.

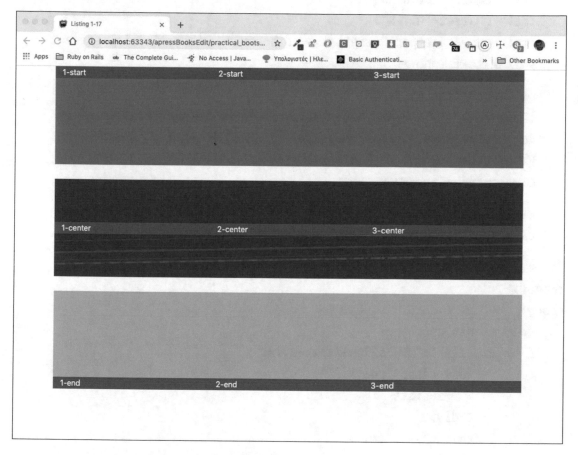

Figure 2-5. *Use Various Vertical Alignments*

As you can see, the middle and bottom rows have alignments `center` and `end`, respectively. I am pretty sure that you write the HTML without my help, but let's include here the code for completeness (Listing 2-5).

Listing 2-5. Align Top, Middle, and Bottom

```
<!DOCTYPE html>
<html lang="en">
<head>
    <!-- Required meta tags -->
    <meta charset="utf-8">
    <meta name="viewport" content="width=device-width, initial-scale=1,
    shrink-to-fit=no">

    <!-- Bootstrap CSS -->
    <link rel="stylesheet" href="https://stackpath.bootstrapcdn.
    com/bootstrap/4.4.1/css/bootstrap.min.css" integrity="sha384-
    Vkoo8x4CGsO3+Hhxv8T/Q5PaXtkKtu6ug5TOeNV6gBiFeWPGFN9MuhOf23Q9Ifjh"
    crossorigin="anonymous">

    <!-- Custom CSS -->
    <link rel="stylesheet" href="stylesheets/index.css" type="text/css">

    <title>Listing 2-5</title>
</head>
<body>
    <div class="container">
        <div class="row align-items-start">
            <div class="col">
                1-start
            </div>
            <div class="col">
                2-start
            </div>
            <div class="col">
                3-start
            </div>
        </div>
        <div class="row align-items-center">
            <div class="col">
                1-center
```

```
        </div>
        <div class="col">
            2-center
        </div>
        <div class="col">
            3-center
        </div>
    </div>
    <div class="row align-items-end">
        <div class="col">
            1-end
        </div>
        <div class="col">
            2-end
        </div>
        <div class="col">
            3-end
        </div>
    </div>
</div>

<!-- Optional JavaScript -->
<!-- jQuery first, then Popper.js, then Bootstrap JS -->
<script src="https://code.jquery.com/jquery-3.4.1.slim.min.js"
integrity="sha384-J6qa4849blE2+poT4WnyKhv5vZF5SrPo0iEjwBvKU7imGFAVOwwj1
yYfoRSJoZ+n" crossorigin="anonymous"></script>
<script src="https://cdn.jsdelivr.net/npm/popper.js@1.16.0/dist/umd/
popper.min.js" integrity="sha384-Q6E9RHvbIyZFJoft+2mJbHaEWldlvI9IOYy5n3
zV9zzTtmI3UksdQRVvoxMfooAo" crossorigin="anonymous"></script>
<script src="https://stackpath.bootstrapcdn.com/bootstrap/4.4.1/js/
bootstrap.min.js" integrity="sha384-wfSDF2E50Y2D1uUdjOO3uMBJnjuUD4Ih7Yw
aYd1iqfktjOUod8GCExl3Og8ifwB6" crossorigin="anonymous"></script>
</body>
</html>
```

Don't forget to make your `index.css` have rules that will make your rows have minimum height so that you can see the vertical alignment. Listing 2-6 contains such rules.

Listing 2-6. index.css File That Gives Rows Minimum Height

```css
.row {
    min-height: 200px;
    margin-bottom: 30px;
    color: white;
}

.align-items-start {
    background-color: #4e9013;
}

.align-items-center {
    background-color: #902e07;
}

.align-items-end {
    background-color: #8DC5CC;
}

.col {
    background-color: #367390;
}
```

Different Vertical Alignments Within the Same Row

Finally, sometimes you want the columns within the same row to have different vertical alignments. Figure 2-6 is an example of such a page.

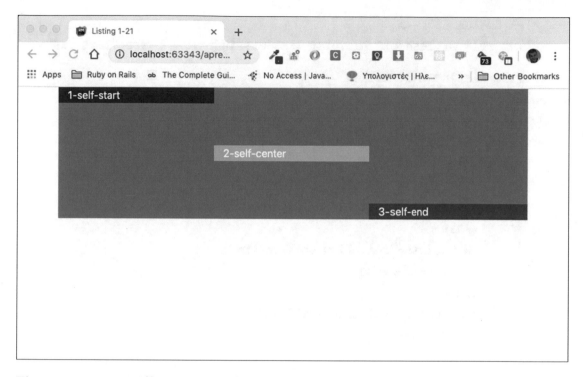

Figure 2-6. *Use Different Vertical Alignments Within the Same Row*

In order to achieve this, I use some special classes at the col level. Here is the HTML code for the preceding page (Listing 2-7).

Listing 2-7. Different Vertical Alignments Within the Same Row

```
<!DOCTYPE html>
<html lang="en">
<head>
    <!-- Required meta tags -->
    <meta charset="utf-8">
    <meta name="viewport" content="width=device-width, initial-scale=1,
    shrink-to-fit=no">

    <!-- Bootstrap CSS -->
    <link rel="stylesheet" href="https://stackpath.bootstrapcdn.
    com/bootstrap/4.4.1/css/bootstrap.min.css" integrity="sha384-
    Vkoo8x4CGsO3+Hhxv8T/Q5PaXtkKtu6ug5TOeNV6gBiFeWPGFN9MuhOf23Q9Ifjh"
    crossorigin="anonymous">
```

```html
    <!-- Custom CSS -->
    <link rel="stylesheet" href="stylesheets/index.css" type="text/css">

    <title>Listing 2-7</title>
</head>
<body>
    <div class="container">
        <div class="row">
            <div class="col align-self-start">
                1-self-start
            </div>
            <div class="col align-self-center">
                2-self-center
            </div>
            <div class="col align-self-end">
                3-self-end
            </div>
        </div>
    </div>

    <!-- Optional JavaScript -->
    <!-- jQuery first, then Popper.js, then Bootstrap JS -->
    <script src="https://code.jquery.com/jquery-3.4.1.slim.min.js"
    integrity="sha384-J6qa4849blE2+poT4WnyKhv5vZF5SrPo0iEjwBvKU7imGFAVOwwj1
    yYfoRSJoZ+n" crossorigin="anonymous"></script>
    <script src="https://cdn.jsdelivr.net/npm/popper.js@1.16.0/dist/umd/
    popper.min.js" integrity="sha384-Q6E9RHvbIyZFJoft+2mJbHaEWldlvI9IOYy5n3
    zV9zzTtmI3UksdQRVvoxMfooAo" crossorigin="anonymous"></script>
    <script src="https://stackpath.bootstrapcdn.com/bootstrap/4.4.1/js/
    bootstrap.min.js" integrity="sha384-wfSDF2E50Y2D1uUdjOO3uMBJnjuUD4Ih7Yw
    aYd1iqfktjOUod8GCExl3Og8ifwB6" crossorigin="anonymous"></script>
</body>
</html>
```

Use the following index.css (Listing 2-8) in order to style the preceding HTML content so that you can get the result presented in Figure 2-6.

Listing 2-8. CSS for Listing 2-7

```
.row {
    background-color: #4e9013;
    min-height: 200px;
    margin-bottom: 30px;
    color: white;
}

.align-self-start {
    background-color: #441180;
}

.align-self-center {
    background-color: #8DC5CC;
}

.align-self-end {
    background-color: #902e07;
}
```

Less Than 12 and Horizontal Alignment

I continue by explaining to you how you can align columns in the horizontal direction, which is more useful when you have content that does not occupy the whole width of the page.

Left Alignment

Until now, your rows had content left to right. They occupied the whole container width. There are cases in which you want to have part of the width occupied. For example, you want to have content on the first two columns and the rest of the horizontal space to be empty. Look at the following example in Figure 2-7.

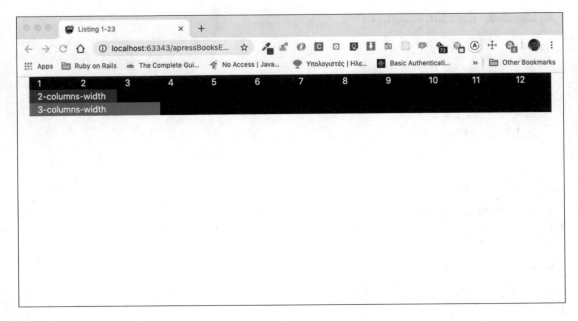

Figure 2-7.   *Left-Aligned Columns*

As you can see in Figure 2-7, the second and third rows have columns that occupy the left side of the grid. The second row occupies the first two columns, and the third row occupies the first three columns. How can you achieve this? The HTML code is given in Listing 2-9.

Listing 2-9.   Left-Aligned Columns

```
<!DOCTYPE html>
<html lang="en">
<head>
    <!-- Required meta tags -->
    <meta charset="utf-8">
    <meta name="viewport" content="width=device-width, initial-scale=1,
    shrink-to-fit=no">

    <!-- Bootstrap CSS -->
    <link rel="stylesheet" href="https://stackpath.bootstrapcdn.
    com/bootstrap/4.4.1/css/bootstrap.min.css" integrity="sha384-
    Vkoo8x4CGsO3+Hhxv8T/Q5PaXtkKtu6ug5TOeNV6gBiFeWPGFN9MuhOf23Q9Ifjh"
    crossorigin="anonymous">
```

```html
    <!-- Custom CSS -->
    <link rel="stylesheet" href="stylesheets/index.css" type="text/css">

    <title>Listing 2-9</title>
</head>
<body>
    <div class="container">
        <div class="row">
            <div class="col">1</div>
            <div class="col">2</div>
            <div class="col">3</div>
            <div class="col">4</div>
            <div class="col">5</div>
            <div class="col">6</div>
            <div class="col">7</div>
            <div class="col">8</div>
            <div class="col">9</div>
            <div class="col">10</div>
            <div class="col">11</div>
            <div class="col">12</div>
        </div>
        <div class="row justify-content-start row-1">
            <div class="col-2 col">
                2-columns-width
            </div>
        </div>
        <div class="row justify-content-start row-2">
            <div class="col-3 col">
                3-columns-width
            </div>
        </div>
    </div>

    <!-- Optional JavaScript -->
    <!-- jQuery first, then Popper.js, then Bootstrap JS -->
```

```
<script src="https://code.jquery.com/jquery-3.4.1.slim.min.js"
integrity="sha384-J6qa4849blE2+poT4WnyKhv5vZF5SrPo0iEjwBvKU7imGFAVOwwj1
yYfoRSJoZ+n" crossorigin="anonymous"></script>
<script src="https://cdn.jsdelivr.net/npm/popper.js@1.16.0/dist/umd/
popper.min.js" integrity="sha384-Q6E9RHvbIyZFJoft+2mJbHaEWldlvI9IOYy5n3
zV9zzTtmI3UksdQRVvoxMfooAo" crossorigin="anonymous"></script>
<script src="https://stackpath.bootstrapcdn.com/bootstrap/4.4.1/js/
bootstrap.min.js" integrity="sha384-wfSDF2E50Y2D1uUdj0O3uMBJnjuUD4Ih7Yw
aYd1iqfktjOUod8GCExl3Og8ifwB6" crossorigin="anonymous"></script>
</body>
</html>
```

Before loading the preceding HTML into your browser, make sure that you have correct CSS rules inside your index.css file, something like that in Listing 2-10.

Listing 2-10. CSS for Listing 2-9

```
* {
    color: white;
}

.row {
    background-color: black;
}

.row-1 .col {
    background-color: #902e07;
}

.row-2 .col {
    background-color: #31907c;
}
```

In Listing 2-9, the class justify-content-start is attached on the second and third row divs.

Center and Right Alignment

But this, in fact, was not very useful. The same would have been accomplished even if you didn't have this class attached to the row divs. Things are getting more interesting when you use the corresponding *-center and *-end classes like in Listing 2-11.

Listing 2-11. Use *-center and *-end Classes

```
<!DOCTYPE html>
<html lang="en">
<head>
    <!-- Required meta tags -->
    <meta charset="utf-8">
    <meta name="viewport" content="width=device-width, initial-scale=1,
    shrink-to-fit=no">

    <!-- Bootstrap CSS -->
    <link rel="stylesheet" href="https://stackpath.bootstrapcdn.
    com/bootstrap/4.4.1/css/bootstrap.min.css" integrity="sha384-
    Vkoo8x4CGsO3+Hhxv8T/Q5PaXtkKtu6ug5TOeNV6gBiFeWPGFN9MuhOf23Q9Ifjh"
    crossorigin="anonymous">

    <!-- Custom CSS -->
    <link rel="stylesheet" href="stylesheets/index.css" type="text/css">

    <title>Listing 2-11</title>
</head>
<body>
    <div class="container">
        <div class="row">
            <div class="col">1</div>
            <div class="col">2</div>
            <div class="col">3</div>
            <div class="col">4</div>
            <div class="col">5</div>
            <div class="col">6</div>
            <div class="col">7</div>
            <div class="col">8</div>
```

```
        <div class="col">9</div>
        <div class="col">10</div>
        <div class="col">11</div>
        <div class="col">12</div>
    </div>
    <div class="row justify-content-center row-1">
        <div class="col-2 col">
            2-columns-width
        </div>
    </div>
    <div class="row justify-content-end row-2">
        <div class="col-3 col">
            3-columns-width
        </div>
    </div>
</div>

<!-- Optional JavaScript -->
<!-- jQuery first, then Popper.js, then Bootstrap JS -->
<script src="https://code.jquery.com/jquery-3.4.1.slim.min.js"
integrity="sha384-J6qa4849blE2+poT4WnyKhv5vZF5SrPo0iEjwBvKU7imGFAVOwwj1
yYfoRSJoZ+n" crossorigin="anonymous"></script>
<script src="https://cdn.jsdelivr.net/npm/popper.js@1.16.0/dist/umd/
popper.min.js" integrity="sha384-Q6E9RHvbIyZFJoft+2mJbHaEWldlvI9IOYy5n3
zV9zzTtmI3UksdQRVvoxMfooAo" crossorigin="anonymous"></script>
<script src="https://stackpath.bootstrapcdn.com/bootstrap/4.4.1/js/
bootstrap.min.js" integrity="sha384-wfSDF2E50Y2D1uUdj0O3uMBJnjuUD4Ih7Yw
aYd1iqfktj0Uod8GCExl30g8ifwB6" crossorigin="anonymous"></script>
</body>
</html>
```

Save the preceding page and load it on your browser. You will see something like what is depicted in Figure 2-8.

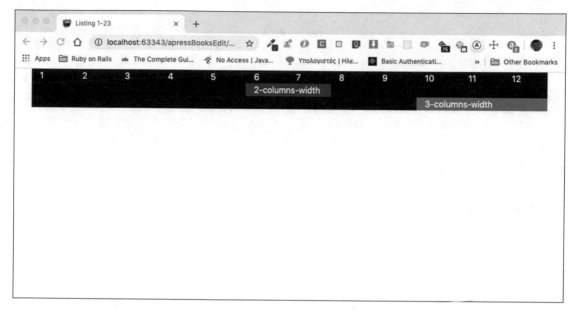

Figure 2-8. *Center and Right Alignment*

Hence, these `justify-content-*` classes at the row `divs` are useful, because they allow you to align without having to use empty divs.

Space Between

What if you had three content columns that you wanted horizontally aligned in such a way that they had equal space between them? Figure 2-9 has an example of such a case.

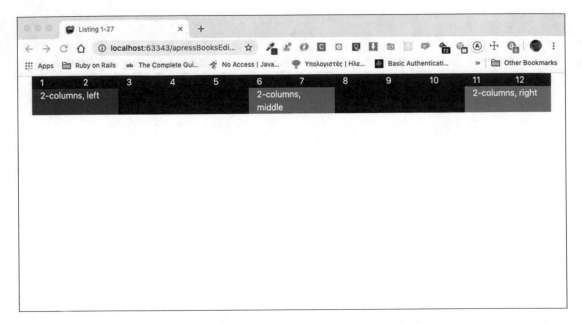

Figure 2-9. *Columns with Space Between*

The class that you have to use in order to achieve is the justify-content-between. The HTML code is given in Listing 2-12.

Listing 2-12. Using justify-content-between

```
<!DOCTYPE html>
<html lang="en">
<head>
    <!-- Required meta tags -->
    <meta charset="utf-8">
    <meta name="viewport" content="width=device-width, initial-scale=1,
    shrink-to-fit=no">

    <!-- Bootstrap CSS -->
    <link rel="stylesheet" href="https://stackpath.bootstrapcdn.
    com/bootstrap/4.4.1/css/bootstrap.min.css" integrity="sha384-
    Vkoo8x4CGsO3+Hhxv8T/Q5PaXtkKtu6ug5TOeNV6gBiFeWPGFN9MuhOf23Q9Ifjh"
    crossorigin="anonymous">
```

```html
    <!-- Custom CSS -->
    <link rel="stylesheet" href="stylesheets/index.css" type="text/css">

    <title>Listing 2-12</title>
</head>
<body>
    <div class="container">
        <div class="row">
            <div class="col">1</div>
            <div class="col">2</div>
            <div class="col">3</div>
            <div class="col">4</div>
            <div class="col">5</div>
            <div class="col">6</div>
            <div class="col">7</div>
            <div class="col">8</div>
            <div class="col">9</div>
            <div class="col">10</div>
            <div class="col">11</div>
            <div class="col">12</div>
        </div>
        <div class="row justify-content-between">
            <div class="col-2">
                2-columns, left
            </div>
            <div class="col-2">
                2-columns, middle
            </div>
            <div class="col-2">
                2-columns, right
            </div>
        </div>
    </div>

    <!-- Optional JavaScript -->
    <!-- jQuery first, then Popper.js, then Bootstrap JS -->
```

```
<script src="https://code.jquery.com/jquery-3.4.1.slim.min.js"
integrity="sha384-J6qa4849blE2+poT4WnyKhv5vZF5SrPo0iEjwBvKU7imGFAVOwwj1
yYfoRSJoZ+n" crossorigin="anonymous"></script>
<script src="https://cdn.jsdelivr.net/npm/popper.js@1.16.0/dist/umd/
popper.min.js" integrity="sha384-Q6E9RHvbIyZFJoft+2mJbHaEWldlvI9IOYy5n3
zV9zzTtmI3UksdQRVvoxMfooAo" crossorigin="anonymous"></script>
<script src="https://stackpath.bootstrapcdn.com/bootstrap/4.4.1/js/
bootstrap.min.js" integrity="sha384-wfSDF2E50Y2D1uUdj0O3uMBJnjuUD4Ih7Yw
aYd1iqfktj0Uod8GCExl3Og8ifwB6" crossorigin="anonymous"></script>
</body>
</html>
```

Space Around

Finally, sometimes you want the space to be around your content. See an example in Figure 2-10.

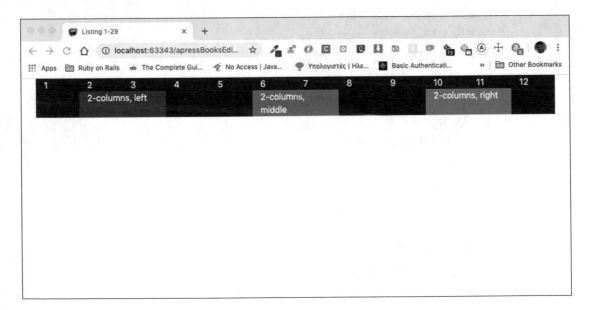

Figure 2-10.   *Content with Space Around*

In order to achieve this, you need to use the class `justify-content-around`. Attach it at the row div level, as in Listing 2-13.

Listing 2-13. Content with Space Around

```
<!DOCTYPE html>
<html lang="en">
<head>
    <!-- Required meta tags -->
    <meta charset="utf-8">
    <meta name="viewport" content="width=device-width, initial-scale=1,
    shrink-to-fit=no">

    <!-- Bootstrap CSS -->
    <link rel="stylesheet" href="https://stackpath.bootstrapcdn.
    com/bootstrap/4.4.1/css/bootstrap.min.css" integrity="sha384-
    Vkoo8x4CGsO3+Hhxv8T/Q5PaXtkKtu6ug5TOeNV6gBiFeWPGFN9MuhOf23Q9Ifjh"
    crossorigin="anonymous">

    <!-- Custom CSS -->
    <link rel="stylesheet" href="stylesheets/index.css" type="text/css">

    <title>Listing 2-13</title>
</head>
<body>
    <div class="container">
        <div class="row">
            <div class="col">1</div>
            <div class="col">2</div>
            <div class="col">3</div>
            <div class="col">4</div>
            <div class="col">5</div>
            <div class="col">6</div>
            <div class="col">7</div>
            <div class="col">8</div>
            <div class="col">9</div>
            <div class="col">10</div>
```

```
            <div class="col">11</div>
            <div class="col">12</div>
        </div>
        <div class="row justify-content-around">
            <div class="col-2">
                2-columns, left
            </div>
            <div class="col-2">
                2-columns, middle
            </div>
            <div class="col-2">
                2-columns, right
            </div>
        </div>
    </div>

<!-- Optional JavaScript -->
<!-- jQuery first, then Popper.js, then Bootstrap JS -->
<script src="https://code.jquery.com/jquery-3.4.1.slim.min.js"
integrity="sha384-J6qa4849blE2+poT4WnyKhv5vZF5SrPo0iEjwBvKU7imGFAVOwwj1
yYfoRSJoZ+n" crossorigin="anonymous"></script>
<script src="https://cdn.jsdelivr.net/npm/popper.js@1.16.0/dist/umd/
popper.min.js" integrity="sha384-Q6E9RHvbIyZFJoft+2mJbHaEWldlvI9IOYy5n3
zV9zzTtmI3UksdQRVvoxMfooAo" crossorigin="anonymous"></script>
<script src="https://stackpath.bootstrapcdn.com/bootstrap/4.4.1/js/
bootstrap.min.js" integrity="sha384-wfSDF2E50Y2D1uUdj0O3uMBJnjuUD4Ih7Yw
aYd1iqfktj0Uod8GCExl3Og8ifwB6" crossorigin="anonymous"></script>
</body>
</html>
```

Load the preceding code using an index.css file like the one given in Listing 2-14.

Listing 2-14. CSS Content for Listing 2-13

```
* {
    color: white;
}

.row {
    background-color: darkblue;
}

.col-2:nth-child(1) {
    background-color: #902e07;
}

.col-2:nth-child(2) {
    background-color: #31907c;
}

.col-2:nth-child(3) {
    background-color: #89906b;
}
```

Nesting

I will close this first encounter with Twitter Bootstrap by giving some advice on how you should nest a grid within another.

Nesting a grid within another is allowed and follows the same rules that apply to the root grid. How would you do it? You have to use a `row` div and child `col` divs inside the parent `col` div.

Figure 2-11 shows an example of a grid inside another.

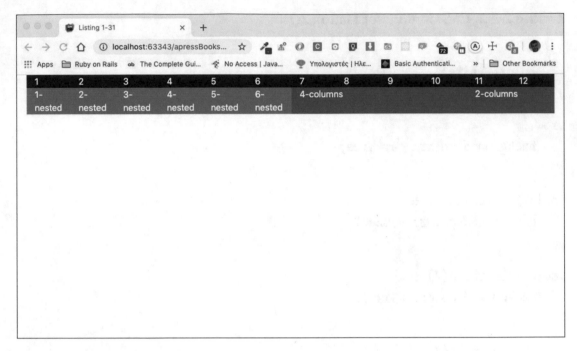

Figure 2-11. *Nested Grid Inside Another*

And let's see the HTML code for this page (Listing 2-15).

Listing 2-15. Nested Grid Inside Another

```
<!DOCTYPE html>
<html lang="en">
<head>
    <!-- Required meta tags -->
    <meta charset="utf-8">
    <meta name="viewport" content="width=device-width, initial-scale=1,
    shrink-to-fit=no">

    <!-- Bootstrap CSS -->
    <link rel="stylesheet" href="https://stackpath.bootstrapcdn.
    com/bootstrap/4.4.1/css/bootstrap.min.css" integrity="sha384-
    Vkoo8x4CGsO3+Hhxv8T/Q5PaXtkKtu6ug5TOeNV6gBiFeWPGFN9MuhOf23Q9Ifjh"
    crossorigin="anonymous">
```

```html
    <!-- Custom CSS -->
    <link rel="stylesheet" href="stylesheets/index.css" type="text/css">

    <title>Listing 2-15</title>
</head>
<body>
    <div class="container">
        <div class="row">
            <div class="col">1</div>
            <div class="col">2</div>
            <div class="col">3</div>
            <div class="col">4</div>
            <div class="col">5</div>
            <div class="col">6</div>
            <div class="col">7</div>
            <div class="col">8</div>
            <div class="col">9</div>
            <div class="col">10</div>
            <div class="col">11</div>
            <div class="col">12</div>
        </div>
        <div class="row parent">
            <div class="col-6">
                <div class="row nested row-cols-md-3 row-cols-lg-6">
                    <div class="col">
                        1-nested
                    </div>
                    <div class="col">
                        2-nested
                    </div>
                    <div class="col">
                        3-nested
                    </div>
                    <div class="col">
                        4-nested
                    </div>
```

```
                    <div class="col">
                        5-nested
                    </div>
                    <div class="col">
                        6-nested
                    </div>
                </div>
            </div>
            <div class="col-4">
                4-columns
            </div>
            <div class="col-2">
                2-columns
            </div>
        </div>
    </div>

    <!-- Optional JavaScript -->
    <!-- jQuery first, then Popper.js, then Bootstrap JS -->
    <script src="https://code.jquery.com/jquery-3.4.1.slim.min.js"
    integrity="sha384-J6qa4849blE2+poT4WnyKhv5vZF5SrPo0iEjwBvKU7imGFAVOwwj1
    yYfoRSJoZ+n" crossorigin="anonymous"></script>
    <script src="https://cdn.jsdelivr.net/npm/popper.js@1.16.0/dist/umd/
    popper.min.js" integrity="sha384-Q6E9RHvbIyZFJoft+2mJbHaEWldlvI9IOYy5n3
    zV9zzTtmI3UksdQRVvoxMfooAo" crossorigin="anonymous"></script>
    <script src="https://stackpath.bootstrapcdn.com/bootstrap/4.4.1/js/
    bootstrap.min.js" integrity="sha384-wfSDF2E50Y2D1uUdjOO3uMBJnjuUD4Ih7Yw
    aYd1iqfktjOUod8GCExl3Og8ifwB6" crossorigin="anonymous"></script>
</body>
</html>
```

As you can see from the preceding code, inside the row div with class parent, I have a col div (with class col-6). This latter div has another row inside it (with class nested) that starts the nested grid.

The classes parent and nested are not Twitter Bootstrap classes. They are my custom CSS classes that help style the page with rules that exist inside index.css (Listing 2-16).

Listing 2-16. index.css for Listing 2-15

```
* {
    color: white;
}

.row {
    background-color: darkblue;
}

.row.parent {
    background-color: #367390;
}

.row.nested {
    background-color: #31907c;
}
```

Look how the nested row div uses the row-cols-* classes to specify the number of columns on different breakpoints. For example, if you shrink your browser window to 780px, which is a medium-size device, you will see the nested grid having a three-column layout, due to the class row-cols-3. See Figure 2-12.

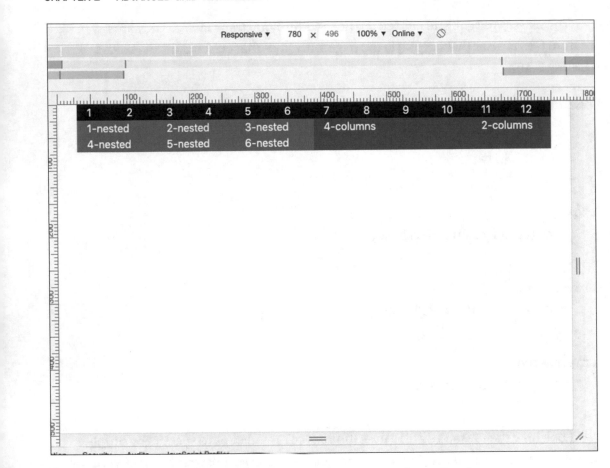

Figure 2-12. *Nested Grid Has Three Columns on Medium Devices*

Twitter Bootstrap Defaults

Before I close this chapter, I would like to quickly walk you through the most important defaults (Table 2-2) that one takes by including Twitter Bootstrap and compare them to the defaults without it.

Table 2-2. *Twitter Bootstrap Default vs. Browser Defaults*

	Twitter Bootstrap	**Without Twitter Bootstrap**
html element box-sizing	border-box	content-box
html element font-family	sans-serif	Times
html element font-size	16px	16px
body element font-family	-apple-system,BlinkMacSystem Font,"Segoe UI",Roboto,"Helvetica Neue",Arial,"Noto Sans",sans-serif,"Apple Color Emoji","Segoe UI Emoji","Segoe UI Symbol","Noto Color Emoji"	Times
body element font-size	16px	16px
body element line-height	24px	normal
body element color	#212529	#000
body element background-color	#fff	rgba(0,0,0,0); hence transparent
body element box-sizing	border-box	content-box
body element margin	0	8px

You can read more about the Twitter Bootstrap defaults if you download Twitter Bootstrap, locally on your computer. You can do that by visiting `https://getbootstrap.com/docs/4.4/getting-started/download/` and then clicking the button Download. This will download, among the others, ready CSS non-minified code (look for file `css/bootstrap.css`).

Tasks and Quizzes

> ## TASK DETAILS

1. You need to implement a page that contains an image roster.

2. You need to use Twitter Bootstrap tools to make it responsive.

3. Here is how the page should look (Figure 2-13) on extralarge displays (>=1200px).

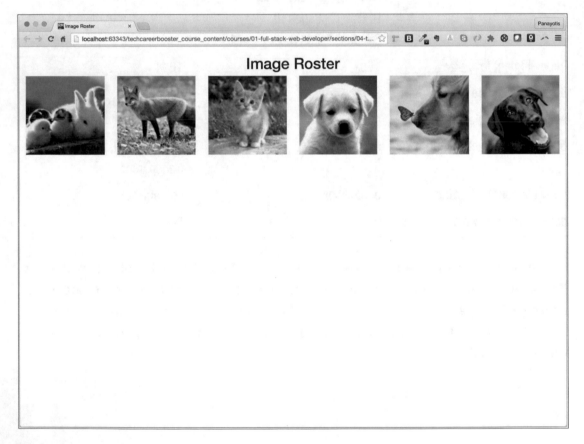

Figure 2-13. *Task: Responsive Image Roster Page*

As you can see, it has six images evenly positioned on the page.

4. The page should look like Figure 2-14 on medium (>=768px) and large (<1200px) devices.

Figure 2-14. *How the Page Should Look on Medium and Large Devices*

As you can see in Figure 2-14, now, the images are arranged so that each row has three images. Hence, all the images are displayed in two rows.

5. The page should look like Figure 2-15 on small and extrasmall devices (<768px).

Figure 2-15. *Page on Small and Extrasmall Devices*

As you can see in Figure 2-15, now each image is displayed on its own row.

6. The header is an h1 element.

7. The img tags should be styled with width and height 100% so that they occupy all the space they are given.

Good luck!

Key Takeaways

Here is a list of the key things you learned:

- How to achieve vertical alignment

- How to achieve horizontal alignment

- How to nest a grid inside another

In the following chapter, you will learn Bootstrap by implementing a real project. It will have a responsive navigation bar that will change its appearance according to the width of the display.

CHAPTER 3

Target Project 1

In the previous chapter, you have learned about the Twitter Bootstrap grid system. In this chapter, you will develop a web page that has a navigation bar fixed at the top as seen in Figure 3-1.

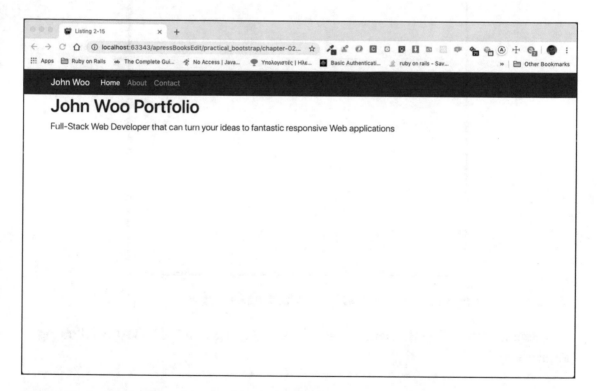

Figure 3-1. *Basic Template with a Top Nav Bar*

This navigation bar is responsive, which means it can be equally displayed on small-display devices. In those cases, the menu is hidden behind a hamburger icon (Figure 3-2).

© Panos Matsinopoulos 2020
P. Matsinopoulos, *Practical Bootstrap*, https://doi.org/10.1007/978-1-4842-6071-5_3

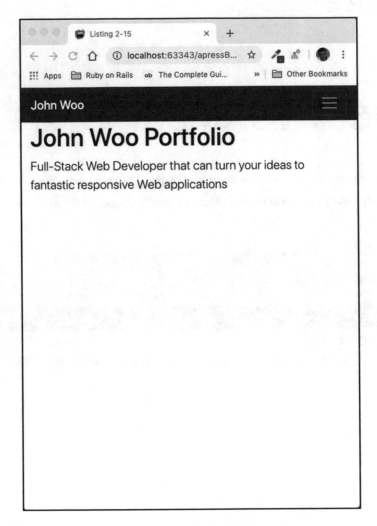

Figure 3-2. *This Is How a Site Looks on Mobile Devices*

When the user clicks the hamburger icon, the menu is unfolded, like the following (Figure 3-3).

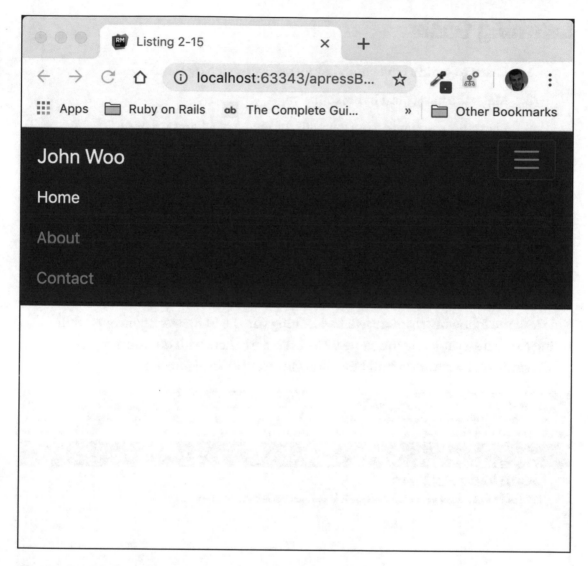

Figure 3-3. Menu Options Appear on Hamburger Icon Click

You will develop this web page, but at the same time, you will understand how the Twitter Bootstrap classes work.

Learning Goals

1. Learn to build a navigation bar for your site, step by step.

2. Make the navigation bar responsive.

3. Learn how to create a button with the shape of a hamburger and how to make it unfold the menu options.

4. Learn how to make the content of a paragraph stand out.

5. Learn about how to make your main content area not be hidden by the navigation bar.

Introduction

This and the following chapters will be teaching you the framework concepts while trying to create a project at the same time. Let's start, then, with our first project.

Assume that we want to build the following website in Figure 3-4.

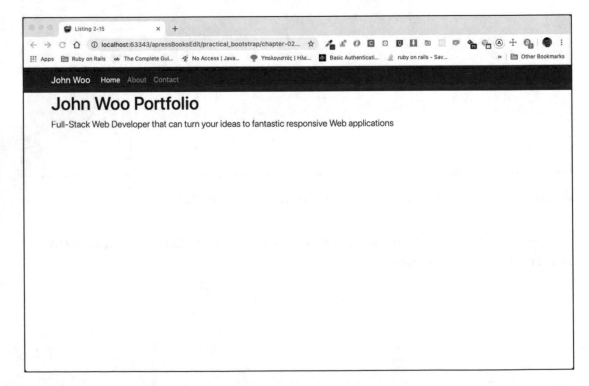

Figure 3-4. *Target Project 1—Basic Template with a Top Nav Bar*

This project has the following characteristics:

1. It has a navigation bar. This navigation bar is responsive. This means that when you resize your browser to mimic the size of a mobile phone, you will see something like Figure 3-5.

Figure 3-5. *This Is How a Site Looks Like on Mobile Devices*

As you can see, the menu options have been collapsed and turned to a hamburger icon. If the user wants to get the list of menu options, they need to click this icon (Figure 3-6).

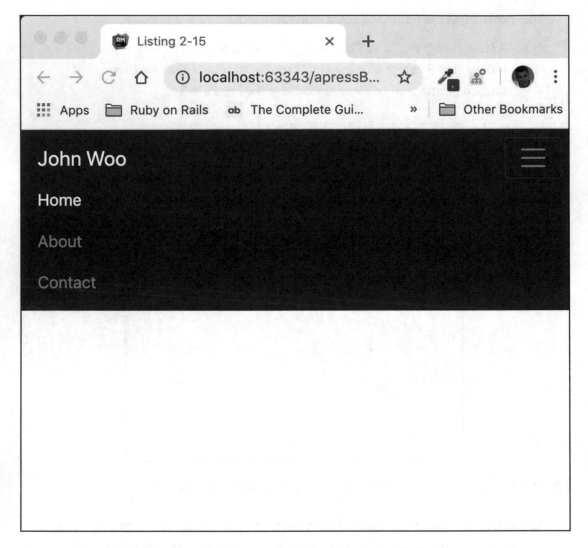

Figure 3-6. Menu Options Appear on Hamburger Icon Click

There are other features on this website that you take for free from Twitter Bootstrap. For example, when you mouse over the options, you will see that the options change color and intensity.

Let's try to build this website from scratch, using Twitter Bootstrap.

Start with HTML

Let's start with the basic HTML that includes a nav bar and a list of items that will be the menu options, like the following (Listing 3-1).

Listing 3-1. Starting with a nav Element and List of Menu Items

```html
<!DOCTYPE html>
<html lang="en">
<head>
    <!-- Required meta tags -->
    <meta charset="utf-8">
    <meta name="viewport" content="width=device-width, initial-scale=1,
    shrink-to-fit=no">

    <!-- Bootstrap CSS -->
    <link rel="stylesheet" href="https://stackpath.bootstrapcdn.
    com/bootstrap/4.4.1/css/bootstrap.min.css" integrity="sha384-
    Vkoo8x4CGsO3+Hhxv8T/Q5PaXtkKtu6ug5TOeNV6gBiFeWPGFN9MuhOf23Q9Ifjh"
    crossorigin="anonymous">

    <!-- Custom CSS -->
    <link rel="stylesheet" href="stylesheets/main.css" type="text/css">

    <title>Listing 3-1</title>
</head>
<body>
    <nav>

        <ul>
            <li ><a href="#">Home</a></li>
            <li><a href="#about">About</a></li>
            <li><a href="#contact">Contact</a></li>
        </ul>

    </nav>
```

```
<!-- Optional JavaScript -->
<!-- jQuery first, then Popper.js, then Bootstrap JS -->
<script src="https://code.jquery.com/jquery-3.4.1.slim.min.js"
integrity="sha384-J6qa4849blE2+poT4WnyKhv5vZF5SrPo0iEjwBvKU7imGFAVOwwj1
yYfoRSJoZ+n" crossorigin="anonymous"></script>
<script src="https://cdn.jsdelivr.net/npm/popper.js@1.16.0/dist/umd/
popper.min.js" integrity="sha384-Q6E9RHvbIyZFJoft+2mJbHaEWldlvI9IOYy5n3
zV9zzTtmI3UksdQRVvoxMfooAo" crossorigin="anonymous"></script>
<script src="https://stackpath.bootstrapcdn.com/bootstrap/4.4.1/js/
bootstrap.min.js" integrity="sha384-wfSDF2E5OY2D1uUdjOO3uMBJnjuUD4Ih7Yw
aYd1iqfktjOUod8GCExl3Og8ifwB6" crossorigin="anonymous"></script>
</body>
</html>
```

Save the preceding code into the file index.html and load the page on your browser. Note that the referenced stylesheets/main.css does not contain anything, for the time being. But create this file so that your page can find it.

You will see the following (Figure 3-7).

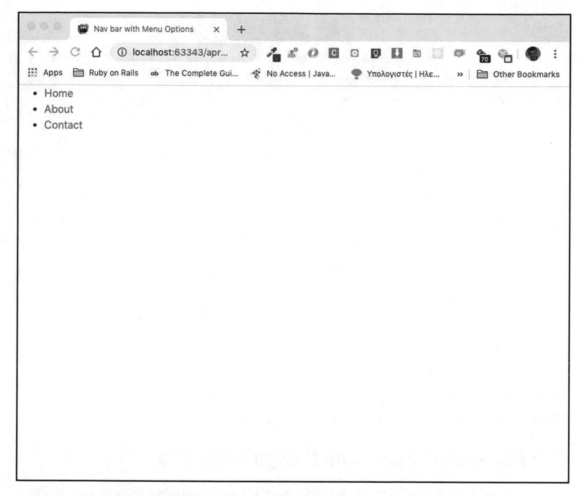

Figure 3-7. *Page with a Nav Bar and Menu Items but Not Styled*

I guess that this was expected. The body element contained nothing but a block element nav and a ul with the menu options. Note that we are using the semantic HTML5 element nav, instead of just a div.

The Class nav

You will first add the class nav on the ul element that holds the menu options. This will remove the bullets from the list. Do the following change. Instead of <ul>, write <ul class="nav">. Save the file and reload the page. You will see the following (Figure 3-8).

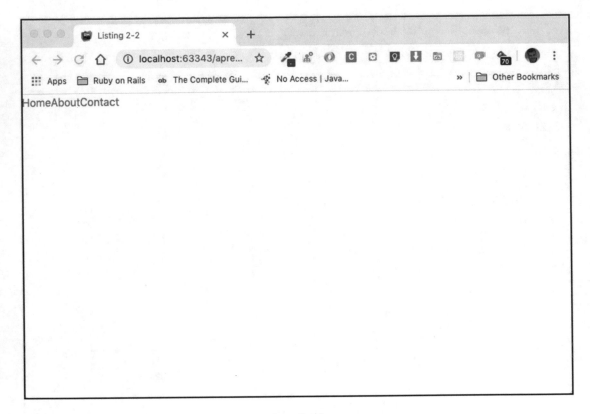

Figure 3-8. *Added the Class nav on the ul Element*

The Navigation Items and Navigation Links

Let's now make the menu items have some space around them, because, now, they are one exactly next to the other.

In order to achieve this, you will add the class nav-item on the li elements and the class nav-link on the anchor a elements. Read Listing 3-2 to see how the current state of your HTML page should be.

Listing 3-2. Menu Items on the Same Line, One Separate from the Other

```
<!DOCTYPE html>
<html lang="en">
<head>
    <!-- Required meta tags -->
    <meta charset="utf-8">
    <meta name="viewport" content="width=device-width, initial-scale=1,
    shrink-to-fit=no">
```

```
<!-- Bootstrap CSS -->
<link rel="stylesheet" href="https://stackpath.bootstrapcdn.
com/bootstrap/4.4.1/css/bootstrap.min.css" integrity="sha384-
Vkoo8x4CGsO3+Hhxv8T/Q5PaXtkKtu6ug5TOeNV6gBiFeWPGFN9MuhOf23Q9Ifjh"
crossorigin="anonymous">

<!-- Custom CSS -->
<link rel="stylesheet" href="stylesheets/main.css" type="text/css">

<title>Listing 3-2</title>
</head>
<body>
    <nav>

        <ul class="nav">
            <li class="nav-item">
                <a class="nav-link" href="#">Home</a>
            </li>
            <li class="nav-item">
                <a class="nav-link" href="#about">About</a>
            </li>
            <li class="nav-item">
                <a class="nav-link" href="#contact">Contact</a>
            </li>
        </ul>

    </nav>
    <!-- Optional JavaScript -->
    <!-- jQuery first, then Popper.js, then Bootstrap JS -->
    <script src="https://code.jquery.com/jquery-3.4.1.slim.min.js"
    integrity="sha384-J6qa4849blE2+poT4WnyKhv5vZF5SrPo0iEjwBvKU7imGFAVOwwj1
    yYfoRSJoZ+n" crossorigin="anonymous"></script>
    <script src="https://cdn.jsdelivr.net/npm/popper.js@1.16.0/dist/umd/
    popper.min.js" integrity="sha384-Q6E9RHvbIyZFJoft+2mJbHaEWldlvI9IOYy5n3
    zV9zzTtmI3UksdQRVvoxMfooAo" crossorigin="anonymous"></script>
```

```
<script src="https://stackpath.bootstrapcdn.com/bootstrap/4.4.1/js/
bootstrap.min.js" integrity="sha384-wfSDF2E50Y2D1uUdjOO3uMBJnjuUD4Ih7Yw
aYd1iqfktjOUod8GCExl30g8ifwB6" crossorigin="anonymous"></script>
</body>
</html>
```

If you load the preceding page on your browser, you will see the following (Figure 3-9).

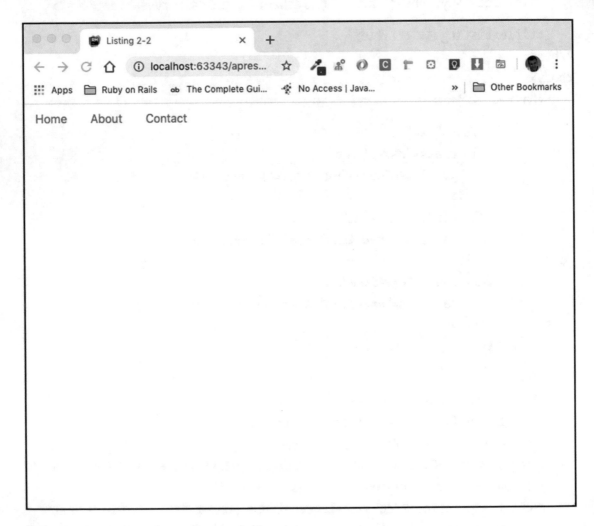

Figure 3-9. *Menu Items Separated*

Collapse and Expand

In order for the list of menu items to be collapsible, that is, to be replaced with a hamburger icon on small devices, which, when clicked, would enlist the menu options, you need to add a special class on the nav element, and you need to wrap the collapsible/expandable content into a div with special classes, like in Listing 3-3.

Listing 3-3. Make Menu Options Collapse and Expand

```
<!DOCTYPE html>
<html lang="en">
<head>
    <!-- Required meta tags -->
    <meta charset="utf-8">
    <meta name="viewport" content="width=device-width, initial-scale=1,
    shrink-to-fit=no">

    <!-- Bootstrap CSS -->
    <link rcl="stylesheet" href-"https://stackpath.bootstrapcdn.
    com/bootstrap/4.4.1/css/bootstrap.min.css" integrity="sha384-
    Vkoo8x4CGsO3+Hhxv8T/Q5PaXtkKtu6ug5TOeNV6gBiFeWPGFN9MuhOf23Q9Ifjh"
    crossorigin="anonymous">

    <!-- Custom CSS -->
    <link rel="stylesheet" href="stylesheets/main.css" type="text/css">

    <title>Listing 3-3</title>
</head>
<body>
    <nav class="navbar-expand-lg">

        <div class="collapse navbar-collapse">
            <ul class="nav">
                <li class="nav-item">
                    <a class="nav-link" href="#">Home</a>
                </li>
                <li class="nav-item">
                    <a class="nav-link" href="#about">About</a>
```

```
                </li>
                <li class="nav-item">
                    <a class="nav-link" href="#contact">Contact</a>
                </li>
            </ul>
        </div>

    </nav>
    <!-- Optional JavaScript -->
    <!-- jQuery first, then Popper.js, then Bootstrap JS -->
    <script src="https://code.jquery.com/jquery-3.4.1.slim.min.js"
    integrity="sha384-J6qa4849blE2+poT4WnyKhv5vZF5SrPo0iEjwBvKU7imGFAVOwwj1
    yYfoRSJoZ+n" crossorigin="anonymous"></script>
    <script src="https://cdn.jsdelivr.net/npm/popper.js@1.16.0/dist/umd/
    popper.min.js" integrity="sha384-Q6E9RHvbIyZFJoft+2mJbHaEWldlvI9IOYy5n3
    zV9zzTtmI3UksdQRVvoxMfooAo" crossorigin="anonymous"></script>
    <script src="https://stackpath.bootstrapcdn.com/bootstrap/4.4.1/js/
    bootstrap.min.js" integrity="sha384-wfSDF2E50Y2D1uUdj0O3uMBJnjuUD4Ih7Yw
    aYd1iqfktj0Uod8GCExl30g8ifwB6" crossorigin="anonymous"></script>
</body>
</html>
```

What you have done in order to make the menu options collapse and expand is the following:

1. You have added the class navbar-expand-lg on the nav element. This instructs the browser to expand the content at the lg breakpoint, that is, for displays greater than or equal to 992px. Apparently, you could have used another breakpoint, for example, the md breakpoint, if you wanted the menu to expand for displays with width >=768px.

2. You have wrapped the ul element into a div element with classes collapse and navbar-collapse. This makes the browser know which content it needs to collapse and expand.

If you load the new HTML content into your browser and set the pixel width to 991px, then you will see a blank page like the following (Figure 3-10).

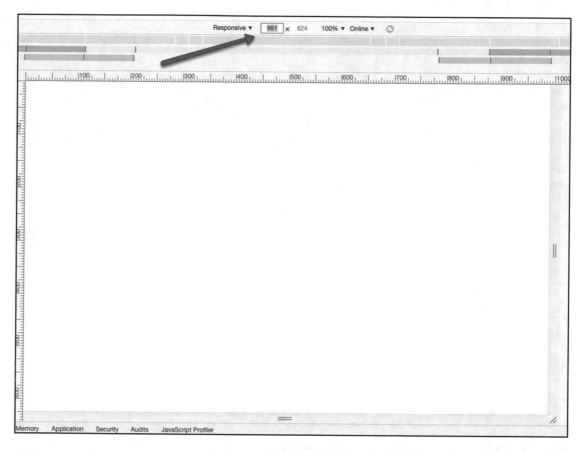

Figure 3-10. *A Blank Page on Width Less Than 992px*

But, if you expand to 992px, then you will see the menu options appearing back again (Figure 3-11).

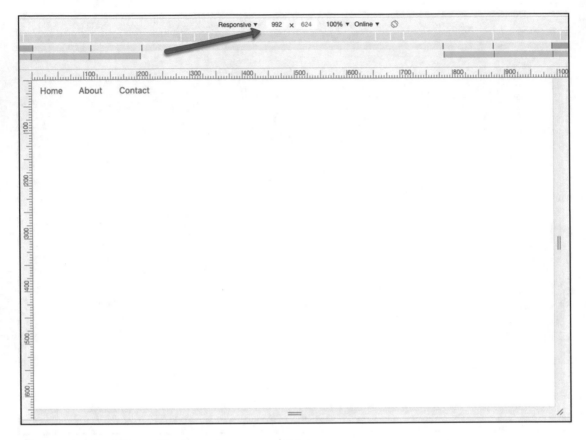

Figure 3-11. *Menu Options Appear on 992px*

The Brand link

If you go back and look again at the final result, you will see that there is the link with text John Woo, which is not hidden when the page shrinks to mobile size. It is always visible, and it is supposed to be a link that would take the user to the home page of the site. It is not part of the list of menu items.

Let's put that above the collapsible div, but still inside the nav element (Listing 3-4).

Listing 3-4. Add the Link That Would Take the User to the Home Page

```
<!DOCTYPE html>
<html lang="en">
<head>
    <!-- Required meta tags -->
    <meta charset="utf-8">
```

```
    <meta name="viewport" content="width=device-width, initial-scale=1,
    shrink-to-fit=no">

    <!-- Bootstrap CSS -->
    <link rel="stylesheet" href="https://stackpath.bootstrapcdn.
    com/bootstrap/4.4.1/css/bootstrap.min.css" integrity="sha384-
    Vkoo8x4CGsO3+Hhxv8T/Q5PaXtkKtu6ug5TOeNV6gBiFeWPGFN9MuhOf23Q9Ifjh"
    crossorigin="anonymous">

    <!-- Custom CSS -->
    <link rel="stylesheet" href="stylesheets/main.css" type="text/css">

    <title>Listing 3-4</title>
</head>
<body>
    <nav class="navbar-expand-lg">

        <a href="#">John Woo</a>

        <div class="collapse navbar-collapse">
            <ul class="nav">
                <li class="nav-item">
                    <a class="nav-link" href="#">Home</a>
                </li>
                <li class="nav-item">
                    <a class="nav-link" href="#about">About</a>
                </li>
                <li class="nav-item">
                    <a class="nav-link" href="#contact">Contact</a>
                </li>
            </ul>
        </div>

    </nav>
    <!-- Optional JavaScript -->
    <!-- jQuery first, then Popper.js, then Bootstrap JS -->
```

```
<script src="https://code.jquery.com/jquery-3.4.1.slim.min.js"
integrity="sha384-J6qa4849blE2+poT4WnyKhv5vZF5SrPo0iEjwBvKU7imGFAVOwwj1
yYfoRSJoZ+n" crossorigin="anonymous"></script>
<script src="https://cdn.jsdelivr.net/npm/popper.js@1.16.0/dist/umd/
popper.min.js" integrity="sha384-Q6E9RHvbIyZFJoft+2mJbHaEWldlvI9IOYy5n3
zV9zzTtmI3UksdQRVvoxMfooAo" crossorigin="anonymous"></script>
<script src="https://stackpath.bootstrapcdn.com/bootstrap/4.4.1/js/
bootstrap.min.js" integrity="sha384-wfSDF2E50Y2D1uUdj0O3uMBJnjuUD4Ih7Yw
aYd1iqfktj0Uod8GCExl3Og8ifwB6" crossorigin="anonymous"></script>
</body>
</html>
```

If you save the preceding code and reload your page, you will see the John Woo link on the left, which, if you shrink the page, remains visible and does not disappear like the menu options do (Figure 3-12).

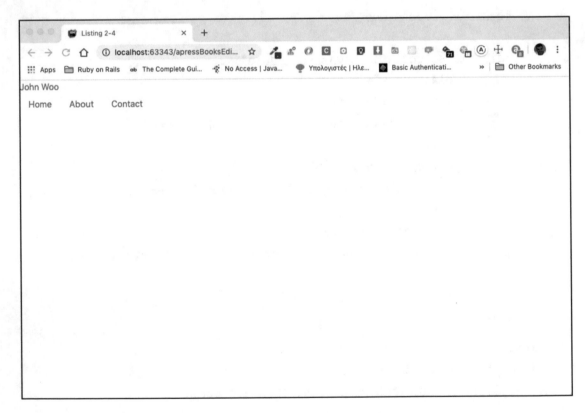

Figure 3-12. *Brand Link Is Separate from Menu Options*

Make the Brand Link Stand Out

The brand link, on the top left, needs to be on the same level as the menu; and it needs to stand out a little bit. Let's do that by

1.   Adding the class navbar to the nav wrapping element

2.   Adding the class navbar-brand to the anchor element

Caution   The navbar class on the nav wrapping element is crucial for the whole styling of the navigation bar, not only for the brand link.

Listing 3-5 is what you need to have in your HTML page in order to make this work.

Listing 3-5. Brand Link on the Same Line and Standing Out

```
<!DOCTYPE html>
<html lang="en">
<head>
    <!-- Required meta tags -->
    <meta charset="utf-8">
    <meta name="viewport" content="width=device-width, initial-scale=1,
    shrink-to-fit=no">

    <!-- Bootstrap CSS -->
    <link rel="stylesheet" href="https://stackpath.bootstrapcdn.
    com/bootstrap/4.4.1/css/bootstrap.min.css" integrity="sha384-
    Vkoo8x4CGsO3+Hhxv8T/Q5PaXtkKtu6ug5TOeNV6gBiFeWPGFN9MuhOf23Q9Ifjh"
    crossorigin="anonymous">

    <!-- Custom CSS -->
    <link rel="stylesheet" href="stylesheets/main.css" type="text/css">

    <title>Listing 3-5</title>
</head>
```

```
<body>
    <nav class="navbar navbar-expand-lg">

        <a class="navbar-brand" href="#">John Woo</a>

        <div class="collapse navbar-collapse">
            <ul class="nav">
                <li class="nav-item">
                    <a class="nav-link" href="#">Home</a>
                </li>
                <li class="nav-item">
                    <a class="nav-link" href="#about">About</a>
                </li>
                <li class="nav-item">
                    <a class="nav-link" href="#contact">Contact</a>
                </li>
            </ul>
        </div>

    </nav>
    <!-- Optional JavaScript -->
    <!-- jQuery first, then Popper.js, then Bootstrap JS -->
    <script src="https://code.jquery.com/jquery-3.4.1.slim.min.js"
    integrity="sha384-J6qa4849blE2+poT4WnyKhv5vZF5SrPo0iEjwBvKU7imGFAVOwwj1
    yYfoRSJoZ+n" crossorigin="anonymous"></script>
    <script src="https://cdn.jsdelivr.net/npm/popper.js@1.16.0/dist/umd/
    popper.min.js" integrity="sha384-Q6E9RHvbIyZFJoft+2mJbHaEWldlvI9IOYy5n3
    zV9zzTtmI3UksdQRVvoxMfooAo" crossorigin="anonymous"></script>
    <script src="https://stackpath.bootstrapcdn.com/bootstrap/4.4.1/js/
    bootstrap.min.js" integrity="sha384-wfSDF2E50Y2D1uUdjOO3uMBJnjuUD4Ih7Yw
    aYd1iqfktjOUod8GCExl3Og8ifwB6" crossorigin="anonymous"></script>
</body>
</html>
```

If you load the preceding HTML page on your browser, you will see what is depicted in Figure 3-13.

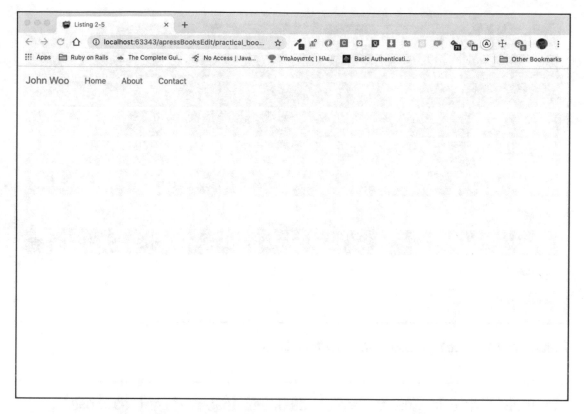

Figure 3-13. *Brand Link Standing Out on the Left*

Add Some Color to Your Nav Bar

Let's add some color to your nav bar. In order to do that, you have to

1. Use one of the navbar-dark or navbar-light classes at the nav element.

2. Combine it with a background color utility class.

The former is basically dealing with the font colors, whereas the latter is dealing with the background colors. Usually you would like to combine the *-dark class with the dark background colors and the *-light class with the light background colors.

The background color utilities are listed in Figure 3-14.

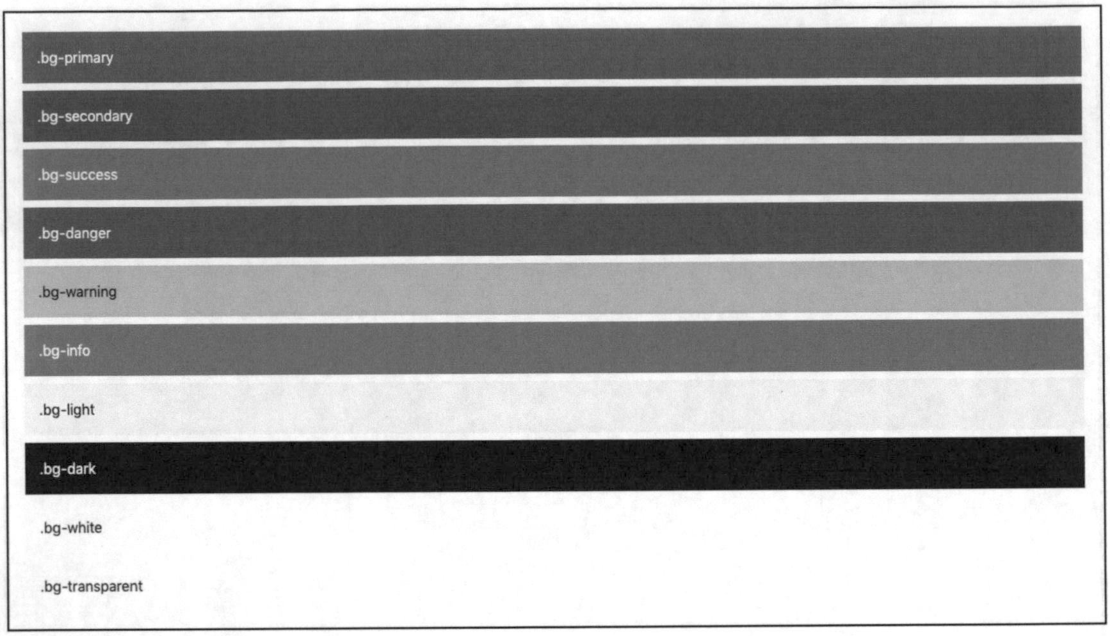

Figure 3-14. *Background Color Utility Classes*

Caution   The color classes, navbar-dark and navbar-light, have been designed to expect the ul element to have the class navbar-nav. So we are going to add that too.

In Listing 3-6, we are applying the bg-dark background color utility class, combined with the navbar-dark color scheme for the navigation bar. We also add the class navbar-nav to the ul element.

Listing 3-6. Coloring the Navigation Bar

```
<!DOCTYPE html>
<html lang="en">
<head>
    <!-- Required meta tags -->
    <meta charset="utf-8">
    <meta name="viewport" content="width=device-width, initial-scale=1,
    shrink-to-fit=no">
```

```html
<!-- Bootstrap CSS -->
<link rel="stylesheet" href="https://stackpath.bootstrapcdn.
com/bootstrap/4.4.1/css/bootstrap.min.css" integrity="sha384-
Vkoo8x4CGsO3+Hhxv8T/Q5PaXtkKtu6ug5TOeNV6gBiFeWPGFN9MuhOf23Q9Ifjh"
crossorigin="anonymous">

<!-- Custom CSS -->
<link rel="stylesheet" href="stylesheets/main.css" type="text/css">

<title>Listing 3-6</title>
</head>
<body>
    <nav class="navbar navbar-expand-lg navbar-dark bg-dark">

        <a class="navbar-brand" href="#">John Woo</a>

        <div class="collapse navbar-collapse">
            <ul class="navbar-nav nav">
                <li class="nav-item">
                    <a class="nav-link" href="#">Home</a>
                </li>
                <li class="nav-item">
                    <a class="nav-link" href="#about">About</a>
                </li>
                <li class="nav-item">
                    <a class="nav-link" href="#contact">Contact</a>
                </li>
            </ul>
        </div>

    </nav>
    <!-- Optional JavaScript -->
    <!-- jQuery first, then Popper.js, then Bootstrap JS -->
    <script src="https://code.jquery.com/jquery-3.4.1.slim.min.js"
integrity="sha384-J6qa4849blE2+poT4WnyKhv5vZF5SrPo0iEjwBvKU7imGFAVOwwj1
yYfoRSJoZ+n" crossorigin="anonymous"></script>
```

```
<script src="https://cdn.jsdelivr.net/npm/popper.js@1.16.0/dist/umd/
popper.min.js" integrity="sha384-Q6E9RHvbIyZFJoft+2mJbHaEWldlvI9IOYy5n3
zV9zzTtmI3UksdQRVvoxMfooAo" crossorigin="anonymous"></script>
<script src="https://stackpath.bootstrapcdn.com/bootstrap/4.4.1/js/
bootstrap.min.js" integrity="sha384-wfSDF2E50Y2D1uUdjOO3uMBJnjuUD4Ih7Yw
aYd1iqfktjOUod8GCExl3Og8ifwB6" crossorigin="anonymous"></script>
</body>
</html>
```

If you load the preceding HTML page on your browser, you will see what is depicted in Figure 3-15.

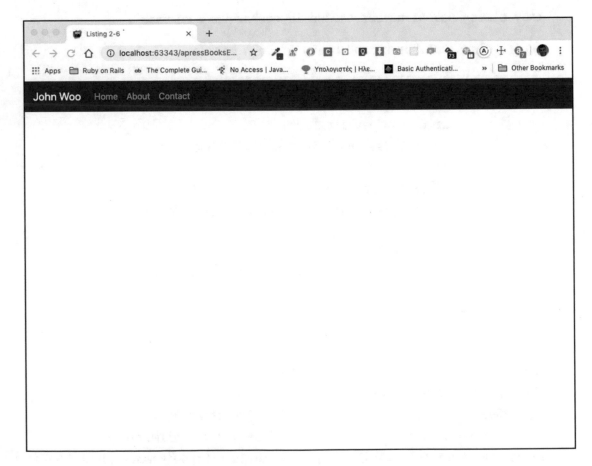

Figure 3-15. *Coloring the Navigation Bar*

Also, hover your mouse pointer over the menu options. You will see how the links are getting lighter.

Adding the Button to Unfold Menu Options on Small Devices

Let's add a button. This will be clicked to unfold the menu options on small devices. See Listing 3-7.

Listing 3-7. Add a Button That Will Toggle the Menu On and Off on Small Devices

```
<!DOCTYPE html>
<html lang="en">
<head>
    <!-- Required meta tags -->
    <meta charset="utf-8">
    <meta name="viewport" content="width=device-width, initial-scale=1,
    shrink-to-fit=no">

    <!-- Bootstrap CSS -->
    <link rel="stylesheet" href="https://stackpath.bootstrapcdn.
    com/bootstrap/4.4.1/css/bootstrap.min.css" integrity="sha384-
    Vkoo8x4CGsO3+Hhxv8T/Q5PaXtkKtu6ug5TOeNV6gBiFeWPGFN9MuhOf23Q9Ifjh"
    crossorigin="anonymous">

    <!-- Custom CSS -->
    <link rel="stylesheet" href="stylesheets/main.css" type="text/css">

    <title>Listing 3-7</title>
</head>
<body>
    <nav class="navbar navbar-expand-lg navbar-dark bg-dark">

        <a class="navbar-brand" href="#">John Woo</a>

        <button type="button">
        </button>
```

```
        <div class="collapse navbar-collapse">
            <ul class="nav navbar-nav">
                <li class="nav-item">
                    <a class="nav-link" href="#">Home</a>
                </li>
                <li class="nav-item">
                    <a class="nav-link" href="#about">About</a>
                </li>
                <li class="nav-item">
                    <a class="nav-link" href="#contact">Contact</a>
                </li>
            </ul>
        </div>

    </nav>
    <!-- Optional JavaScript -->
    <!-- jQuery first, then Popper.js, then Bootstrap JS -->
    <script src="https://code.jquery.com/jquery-3.4.1.slim.min.js"
    integrity="sha384-J6qa4849blE2+poT4WnyKhv5vZF5SrPo0iEjwBvKU7imGFAVOwwj1
    yYfoRSJoZ+n" crossorigin="anonymous"></script>
    <script src="https://cdn.jsdelivr.net/npm/popper.js@1.16.0/dist/umd/
    popper.min.js" integrity="sha384-Q6E9RHvbIyZFJoft+2mJbHaEWldlvI9IOYy5n3
    zV9zzTtmI3UksdQRVvoxMfooAo" crossorigin="anonymous"></script>
    <script src="https://stackpath.bootstrapcdn.com/bootstrap/4.4.1/js/
    bootstrap.min.js" integrity="sha384-wfSDF2E50Y2D1uUdj0O3uMBJnjuUD4Ih7Yw
    aYd1iqfktjOUod8GCExl3Og8ifwB6" crossorigin="anonymous"></script>
</body>
</html>
```

You have added the button as a sibling of the brand anchor, but after it. If you load this HTML page on your browser, you will see the following (Figure 3-16).

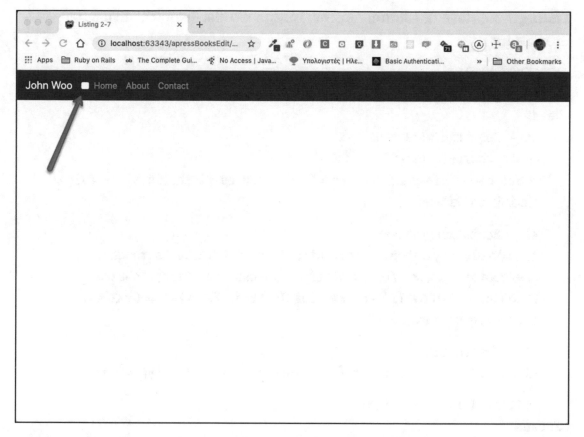

Figure 3-16. *Unstyled Button to Toggle the Menu On and Off*

This is pretty bad. Indeed. But it's a start.

Making the Button Appear Only on Small Devices

The problem you have with the button, at the moment, is that it always appears. What you want is that it appears only on devices with width below the expanded breakpoint that you have set on the nav element. The breakpoint that you have set is lg, which means that you want the button to appear for displays with width <992px.

In order to do that, you can add the class navbar-toggler. Let's do that. See Listing 3-8.

Listing 3-8. Make the Button Appear Only on Widths Below the Expanded
Breakpoint

```
<!DOCTYPE html>
<html lang="en">
<head>
    <!-- Required meta tags -->
    <meta charset="utf-8">
    <meta name="viewport" content="width=device-width, initial-scale=1,
    shrink-to-fit=no">

    <!-- Bootstrap CSS -->
    <link rel="stylesheet" href="https://stackpath.bootstrapcdn.
    com/bootstrap/4.4.1/css/bootstrap.min.css" integrity="sha384-
    Vkoo8x4CGsO3+Hhxv8T/Q5PaXtkKtu6ug5TOeNV6gBiFeWPGFN9MuhOf23Q9Ifjh"
    crossorigin="anonymous">

    <!-- Custom CSS -->
    <link rel="stylesheet" href="stylesheets/main.css" type="text/css">

    <title>Listing 3-8</title>
</head>
<body>
    <nav class="navbar navbar-expand-lg navbar-dark bg-dark">

        <a class="navbar-brand" href="#">John Woo</a>

        <button type="button" class="navbar-toggler">
        </button>

        <div class="collapse navbar-collapse">
            <ul class="nav navbar-nav">
                <li class="nav-item">
                    <a class="nav-link" href="#">Home</a>
                </li>
                <li class="nav-item">
                    <a class="nav-link" href="#about">About</a>
                </li>
                <li class="nav-item">
```

```
            <a class="nav-link" href="#contact">Contact</a>
         </li>
      </ul>
   </div>

</nav>
<!-- Optional JavaScript -->
<!-- jQuery first, then Popper.js, then Bootstrap JS -->
<script src="https://code.jquery.com/jquery-3.4.1.slim.min.js"
integrity="sha384-J6qa4849blE2+poT4WnyKhv5vZF5SrPo0iEjwBvKU7imGFAVOwwj1
yYfoRSJoZ+n" crossorigin="anonymous"></script>
<script src="https://cdn.jsdelivr.net/npm/popper.js@1.16.0/dist/umd/
popper.min.js" integrity="sha384-Q6E9RHvbIyZFJoft+2mJbHaEWldlvI9IOYy5n3
zV9zzTtmI3UksdQRVvoxMfooAo" crossorigin="anonymous"></script>
<script src="https://stackpath.bootstrapcdn.com/bootstrap/4.4.1/js/
bootstrap.min.js" integrity="sha384-wfSDF2E50Y2D1uUdj0O3uMBJnjuUD4Ih7Yw
aYd1iqfktj0Uod8GCExl3Og8ifwB6" crossorigin="anonymous"></script>
</body>
</html>
```

Now, when you have a display >=992px, the button does not appear (Figure 3-17).

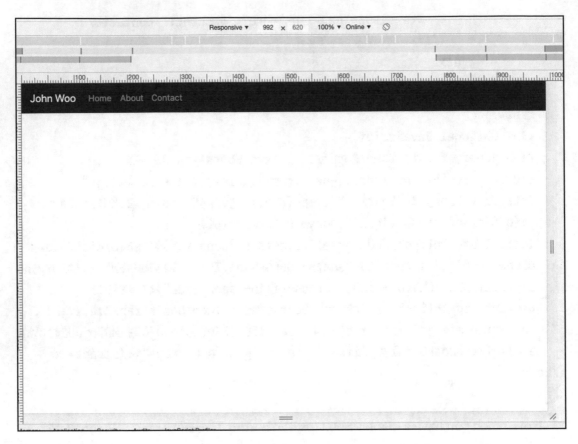

Figure 3-17. *Menu Is Visible; Button to Toggle Is Not Visible (>=992px)*

When you shrink by 1 pixel, to 991px, then you will see the menu disappearing and the button appearing (Figure 3-18).

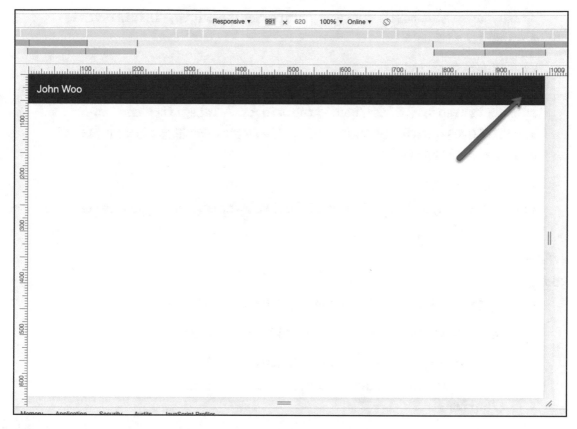

Figure 3-18. *Menu Hidden, but Button Present (<992px)*

The button appears in a way that is very hard to see. This is fixed next.

Creating the Hamburger Icon

The button does not look good on small devices, and this is because it does not have actual content inside. In order to create the visual icon of the hamburger, Twitter Bootstrap gives you the class `navbar-toggler-icon`. You need to apply that on a `span` element inside the `button` element. See Listing 3-9.

Listing 3-9. Creating the Hamburger Icon

```
<!DOCTYPE html>
<html lang="en">
<head>
    <!-- Required meta tags -->
    <meta charset="utf-8">
```

```html
    <meta name="viewport" content="width=device-width, initial-scale=1,
    shrink-to-fit=no">

    <!-- Bootstrap CSS -->
    <link rel="stylesheet" href="https://stackpath.bootstrapcdn.
    com/bootstrap/4.4.1/css/bootstrap.min.css" integrity="sha384-
    Vkoo8x4CGsO3+Hhxv8T/Q5PaXtkKtu6ug5TOeNV6gBiFeWPGFN9MuhOf23Q9Ifjh"
    crossorigin="anonymous">

    <!-- Custom CSS -->
    <link rel="stylesheet" href="stylesheets/main.css" type="text/css">

    <title>Listing 3-9</title>
</head>
<body>
    <nav class="navbar navbar-expand-lg navbar-dark bg-dark">

        <a class="navbar-brand" href="#">John Woo</a>

        <button type="button" class="navbar-toggler">
            <span class="navbar-toggler-icon"></span>
        </button>

        <div class="collapse navbar-collapse">
            <ul class="nav navbar-nav">
                <li class="nav-item">
                    <a class="nav-link" href="#">Home</a>
                </li>
                <li class="nav-item">
                    <a class="nav-link" href="#about">About</a>
                </li>
                <li class="nav-item">
                    <a class="nav-link" href="#contact">Contact</a>
                </li>
            </ul>
        </div>

    </nav>
    <!-- Optional JavaScript -->
    <!-- jQuery first, then Popper.js, then Bootstrap JS -->
```

```
<script src="https://code.jquery.com/jquery-3.4.1.slim.min.js"
integrity="sha384-J6qa4849blE2+poT4WnyKhv5vZF5SrPo0iEjwBvKU7imGFAVOwwj1
yYfoRSJoZ+n" crossorigin="anonymous"></script>
<script src="https://cdn.jsdelivr.net/npm/popper.js@1.16.0/dist/umd/
popper.min.js" integrity="sha384-Q6E9RHvbIyZFJoft+2mJbHaEWldlvI9IOYy5n3
zV9zzTtmI3UksdQRVvoxMfooAo" crossorigin="anonymous"></script>
<script src="https://stackpath.bootstrapcdn.com/bootstrap/4.4.1/js/
bootstrap.min.js" integrity="sha384-wfSDF2E50Y2D1uUdj0O3uMBJnjuUD4Ih7Yw
aYd1iqfktj0Uod8GCExl3Og8ifwB6" crossorigin="anonymous"></script>
</body>
</html>
```

If you load the preceding HTML page on a display with 991px width, you will see the following (Figure 3-19).

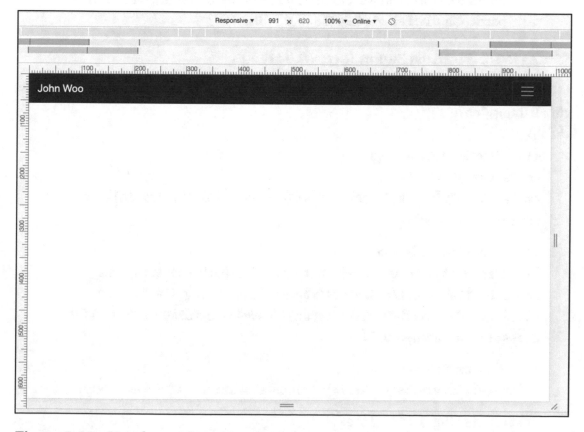

Figure 3-19. *Hamburger Icon Now Present*

Adding Behavior to the Button

If you try to click the hamburger button, nothing happens. You now need to add behavior to the button. When the button is clicked, the menu options unfold. You will do that by adding two data-* attributes to the button element:

- data-toggle="collapse", which tells Twitter Bootstrap that this button is used to collapse/unfold a specific area of the HTML document

- data-target="#navbar", which tells Twitter Bootstrap that the specific area that needs to be collapsed/unfolded is the one that is selected with the CSS selector #navbar. Of course, since there is no such element (with id navbar) in your HTML document, but the element that you want to fold/unfold is the container that holds the menu items list, you will add the id attribute with value navbar to this particular div. Let's do that (Listing 3-10).

Listing 3-10. Make the Button Toggle the Menu

```
<!DOCTYPE html>
<html lang="en">
<head>
    <!-- Required meta tags -->
    <meta charset="utf-8">
    <meta name="viewport" content="width=device-width, initial-scale=1,
    shrink-to-fit=no">

    <!-- Bootstrap CSS -->
    <link rel="stylesheet" href="https://stackpath.bootstrapcdn.
    com/bootstrap/4.4.1/css/bootstrap.min.css" integrity="sha384-
    Vkoo8x4CGsO3+Hhxv8T/Q5PaXtkKtu6ug5TOeNV6gBiFeWPGFN9MuhOf23Q9Ifjh"
    crossorigin="anonymous">

    <!-- Custom CSS -->
    <link rel="stylesheet" href="stylesheets/main.css" type="text/css">

    <title>Listing 3-10</title>
</head>
```

```
<body>
    <nav class="navbar navbar-expand-lg navbar-dark bg-dark">

        <a class="navbar-brand" href="#">John Woo</a>

        <button type="button" class="navbar-toggler" data-toggle="collapse"
        data-target="#navbar">
            <span class="navbar-toggler-icon"></span>
        </button>

        <div class="collapse navbar-collapse" id="navbar">
            <ul class="nav navbar-nav">
                <li class="nav-item">
                    <a class="nav-link" href="#">Home</a>
                </li>
                <li class="nav-item">
                    <a class="nav-link" href="#about">About</a>
                </li>
                <li class="nav-item">
                    <a class="nav-link" href="#contact">Contact</a>
                </li>
            </ul>
        </div>

    </nav>
    <!-- Optional JavaScript -->
    <!-- jQuery first, then Popper.js, then Bootstrap JS -->
    <script src="https://code.jquery.com/jquery-3.4.1.slim.min.js"
    integrity="sha384-J6qa4849blE2+poT4WnyKhv5vZF5SrPo0iEjwBvKU7imGFAVOwwj1
    yYfoRSJoZ+n" crossorigin="anonymous"></script>
    <script src="https://cdn.jsdelivr.net/npm/popper.js@1.16.0/dist/umd/
    popper.min.js" integrity="sha384-Q6E9RHvbIyZFJoft+2mJbHaEWldlvI9IOYy5n3
    zV9zzTtmI3UksdQRVvoxMfooAo" crossorigin="anonymous"></script>
    <script src="https://stackpath.bootstrapcdn.com/bootstrap/4.4.1/js/
    bootstrap.min.js" integrity="sha384-wfSDF2E50Y2D1uUdjOO3uMBJnjuUD4Ih7Yw
    aYd1iqfktjOUod8GCExl3Og8ifwB6" crossorigin="anonymous"></script>
</body>
</html>
```

If you save the preceding content and load the page on your browser, you will now see that the button toggles the menu on and off. In Figure 3-20, I display how it looks like with the menu expanded.

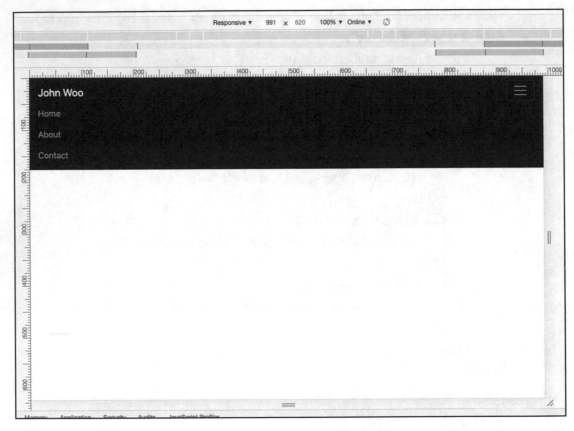

Figure 3-20. *Menu Expanded After Clicking the Button*

Final Touches to Our Navigation Bar

- `fixed-top` on `nav` element will fix the position of the navigation bar at the top of the page.

- You will also add some elements and attributes to make the whole navigation bar ready to be used with assistive technologies, for example, with screen readers.

- You will also add the class `active` to the first menu item, to indicate that you are on the page that this link corresponds to.

Here is the final version of your page with the navigation bar ready (Listing 3-11).

Listing 3-11. Final HTML Page

```
<!DOCTYPE html>
<html lang="en">
<head>
    <!-- Required meta tags -->
    <meta charset="utf-8">
    <meta name="viewport" content="width=device-width, initial-scale=1,
    shrink-to-fit=no">

    <!-- Bootstrap CSS -->
    <link rel="stylesheet" href="https://stackpath.bootstrapcdn.
    com/bootstrap/4.4.1/css/bootstrap.min.css" integrity="sha384-
    Vkoo8x4CGsO3+Hhxv8T/Q5PaXtkKtu6ug5TOeNV6gBiFeWPGFN9MuhOf23Q9Ifjh"
    crossorigin="anonymous">

    <!-- Custom CSS -->
    <link rel="stylesheet" href="stylesheets/main.css" type="text/css">

    <title>Listing 3-11</title>
</head>
<body>
    <nav class="navbar navbar-expand-lg navbar-dark bg-dark fixed-top">
        <a class="navbar-brand" href="#">John Woo</a>

        <button type="button" class="navbar-toggler" data-toggle="collapse"
        data-target="#navbar"
                aria-controls="navbar"
                aria-expanded="false"
                aria-label="Toggle navigation">
            <span class="navbar-toggler-icon"></span>
        </button>

        <div class="collapse navbar-collapse" id="navbar">
            <ul class="nav navbar-nav">
                <li class="nav-item">
```

```
                        <a class="nav-link active" href="#">Home <span
                        class="sr-only">(current)</span></a>
                    </li>
                    <li class="nav-item">
                        <a class="nav-link" href="#about">About</a>
                    </li>
                    <li class="nav-item">
                        <a class="nav-link" href="#contact">Contact</a>
                    </li>
                </ul>
            </div>
        </nav>

        <!-- Optional JavaScript -->
        <!-- jQuery first, then Popper.js, then Bootstrap JS -->
        <script src="https://code.jquery.com/jquery-3.4.1.slim.min.js"
        integrity="sha384-J6qa4849blE2+poT4WnyKhv5vZF5SrPo0iEjwBvKU7imGFAVOwwj1
        yYfoRSJoZ+n" crossorigin="anonymous"></script>
        <script src="https://cdn.jsdelivr.net/npm/popper.js@1.16.0/dist/umd/
        popper.min.js" integrity="sha384-Q6E9RHvbIyZFJoft+2mJbHaEWldlvI9IOYy5n3
        zV9zzTtmI3UksdQRVvoxMfooAo" crossorigin="anonymous"></script>
        <script src="https://stackpath.bootstrapcdn.com/bootstrap/4.4.1/js/
        bootstrap.min.js" integrity="sha384-wfSDF2E50Y2D1uUdjOO3uMBJnjuUD4Ih7Yw
        aYd1iqfktjOUod8GCExl30g8ifwB6" crossorigin="anonymous"></script>
    </body>
</html>
```

If you save the preceding content and load the page on a display of 992px width, you will see Figure 3-21.

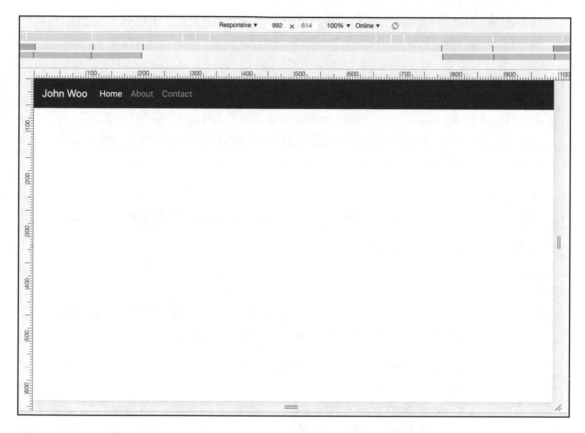

Figure 3-21. *Final Page with a Navigation Bar on 992px*

Your navigation bar works perfectly, and you have not written a single line of CSS or JavaScript code. Isn't it amazing? All thanks to Twitter Bootstrap.

Adding the Main Content

You have added/created the navigation bar. Let's now add the main content of your page (Listing 3-12).

Listing 3-12. We Add the Main Content

```
<!DOCTYPE html>
<html lang="en">
<head>
    <!-- Required meta tags -->
    <meta charset="utf-8">
```

```
    <meta name="viewport" content="width=device-width, initial-scale=1,
    shrink-to-fit=no">

    <!-- Bootstrap CSS -->
    <link rel="stylesheet" href="https://stackpath.bootstrapcdn.
    com/bootstrap/4.4.1/css/bootstrap.min.css" integrity="sha384-
    Vkoo8x4CGsO3+Hhxv8T/Q5PaXtkKtu6ug5TOeNV6gBiFeWPGFN9MuhOf23Q9Ifjh"
    crossorigin="anonymous">

    <!-- Custom CSS -->
    <link rel="stylesheet" href="stylesheets/main.css" type="text/css">

    <title>Listing 3-12</title>
</head>
<body>
    <nav class="navbar navbar-expand-lg navbar-dark bg-dark fixed-top">
        <a class="navbar-brand" href="#">John Woo</a>

        <button type="button" class="navbar-toggler" data-toggle="collapse"
        data-target="#navbar"
                aria-controls="navbar"
                aria-expanded="false"
                aria-label="Toggle navigation">
            <span class="navbar-toggler-icon"></span>
        </button>

        <div class="collapse navbar-collapse" id="navbar">
            <ul class="nav navbar-nav">
                <li class="nav-item">
                    <a class="nav-link active" href="#">Home <span
                    class="sr-only">(current)</span></a>
                </li>
                <li class="nav-item">
                    <a class="nav-link" href="#about">About</a>
                </li>
                <li class="nav-item">
                    <a class="nav-link" href="#contact">Contact</a>
                </li>
```

```
        </ul>
      </div>
    </nav>

    <div class="container">

      <h1>John Woo Portfolio</h1>
      <p>Full-Stack Web Developer that can turn your ideas to fantastic
      responsive Web applications</p>

    </div>

    <!-- Optional JavaScript -->
    <!-- jQuery first, then Popper.js, then Bootstrap JS -->
    <script src="https://code.jquery.com/jquery-3.4.1.slim.min.js"
    integrity="sha384-J6qa4849blE2+poT4WnyKhv5vZF5SrPo0iEjwBvKU7imGFAVOwwj1
    yYfoRSJoZ+n" crossorigin="anonymous"></script>
    <script src="https://cdn.jsdelivr.net/npm/popper.js@1.16.0/dist/umd/
    popper.min.js" integrity="sha384-Q6E9RHvbIyZFJoft+2mJbHaEWldlvI9IOYy5n3
    zV9zzTtmI3UksdQRVvoxMfooAo" crossorigin="anonymous"></script>
    <script src="https://stackpath.bootstrapcdn.com/bootstrap/4.4.1/js/
    bootstrap.min.js" integrity="sha384-wfSDF2E50Y2D1uUdj0O3uMBJnjuUD4Ih7Yw
    aYd1iqfktjOUod8GCExl3Og8ifwB6" crossorigin="anonymous"></script>
  </body>
</html>
```

You have added a div with the class container below the nav element. Inside this new div, you have added an h1 and a p element with some content inside them.

Let's save the content and load the page on the browser. You will see the following (Figure 3-22).

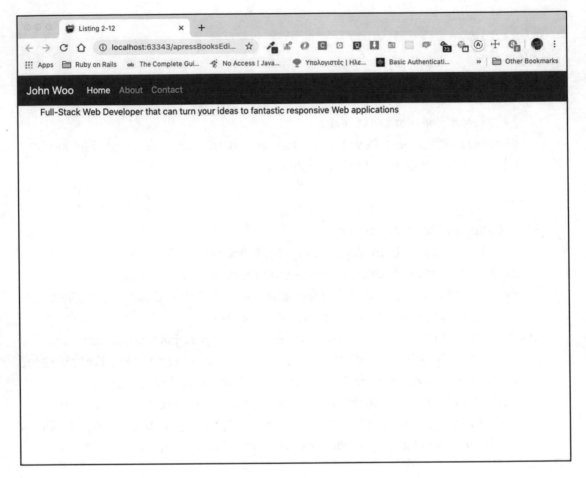

Figure 3-22. *Main Content Hidden Behind the Top Nav Bar*

You can see the problem, I guess. The h1 header is hidden behind the top navigation bar.

In order to resolve this, we will have to add some custom CSS. You will have to ask the body to position its actual content so many pixels below the top, as the height of the navigation bar. Figure 3-23 is depicting how you can find out the height of the top navigation bar, with the help of the developer tools.

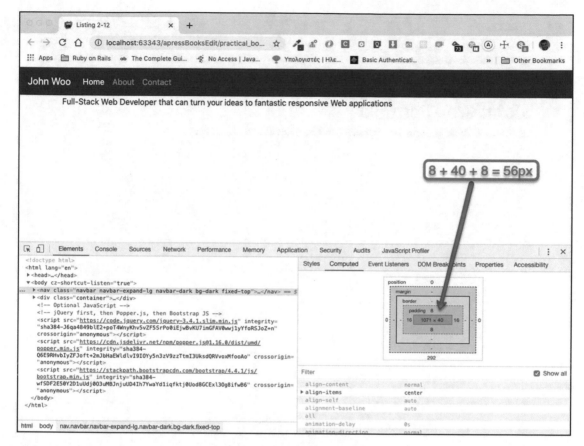

Figure 3-23. *Calculate the Height of the Top Navigation Bar*

As you can see from the developer tools, the height of the top navigation bar is 56px, calculated by adding the top and bottom paddings and content height.

With 56px at hand, let's add some content inside the stylesheets/main.css file (Listing 3-13).

Listing 3-13. Content of the main.css File

```css
body {
    padding-top: 56px;
}
```

Now, if you load your page again (make sure that it references the stylesheets/main.css), it will look like the following (Figure 3-24).

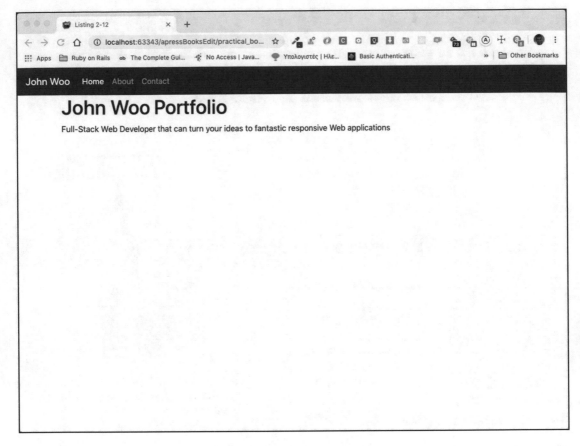

Figure 3-24. *h1 Is Now Visible*

Making the Paragraph Content Stand Out

There are some small differences to the original site. One is that the paragraph content is plain, normal-size text. You want to make it stand out. You will use the class lead for that (again provided to us by Twitter Bootstrap).

Make the p element have that class (Listing 3-14).

Listing 3-14. Make the Paragraph Stand Out

```
<!DOCTYPE html>
<html lang="en">
<head>
    <!-- Required meta tags -->
    <meta charset="utf-8">
```

```
<meta name="viewport" content="width=device-width, initial-scale=1,
shrink-to-fit=no">

<!-- Bootstrap CSS -->
<link rel="stylesheet" href="https://stackpath.bootstrapcdn.
com/bootstrap/4.4.1/css/bootstrap.min.css" integrity="sha384-
Vkoo8x4CGsO3+Hhxv8T/Q5PaXtkKtu6ug5TOeNV6gBiFeWPGFN9MuhOf23Q9Ifjh"
crossorigin="anonymous">

<!-- Custom CSS -->
<link rel="stylesheet" href="stylesheets/main.css" type="text/css">

<title>Listing 3-14</title>
</head>
<body>
    <nav class="navbar navbar-expand-lg navbar-dark bg-dark fixed-top">
        <a class="navbar-brand" href="#">John Woo</a>

        <button type="button" class="navbar-toggler" data-toggle="collapse"
        data-target="#navbar"
                aria-controls="navbar"
                aria-expanded="false"
                aria-label="Toggle navigation">
            <span class="navbar-toggler-icon"></span>
        </button>

        <div class="collapse navbar-collapse" id="navbar">
            <ul class="nav navbar-nav">
                <li class="nav-item">
                    <a class="nav-link active" href="#">Home <span
                    class="sr-only">(current)</span></a>
                </li>
                <li class="nav-item">
                    <a class="nav-link" href="#about">About</a>
                </li>
                <li class="nav-item">
                    <a class="nav-link" href="#contact">Contact</a>
                </li>
```

```
            </ul>
        </div>
    </nav>

    <div class="container">

        <h1>John Woo Portfolio</h1>
        <p class="lead">Full-Stack Web Developer that can turn your ideas
        to fantastic responsive Web applications</p>

    </div>

    <!-- Optional JavaScript -->
    <!-- jQuery first, then Popper.js, then Bootstrap JS -->
    <script src="https://code.jquery.com/jquery-3.4.1.slim.min.js"
    integrity="sha384-J6qa4849blE2+poT4WnyKhv5vZF5SrPo0iEjwBvKU7imGFAVOwwj1
    yYfoRSJoZ+n" crossorigin="anonymous"></script>
    <script src="https://cdn.jsdelivr.net/npm/popper.js@1.16.0/dist/umd/
    popper.min.js" integrity="sha384-Q6E9RHvbIyZFJoft+2mJbHaEWldlvI9IOYy5n3
    zV9zzTtmI3UksdQRVvoxMfooAo" crossorigin="anonymous"></script>
    <script src="https://stackpath.bootstrapcdn.com/bootstrap/4.4.1/js/
    bootstrap.min.js" integrity="sha384-wfSDF2E50Y2D1uUdjOO3uMBJnjuUD4Ih7Yw
    aYd1iqfktjOUod8GCExl3Og8ifwB6" crossorigin="anonymous"></script>
</body>
</html>
```

If you save and load your page again, you will see Figure 3-25.

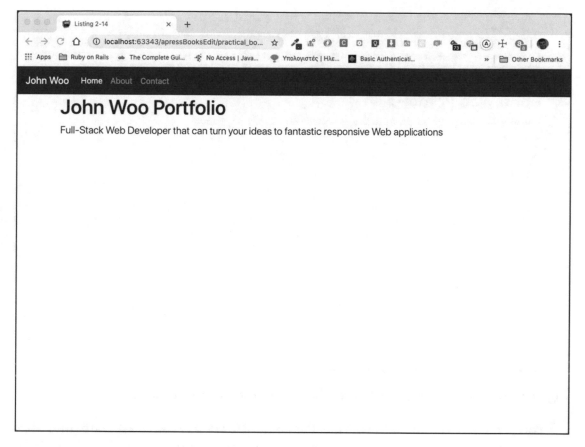

Figure 3-25. *Paragraph Stands Out*

Aligning Nav Bar Content with Page Main Content

So far, so good, but there is one more thing to fix. The content of the nav bar is not aligned with the main content of the page. See the problem in Figure 3-26.

Figure 3-26. *Nav Bar Content Misaligned with Page Main Content*

You can fix this by wrapping the nav bar content into a div with class container, like you have done with the main content of the page (Listing 3-15).

Listing 3-15. Wrap Nav Bar Content into a Container

```
<!DOCTYPE html>
<html lang="en">
<head>
    <!-- Required meta tags -->
    <meta charset="utf-8">
    <meta name="viewport" content="width=device-width, initial-scale=1,
    shrink-to-fit=no">

    <!-- Bootstrap CSS -->
    <link rel="stylesheet" href="https://stackpath.bootstrapcdn.
    com/bootstrap/4.4.1/css/bootstrap.min.css" integrity="sha384-
    Vkoo8x4CGsO3+Hhxv8T/Q5PaXtkKtu6ug5TOeNV6gBiFeWPGFN9MuhOf23Q9Ifjh"
    crossorigin="anonymous">
```

```html
    <!-- Custom CSS -->
    <link rel="stylesheet" href="stylesheets/main.css" type="text/css">

    <title>Listing 3-15</title>
</head>
<body>
    <nav class="navbar navbar-expand-lg navbar-dark bg-dark fixed-top">
        <div class="container">
            <a class="navbar-brand" href="#">John Woo</a>

            <button type="button" class="navbar-toggler" data-
            toggle="collapse" data-target="#navbar"
                    aria-controls="navbar"
                    aria-expanded="false"
                    aria-label="Toggle navigation">
                <span class="navbar-toggler-icon"></span>
            </button>

            <div class="collapse navbar-collapse" id="navbar">
                <ul class="nav navbar-nav">
                    <li class="nav-item">
                        <a class="nav-link active" href="#">Home <span
                        class="sr-only">(current)</span></a>
                    </li>
                    <li class="nav-item">
                        <a class="nav-link" href="#about">About</a>
                    </li>
                    <li class="nav-item">
                        <a class="nav-link" href="#contact">Contact</a>
                    </li>
                </ul>
            </div>
        </div>
    </nav>
```

```
<div class="container">

    <h1>John Woo Portfolio</h1>
    <p class="lead">Full-Stack Web Developer that can turn your ideas
    to fantastic responsive Web applications</p>

</div>

<!-- Optional JavaScript -->
<!-- jQuery first, then Popper.js, then Bootstrap JS -->
<script src="https://code.jquery.com/jquery-3.4.1.slim.min.js"
integrity="sha384-J6qa4849blE2+poT4WnyKhv5vZF5SrPoOiEjwBvKU7imGFAVOwwj1
yYfoRSJoZ+n" crossorigin="anonymous"></script>
<script src="https://cdn.jsdelivr.net/npm/popper.js@1.16.0/dist/umd/
popper.min.js" integrity="sha384-Q6E9RHvbIyZFJoft+2mJbHaEWldlvI9IOYy5n3
zV9zzTtmI3UksdQRVvoxMfooAo" crossorigin="anonymous"></script>
<script src="https://stackpath.bootstrapcdn.com/bootstrap/4.4.1/js/
bootstrap.min.js" integrity="sha384-wfSDF2E5OY2D1uUdjOO3uMBJnjuUD4Ih7Yw
aYd1iqfktjOUod8GCExl3Og8ifwB6" crossorigin="anonymous"></script>
</body>
</html>
```

If you save and load this page on your browser, you will see the following (Figure 3-27).

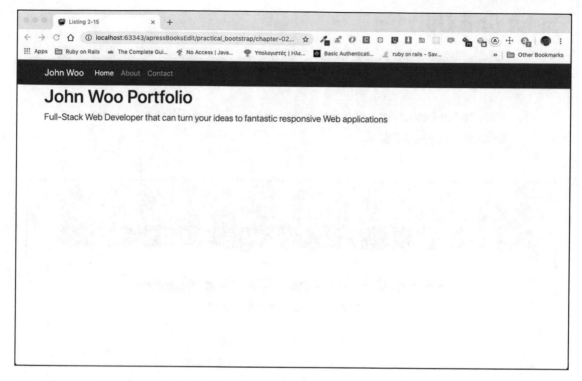

Figure 3-27. *Nav Bar Content Aligned with Page Main Content*

Well done! This matches the original page that you wanted to build.

Closing Notes

You have created a website with a responsive navigation bar, without writing any single piece of CSS code. Twitter Bootstrap has provided everything to you. You only had to use the correct classes (and in one case, two `data-*` attributes).

Tasks and Quizzes

TASK DETAILS

---

1. You need to implement a web page with a responsive navigation bar, like the following (Figure 3-28).

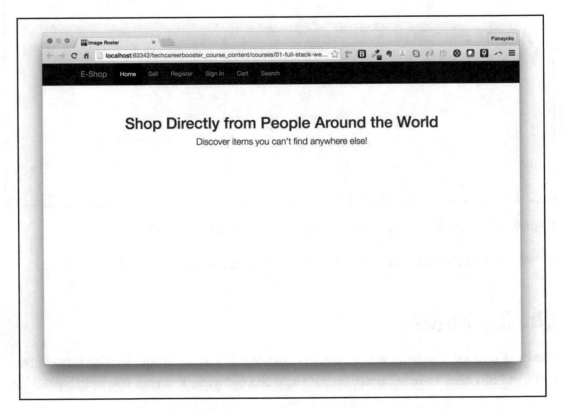

Figure 3-28. *Task Project with a Navigation Bar*

2. Watch out for the following:

    1. The main content should be centered.

    2. There is a lot of blank space above the main content and below the navigation bar. Make sure that you have the same on your page.

3. The navigation bar should be responsive, and when you load your page on small displays, the menu items should be hidden. In their place, a hamburger icon should be displayed. The icon, when clicked, will unfold the list with the menu options.

Good luck!

Key Takeaways

Congratulations! You now know how to implement a responsive navigation bar. Here is a list of the key things you learned:

- How to implement a navigation bar with menu options that are hidden on small devices and visible on large devices.

- For small devices, you have implemented a button that when clicked toggles on/off the menu with the options.

- You have also learned how to color the navigation bar and how to position it.

- You have learned how to put content on the main page without it being hidden by the top navigation bar.

- You have learned how to make a paragraph stand out.

In the following chapter, you are going to get acquainted with the most popular Twitter Bootstrap components, like buttons, badges, tabs, and so on.

CHAPTER 4

Theme Reference: Part 1

In the previous chapter, you have created a small Twitter Bootstrap project. Now, you are going to create a page that would reference some of the most commonly used Twitter Bootstrap components.

In the first part of this Theme Reference project, you will learn how to create dropdown menus in the navigation bar (Figure 4-1).

Figure 4-1. *Dropdown Menu in the Navigation Bar*

P. Matsinopoulos, *Practical Bootstrap*, https://doi.org/10.1007/978-1-4842-6071-5_4

You will learn how to create standout text areas, called jumbotrons (Figure 4-2).

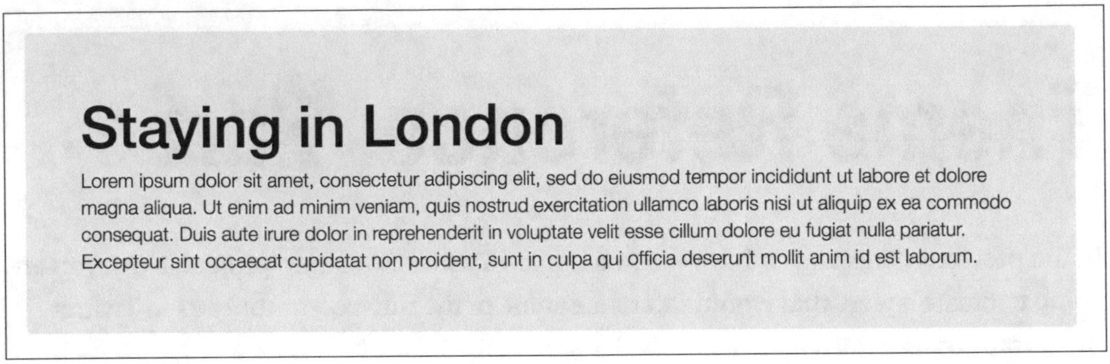

Staying in London
Lorem ipsum dolor sit amet, consectetur adipiscing elit, sed do eiusmod tempor incididunt ut labore et dolore magna aliqua. Ut enim ad minim veniam, quis nostrud exercitation ullamco laboris nisi ut aliquip ex ea commodo consequat. Duis aute irure dolor in reprehenderit in voluptate velit esse cillum dolore eu fugiat nulla pariatur. Excepteur sint occaecat cupidatat non proident, sunt in culpa qui officia deserunt mollit anim id est laborum.

Figure 4-2. *Jumbotron Example*

You will learn how to quickly create nice-looking buttons, like the following (Figure 4-3)

at eros. Praesent commodo cursu
View details »

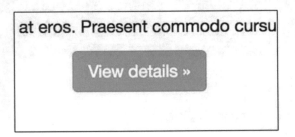

Figure 4-3. *Button Example*

and tables as in Figure 4-4.

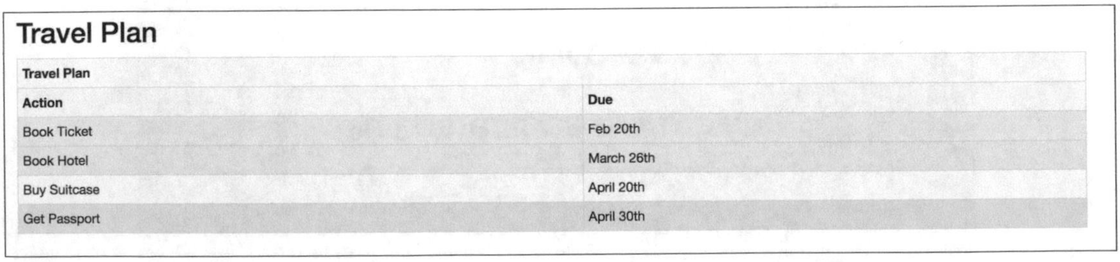

Travel Plan

Travel Plan	
Action	**Due**
Book Ticket	Feb 20th
Book Hotel	March 26th
Buy Suitcase	April 20th
Get Passport	April 30th

Figure 4-4. *Table Example*

You will also learn how to create nice-looking labels and tags (Figure 4-5)

Figure 4-5. *Label Example*

and badges (Figure 4-6).

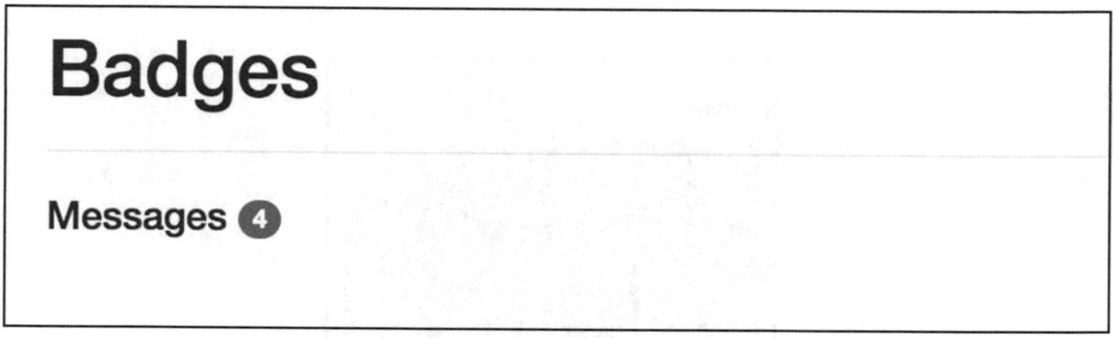

Badges

Messages ④

Figure 4-6. *Badge Example*

In the second part of the Theme Reference project, you will learn how to group information under tabs (Figure 4-7).

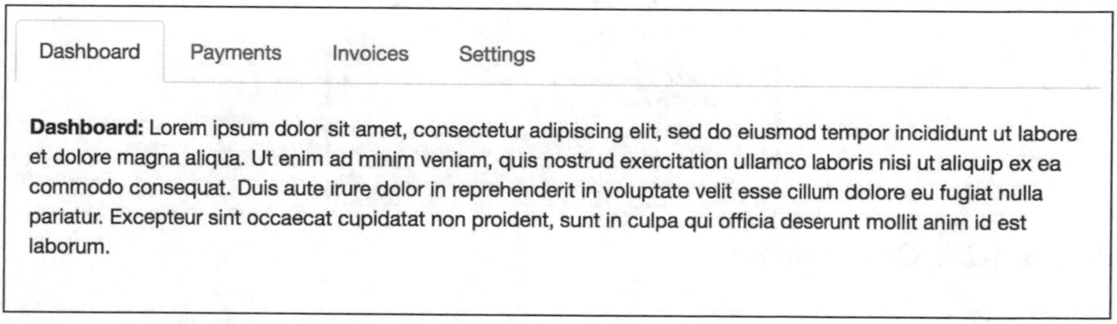

| Dashboard | Payments | Invoices | Settings |

Dashboard: Lorem ipsum dolor sit amet, consectetur adipiscing elit, sed do eiusmod tempor incididunt ut labore et dolore magna aliqua. Ut enim ad minim veniam, quis nostrud exercitation ullamco laboris nisi ut aliquip ex ea commodo consequat. Duis aute irure dolor in reprehenderit in voluptate velit esse cillum dolore eu fugiat nulla pariatur. Excepteur sint occaecat cupidatat non proident, sunt in culpa qui officia deserunt mollit anim id est laborum.

Figure 4-7. *Tabs Example*

You will learn how to create alerts (Figure 4-8)

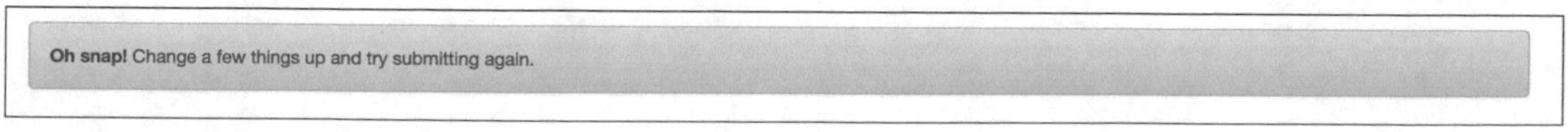

Oh snap! Change a few things up and try submitting again.

Figure 4-8. *Alert Example*

and nice-looking progress bars (Figure 4-9).

Figure 4-9. *Progress Bar Example*

You will learn how to create cards, with standout heading and separate body (Figure 4-10).

Figure 4-10. *Card Example*

And finally, you will learn how to create the impressive image carousels.

At the end of the second part, you will be asked to create a page that will require you to use most of the preceding components (Figure 4-11).

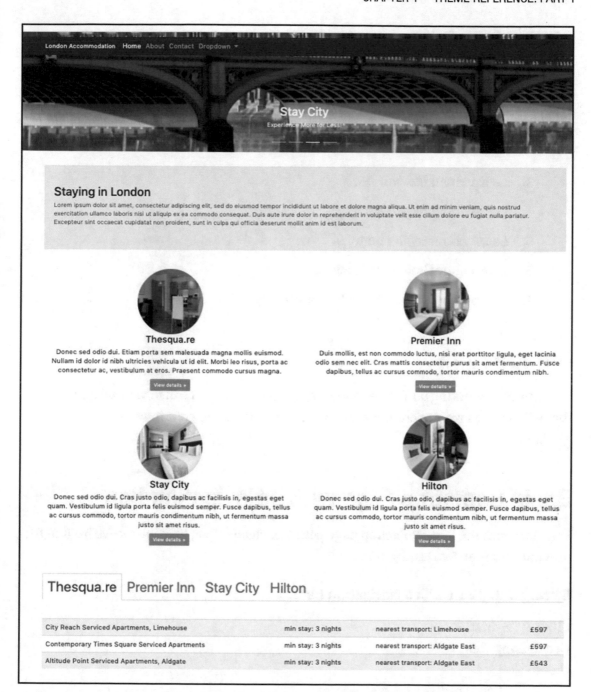

Figure 4-11. *Twitter Bootstrap Example Page with Various Elements*

Learning Goals

This is the list of things you will learn in the first part:

1. Learn how to add a dropdown menu in the navigation bar.

2. Learn about the various dropdown menu components and classes.

3. Learn about *jumbotrons*.

4. Learn about page headers.

5. Learn about styling buttons.

6. Learn about how to style tables.

7. Learn how you can create labels and tags.

Introduction

You continue working on Twitter Bootstrap projects, and you will now build a project that will work as your reference to various Twitter Bootstrap components.

Let's start.

Basic Bootstrap Page with a Navigation Bar

You start with the basic Bootstrap page with a navigation bar, like the one we built in the previous chapter. See Listing 4-1.

Listing 4-1. Start with a Navigation Bar

```
<!DOCTYPE html>
<html lang="en">
<head>
    <!-- Required meta tags -->
    <meta charset="utf-8">
    <meta name="viewport" content="width=device-width, initial-scale=1,
    shrink-to-fit=no">
```

```html
<!-- Bootstrap CSS -->
<link rel="stylesheet" href="https://stackpath.bootstrapcdn.
com/bootstrap/4.4.1/css/bootstrap.min.css" integrity="sha384-
Vkoo8x4CGsO3+Hhxv8T/Q5PaXtkKtu6ug5TOeNV6gBiFeWPGFN9MuhOf23Q9Ifjh"
crossorigin="anonymous">

<!-- Custom CSS -->
<link rel="stylesheet" href="stylesheets/main.css" type="text/css">

<title>Twitter Bootstrap Reference Page</title>
</head>
<body>
    <nav class="navbar navbar-expand-lg navbar-dark bg-dark fixed-top">
        <div class="container">
            <a class="navbar-brand" href="#">Bootstrap Ref. Page</a>

            <button type="button" class="navbar-toggler" data-
            toggle="collapse" data-target="#navbar"
                    aria-controls="navbar"
                    aria-expanded="false"
                    aria-label="Toggle navigation">
                <span class="navbar-toggler-icon"></span>
            </button>

            <div class="collapse navbar-collapse" id="navbar">
                <ul class="nav navbar-nav">
                    <li class="nav-item">
                        <a class="nav-link active" href="#">Home <span
                        class="sr-only">(current)</span></a>
                    </li>
                    <li class="nav-item">
                        <a class="nav-link" href="#about">About</a>
                    </li>
                    <li class="nav-item">
                        <a class="nav-link" href="#contact">Contact</a>
                    </li>
                </ul>
```

```
                </div>
            </div>
        </nav>

        <!-- Optional JavaScript -->
        <!-- jQuery first, then Popper.js, then Bootstrap JS -->
        <script src="https://code.jquery.com/jquery-3.4.1.slim.min.js"
        integrity="sha384-J6qa4849blE2+poT4WnyKhv5vZF5SrPo0iEjwBvKU7imGFAVOwwj1
        yYfoRSJoZ+n" crossorigin="anonymous"></script>
        <script src="https://cdn.jsdelivr.net/npm/popper.js@1.16.0/dist/umd/
        popper.min.js" integrity="sha384-Q6E9RHvbIyZFJoft+2mJbHaEWldlvI9IOYy5n3
        zV9zzTtmI3UksdQRVvoxMfooAo" crossorigin="anonymous"></script>
        <script src="https://stackpath.bootstrapcdn.com/bootstrap/4.4.1/js/
        bootstrap.min.js" integrity="sha384-wfSDF2E50Y2D1uUdj0O3uMBJnjuUD4Ih7Yw
        aYd1iqfktj0Uod8GCExl3Og8ifwB6" crossorigin="anonymous"></script>
    </body>
</html>
```

Make sure that you have your `stylesheets/main.css` file containing the necessary body padding that will allow the main content of the page to be displayed below the navigation bar (Listing 4-2).

Listing 4-2. stylesheets/main.css for Listing 4-1

```
body {
    padding-top: 56px;
}
```

If you save the preceding content and load the page on your browser, you will see the following (Figure 4-12).

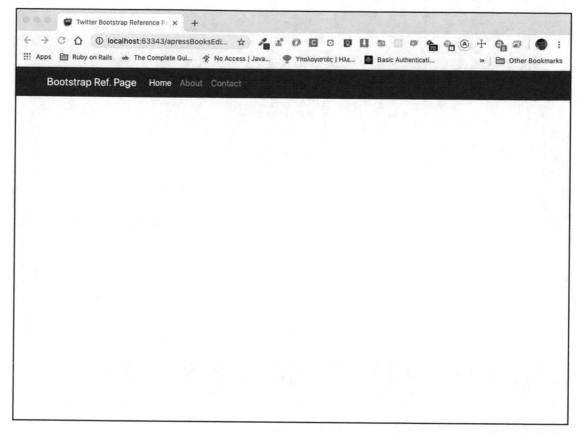

Figure 4-12. *Starting Page*

Adding a Dropdown Menu

You will now learn how you can add a dropdown menu, like the following (Figure 4-13).

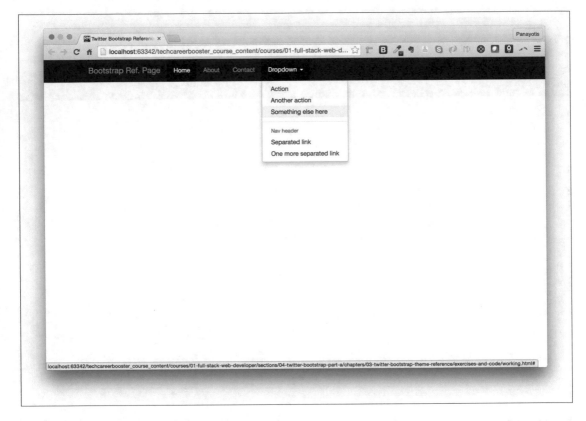

Figure 4-13. *Page with a Dropdown Menu*

This is very easy. One has to add an extra li item to the list of menu items. This new li item needs to have another list included that will be the list of options inside the dropdown menu, like the following (Listing 4-3).

Listing 4-3. Dropdown Menu in the Navigation Bar

```
<!DOCTYPE html>
<html lang="en">
<head>
    <!-- Required meta tags -->
    <meta charset="utf-8">
    <meta name="viewport" content="width=device-width, initial-scale=1,
    shrink-to-fit=no">

    <!-- Bootstrap CSS -->
```

```
<link rel="stylesheet" href="https://stackpath.bootstrapcdn.
com/bootstrap/4.4.1/css/bootstrap.min.css" integrity="sha384-
Vkoo8x4CGsO3+Hhxv8T/Q5PaXtkKtu6ug5TOeNV6gBiFeWPGFN9MuhOf23Q9Ifjh"
crossorigin="anonymous">

<!-- Custom CSS -->
<link rel="stylesheet" href="stylesheets/main.css" type="text/css">

<title>Twitter Bootstrap Reference Page</title>
</head>
<body>
    <nav class="navbar navbar-expand-lg navbar-dark bg-dark fixed-top">
        <div class="container">
            <a class="navbar-brand" href="#">Bootstrap Ref. Page</a>

            <button type="button" class="navbar-toggler" data-
            toggle="collapse" data-target="#navbar"
                    aria-controls="navbar"
                    aria-expanded="false"
                    aria-label="Toggle navigation">
                <span class="navbar-toggler-icon"></span>
            </button>

            <div class="collapse navbar-collapse" id="navbar">
                <ul class="nav navbar-nav">
                    <li class="nav-item">
                        <a class="nav-link active" href="#">Home <span
                        class="sr-only">(current)</span></a>
                    </li>
                    <li class="nav-item">
                        <a class="nav-link" href="#about">About</a>
                    </li>
                    <li class="nav-item">
                        <a class="nav-link" href="#contact">Contact</a>
                    </li>

                    <!-- Drop down Menu -->
                    <li class="nav-item dropdown">
```

153

```
                      <a href="#"
                         class="nav-link dropdown-toggle"
                         data-toggle="dropdown">
                         Dropdown <span class="caret"></span>
                      </a>
                      <div class="dropdown-menu">
                          <a href="#" class="dropdown-item">Action</a>
                          <a href="#" class="dropdown-item">Another
                          action</a>
                          <a href="#" class="dropdown-item">Something
                          else here</a>
                          <div class="dropdown-divider"></div>
                          <div class="dropdown-header">Nav header</div>
                          <a href="#" class="dropdown-item">Separated
                          link</a>
                          <a href="#" class="dropdown-item">One more
                          separated link</a>
                      </div>
                  </li>
              </ul>
          </div>
      </div>
  </nav>

  <!-- Optional JavaScript -->
  <!-- jQuery first, then Popper.js, then Bootstrap JS -->
  <script src="https://code.jquery.com/jquery-3.4.1.slim.min.js"
  integrity="sha384-J6qa4849blE2+poT4WnyKhv5vZF5SrPo0iEjwBvKU7imGFAVOwwj1
  yYfoRSJoZ+n" crossorigin="anonymous"></script>
  <script src="https://cdn.jsdelivr.net/npm/popper.js@1.16.0/dist/umd/
  popper.min.js" integrity="sha384-Q6E9RHvbIyZFJoft+2mJbHaEWldlvI9IOYy5n3
  zV9zzTtmI3UksdQRVvoxMfooAo" crossorigin="anonymous"></script>
  <script src="https://stackpath.bootstrapcdn.com/bootstrap/4.4.1/js/
  bootstrap.min.js" integrity="sha384-wfSDF2E50Y2D1uUdj0O3uMBJnjuUD4Ih7Yw
  aYd1iqfktj0Uod8GCExl3Og8ifwB6" crossorigin="anonymous"></script>
</body>
</html>
```

If you save the preceding code and load the page on your browser, you will see the new dropdown menu on the far right.

Let's give some notes about the code that has been used to build that dropdown menu (Listing 4-4).

Listing 4-4. Looking into the Details of the Dropdown Menu

```html
<!-- Drop down Menu -->
<li class="nav-item dropdown">
  <a href="#"
    class="nav-link dropdown-toggle"
    data-toggle="dropdown">
    Dropdown
  </a>
  <div class="dropdown-menu">
    <a href="#" class="dropdown-item">Action</a>
    <a href="#" class="dropdown-item">Another action</a>
    <a href="#" class="dropdown-item">Something else here</a>
    <div class="dropdown-divider"></div>
    <div class="dropdown-header">Nav header</div>
    <a href="#" class="dropdown-item">Separated link</a>
    <a href="#" class="dropdown-item">One more separated link</a>
  </div>
</li>
```

1. The list item (li) that will work as a dropdown menu needs to have the class dropdown.

2. The dropdown list item text, in our case Dropdown, needs to be wrapped into an anchor <a> HTML element. This will make the pointer change, when the user hovers over it. Note that the anchor needs to have the class dropdown-toggle and the data-toggle attribute equal to dropdown.

3. The list of options of the dropdown menu can be given inside a div.

4. The div needs to have the class dropdown-menu.

5. Each menu option is given with an anchor a that has the class
   `dropdown-item`.

6. You can use a special, empty `div` with the class `divider` if you
   want to create a line in between menu items that would function
   as a divider.

7. You can also use another special `div` that would function as a
   submenu header and will not actually be part of the user options,
   that is, wouldn't be possible to click and select. This can be done if
   the div has the class `dropdown-header`.

Jumbotron

Twitter Bootstrap allows you to create jumbotrons, big areas that display a message, a
header, or both with a very big font size. Let's do that:

1. After the nav, you are creating a `.container` `div` to include the
   content of your page.

2. The first thing that you create is a div with class `.jumbotron`.

Let's see Listing 4-5 that has your page with the jumbotron in.

Listing 4-5. Page with Jumbotron

```
<!DOCTYPE html>
<html lang="en">
<head>
    <!-- Required meta tags -->
    <meta charset="utf-8">
    <meta name="viewport" content="width=device-width, initial-scale=1,
    shrink-to-fit=no">

    <!-- Bootstrap CSS -->
    <link rel="stylesheet" href="https://stackpath.bootstrapcdn.
    com/bootstrap/4.4.1/css/bootstrap.min.css" integrity="sha384-
    Vkoo8x4CGsO3+Hhxv8T/Q5PaXtkKtu6ug5TOeNV6gBiFeWPGFN9MuhOf23Q9Ifjh"
    crossorigin="anonymous">
```

```html
<!-- Custom CSS -->
<link rel="stylesheet" href="stylesheets/main.css" type="text/css">

<title>Twitter Bootstrap Reference Page</title>
</head>
<body>
    <nav class="navbar navbar-expand-lg navbar-dark bg-dark fixed-top">
        <div class="container">
            <a class="navbar-brand" href="#">Bootstrap Ref. Page</a>

            <button type="button" class="navbar-toggler" data-
            toggle="collapse" data-target="#navbar"
                    aria-controls="navbar"
                    aria-expanded="false"
                    aria-label="Toggle navigation">
                <span class="navbar-toggler-icon"></span>
            </button>

            <div class="collapse navbar-collapse" id="navbar">
                <ul class="nav navbar-nav">
                    <li class="nav-item">
                        <a class="nav-link active" href="#">Home <span
                        class="sr-only">(current)</span></a>
                    </li>
                    <li class="nav-item">
                        <a class="nav-link" href="#about">About</a>
                    </li>
                    <li class="nav-item">
                        <a class="nav-link" href="#contact">Contact</a>
                    </li>

                    <!-- Drop down Menu -->
                    <li class="nav-item dropdown">
                        <a href="#"
                            class="nav-link dropdown-toggle"
                            data-toggle="dropdown">
                          Dropdown
```

```
                    </a>
                    <div class="dropdown-menu">
                        <a href="#" class="dropdown-item">Action</a>
                        <a href="#" class="dropdown-item">Another
                        action</a>
                        <a href="#" class="dropdown-item">Something
                        else here</a>
                        <div class="dropdown-divider"></div>
                        <div class="dropdown-header">Nav header</div>
                        <a href="#" class="dropdown-item">Separated
                        link</a>
                        <a href="#" class="dropdown-item">One more
                        separated link</a>
                    </div>
                </li>
            </ul>
        </div>
    </div>
</nav>

<!-- main content container -->
<div class="container">
    <div class="jumbotron">
        <h1>Jumbotron</h1>
        <p class="lead">
            Lorem ipsum dolor sit amet, consectetur adipiscing elit,
            sed do eiusmod tempor incididunt ut labore et dolore magna
            aliqua. Ut enim ad minim veniam, quis nostrud
            exercitation ullamco laboris nisi ut aliquip ex ea commodo
            consequat. Duis aute irure dolor in reprehenderit in
            voluptate velit esse cillum dolore eu fugiat nulla
            pariatur. Excepteur sint occaecat cupidatat non proident,
            sunt in culpa qui officia deserunt mollit anim id est
            laborum.
        </p>
    </div>
</div>
```

```
<!-- end of main content container -->

<!-- Optional JavaScript -->
<!-- jQuery first, then Popper.js, then Bootstrap JS -->
<script src="https://code.jquery.com/jquery-3.4.1.slim.min.js"
integrity="sha384-J6qa4849blE2+poT4WnyKhv5vZF5SrPo0iEjwBvKU7imGFAVOwwj1
yYfoRSJoZ+n" crossorigin="anonymous"></script>
<script src="https://cdn.jsdelivr.net/npm/popper.js@1.16.0/dist/umd/
popper.min.js" integrity="sha384-Q6E9RHvbIyZFJoft+2mJbHaEWldlvI9IOYy5n3
zV9zzTtmI3UksdQRVvoxMfooAo" crossorigin="anonymous"></script>
<script src="https://stackpath.bootstrapcdn.com/bootstrap/4.4.1/js/
bootstrap.min.js" integrity="sha384-wfSDF2E50Y2D1uUdj0O3uMBJnjuUD4Ih7Yw
aYd1iqfktjOUod8GCExl3Og8ifwB6" crossorigin="anonymous"></script>
</body>
</html>
```

Before you save and load this page on your browser, make sure that your
stylesheets/main.css file has the following content (Listing 4-6).

Listing 4-6. CSS File for Listing 4-5

```
body {
    padding-top: 70px;
        padding-bottom: 70px;
}
```

If you do that and save your page, you will see the following on your browser
(Figure 4-14).

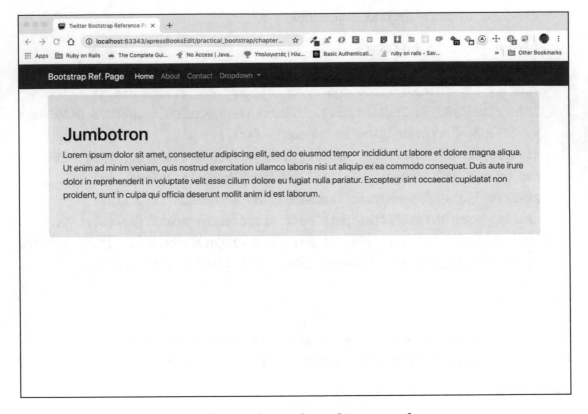

Figure 4-14. *Jumbotron with Header and Lead Paragraph*

Note that the space between the bottom side of the navigation bar and the top side of the jumbotron is created by the padding-top rule inside the main.css file.

The approach here is very simple. We use the class jumbotron for the div. We also use the header h1 for the header text inside the jumbotron.

Finally, we have already seen, in the previous chapter, the class lead that is applied on the p element to make the text stand out.

Headers with Horizontal Lines: Page Headers

There are times that you want to create a header, that is, a piece of text that stands out like a header, for example, h1 or h2, and below that a horizontal line.

You can quickly do that with the help of an hr element below your h1 element. Add the following as the last element inside the main content container (Listing 4-7).

Listing 4-7. How to Have a Header with a Horizontal Line Below It

```
<h1>Page Header</h1>
<hr class="my-4">
```

If you save this and reload your page, you should have something like the following (Figure 4-15).

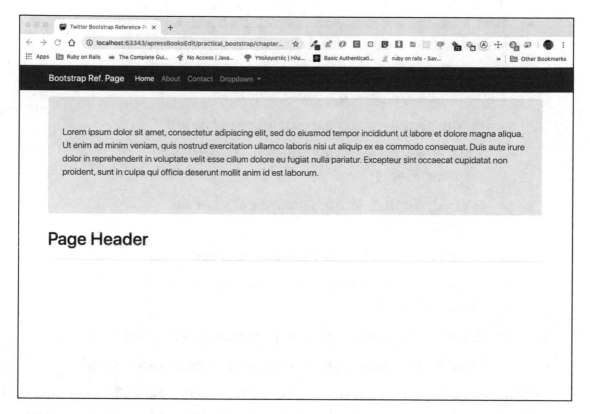

Figure 4-15. *Page Header with Horizontal Line*

You have used the hr element with the class my-4. What's the deal with this class? This is one of the classes that Bootstrap calls utility classes. This particular one belongs to the *spacing* category, which has to do with margins and paddings for the element it is attached to. In particular

- The prefix m stands for margin. Hence, in your example, you are applying some margin to the hr element.

- The y refers to the vertical y-axis. Essentially, it is about the top and bottom sides of the element. Hence, in your example, you are applying some top and bottom margins to the hr element.

- The number 4 is the size. The sizes can be one

  - 0: Which sets the size of the margin or padding to 0

  - 1: Which sets the size to 0.25 times the $spacer size ($spacer * 0.25)

  - 2: Which sets the size to 0.5 times the $spacer size ($spacer * 0.5)

  - 3: Which sets the size equal to the $spacer size

  - 4: Which sets the size to 1.5 times the $spacer size ($spacer * 1.5)

  - 5: Which sets the size to 3 times the $spacer size ($spacer * 3)

  - Auto: Which automatically sets the size (applies to margins only)

OK! Hold on! What is the $spacer? The $spacer is a Sass (Syntactically Awesome Style Sheets) variable. Note Bootstrap is written in Sass and then it is compiled to actual CSS. The default value of the $spacer variable is 1rem.

If this is too complicated, there is no other way to clarify it but to play and try things out. Also, your best friend is the developer tools of your browser.

For example, open the developer tools while you are on your jumbotron page and locate the element hr. See how the top and bottom margins have been set, thanks to the my-4 class attached to it (Figure 4-16).

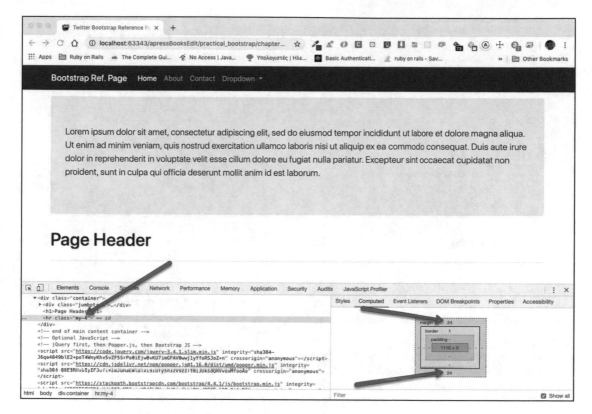

Figure 4-16. *24px Margin Top and Bottom, Thanks to my-4*

Why 24px? This is because the 4 on my-4 is interpreted as $spacer * 1.5, and because $spacer is 1rem, we finally get 1.5rem. You can also see that if you switch your developer tools' selected tab to Styles, instead of Computed (Figure 4-17).

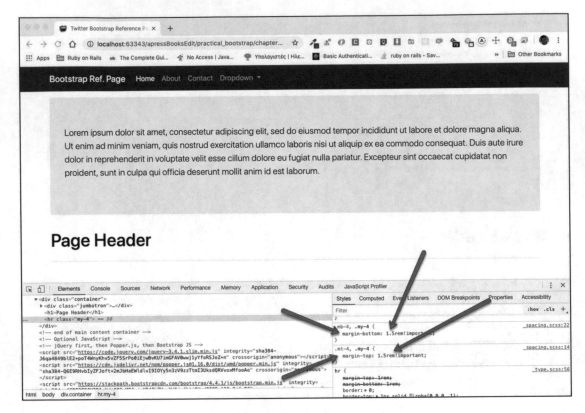

Figure 4-17. *my-4 Gives 1.5rem Top and Bottom Margins*

And why is 1.5rem computed to be 24px? rem is a CSS unit that calculates the size of an element relative to the font-size of the root element of the page, that is, of the html element. If you inspect the font-size property of the html element using the developer tools, you will see that it has size equal to 16px (Figure 4-18).

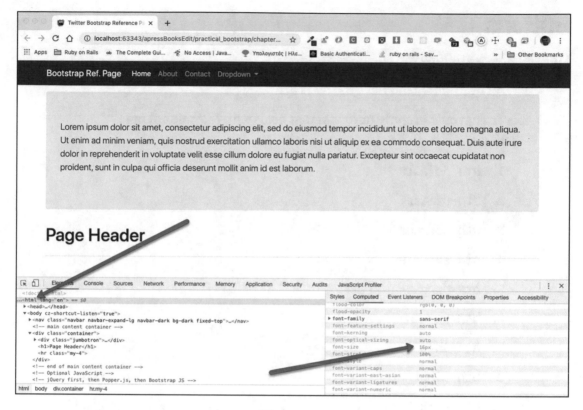

Figure 4-18. *The font-size of the Root Element Is 16px*

Hence, 16px * 1.5 calculates to 24px.

Note   I did a small deviation to discuss CSS units and how they are used in an HTML document. This is not part of Twitter Bootstrap. You can learn more about HTML and CSS in my book *Master HTML & CSS*.

Buttons

You will now learn how you can create buttons:

1. All buttons should have the class `btn`.

2. Then, you can apply one class that deals with the color of the button:

   1. `btn-default`

   2. `btn-primary`

   3. `btn-secondary`

   4. `btn-success`

   5. `btn-danger`

   6. `btn-warning`

   7. `btn-info`

   8. `btn-light`

   9. `btn-dark`

3. Instead of a color, you can also apply a class to turn a button into a link: `btn-link`.

4. Or you can interpolate the *-outline-* word in the class name in order to style a transparent background color button with a border, for example, `btn-outline-primary`.

5. Then you can specify the size of the button using a corresponding class:

   1. `btn-lg` for large buttons.

   2. Specify no class for normal-size buttons.

   3. `btn-sm` for small buttons.

   4. `btn-block` for blocks that span the whole available width.

Let's see that in action. Listing 4-8 is the code that your page should now have.

Listing 4-8. Page Demonstrating Buttons

```
<!DOCTYPE html>
<html lang="en">
<head>
    <!-- Required meta tags -->
    <meta charset="utf-8">
    <meta name="viewport" content="width=device-width, initial-scale=1,
    shrink-to-fit=no">

    <!-- Bootstrap CSS -->
    <link rel="stylesheet" href="https://stackpath.bootstrapcdn.
    com/bootstrap/4.4.1/css/bootstrap.min.css" integrity="sha384-
    Vkoo8x4CGsO3+Hhxv8T/Q5PaXtkKtu6ug5TOeNV6gBiFeWPGFN9MuhOf23Q9Ifjh"
    crossorigin="anonymous">

    <!-- Custom CSS -->
    <link rel="stylesheet" href="stylesheets/main.css" type="text/css">

    <title>Twitter Bootstrap Reference Page</title>
</head>
<body>
    <nav class="navbar navbar-expand-lg navbar-dark bg-dark fixed-top">
        <div class="container">
            <a class="navbar-brand" href="#">Bootstrap Ref. Page</a>

            <button type="button" class="navbar-toggler" data-
            toggle="collapse" data-target="#navbar"
                    aria-controls="navbar"
                    aria-expanded="false"
                    aria-label="Toggle navigation">
                <span class="navbar-toggler-icon"></span>
            </button>

            <div class="collapse navbar-collapse" id="navbar">
                <ul class="nav navbar-nav">
                    <li class="nav-item">
```

```
                              <a class="nav-link active" href="#">Home <span
                              class="sr-only">(current)</span></a>
                      </li>
                      <li class="nav-item">
                          <a class="nav-link" href="#about">About</a>
                      </li>
                      <li class="nav-item">
                          <a class="nav-link" href="#contact">Contact</a>
                      </li>

                      <!-- Drop down Menu -->
                      <li class="nav-item dropdown">
                          <a href="#"
                             class="nav-link dropdown-toggle"
                             data-toggle="dropdown">
                              Dropdown
                          </a>
                          <div class="dropdown-menu">
                              <a href="#" class="dropdown-item">Action</a>
                              <a href="#" class="dropdown-item">Another
                              action</a>
                              <a href="#" class="dropdown-item">Something
                              else here</a>
                              <div class="dropdown-divider"></div>
                              <div class="dropdown-header">Nav header</div>
                              <a href="#" class="dropdown-item">Separated
                              link</a>
                              <a href="#" class="dropdown-item">One more
                              separated link</a>
                          </div>
                      </li>
                  </ul>
              </div>
          </div>
      </nav>
```

```
<!-- main content container -->
<div class="container">
    <div class="jumbotron">
        <p class="lead">
            Lorem ipsum dolor sit amet, consectetur adipiscing elit,
            sed do eiusmod tempor incididunt ut labore et dolore magna
            aliqua. Ut enim ad minim veniam, quis nostrud
            exercitation ullamco laboris nisi ut aliquip ex ea commodo
            consequat. Duis aute irure dolor in reprehenderit in
            voluptate velit esse cillum dolore eu fugiat nulla
            pariatur. Excepteur sint occaecat cupidatat non proident,
            sunt in culpa qui officia deserunt mollit anim id est
            laborum.
        </p>
    </div>

    <h1>Buttons</h1>
    <hr class="my-4">

    <h2>Small Sizes</h2>
    <p>
        <button type="button" class="btn btn-sm btn-primary">btn btn-sm
        btn-primary</button>
        <button type="button" class="btn btn-sm btn-secondary">btn
        btn-sm btn-secondary</button>
        <button type="button" class="btn btn-sm btn-success">btn btn-sm
        btn-success</button>
        <button type="button" class="btn btn-sm btn-danger">btn btn-sm
        btn-danger</button>
        <button type="button" class="btn btn-sm btn-warning">btn btn-sm
        btn-warning</button>
        <button type="button" class="btn btn-sm btn-info">btn btn-sm
        btn-info</button>
        <button type="button" class="btn btn-sm btn-light">btn btn-sm
        btn-light</button>
```

```
    <button type="button" class="btn btn-sm btn-dark">btn btn-sm
    btn-dark</button>
    <button type="button" class="btn btn-sm btn-link">btn btn-sm
    btn-link</button>
</p>

<h2>Normal Sizes</h2>
<p>
    <button type="button" class="btn btn-primary">btn btn-primary
    </button>
    <button type="button" class="btn btn-secondary">btn btn-
    secondary</button>
    <button type="button" class="btn btn-success">btn btn-success
    </button>
    <button type="button" class="btn btn-danger">btn btn-danger
    </button>
    <button type="button" class="btn btn-warning">btn btn-warning
    </button>
    <button type="button" class="btn btn-info">btn btn-info</button>
    <button type="button" class="btn btn-light">btn btn-light
    </button>
    <button type="button" class="btn btn-dark">btn btn-dark</button>
    <button type="button" class="btn btn-link">btn btn-link</button>
</p>

<h2>Large Sizes</h2>
<p>
    <button type="button" class="btn btn-lg btn-primary">btn btn-lg
    btn-primary</button>
    <button type="button" class="btn btn-lg btn-secondary">btn btn-
    lg btn-secondary</button>
    <button type="button" class="btn btn-lg btn-success">btn btn-lg
    btn-success</button>
    <button type="button" class="btn btn-lg btn-danger">btn btn-lg
    btn-danger</button>
    <button type="button" class="btn btn-lg btn-warning">btn btn-lg
    btn-warning</button>
```

```
    <button type="button" class="btn btn-lg btn-info">btn btn-lg
    btn-info</button>
    <button type="button" class="btn btn-lg btn-light">btn btn-lg
    btn-light</button>
    <button type="button" class="btn btn-lg btn-dark">btn btn-lg
    btn-dark</button>
    <button type="button" class="btn btn-lg btn-link">btn btn-lg
    btn-link</button>
</p>

<h2>Block Sizes</h2>
<p>
    <button type="button" class="btn btn-block btn-primary">btn
    btn-block btn-primary</button>
    <button type="button" class="btn btn-block btn-secondary">btn
    btn-block btn-secondary</button>
    <button type="button" class="btn btn-block btn-success">btn
    btn-block btn-success</button>
    <button type="button" class="btn btn-block btn-danger">btn btn-
    block btn-danger</button>
    <button type="button" class="btn btn-block btn-warning">btn
    btn-block btn-warning</button>
    <button type="button" class="btn btn-block btn-info">btn btn-
    block btn-info</button>
    <button type="button" class="btn btn-block btn-light">btn btn-
    block btn-light</button>
    <button type="button" class="btn btn-block btn-dark">btn btn-
    block btn-dark</button>
    <button type="button" class="btn btn-block btn-link">btn btn-
    block btn-link</button>
</p>

<h2>Outline buttons (Normal Sizes)</h2>
<p>
    <button type="button" class="btn btn-outline-primary">btn btn-
    outline-primary</button>
```

```
        <button type="button" class="btn btn-outline-secondary">btn
        btn-outline-secondary</button>
        <button type="button" class="btn btn-outline-success">btn btn-
        outline-success</button>
        <button type="button" class="btn btn-outline-danger">btn btn-
        outline-danger</button>
        <button type="button" class="btn btn-outline-warning">btn btn-
        outline-warning</button>
        <button type="button" class="btn btn-outline-info">btn btn-
        outline-info</button>
        <button type="button" class="btn btn-outline-light">btn btn-
        outline-light</button>
        <button type="button" class="btn btn-outline-dark">btn btn-
        outline-dark</button>
        <button type="button" class="btn btn-outline-link">btn btn-
        outline-link</button>
    </p>
  </div>
  <!-- end of main content container -->

  <!-- Optional JavaScript -->
  <!-- jQuery first, then Popper.js, then Bootstrap JS -->
  <script src="https://code.jquery.com/jquery-3.4.1.slim.min.js"
  integrity="sha384-J6qa4849blE2+poT4WnyKhv5vZF5SrPo0iEjwBvKU7imGFAVOwwj1
  yYfoRSJoZ+n" crossorigin="anonymous"></script>
  <script src="https://cdn.jsdelivr.net/npm/popper.js@1.16.0/dist/umd/
  popper.min.js" integrity="sha384-Q6E9RHvbIyZFJoft+2mJbHaEWldlvI9IOYy5n3
  zV9zzTtmI3UksdQRVvoxMfooAo" crossorigin="anonymous"></script>
  <script src="https://stackpath.bootstrapcdn.com/bootstrap/4.4.1/js/
  bootstrap.min.js" integrity="sha384-wfSDF2E5OY2D1uUdjOO3uMBJnjuUD4Ih7Yw
  aYd1iqfktjOUod8GCExl3Og8ifwB6" crossorigin="anonymous"></script>
</body>
</html>
```

As you can see in the preceding code, this is a series of header h2 and p elements that apply to all the combinations of classes I talked about earlier.

Save your file and reload the page on your browser. You will see something like the following (Figure 4-19).

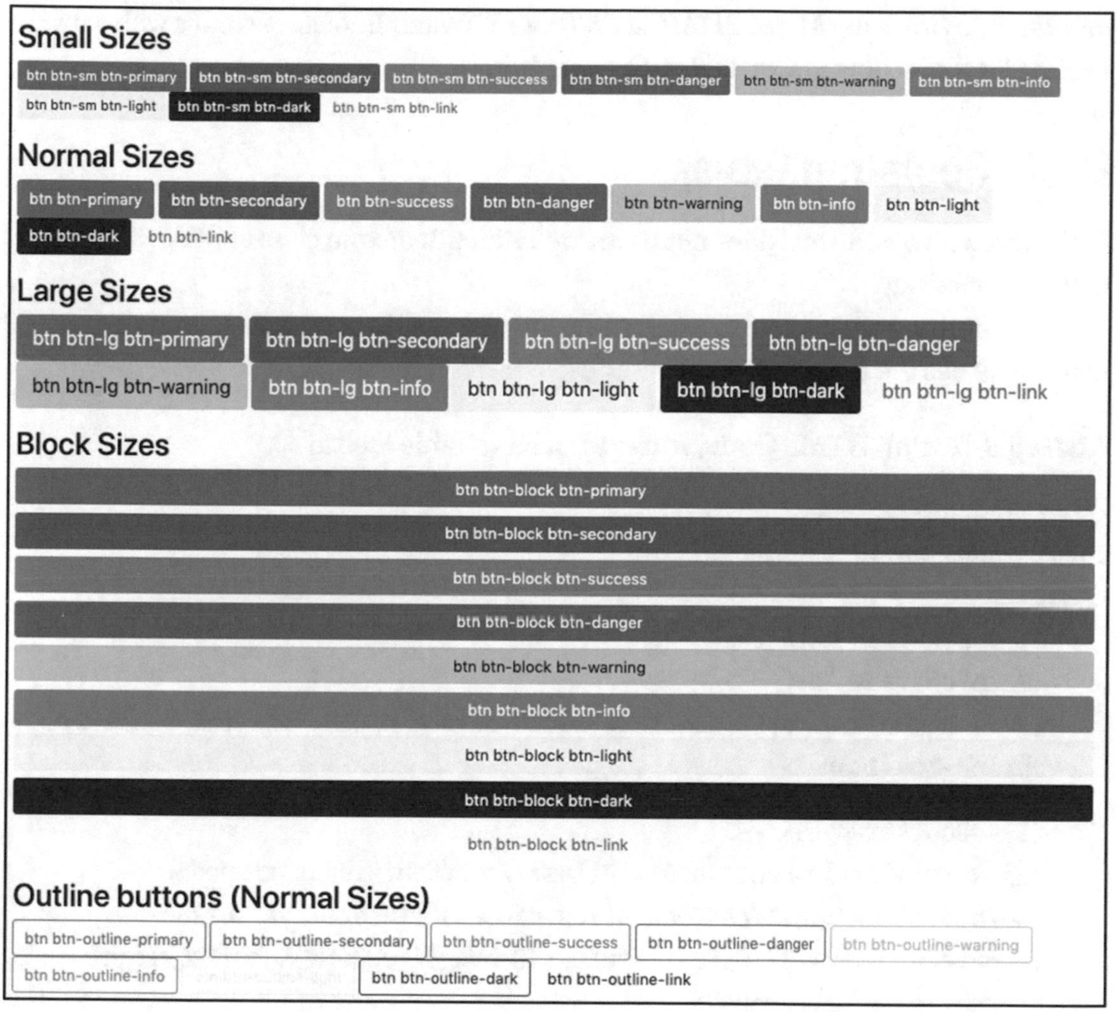

Figure 4-19. *Page Demonstrating Buttons*

On this page, you can see how each button is displayed, according to the Twitter Bootstrap button classes that you have applied. It is really impressive, because without a single line of CSS code, you have so much functionality for free. You only have to learn the various Twitter Bootstrap classes.

Tables

You have already learned about the tables and how they should be used to display tabular data (from my *Master HTML & CSS* book). Twitter Bootstrap comes with some useful classes on how to style tables. Let's see how.

Basic Bootstrap Tables

Let's start with a table that does not have any Twitter Bootstrap class applied. So it is only with its default style.

You continue appending content at the end of the main container. However, Listing 4-9 has the full HTML code.

Listing 4-9. Full HTML Code, Includes a New Table Demo

```
<!DOCTYPE html>
<html lang="en">
<head>
    <!-- Required meta tags -->
    <meta charset="utf-8">
    <meta name="viewport" content="width=device-width, initial-scale=1,
    shrink-to-fit=no">

    <!-- Bootstrap CSS -->
    <link rel="stylesheet" href="https://stackpath.bootstrapcdn.
    com/bootstrap/4.4.1/css/bootstrap.min.css" integrity="sha384-
    Vkoo8x4CGsO3+Hhxv8T/Q5PaXtkKtu6ug5TOeNV6gBiFeWPGFN9MuhOf23Q9Ifjh"
    crossorigin="anonymous">

    <!-- Custom CSS -->
    <link rel="stylesheet" href="stylesheets/main.css" type="text/css">

    <title>Twitter Bootstrap Reference Page</title>
</head>
<body>
    <nav class="navbar navbar-expand-lg navbar-dark bg-dark fixed-top">
        <div class="container">
```

```
<a class="navbar-brand" href="#">Bootstrap Ref. Page</a>

<button type="button" class="navbar-toggler" data-
toggle="collapse" data-target="#navbar"
        aria-controls="navbar"
        aria-expanded="false"
        aria-label="Toggle navigation">
    <span class="navbar-toggler-icon"></span>
</button>

<div class="collapse navbar-collapse" id="navbar">
    <ul class="nav navbar-nav">
        <li class="nav-item">
            <a class="nav-link active" href="#">Home <span
            class="sr-only">(current)</span></a>
        </li>
        <li class="nav-item">
            <a class="nav-link" href="#about">About</a>
        </li>
        <li class="nav-item">
            <a class="nav-link" href="#contact">Contact</a>
        </li>

        <!-- Drop down Menu -->
        <li class="nav-item dropdown">
            <a href="#"
               class="nav-link dropdown-toggle"
               data-toggle="dropdown">
                Dropdown
            </a>
            <div class="dropdown-menu">
                <a href="#" class="dropdown-item">Action</a>
                <a href="#" class="dropdown-item">Another
                action</a>
                <a href="#" class="dropdown-item">Something
                else here</a>
                <div class="dropdown-divider"></div>
```

```
                            <div class="dropdown-header">Nav header</div>
                            <a href="#" class="dropdown-item">Separated
                            link</a>
                            <a href="#" class="dropdown-item">One more
                            separated link</a>
                        </div>
                    </li>
                </ul>
            </div>
        </div>
    </nav>

    <!-- main content container -->
    <div class="container">
        <div class="jumbotron">
            <p class="lead">
                Lorem ipsum dolor sit amet, consectetur adipiscing elit,
                sed do eiusmod tempor incididunt ut labore et dolore magna
                aliqua. Ut enim ad minim veniam, quis nostrud
                exercitation ullamco laboris nisi ut aliquip ex ea commodo
                consequat. Duis aute irure dolor in reprehenderit in
                voluptate velit esse cillum dolore eu fugiat nulla
                pariatur. Excepteur sint occaecat cupidatat non proident,
                sunt in culpa qui officia deserunt mollit anim id est
                laborum.
            </p>
        </div>

        <h1>Buttons</h1>
        <hr class="my-4">

        <h2>Small Sizes</h2>
        <p>
            <button type="button" class="btn btn-sm btn-primary">btn btn-sm
            btn-primary</button>
            <button type="button" class="btn btn-sm btn-secondary">btn btn-
            sm btn-secondary</button>
```

```
    <button type="button" class="btn btn-sm btn-success">btn btn-sm
    btn-success</button>
    <button type="button" class="btn btn-sm btn-danger">btn btn-sm
    btn-danger</button>
    <button type="button" class="btn btn-sm btn-warning">btn btn-sm
    btn-warning</button>
    <button type="button" class="btn btn-sm btn-info">btn btn-sm
    btn-info</button>
    <button type="button" class="btn btn-sm btn-light">btn btn-sm
    btn-light</button>
    <button type="button" class="btn btn-sm btn-dark">btn btn-sm
    btn-dark</button>
    <button type="button" class="btn btn-sm btn-link">btn btn-sm
    btn-link</button>
</p>

<h2>Normal Sizes</h2>
<p>
    <button type="button" class="btn btn-primary">btn btn-primary
    </button>
    <button type="button" class="btn btn-secondary">btn btn-
    secondary</button>
    <button type="button" class="btn btn-success">btn btn-success
    </button>
    <button type="button" class="btn btn-danger">btn btn-danger
    </button>
    <button type="button" class="btn btn-warning">btn btn-warning
    </button>
    <button type="button" class="btn btn-info">btn btn-info</button>
    <button type="button" class="btn btn-light">btn btn-light
    </button>
    <button type="button" class="btn btn-dark">btn btn-dark</button>
    <button type="button" class="btn btn-link">btn btn-link</button>
</p>
```

```
<h2>Large Sizes</h2>
<p>
    <button type="button" class="btn btn-lg btn-primary">btn btn-lg
    btn-primary</button>
    <button type="button" class="btn btn-lg btn-secondary">btn btn-
    lg btn-secondary</button>
    <button type="button" class="btn btn-lg btn-success">btn btn-lg
    btn-success</button>
    <button type="button" class="btn btn-lg btn-danger">btn btn-lg
    btn-danger</button>
    <button type="button" class="btn btn-lg btn-warning">btn btn-lg
    btn-warning</button>
    <button type="button" class="btn btn-lg btn-info">btn btn-lg
    btn-info</button>
    <button type="button" class="btn btn-lg btn-light">btn btn-lg
    btn-light</button>
    <button type="button" class="btn btn-lg btn-dark">btn btn-lg
    btn-dark</button>
    <button type="button" class="btn btn-lg btn-link">btn btn-lg
    btn-link</button>
</p>

<h2>Block Sizes</h2>
<p>
    <button type="button" class="btn btn-block btn-primary">btn
    btn-block btn-primary</button>
    <button type="button" class="btn btn-block btn-secondary">btn
    btn-block btn-secondary</button>
    <button type="button" class="btn btn-block btn-success">btn
    btn-block btn-success</button>
    <button type="button" class="btn btn-block btn-danger">btn btn-
    block btn-danger</button>
    <button type="button" class="btn btn-block btn-warning">btn
    btn-block btn-warning</button>
    <button type="button" class="btn btn-block btn-info">btn btn-
    block btn-info</button>
```

```
    <button type="button" class="btn btn-block btn-light">btn btn-
    block btn-light</button>
    <button type="button" class="btn btn-block btn-dark">btn btn-
    block btn-dark</button>
    <button type="button" class="btn btn-block btn-link">btn btn-
    block btn-link</button>
</p>

<h2>Outline buttons (Normal Sizes)</h2>
<p>
    <button type="button" class="btn btn-outline-primary">btn btn-
    outline-primary</button>
    <button type="button" class="btn btn-outline-secondary">btn
    btn-outline-secondary</button>
    <button type="button" class="btn btn-outline-success">btn btn-
    outline-success</button>
    <button type="button" class="btn btn-outline-danger">btn btn-
    outline-danger</button>
    <button type="button" class="btn btn-outline-warning">btn btn-
    outline-warning</button>
    <button type="button" class="btn btn-outline-info">btn btn-
    outline-info</button>
    <button type="button" class="btn btn-outline-light">btn btn-
    outline-light</button>
    <button type="button" class="btn btn-outline-dark">btn btn-
    outline-dark</button>
    <button type="button" class="btn btn-outline-link">btn btn-
    outline-link</button>
</p>

<h1>Tables</h1>
<hr class="my-4">

<h2>Shopping List</h2>
<table>
    <tr><th colspan="2">Shopping List</th></tr>
    <tr><th>Item</th><th>Qt</th></tr>
```

```
            <tr><td>Cheese</td><td>1 kgr</td></tr>
            <tr><td>Rice</td><td>1.5 kgr</td></tr>
            <tr><td>Coffee</td><td>0.5 kgr</td></tr>
            <tr><td>Milk</td><td>1 ltr</td></tr>
            <tr><td>Wine</td><td>1 btl</td></tr>
        </table>

        <h2>Travel Plan</h2>
        <table>
            <tr><th colspan="2">Travel Plan</th></tr>
            <tr><th>Action</th><th>Due</th></tr>
            <tr><td>Book Ticket</td><td>Feb 20th</td></tr>
            <tr><td>Book Hotel</td><td>March 26th</td></tr>
            <tr><td>Buy Suitcase</td><td>April 20th</td></tr>
            <tr><td>Get Passport</td><td>April 30th</td></tr>
        </table>
    </div>
    <!-- end of main content container -->

    <!-- Optional JavaScript -->
    <!-- jQuery first, then Popper.js, then Bootstrap JS -->
    <script src="https://code.jquery.com/jquery-3.4.1.slim.min.js"
    integrity="sha384-J6qa4849blE2+poT4WnyKhv5vZF5SrPo0iEjwBvKU7imGFAV0wwj1
    yYfoRSJoZ+n" crossorigin="anonymous"></script>
    <script src="https://cdn.jsdelivr.net/npm/popper.js@1.16.0/dist/umd/
    popper.min.js" integrity="sha384-Q6E9RHvbIyZFJoft+2mJbHaEWldlvI9IOYy5n3
    zV9zzTtmI3UksdQRVvoxMfooAo" crossorigin="anonymous"></script>
    <script src="https://stackpath.bootstrapcdn.com/bootstrap/4.4.1/js/
    bootstrap.min.js" integrity="sha384-wfSDF2E50Y2D1uUdj0O3uMBJnjuUD4Ih7Yw
    aYd1iqfktjOUod8GCExl3Og8ifwB6" crossorigin="anonymous"></script>
</body>
</html>
```

As you can see in the preceding code, you have only added two simple table elements. If you save it and reload the page, you will see the following (Figure 4-20).

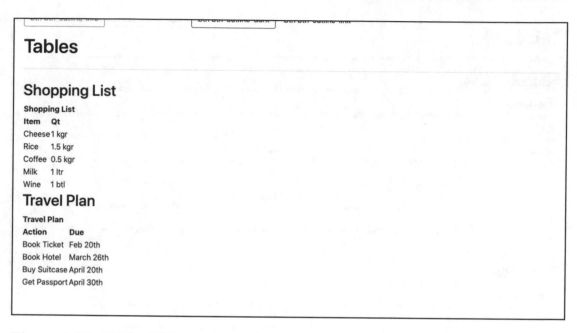

Figure 4-20. *Tables Without Any Extra Styling*

Styling Bootstrap Tables

Let's try to apply some Twitter Bootstrap classes in order to style it. You would have a decent example without too much effort, if you only applied the class table on the table elements. Let's do that. Instead of just

```
<table>
```

write

```
<table class="table">
```

If you reload the page on your browser, you will see that tables are displayed very nicely (Figure 4-21).

```
Pretty cool! Eh?
```

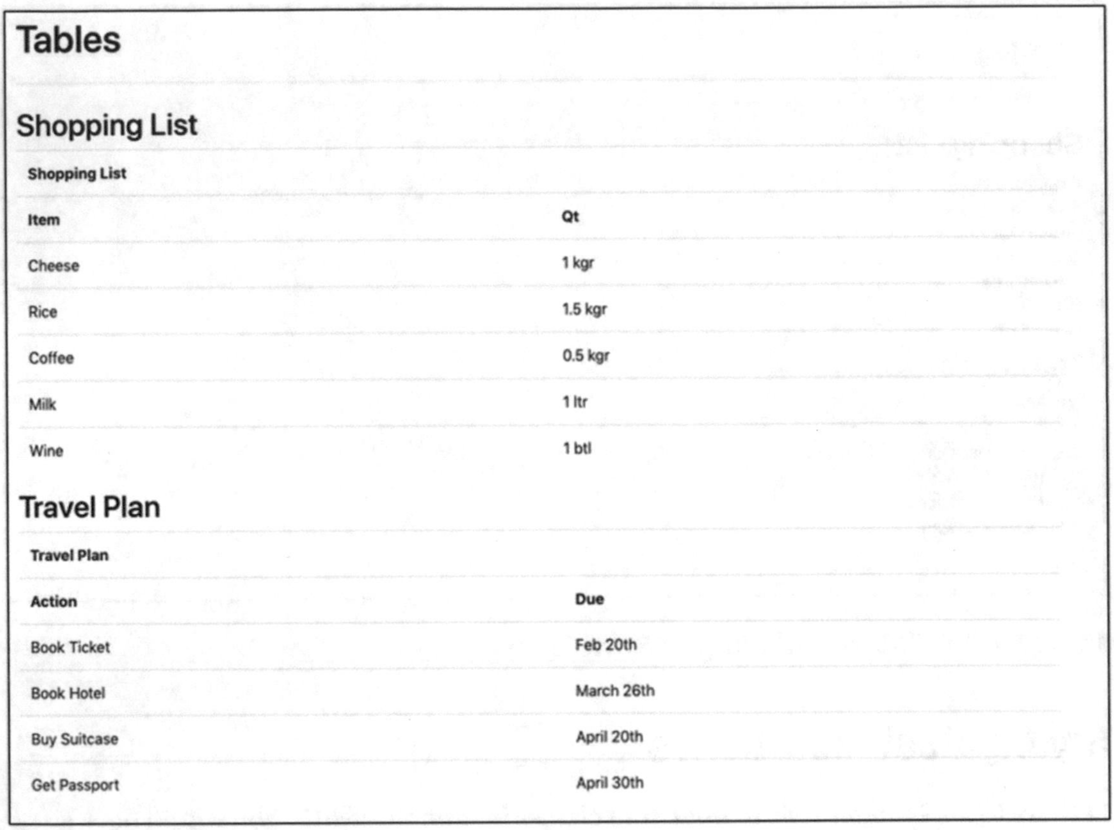

Tables

Shopping List

Shopping List	
Item	**Qt**
Cheese	1 kgr
Rice	1.5 kgr
Coffee	0.5 kgr
Milk	1 ltr
Wine	1 btl

Travel Plan

Travel Plan	
Action	**Due**
Book Ticket	Feb 20th
Book Hotel	March 26th
Buy Suitcase	April 20th
Get Passport	April 30th

Figure 4-21. *Tables with the "table" Class Only*

There are some more classes that you can try on tables, alongside the table class. Try to attach the class table-striped on the first table and the class table-bordered on the second one. So instead of

```
<table class="table">
```

turn it to

```
<table class="table table-striped">
```

for the first table and to

```
<table class="table table-bordered">
```

for the second table.

If you save and reload your page, you will see the following (Figure 4-22).

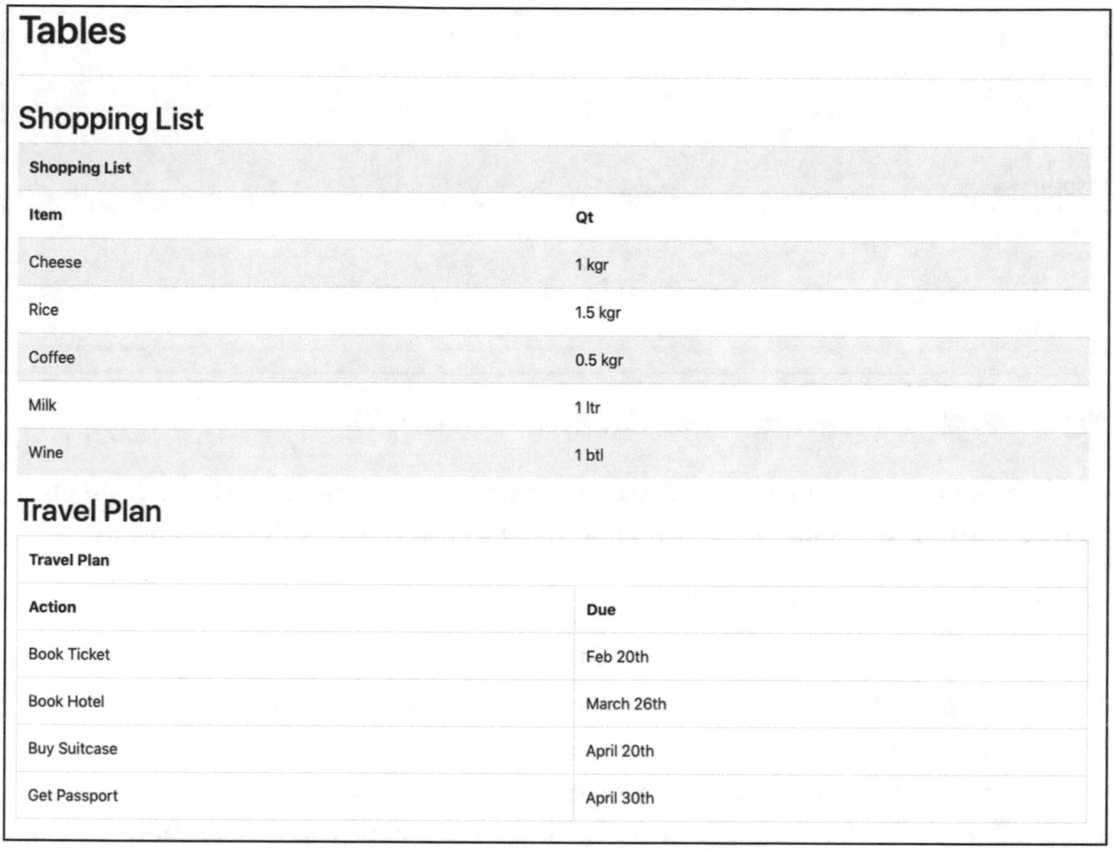

Tables

Shopping List

Shopping List	
Item	Qt
Cheese	1 kgr
Rice	1.5 kgr
Coffee	0.5 kgr
Milk	1 ltr
Wine	1 btl

Travel Plan

Travel Plan	
Action	Due
Book Ticket	Feb 20th
Book Hotel	March 26th
Buy Suitcase	April 20th
Get Passport	April 30th

Figure 4-22. *Striped and Bordered Tables*

The `table-striped` class makes the table have stripes, one row being with a dark background and the next one with a bright one. The `table-bordered` class adds borders to the table.

You can definitely combine table classes. For example, try `table table-striped table-bordered` for the second table. You will get the following (Figure 4-23).

Travel Plan	
Travel Plan	
Action	**Due**
Book Ticket	Feb 20th
Book Hotel	March 26th
Buy Suitcase	April 20th
Get Passport	April 30th

Figure 4-23. *Table Bordered and Striped at the Same Time*

Another one of the nice table classes is the class `table-hover`, which will highlight the row the mouse hovers on. Let's try that. Set the class value for the first table to

```
<table class="table table-hover">
```

If you save and load the page on your browser, you will see the table as it was with the `table` class only. But if you try to move your mouse pointer over the rows, you will see how rows are highlighted as the mouse moves over them.

Another useful class is `table-sm` which will make sure that the rows have quite small height. Try that on the second table alongside the other table classes that it already has:

```
<table class="table table-striped table-bordered table-sm">
```

If you reload the page on your browser, you will see the following (Figure 4-24).

Travel Plan	
Travel Plan	
Action	**Due**
Book Ticket	Feb 20th
Book Hotel	March 26th
Buy Suitcase	April 20th
Get Passport	April 30th

Figure 4-24. *Small Height with the `table-sm` Class*

As you can see in Figure 4-24, the second table with its condensed style has significantly smaller height for its rows, if compared to the height of the rows of the first table.

Coloring Table Rows

Furthermore, Twitter Bootstrap offers a series of semantic classes that correspond to specific colors. When you apply those classes, you quickly set the background color of the corresponding row (tr) or the corresponding cell (td or th).

These classes are

1. table-active

2. table-primary

3. table-secondary

4. table-success

5. table-danger

6. table-warning

7. table-info

8. table-light

9. table-dark

Let's apply some of them to the rows of the second table on your page. So the second table HTML fragment becomes as follows (Listing 4-10).

Listing 4-10. Second Table with Various Classes at Row Level

```
<table class="table table-bordered table-striped table-sm">
    <tr><th colspan="2">Travel Plan</th></tr>
    <tr class="table-active"><th>(active) Action</th><th>Due</th></tr>
    <tr class="table-success"><td>(success) Book Ticket</td><td>Feb 20th
    </td></tr>
    <tr class="table-info"><td>(info) Book Hotel</td><td>March 26th</td>
    </tr>
    <tr class="table-warning"><td>(warning) Buy Suitcase</td><td>April
    20th</td></tr>
    <tr class="table-danger"><td>(danger) Get Passport</td><td>April 30th
    </td></tr>
</table>
```

If you save the preceding code and reload the page on your browser, you will see the following (Figure 4-25).

Travel Plan	
Travel Plan	
(active) Action	**Due**
(success) Book Ticket	Feb 20th
(info) Book Hotel	March 26th
(warning) Buy Suitcase	April 20th
(danger) Get Passport	April 30th

Figure 4-25. *Table with Different Classes at Row Level*

Labels and Badges

Bootstrap allows you to create labels and badges very easily.

Labels

There are times that you want to create some kind of visual label, a tag, like the following (Figure 4-26).

Figure 4-26. *Tag Example*

This is very easily achieved with Twitter Bootstrap. You only have to enclose the content inside a span element and apply the class badge plus one class for the color of the label (any of the following badge-* classes):

1. badge-primary

2. badge-secondary

3. badge-success

4. badge-danger

5. badge-warning

6. `badge-info`

7. `badge-light`

8. `badge-dark`

Let's add the following content at the end of the main content container (Listing 4-11).

Listing 4-11. HTML Fragment That Creates Labels

```
<h1>Labels & Badges</h1>
<hr class="my-4">

<h4>
    <span class="badge badge-primary">€20.00 - Primary</span>
    <span class="badge badge-secondary">€20.00 - Secondary</span>
    <span class="badge badge-success">€20.00 - Success</span>
    <span class="badge badge-danger">€20.00 - Danger</span>
    <span class="badge badge-warning">€20.00 - Warning</span>
    <span class="badge badge-info">€20.00 - Info</span>
    <span class="badge badge-light">€20.00 - Light</span>
    <span class="badge badge-dark">€20.00 - Dark</span>
</h4>
```

Save the whole content and reload the page on your browser. You will see what is depicted in Figure 4-27.

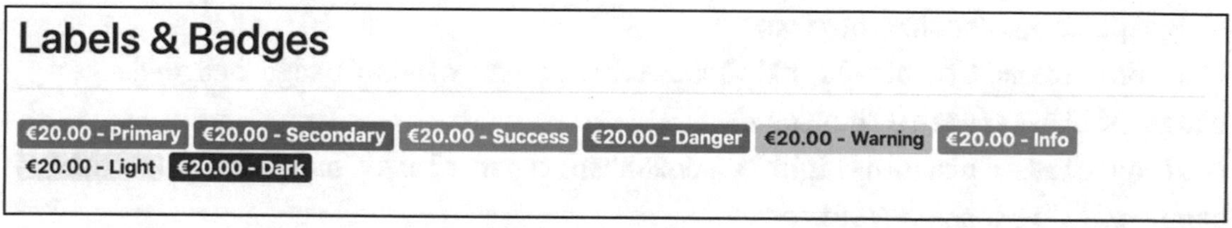

Labels & Badges

€20.00 - Primary €20.00 - Secondary €20.00 - Success €20.00 - Danger €20.00 - Warning €20.00 - Info
€20.00 - Light €20.00 - Dark

Figure 4-27. *Labels Demonstration*

Pretty clear. Please, keep note that you have enclosed the spans inside an h4 element just to make them a little bit bigger.

Badges

But what about badges? Quite often, you want to display a small, or larger, badge, like a number inside a circle, for example, to indicate the number of unread messages, as in Figure 4-28.

Figure 4-28. *Badge Example*

These are not different from the labels we have created earlier. The only difference is that they are more rounded. You can achieve this by adding the class badge-pill alongside the other badge-* classes.

Listing 4-12 is an HTML fragment that creates buttons with badges. Imagine a button that would allow the user to click and go to their inbox. The button would display the number of unread messages.

Listing 4-12. Buttons with Badges

```
<button class="btn btn-light">Inbox <span class="badge badge-primary
badge-pill">1</span></button>
<button class="btn btn-light">Inbox <span class="badge badge-secondary
badge-pill">2</span></button>
<button class="btn btn-light">Inbox <span class="badge badge-success
badge-pill">3</span></button>
<button class="btn btn-light">Inbox <span class="badge badge-danger
badge-pill">4</span></button>
<button class="btn btn-light">Inbox <span class="badge badge-warning
badge-pill">5</span></button>
<button class="btn btn-light">Inbox <span class="badge badge-info
badge-pill">6</span></button>
<button class="btn btn-light">Inbox <span class="badge badge-light
badge-pill">7</span></button>
<button class="btn btn-light">Inbox <span class="badge badge-dark
badge-pill">8</span></button>
```

Add this HTML fragment at the bottom of the main container and then reload the page on your browser. You will see the buttons with badges being displayed like the following (Figure 4-29).

Figure 4-29. *Buttons with Badges*

Key Takeaways

- Navigation bars with dropdown menu lists

- Buttons, with various sizes and colors

- Tables with different styles

- Labels and badges

This is the end of the first part of the Theme Reference project. In the following chapter, the second part of the project, you will continue learning more about Twitter Bootstrap components.

CHAPTER 5

Theme Reference: Part 2

In Chapter 4, "Theme Reference: Part 1," you have learned about some of the most important Twitter Bootstrap components, and you have started creating a reference page for all of them. In this chapter, the second part, you continue with some more components, within the same reference project.

In particular, the remaining components that I promised to present you are

- Tabs, which are used to group information

- Alerts, which are used to display a standout message

- Progress bars, which are used to visually show to the user the percentage of a work under process already done

- Cards, beautiful rectangular areas with rich content that draws viewers' attention

- Carousel, a component that works like an image or some other rich content slideshow

At the end, you will be asked to create a page that would require you to use most of the preceding components (Figure 5-1).

© Panos Matsinopoulos 2020
P. Matsinopoulos, *Practical Bootstrap*, https://doi.org/10.1007/978-1-4842-6071-5_5

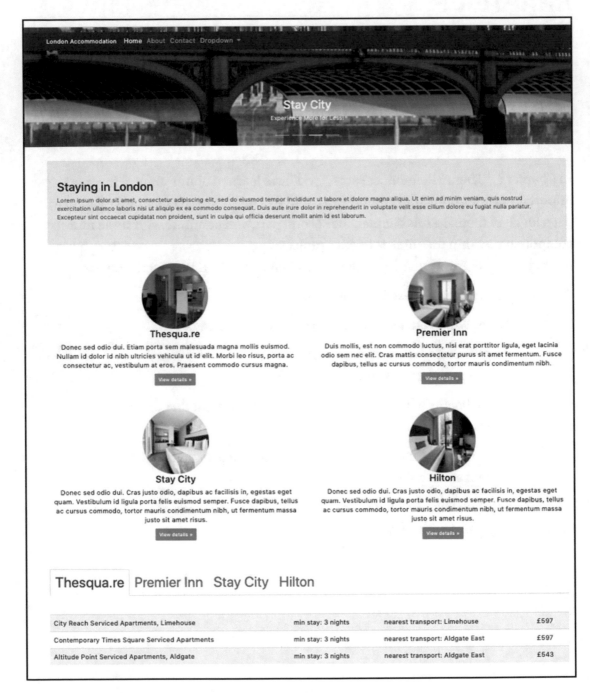

Figure 5-1. *Twitter Bootstrap Example Page with Various Elements*

Learning Goals

1. Learn how you can create tabs.

2. Learn how you can create alerts.

3. Learn how you can create progress bars.

4. Learn how you can create cards.

5. Learn how you can create carousels.

Introduction

You continue working on the Twitter Bootstrap Theme Reference project that you started in the previous chapter. Let's start adding more components into it.

Tabs

Sometimes you want to organize the information on your page using tabs. The tabs are good because they group parts of the information under a title and they do not display all the information at the same time. The user selects which information group to see/read by clicking the corresponding tab header.

For example, see some tabs in Figure 5-2.

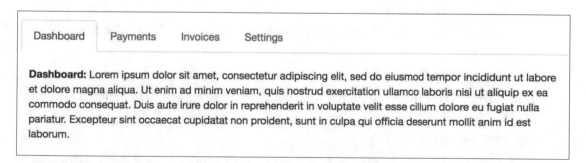

Figure 5-2. *Example of Tabs*

The information displayed is changed according to the tab header being clicked. Let's see how we can implement the preceding tabs example.

First, you need to understand that there are two parts in the HTML implementation of a tabs feature:

1. The tab headers

2. The different contents with the actual information

The Tab Headers

The tab headers are an unsorted list ul with class nav nav-tabs. Each element in the list (li) corresponds to a tab header, and it has to have the class nav-item. The content of each li is an anchor with class nav-link and the data attribute data-toggle with value tab. Also, each anchor has an href value pointing to the corresponding information container. When this anchor is clicked, that information container is going to be displayed to the user. Note that the li corresponding to the information container that should be displayed to the user needs to have the class active too.

Here is the HTML fragment for tab headers for the preceding example (Listing 5-1).

Listing 5-1. The ul HTML Fragment for the Tabs Example

```
<ul class="nav nav-tabs">
    <li class="nav-item">
      <a class="nav-link active" href="#dashboard" data-
      toggle="tab">Dashboard</a>
    </li>
    <li class="nav-item">
      <a class="nav-link" href="#payments" data-toggle="tab">Payments</a>
    </li>
    <li class="nav-item">
      <a class="nav-link" href="#invoices" data-toggle="tab">Invoices</a>
    </li>
    <li class="nav-item">
      <a class="nav-link" href="#settings" data-toggle="tab">Settings</a>
    </li>
</ul>
```

Let's change your main HTML page using the preceding fragment. Add it to the bottom of the container. Before this ul list, add the header for the Tabs like you did for the other headers (Listing 5-2).

Listing 5-2. Tabs Header

```
<h1>Tabs</h1>
<hr class="my-4">
```

If you save the page and load it on your browser, the Tabs part will be the one shown in Figure 5-3.

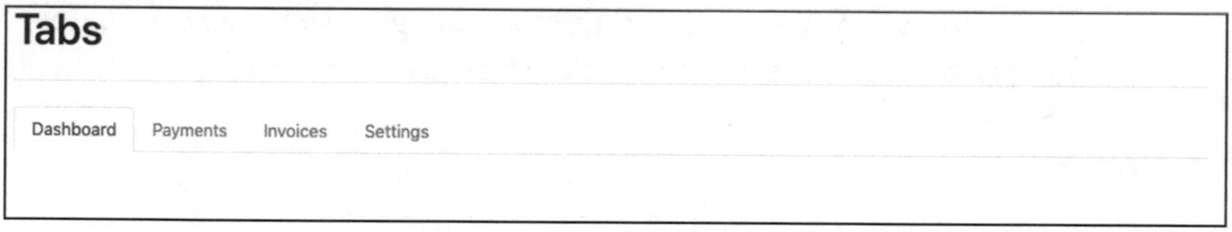

Figure 5-3. *Tabs with Empty Content*

That's a good step. You can see how the tabs are well put on the page. You can even click the headers in order to see how the active tab changes according to the tab that you click.

What is missing now is the information that should be attached at each tab.

The Tab Information

You put the tab information inside a div with class tab-content. Inside that, we create one div per information group/tab header. This div needs to have a class tab-pane. Also, it needs to have the correct id, different for each tab information panel and corresponding to the href value of the corresponding tab.

Let's add the following piece of HTML code (Listing 5-3) at the end of the main content container, after the unsorted list that we have created for the tab headers.

Listing 5-3. HTML Fragment for Tab Content

```
<div class="tab-content">
    <div id="dashboard" class="tab-pane active">
        <p>
            <strong>Dashboard:</strong> Lorem ipsum dolor sit amet,
            consectetur adipiscing elit, sed do eiusmod tempor incididunt
            ut labore et dolore magna aliqua. Ut enim ad minim veniam, quis
            nostrud exercitation ullamco laboris nisi ut aliquip ex ea
            commodo consequat. Duis aute irure dolor in reprehenderit in
            voluptate velit esse cillum dolore eu fugiat nulla pariatur.
            Excepteur sint occaecat cupidatat non proident, sunt in culpa
            qui officia deserunt mollit anim id est laborum.
        </p>
    </div>

    <div id="payments" class="tab-pane">
        <p>
            <strong>Payments:</strong> Lorem ipsum dolor sit amet,
            consectetur adipiscing elit, sed do eiusmod tempor incididunt
            ut labore et dolore magna aliqua. Ut enim ad minim veniam, quis
            nostrud exercitation ullamco laboris nisi ut aliquip ex ea
            commodo consequat. Duis aute irure dolor in reprehenderit in
            voluptate velit esse cillum dolore eu fugiat nulla pariatur.
            Excepteur sint occaecat cupidatat non proident, sunt in culpa
            qui officia deserunt mollit anim id est laborum.
        </p>
    </div>

    <div id="invoices" class="tab-pane">
        <p>
            <strong>Invoices:</strong> Lorem ipsum dolor sit amet,
            consectetur adipiscing elit, sed do eiusmod tempor incididunt
            ut labore et dolore magna aliqua. Ut enim ad minim veniam, quis
            nostrud exercitation ullamco laboris nisi ut aliquip ex ea
            commodo consequat. Duis aute irure dolor in reprehenderit in
            voluptate velit esse cillum dolore eu fugiat nulla pariatur.
```

```
            Excepteur sint occaecat cupidatat non proident, sunt in culpa
            qui officia deserunt mollit anim id est laborum.
        </p>
    </div>

    <div id="settings" class="tab-pane">
        <p>
            <strong>Settings:</strong> Lorem ipsum dolor sit amet,
            consectetur adipiscing elit, sed do eiusmod tempor incididunt
            ut labore et dolore magna aliqua. Ut enim ad minim veniam, quis
            nostrud exercitation ullamco laboris nisi ut aliquip ex ea
            commodo consequat. Duis aute irure dolor in reprehenderit in
            voluptate velit esse cillum dolore eu fugiat nulla pariatur.
            Excepteur sint occaecat cupidatat non proident, sunt in culpa
            qui officia deserunt mollit anim id est laborum.
        </p>
    </div>
</div>
```

As you can see in the preceding code

1. You have a div that contains all the other individual divs.

2. This parent div has class tab-content.

3. Each div has id value equal to the href of the corresponding tab header anchor.

4. Each div has the class tab-pane.

5. The first div has the class active too, because this is the first information box that is displayed for the first tab header, which is also, initially, active.

If you save the preceding information and reload the page, you will see the following (Figure 5-4).

Tabs

| Dashboard | Payments | Invoices | Settings |

Dashboard: Lorem ipsum dolor sit amet, consectetur adipiscing elit, sed do eiusmod tempor incididunt ut labore et dolore magna aliqua. Ut enim ad minim veniam, quis nostrud exercitation ullamco laboris nisi ut aliquip ex ea commodo consequat. Duis aute irure dolor in reprehenderit in voluptate velit esse cillum dolore eu fugiat nulla pariatur. Excepteur sint occaecat cupidatat non proident, sunt in culpa qui officia deserunt mollit anim id est laborum.

Figure 5-4. Tabs with Content

As you can see, the tab information is clearly displayed below the tab headers. Also, if you try to click different tab headers, you will see how the following information changes accordingly.

However, there is a problem with the content being too close to the tab headers (Figure 5-5).

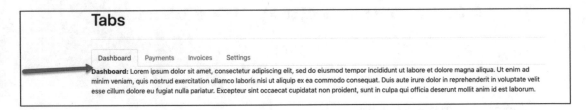

Figure 5-5. Problem with the Tab Content Being Too Close to Tab Headers

In order to fix this, you need some bottom margin on the `ul` that includes the headers. You can achieve that by adding the utility class `mb-3` to the `ul` element.

Now if you load the page on your browser, you will see the following (Figure 5-6).

Tabs

| Dashboard | Payments | Invoices | Settings |

Dashboard: Lorem ipsum dolor sit amet, consectetur adipiscing elit, sed do eiusmod tempor incididunt ut labore et dolore magna aliqua. Ut enim ad minim veniam, quis nostrud exercitation ullamco laboris nisi ut aliquip ex ea commodo consequat. Duis aute irure dolor in reprehenderit in voluptate velit esse cillum dolore eu fugiat nulla pariatur. Excepteur sint occaecat cupidatat non proident, sunt in culpa qui officia deserunt mollit anim id est laborum.

Figure 5-6. Tab Content Now Has Some Free Space Above It

Note   Twitter Bootstrap is encouraging the authors to make their content compatible with assistive technologies, such as screen readers. This means that instead of just using the styling classes, you may also have to add some extra HTML attributes specially designed for this purpose. For example, the role HTML attribute for the `ul` element with the tab list needs to have the value `tablist`. If you want to learn about how you can create accessible rich Internet applications, you have to read and apply the practices given here: WAI-ARIA Authoring Practices.

Checkpoint

You have done a lot of work on this page. Before you continue, let's make sure that it has the following content as in Listing 5-4.

Listing 5-4. Twitter Bootstrap Reference Page Checkpoint

```
<!DOCTYPE html>
<html lang="en">
<head>
    <!-- Required meta tags -->
    <meta charset="utf-8">
    <meta name="viewport" content="width=device-width, initial-scale=1,
    shrink-to-fit=no">

    <!-- Bootstrap CSS -->
    <link rel="stylesheet" href="https://stackpath.bootstrapcdn.
    com/bootstrap/4.4.1/css/bootstrap.min.css" integrity="sha384-
    Vkoo8x4CGsO3+Hhxv8T/Q5PaXtkKtu6ug5TOeNV6gBiFeWPGFN9MuhOf23Q9Ifjh"
    crossorigin="anonymous">

    <!-- Custom CSS -->
    <link rel="stylesheet" href="stylesheets/main.css" type="text/css">

    <title>Twitter Bootstrap Reference Page</title>
</head>
```

```
<body>
    <nav class="navbar navbar-expand-lg navbar-dark bg-dark fixed-top">
        <div class="container">
            <a class="navbar-brand" href="#">Bootstrap Ref. Page</a>

            <button type="button" class="navbar-toggler" data-
            toggle="collapse" data-target="#navbar"
                    aria-controls="navbar"
                    aria-expanded="false"
                    aria-label="Toggle navigation">
                <span class="navbar-toggler-icon"></span>
            </button>

            <div class="collapse navbar-collapse" id="navbar">
                <ul class="nav navbar-nav">
                    <li class="nav-item">
                        <a class="nav-link active" href="#">Home <span
                        class="sr-only">(current)</span></a>
                    </li>
                    <li class="nav-item">
                        <a class="nav-link" href="#about">About</a>
                    </li>
                    <li class="nav-item">
                        <a class="nav-link" href="#contact">Contact</a>
                    </li>

                    <!-- Drop down Menu -->
                    <li class="nav-item dropdown">
                        <a href="#"
                           class="nav-link dropdown-toggle"
                           data-toggle="dropdown">
                            Dropdown
                        </a>
                        <div class="dropdown-menu">
                            <a href="#" class="dropdown-item">Action</a>
                            <a href="#" class="dropdown-item">Another
                            action</a>
```

```
                    <a href="#" class="dropdown-item">Something
                    else here</a>
                    <div class="dropdown-divider"></div>
                    <div class="dropdown-header">Nav header</div>
                    <a href="#" class="dropdown-item">Separated
                    link</a>
                    <a href="#" class="dropdown-item">One more
                    separated link</a>
                </div>
            </li>
        </ul>
    </div>
</div>
</nav>

<!-- main content container -->
<div class="container">
    <div class="jumbotron">
        <p class="lead">
            Lorem ipsum dolor sit amet, consectetur adipiscing elit,
            sed do eiusmod tempor incididunt ut labore et dolore magna
            aliqua. Ut enim ad minim veniam, quis nostrud
            exercitation ullamco laboris nisi ut aliquip ex ea commodo
            consequat. Duis aute irure dolor in reprehenderit in
            voluptate velit esse cillum dolore eu fugiat nulla
            pariatur. Excepteur sint occaecat cupidatat non proident,
            sunt in culpa qui officia deserunt mollit anim id est
            laborum.
        </p>
    </div>

    <h1>Buttons</h1>
    <hr class="my-4">

    <h2>Small Sizes</h2>
    <p>
```

```
    <button type="button" class="btn btn-sm btn-primary">btn btn-sm
    btn-primary</button>
    <button type="button" class="btn btn-sm btn-secondary">btn btn-
    sm btn-secondary</button>
    <button type="button" class="btn btn-sm btn-success">btn btn-sm
    btn-success</button>
    <button type="button" class="btn btn-sm btn-danger">btn btn-sm
    btn-danger</button>
    <button type="button" class="btn btn-sm btn-warning">btn btn-sm
    btn-warning</button>
    <button type="button" class="btn btn-sm btn-info">btn btn-sm
    btn-info</button>
    <button type="button" class="btn btn-sm btn-light">btn btn-sm
    btn-light</button>
    <button type="button" class="btn btn-sm btn-dark">btn btn-sm
    btn-dark</button>
    <button type="button" class="btn btn-sm btn-link">btn btn-sm
    btn-link</button>
</p>

<h2>Normal Sizes</h2>
<p>
    <button type="button" class="btn btn-primary">btn btn-primary</
    button>
    <button type="button" class="btn btn-secondary">btn btn-
    secondary</button>
    <button type="button" class="btn btn-success">btn btn-success</
    button>
    <button type="button" class="btn btn-danger">btn btn-danger</
    button>
    <button type="button" class="btn btn-warning">btn btn-warning</
    button>
    <button type="button" class="btn btn-info">btn btn-info</button>
    <button type="button" class="btn btn-light">btn btn-light</button>
```

```
    <button type="button" class="btn btn-dark">btn btn-dark</button>
    <button type="button" class="btn btn-link">btn btn-link</button>
</p>
```

Large Sizes

```
<p>
    <button type="button" class="btn btn-lg btn-primary">btn btn-lg
    btn-primary</button>
    <button type="button" class="btn btn-lg btn-secondary">btn btn-
    lg btn-secondary</button>
    <button type="button" class="btn btn-lg btn-success">btn btn-lg
    btn-success</button>
    <button type="button" class="btn btn-lg btn-danger">btn btn-lg
    btn-danger</button>
    <button type="button" class="btn btn-lg btn-warning">btn btn-lg
    btn-warning</button>
    <button type="button" class="btn btn-lg btn-info">btn btn-lg
    btn-info</button>
    <button type="button" class="btn btn-lg btn-light">btn btn-lg
    btn-light</button>
    <button type="button" class="btn btn-lg btn-dark">btn btn-lg
    btn-dark</button>
    <button type="button" class="btn btn-lg btn-link">btn btn-lg
    btn-link</button>
</p>
```

Block Sizes

```
<p>
    <button type="button" class="btn btn-block btn-primary">btn
    btn-block btn-primary</button>
    <button type="button" class="btn btn-block btn-secondary">btn
    btn-block btn-secondary</button>
    <button type="button" class="btn btn-block btn-success">btn
    btn-block btn-success</button>
    <button type="button" class="btn btn-block btn-danger">btn btn-
    block btn-danger</button>
```

```
        <button type="button" class="btn btn-block btn-warning">btn
        btn-block btn-warning</button>
        <button type="button" class="btn btn-block btn-info">btn btn-
        block btn-info</button>
        <button type="button" class="btn btn-block btn-light">btn btn-
        block btn-light</button>
        <button type="button" class="btn btn-block btn-dark">btn btn-
        block btn-dark</button>
        <button type="button" class="btn btn-block btn-link">btn btn-
        block btn-link</button>
    </p>

    <h2>Outline buttons (Normal Sizes)</h2>
    <p>
        <button type="button" class="btn btn-outline-primary">btn btn-
        outline-primary</button>
        <button type="button" class="btn btn-outline-secondary">btn
        btn-outline-secondary</button>
        <button type="button" class="btn btn-outline-success">btn btn-
        outline-success</button>
        <button type="button" class="btn btn-outline-danger">btn btn-
        outline-danger</button>
        <button type="button" class="btn btn-outline-warning">btn btn-
        outline-warning</button>
        <button type="button" class="btn btn-outline-info">btn btn-
        outline-info</button>
        <button type="button" class="btn btn-outline-light">btn btn-
        outline-light</button>
        <button type="button" class="btn btn-outline-dark">btn btn-
        outline-dark</button>
        <button type="button" class="btn btn-outline-link">btn btn-
        outline-link</button>
    </p>

    <h1>Tables</h1>
    <hr class="my-4">
```

```
<h2>Shopping List</h2>
<table class="table">
    <tr><th colspan="2">Shopping List</th></tr>
    <tr><th>Item</th><th>Qt</th></tr>
    <tr><td>Cheese</td><td>1 kgr</td></tr>
    <tr><td>Rice</td><td>1.5 kgr</td></tr>
    <tr><td>Coffee</td><td>0.5 kgr</td></tr>
    <tr><td>Milk</td><td>1 ltr</td></tr>
    <tr><td>Wine</td><td>1 btl</td></tr>
</table>

<h2>Travel Plan</h2>
<table class="table table-bordered table-striped table-sm">
    <tr><th colspan="2">Travel Plan</th></tr>
    <tr class="table-active"><th>(active) Action</th><th>Due</th></tr>
    <tr class="table-success"><td>(success) Book Ticket</td><td>Feb
    20th</td></tr>
    <tr class="table-info"><td>(info) Book Hotel</td><td>March
    26th</td></tr>
    <tr class="table-warning"><td>(warning) Buy Suitcase</td>
    <td>April 20th</td></tr>
    <tr class="table-danger"><td>(danger) Get Passport</td>
    <td>April 30th</td></tr>
</table>

<h1>Labels & Badges</h1>
<hr class="my-4">

<h4>
    <span class="badge badge-primary">€20.00 - Primary</span>
    <span class="badge badge-secondary">€20.00 - Secondary</span>
    <span class="badge badge-success">€20.00 - Success</span>
    <span class="badge badge-danger">€20.00 - Danger</span>
    <span class="badge badge-warning">€20.00 - Warning</span>
    <span class="badge badge-info">€20.00 - Info</span>
    <span class="badge badge-light">€20.00 - Light</span>
    <span class="badge badge-dark">€20.00 - Dark</span>
</h4>
```

```
<button class="btn btn-light">Inbox <span class="badge badge-
primary badge-pill">1</span></button>
<button class="btn btn-light">Inbox <span class="badge badge-
secondary badge-pill">2</span></button>
<button class="btn btn-light">Inbox <span class="badge badge-
success badge-pill">3</span></button>
<button class="btn btn-light">Inbox <span class="badge badge-
danger badge-pill">4</span></button>
<button class="btn btn-light">Inbox <span class="badge badge-
warning badge-pill">5</span></button>
<button class="btn btn-light">Inbox <span class="badge badge-
info badge-pill">6</span></button>
<button class="btn btn-light">Inbox <span class="badge badge-
light badge-pill">7</span></button>
<button class="btn btn-light">Inbox <span class="badge badge-
dark badge-pill">8</span></button>

<h1>Tabs</h1>
<hr class="my-4">

<ul class="nav nav-tabs mb-4">
    <li class="nav-item"><a class="nav-link active"
    href="#dashboard" data-toggle="tab">Dashboard</a></li>
    <li class="nav-item"><a class="nav-link" href="#payments" data-
    toggle="tab">Payments</a></li>
    <li class="nav-item"><a class="nav-link" href="#invoices" data-
    toggle="tab">Invoices</a></li>
    <li class="nav-item"><a class="nav-link" href="#settings" data-
    toggle="tab">Settings</a></li>
</ul>

<div class="tab-content">
    <div id="dashboard" class="tab-pane active">
        <p>
            <strong>Dashboard:</strong> Lorem ipsum dolor sit amet,
            consectetur adipiscing elit, sed do eiusmod tempor
            incididunt ut labore et dolore magna aliqua. Ut enim
```

```
        ad minim veniam, quis nostrud exercitation ullamco
        laboris nisi ut aliquip ex ea commodo consequat. Duis
        aute irure dolor in reprehenderit in voluptate velit
        esse cillum dolore eu fugiat nulla pariatur. Excepteur
        sint occaecat cupidatat non proident, sunt in culpa qui
        officia deserunt mollit anim id est laborum.
    </p>
</div>

<div id="payments" class="tab-pane">
    <p>
        <strong>Payments:</strong> Lorem ipsum dolor sit amet,
        consectetur adipiscing elit, sed do eiusmod tempor
        incididunt ut labore et dolore magna aliqua. Ut enim
        ad minim veniam, quis nostrud exercitation ullamco
        laboris nisi ut aliquip ex ea commodo consequat. Duis
        aute irure dolor in reprehenderit in voluptate velit
        esse cillum dolore eu fugiat nulla pariatur. Excepteur
        sint occaecat cupidatat non proident, sunt in culpa qui
        officia deserunt mollit anim id est laborum.
    </p>
</div>

<div id="invoices" class="tab-pane">
    <p>
        <strong>Invoices:</strong> Lorem ipsum dolor sit amet,
        consectetur adipiscing elit, sed do eiusmod tempor
        incididunt ut labore et dolore magna aliqua. Ut enim
        ad minim veniam, quis nostrud exercitation ullamco
        laboris nisi ut aliquip ex ea commodo consequat. Duis
        aute irure dolor in reprehenderit in voluptate velit
        esse cillum dolore eu fugiat nulla pariatur. Excepteur
        sint occaecat cupidatat non proident, sunt in culpa qui
        officia deserunt mollit anim id est laborum.
    </p>
</div>
```

```
            <div id="settings" class="tab-pane">
               <p>
                    <strong>Settings:</strong> Lorem ipsum dolor sit amet,
                    consectetur adipiscing elit, sed do eiusmod tempor
                    incididunt ut labore et dolore magna aliqua. Ut enim
                    ad minim veniam, quis nostrud exercitation ullamco
                    laboris nisi ut aliquip ex ea commodo consequat. Duis
                    aute irure dolor in reprehenderit in voluptate velit
                    esse cillum dolore eu fugiat nulla pariatur. Excepteur
                    sint occaecat cupidatat non proident, sunt in culpa qui
                    officia deserunt mollit anim id est laborum.
               </p>
            </div>
         </div>
    </div>
    <!-- end of main content container -->

    <!-- Optional JavaScript -->
    <!-- jQuery first, then Popper.js, then Bootstrap JS -->
    <script src="https://code.jquery.com/jquery-3.4.1.slim.min.js"
    integrity="sha384-J6qa4849blE2+poT4WnyKhv5vZF5SrPo0iEjwBvKU7imGFAVOwwj1
    yYfoRSJoZ+n" crossorigin="anonymous"></script>
    <script src="https://cdn.jsdelivr.net/npm/popper.js@1.16.0/dist/umd/
    popper.min.js" integrity="sha384-Q6E9RHvbIyZFJoft+2mJbHaEWldlvI9IOYy5n3
    zV9zzTtmI3UksdQRVvoxMfooAo" crossorigin="anonymous"></script>
    <script src="https://stackpath.bootstrapcdn.com/bootstrap/4.4.1/js/
    bootstrap.min.js" integrity="sha384-wfSDF2E50Y2D1uUdj0O3uMBJnjuUD4Ih7Yw
    aYd1iqfktjOUod8GCExl3Og8ifwB6" crossorigin="anonymous"></script>
</body>
</html>
```

Alerts

There are times that you want to display a message that will attract users' attention. These are called alerts. The following is an example (Figure 5-7).

Ooops! Something went wrong with the data you provided. Please, correct and submit again.

Figure 5-7. *Alert Example*

These messages are usually displayed at the top of the page, but not necessarily only there.

Twitter Bootstrap gives the class `alert` that should be used on a block element (like a div) in order to turn it into an alert block. Alongside that, you also need to specify a class that would color the alert so that it better conveys the message to the user. So, for a message that would indicate warning, you could use the `alert-warning` class, alongside the `alert` one.

The color classes related to alerts are

1. `alert-primary`

2. `alert-secondary`

3. `alert-success`

4. `alert-danger`

5. `alert-warning`

6. `alert-info`

7. `alert-light`

8. `alert-dark`

Let's see these alerts in action. Add the following HTML fragment exactly before the end of the main content container (Listing 5-5).

Listing 5-5. HTML Fragment for Alerts Demo

```
<h1>Alerts</h1>
<hr class="my-4">

<div class="alert alert-primary">
    A simple primary alert.
</div>
```

```
<div class="alert alert-secondary">
    A simple secondary alert.
</div>
<div class="alert alert-success">
    A simple success alert.
</div>
<div class="alert alert-danger">
    A simple danger alert.
</div>
<div class="alert alert-warning">
    A simple warning alert.
</div>
<div class="alert alert-info">
    A simple info alert.
</div>
<div class="alert alert-light">
    A simple light alert.
</div>
<div class="alert alert-dark">
    A simple dark alert.
</div>
```

If you save the preceding code and reload your page on your browser, you will see the following at the Alerts part of the page (Figure 5-8).

Alerts

A simple primary alert.

A simple secondary alert.

A simple success alert.

A simple danger alert.

A simple warning alert.

A simple info alert.

A simple light alert.

A simple dark alert.

Figure 5-8. *Alerts Demo*

Inside your alert, you can have any valid HTML content. For example, you can have a link to another page. Let's add the following HTML fragment (Listing 5-6).

Listing 5-6. Add an Alert with HTML Inside

```
<div class="alert alert-info">
    <strong>London</strong> Read more about London from <a href="https://
    en.wikipedia.org/wiki/London">Wikipedia London Link</a>.
</div>
```

If you reload your HTML page, the new alert will be displayed as follows (Figure 5-9).

There is a small styling issue here that has to do with the color of the link inside the alert. It just doesn't look good. Bootstrap recommends that you use the class alert-link on your anchor a. This will provide matching color according to the background of your alert. Let's add it like in Listing 5-7.

London Read more about London from Wikipedia London Link.

Figure 5-9. *Alert with Hyperlink Inside*

211

Listing 5-7. Use the alert-link Class

```
<div class="alert alert-info">
    <strong>London</strong> Read more about London from <a class="alert-
    link" href="https://en.wikipedia.org/wiki/London">Wikipedia London
    Link</a>.
</div>
```

If you save the HTML content and reload the page on your browser, you will see the alert with the hyperlink being displayed as in Figure 5-10.

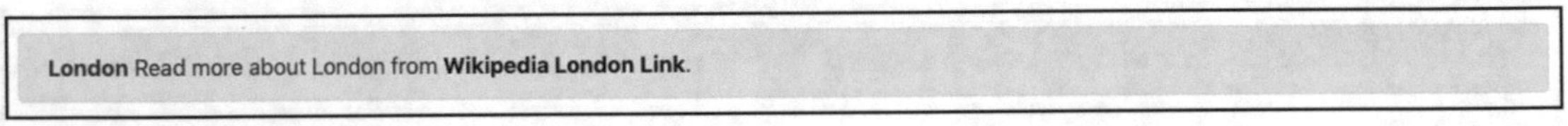

London Read more about London from **Wikipedia London Link**.

Figure 5-10. *Styling Links with* `alert-link`

Progress Bars

Progress bars indicate how much of a given task has been completed and how much remains to be done. See, for example, Figure 5-11.

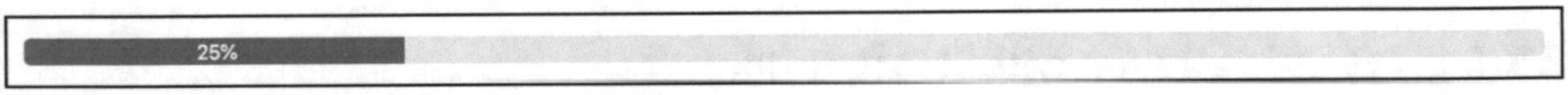

25%

Figure 5-11. *Progress Bar Example*

As you can see in Figure 5-11, the progress bar has both a color and a text indication of how much of the process has been completed and how much is left to be done.

Twitter Bootstrap has two classes that are related to this tool, the `progress` and the `progress-bar`. Let's see how they should be used by appending the following HTML content to the end of the main content container (Listing 5-8).

Listing 5-8. HTML Fragment to Add a Progress Bar

```
<h1>Progress Bars</h1>
<hr class="my-4">

<div class="progress">
    <div class="progress-bar" style="width: 60%;">60% Complete</div>
</div>
```

As you can see from the preceding fragment, the progress bars are very easy to build. A div has the class progress; and another div, inside the first, has the class progress-bar. The child div has the text that is displayed to give a textual info about the current progress. This text is not necessary. It might be empty. The important part here is that you correctly set the value for the width attribute of the child div, so that it is that big to indicate the actual progress. A good approach is to use a percentage here, because the percentage will make the child width be a percentage of the width of the parent div. The progress class on the parent div makes sure that the parent div occupies all the available width of the page, whereas the style="width: 60%" on the child div makes sure that the child div occupies exactly 60% of the parent div, hence these two div elements working as one to give the visual effect of the progress bar.

If you save the HTML page and reload it on your browser, you will see the following (Figure 5-12).

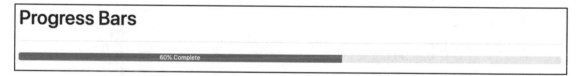

Figure 5-12. *Standard Progress Bar*

Progress Bar Height

If this bar looks short to you, then you can adjust the height of the parent div, the one that has the class progress. Let's add the style attribute as follows (Listing 5-9).

Listing 5-9. Adjust the Height of the Progress Bar

```
<div class="progress" style="height: 1.8rem;">
    <div class="progress-bar" style="width: 60%;">60% Complete</div>
</div>
```

If you save the preceding content and reload the page on your browser, you will see the following (Figure 5-13).

213

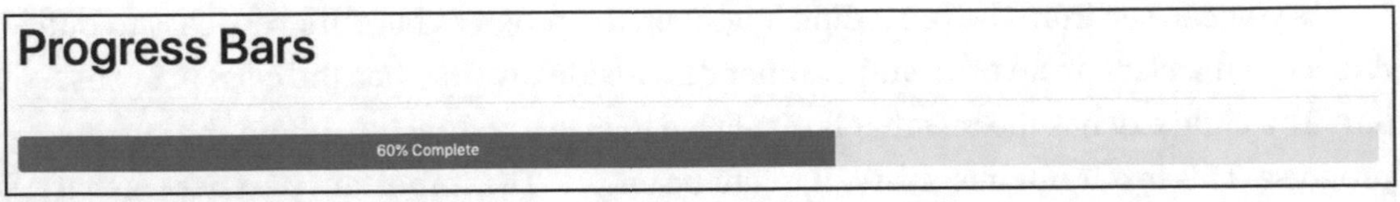

Progress Bars

60% Complete

Figure 5-13. *Adjust the Height of the Progress Bar*

Progress Bar Colors

Besides the plain progress bar that you see in Figure 5-13, you can use the Bootstrap background color utility classes to change the color of the progress bar. These classes are

- `bg-primary`
- `bg-secondary`
- `bg-success`
- `bg-danger`
- `bg-warning`
- `bg-info`
- `bg-light`
- `bg-dark`

You need to set this class on the inner `div`, alongside the `progress-bar` class. Let's change the progress bar demo code in your HTML page to be the following (Listing 5-10).

Listing 5-10. Progress Bar Demo Code Fragment

```
<h1>Progress Bars</h1>
<hr class="my-4">

<div class="progress mb-1 h-4">
    <div class="progress-bar bg-primary" style="width: 60%;">60% Complete -
    primary</div>
</div>
<div class="progress mb-1 h-4">
    <div class="progress-bar bg-secondary" style="width: 60%;">60%
    Complete - secondary</div>
</div>
```

```
<div class="progress mb-1 h-4">
    <div class="progress-bar bg-success" style="width: 60%;">60% Complete -
    success</div>
</div>
<div class="progress mb-1 h-4">
    <div class="progress-bar bg-danger" style="width: 60%;">60% Complete -
    danger</div>
</div>
<div class="progress mb-1 h-4">
    <div class="progress-bar bg-warning" style="width: 60%;">60% Complete -
    warning</div>
</div>
<div class="progress mb-1 h-4">
    <div class="progress-bar bg-info" style="width: 60%;">60% Complete -
    info</div>
</div>
<div class="progress mb-1 h-4">
    <div class="progress-bar bg-light" style="width: 60%;">60% Complete -
    light</div>
</div>
<div class="progress mb-1 h-4">
    <div class="progress-bar bg-dark" style="width: 60%;">60% Complete -
    dark</div>
</div>
```

Also, make sure that your stylesheets/main.css file has the following class definition (Listing 5-11).

Listing 5-11. Class h-4 Which Is Used in Listing 5-10

```
.h-4 {
    height: 1.5rem;
}
```

If you save the HTML page and reload it on your browser, you will see the following (Figure 5-14).

Progress Bars

60% Complete - primary	
60% Complete - secondary	
60% Complete - success	
60% Complete - danger	
60% Complete - warning	
60% Complete - info	
60% Complete - dark	

Figure 5-14. *Progress Bars with Various Colors*

Multicolored Progress Bar

Finally, there is another trick that you can do with progress bars. You can use different colors on the same progress bar. You can create an effect like the following (Figure 5-15).

Figure 5-15. *Multicolored Progress Bar*

This is easily achieved by including more than one child `div` with the `progress-bar` class. In order to see this in action, append the following HTML fragment at the end of the main content container (Listing 5-12).

Listing 5-12. Multicolored Progress Bar HTML Fragment

```
<div class="progress mb-1 h-4">
    <div class="progress-bar bg-primary" style="width: 30%;">30% primary</div>
    <div class="progress-bar bg-success" style="width: 50%;">50% success</div>
    <div class="progress-bar bg-warning" style="width: 10%;">10% warning</div>
</div>
```

As you can see in the preceding code, all three different color `div`s are inside the parent `div`. Twitter Bootstrap is clever enough to draw each one of them at the correct position and, given the classes for the color of the progress bars, to draw them with the correct color.

Cards

A card is a container that has some specific structure to create very attractive content, with headers and footers. In Figure 5-16, you can see an example of a card.

Figure 5-16. *Card Example*

A card usually has an image, a title, and a body. But it can also contain headers and footers.

Three-Card Layout

Let's try to create the following in your Twitter Bootstrap reference page (Figure 5-17).

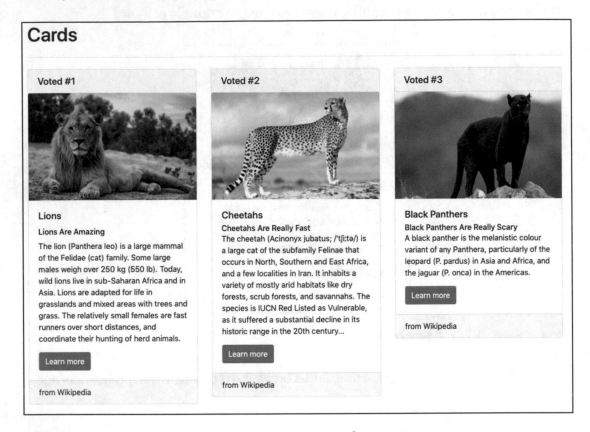

Figure 5-17. *Cards in Your Twitter Bootstrap Reference Page*

- You are going to add three cards.

- The layout you will choose is responsive:

  - For displays up to 767px, it will display one card per row.

  - For displays up to 991px, it will display two cards per row.

  - For displays with width >=992px, it will display the three cards on the same row.

Listing 5-13 contains the HTML code that you have to add at the bottom of the main container of your page.

Listing 5-13. Three Cards

```
<h1>Cards</h1>
<hr class="my-4">

<div class="row row-cols-1 row-cols-md-2 row-cols-lg-3">
    <div class="col">
        <div class="card">
            <h5 class="card-header">Voted #1</h5>
            <img src="https://live.staticflickr.com/3869/14437071224_43fb23
            705b_h.jpg" class="card-img-top" alt="lion sitting and looking
            around" style="height: 220px"/>
            <div class="card-body">
                <h5 class="card-title">Lions</h5>
                <h6 class="card-subtitle">Lions Are Amazing</h6>
                <p class="card-text">
                    The lion (Panthera leo) is a large mammal of the
                    Felidae (cat) family. Some large males weigh over
                    250 kg (550 lb). Today, wild lions live in sub-
                    Saharan Africa and in Asia. Lions are adapted for life
                    in grasslands and mixed areas with trees and grass.
                    The relatively small females are fast runners over
                    short distances, and coordinate their hunting of herd
                    animals.
                </p>
                <a href="https://simple.wikipedia.org/wiki/Lion" class="btn
                btn-primary">Learn more</a>
            </div>
            <div class="card-footer">
                from Wikipedia
            </div>
        </div>
    </div>
    <div class="col">
        <div class="card">
```

```
            <h5 class="card-header">Voted #2</h5>
            <img src="http://www.felineworlds.com/wp-content/uploads/
            Cheetah_Looking_Around_600.jpg" class="card-img-top"
            alt="cheetah looking around" style="height: 220px"/>
            <div class="card-body">
                <h5 class="card-title">Cheetahs</h5>
                <h6 class="card-subtitle">Cheetahs Are Really Fast</h6>
                <p class="card-text">
                    The cheetah (Acinonyx jubatus; /'tʃiːtə/) is a large cat
                    of the subfamily Felinae that occurs in North, Southern
                    and East Africa, and a few localities in Iran.
                    It inhabits a variety of mostly arid habitats like dry
                    forests, scrub forests, and savannahs. The species is
                    IUCN Red Listed as Vulnerable, as it suffered a
                    substantial decline in its historic range in the 20th
                    century...
                </p>
                <a href="https://en.wikipedia.org/wiki/Cheetah" class="btn
                btn-primary">Learn more</a>
            </div>
            <div class="card-footer">
                from Wikipedia
            </div>
        </div>
    </div>
    <div class="col">
        <div class="card">
            <h5 class="card-header">Voted #3</h5>
            <img src="https://cdn.thinglink.me/api/
            image/601481335449583616/1240/10/scaletowidth" class="card-img-
            top" alt="panther looking around" style="height: 220px"/>
            <div class="card-body">
                <h5 class="card-title">Black Panthers</h5>
                <h6 class="card-subtitle">Black Panthers Are Really
                Scary</h6>
```

```
        <p class="card-text">
            A black panther is the melanistic colour variant of
            any Panthera, particularly of the leopard (P. pardus)
            in Asia and Africa, and the jaguar (P. onca) in the
            Americas.
        </p>
        <a href="https://en.wikipedia.org/wiki/Black_panther"
        class="btn btn-primary">Learn more</a>
    </div>
    <div class="card-footer">
        from Wikipedia
    </div>
  </div>
 </div>
</div>
```

The Layout

The layout is simple. It is achieved with this div:

```
<div class="row row-cols-1 row-cols-md-2 row-cols-lg-3">
```

The row-cols-* are the ones needed in order to lay out one or two or three columns on the desired breakpoints.

Then each card is being enclosed inside a col div:

```
<div class="col">
```

All of this is needed so that you can achieve the responsive layout that is required.

The HTML of Each Card

Each card has HTML code similar to the following:

- The whole card is enclosed inside a div with the class card.

- Each card has a header, which is an h* element with class card-header.

- The image is constructed with a standard img element that has the class card-img-top. You have also given a specific height so that all the images of all the cards are displayed on a specific height, but taking all the available width.

- Then, the main content of the card, the one that follows the image, is put inside a div with class card-body.

- Inside the body, you can generally put any HTML code that you want. We have put

  - A card title using an h* and a class card-title.

  - A card subtitle using an h* and a class card-subtitle.

  - A paragraph with the main text. This has the class card-text.

  - A hyperlink with class card-link and some extra classes to make it look like a button.

- After the body, we attach a div with the class card-footer. This is used to create the footer of the card.

That was it. If you save the HTML page and load it on your browser, you will see the cards that you have already seen in Figure 5-17.

Carousels

You will close this long Twitter Bootstrap reference page with a really cool feature which is called a carousel. Twitter Bootstrap allows you to create image and video carousels. Carousels are areas of the page that display a series of images (and/or videos) one by one. Each image stays visible for a while (about 5 seconds) before being replaced by the next one.

A typical carousel is composed of the following:

1. Small indicators usually displayed at the bottom (Figure 5-18)

Figure 5-18. *Carousel Indicators*

The number of indicators is equal to the number of items in the carousel. In the preceding example, there is a carousel with three items. Hence, you can see three bars. The one that is filled with white color indicates which item is currently displayed. You can also click a bar to quickly display the item at the corresponding position.

2. Next and previous controls (Figure 5-19)

Figure 5-19. *Carousel Next and Previous Controls*

223

Next and previous buttons, like arrows, allow you to navigate, slide, from item to item, in either direction, left or right.

3. The items (Figure 5-20)

Figure 5-20. *Carousel Items and Titles*

The carousel has a list of items, each one referencing an image and having a title.

Having said all that, it is easy to identify and understand the following HTML fragment that implements the preceding carousel. Amend that as the last portion of HTML code at the main content container (Listing 5-14).

Listing 5-14. HTML Fragment for the Carousel

```
<div class="page-header">
    <h1>Carousels</h1>
</div>

<div id="carousel-example-generic" class="carousel slide carousel-fade"
data-ride="carousel">
    <!-- Indicators -->
    <ol class="carousel-indicators">
```

```
    <li data-target="#carousel-example-generic" data-slide-to="0"
    class="active"></li>
    <li data-target="#carousel-example-generic" data-slide-to="1"></li>
    <li data-target="#carousel-example-generic" data-slide-to="2"></li>
</ol>

<!-- Wrapper for slides -->
<div class="carousel-inner" role="listbox">

    <div class="carousel-item active">
        <img src="https://tclf.org/sites/default/files/styles/
        crop_2000x700/public/thumbnails/image/GovernorsIsland_hero_
        CharlesABirnbaum_2016_0.jpg"
            alt="New York Landscape Image"
            class="d-block w-100"
            style="height: 500px;">
        <div class="carousel-caption d-none d-md-block">
            New York
        </div>
    </div>

    <div class="carousel-item">
        <img src="https://1920x1080hdwallpapers.com/image/201502/
        city/338/tokyo-night-landscape-top-view.jpg"
            alt="Tokyo Landscape Image"
            class="d-block w-100"
            style="height: 500px;">
        <div class="carousel-caption d-none d-md-block">
            Tokyo
        </div>
    </div>

    <div class="carousel-item">
        <img src="https://thumbor.forbes.com/thumbor/960x0/
        https%3A%2F%2Fspecials-images.forbesimg.com%2Fdam%2Fimageserve%
        2F1154977741%2F960x0.jpg"
            alt="Athens Landscape Image"
```

```
                class="d-block w-100"
                style="height: 500px;">
        <div class="carousel-caption d-none d-md-block">
            Athens
        </div>
    </div>
</div>

</div>

<!-- Controls -->
<a class="carousel-control-prev" href="#carousel-example-generic"
role="button" data-slide="prev">
    <span class="carousel-control-prev-icon" aria-hidden="true"></span>
    <span class="sr-only">Previous</span>
</a>
<a class="carousel-control-next" href="#carousel-example-generic"
role="button" data-slide="next">
    <span class="carousel-control-next-icon" aria-hidden="true"></span>
    <span class="sr-only">Next</span>
</a>
</div>
```

The following is a list of items that you, further, need to be aware of when you create a Twitter Bootstrap carousel:

1. The carousel needs to be enclosed inside a div with classes carousel and slide. If you also want to transition from one slide to the next with a fade effect, then you have to add the class carousel-fade too.

2. The main div needs to have an id, like the one we have in the preceding HTML fragment (carousel-example-generic). This is necessary because it is then referenced by the indicators and the controls. This requirement becomes more important if you have more than one carousel on the same page.

3. For the indicators

    1. They need to be an ordered list (ol) with class `carousel-indicators`.

    2. Each item (li) is an indicator, and you need to have as many indicators as the number of your items. If you have three images, then you have to have three indicators, that is, li items.

    3. Each indicator needs to have a `data-target` attribute with the id of the carousel. Also, it needs to have a `data-slide-to` attribute with value equal to the index/position of the item it corresponds to. Note that indexing/positioning starts from 0. That is, the first carousel item is referenced with index 0, then the second with index 1, and so on.

    4. The first indicator needs to have the class `active`.

4. All the carousel items need to be wrapped in a single div with class `carousel-inner`.

5. For the carousel items

    1. Each one is a div that has the class `carousel-item`.

    2. The first one needs to have the class `active`; otherwise, the carousel will not be displayed.

    3. Note that the images of the carousel need to have classes and styles that take care of their height and display attribute. In particular

        1. Classes `d-block` and `w-100`: The first (`d-block`) sets the image `display` attribute `block` value. The second (`w-100`) sets the image width to be 100%. Hence, the image will occupy the whole width available. Note that these are display and sizing Bootstrap utility classes.

        2. Style that sets the height of all images to be the same. In the example, it is set to 500px.

4. Finally, the carousel items can have a `div` with class `carousel-caption` that works as the title/caption of the item. Note that you have set two extra display utility classes on the captions:

   1. `d-none`, which hides the captions.

   2. `d-md-block`, which displays the captions for medium displays and wider. In other words, you want the captions to be displayed on devices with width >=768px. Otherwise, they will not be displayed.

6. Below the inner content of the carousel (the `div` with class `carousel-inner`), you set the HTML content for controls, which are two anchor `a` elements:

   1. The first has the class `carousel-control-prev,` and it is used to navigate to the previous/left slide.

   2. The second has the class `carousel-control-next,` and it is used to navigate to the next/right slide.

   3. Both have attribute `href` pointing to the carousel id (`#carousel-example-generic`).

   4. Both have a child/content that is a `span`. This `span` is used to display the left (for the first control) and the right (for the second control) arrows. For the first control, the span needs to have the class `carousel-control-prev-icon`, so that it displays the left arrow. For the second control, the span needs to have the class `carousel-control-next-icon`, so that it displays the right arrow.

Final Checkpoint

For your convenience and double-checking with your work, here is the full content of the page that you have created (Listing 5-15).

Listing 5-15. Twitter Bootstrap Reference Page

```
<!DOCTYPE html>
<html lang="en">
<head>
    <!-- Required meta tags -->
    <meta charset="utf-8">
    <meta name="viewport" content="width=device-width, initial-scale=1,
    shrink-to-fit=no">

    <!-- Bootstrap CSS -->
    <link rel="stylesheet" href="https://stackpath.bootstrapcdn.
    com/bootstrap/4.4.1/css/bootstrap.min.css" integrity="sha384-
    Vkoo8x4CGsO3+Hhxv8T/Q5PaXtkKtu6ug5TOeNV6gBiFeWPGFN9MuhOf23Q9Ifjh"
    crossorigin="anonymous">

    <!-- Custom CSS -->
    <link rel="stylesheet" href="stylesheets/main.css" type="text/css">

    <title>Twitter Bootstrap Reference Page</title>
</head>
<body>
    <nav class="navbar navbar-expand-lg navbar-dark bg-dark fixed-top">
        <div class="container">
            <a class="navbar-brand" href="#">Bootstrap Ref. Page</a>

            <button type="button" class="navbar-toggler" data-
            toggle="collapse" data-target="#navbar"
                    aria-controls="navbar"
                    aria-expanded="false"
                    aria-label="Toggle navigation">
                <span class="navbar-toggler-icon"></span>
            </button>

            <div class="collapse navbar-collapse" id="navbar">
                <ul class="nav navbar-nav">
                    <li class="nav-item">
```

```
                    <a class="nav-link active" href="#">Home <span
                    class="sr-only">(current)</span></a>
                </li>
                <li class="nav-item">
                    <a class="nav-link" href="#about">About</a>
                </li>
                <li class="nav-item">
                    <a class="nav-link" href="#contact">Contact</a>
                </li>

                <!-- Drop down Menu -->
                <li class="nav-item dropdown">
                    <a href="#"
                        class="nav-link dropdown-toggle"
                        data-toggle="dropdown">
                         Dropdown
                    </a>
                    <div class="dropdown-menu">
                        <a href="#" class="dropdown-item">Action</a>
                        <a href="#" class="dropdown-item">Another
                        action</a>
                        <a href="#" class="dropdown-item">Something
                        else here</a>
                        <div class="dropdown-divider"></div>
                        <div class="dropdown-header">Nav header</div>
                        <a href="#" class="dropdown-item">Separated
                        link</a>
                        <a href="#" class="dropdown-item">One more
                        separated link</a>
                    </div>
                </li>
            </ul>
        </div>
    </div>
</nav>
```

```html
<!-- main content container -->
<div class="container">
    <div class="jumbotron">
        <p class="lead">
            Lorem ipsum dolor sit amet, consectetur adipiscing elit,
            sed do eiusmod tempor incididunt ut labore et dolore magna
            aliqua. Ut enim ad minim veniam, quis nostrud
            exercitation ullamco laboris nisi ut aliquip ex ea commodo
            consequat. Duis aute irure dolor in reprehenderit in
            voluptate velit esse cillum dolore eu fugiat nulla
            pariatur. Excepteur sint occaecat cupidatat non proident,
            sunt in culpa qui officia deserunt mollit anim id est
            laborum.
        </p>
    </div>

    <h1>Buttons</h1>
    <hr class="my-4">

    <h2>Small Sizes</h2>
    <p>
        <button type="button" class="btn btn-sm btn-primary">btn btn-sm
        btn-primary</button>
        <button type="button" class="btn btn-sm btn-secondary">btn btn-sm
        btn-secondary</button>
        <button type="button" class="btn btn-sm btn-success">btn btn-sm
        btn-success</button>
        <button type="button" class="btn btn-sm btn-danger">btn btn-sm
        btn-danger</button>
        <button type="button" class="btn btn-sm btn-warning">btn btn-sm
        btn-warning</button>
        <button type="button" class="btn btn-sm btn-info">btn btn-sm
        btn-info</button>
        <button type="button" class="btn btn-sm btn-light">btn btn-sm
        btn-light</button>
```

```
    <button type="button" class="btn btn-sm btn-dark">btn btn-sm
    btn-dark</button>
    <button type="button" class="btn btn-sm btn-link">btn btn-sm
    btn-link</button>
</p>

<h2>Normal Sizes</h2>
<p>
    <button type="button" class="btn btn-primary">btn btn-primary</
    button>
    <button type="button" class="btn btn-secondary">btn btn-
    secondary</button>
    <button type="button" class="btn btn-success">btn btn-success
    </button>
    <button type="button" class="btn btn-danger">btn btn-danger
    </button>
    <button type="button" class="btn btn-warning">btn btn-warning
    </button>
    <button type="button" class="btn btn-info">btn btn-info
    </button>
    <button type="button" class="btn btn-light">btn btn-light
    </button>
    <button type="button" class="btn btn-dark">btn btn-dark
    </button>
    <button type="button" class="btn btn-link">btn btn-link
    </button>
</p>

<h2>Large Sizes</h2>
<p>
    <button type="button" class="btn btn-lg btn-primary">btn btn-lg
    btn-primary</button>
    <button type="button" class="btn btn-lg btn-secondary">btn btn-lg
    btn-secondary</button>
    <button type="button" class="btn btn-lg btn-success">btn btn-lg
    btn-success</button>
```

```
    <button type="button" class="btn btn-lg btn-danger">btn btn-lg
    btn-danger</button>
    <button type="button" class="btn btn-lg btn-warning">btn btn-lg
    btn-warning</button>
    <button type="button" class="btn btn-lg btn-info">btn btn-lg
    btn-info</button>
    <button type="button" class="btn btn-lg btn-light">btn btn-lg
    btn-light</button>
    <button type="button" class="btn btn-lg btn-dark">btn btn-lg
    btn-dark</button>
    <button type="button" class="btn btn-lg btn-link">btn btn-lg
    btn-link</button>
</p>

<h2>Block Sizes</h2>
<p>
    <button type="button" class="btn btn-block btn-primary">btn
    btn-block btn-primary</button>
    <button type="button" class="btn btn-block btn-secondary">btn
    btn-block btn-secondary</button>
    <button type="button" class="btn btn-block btn-success">btn
    btn-block btn-success</button>
    <button type="button" class="btn btn-block btn-danger">btn
    btn-block btn-danger</button>
    <button type="button" class="btn btn-block btn-warning">btn
    btn-block btn-warning</button>
    <button type="button" class="btn btn-block btn-info">btn
    btn-block btn-info</button>
    <button type="button" class="btn btn-block btn-light">btn
    btn-block btn-light</button>
    <button type="button" class="btn btn-block btn-dark">btn
    btn-block btn-dark</button>
    <button type="button" class="btn btn-block btn-link">btn
    btn-block btn-link</button>
</p>
```

```
<h2>Outline buttons (Normal Sizes)</h2>
<p>
    <button type="button" class="btn btn-outline-primary">btn btn-
    outline-primary</button>
    <button type="button" class="btn btn-outline-secondary">btn btn-
    outline-secondary</button>
    <button type="button" class="btn btn-outline-success">btn btn-
    outline-success</button>
    <button type="button" class="btn btn-outline-danger">btn btn-
    outline-danger</button>
    <button type="button" class="btn btn-outline-warning">btn btn-
    outline-warning</button>
    <button type="button" class="btn btn-outline-info">btn btn-
    outline-info</button>
    <button type="button" class="btn btn-outline-light">btn btn-
    outline-light</button>
    <button type="button" class="btn btn-outline-dark">btn btn-
    outline-dark</button>
    <button type="button" class="btn btn-outline-link">btn btn-
    outline-link</button>
</p>

<h1>Tables</h1>
<hr class="my-4">

<h2>Shopping List</h2>
<table class="table">
    <tr><th colspan="2">Shopping List</th></tr>
    <tr><th>Item</th><th>Qt</th></tr>
    <tr><td>Cheese</td><td>1 kgr</td></tr>
    <tr><td>Rice</td><td>1.5 kgr</td></tr>
    <tr><td>Coffee</td><td>0.5 kgr</td></tr>
    <tr><td>Milk</td><td>1 ltr</td></tr>
    <tr><td>Wine</td><td>1 btl</td></tr>
</table>

<h2>Travel Plan</h2>
```

```
<table class="table table-bordered table-striped table-sm">
    <tr><th colspan="2">Travel Plan</th></tr>
    <tr class="table-active"><th>(active) Action</th><th>Due</th></tr>
    <tr class="table-success"><td>(success) Book Ticket</td><td>Feb
    20th</td></tr>
    <tr class="table-info"><td>(info) Book Hotel</td><td>March
    26th</td></tr>
    <tr class="table-warning"><td>(warning) Buy Suitcase</td>
    <td>April 20th</td></tr>
    <tr class="table-danger"><td>(danger) Get Passport</td>
    <td>April 30th</td></tr>
</table>

<h1>Labels & Badges</h1>
<hr class="my-4">

<h4>
    <span class="badge badge-primary">€20.00 - Primary</span>
    <span class="badge badge-secondary">€20.00 - Secondary</span>
    <span class="badge badge-success">€20.00 - Success</span>
    <span class="badge badge-danger">€20.00 - Danger</span>
    <span class="badge badge-warning">€20.00 - Warning</span>
    <span class="badge badge-info">€20.00 - Info</span>
    <span class="badge badge-light">€20.00 - Light</span>
    <span class="badge badge-dark">€20.00 - Dark</span>
</h4>

<button class="btn btn-light">Inbox <span class="badge badge-
primary badge-pill">1</span></button>
<button class="btn btn-light">Inbox <span class="badge badge-
secondary badge-pill">2</span></button>
<button class="btn btn-light">Inbox <span class="badge badge-
success badge-pill">3</span></button>
<button class="btn btn-light">Inbox <span class="badge badge-
danger badge-pill">4</span></button>
<button class="btn btn-light">Inbox <span class="badge badge-
warning badge-pill">5</span></button>
```

```
<button class="btn btn-light">Inbox <span class="badge badge-
info badge-pill">6</span></button>
<button class="btn btn-light">Inbox <span class="badge badge-
light badge-pill">7</span></button>
<button class="btn btn-light">Inbox <span class="badge badge-
dark badge-pill">8</span></button>

<h1>Tabs</h1>
<hr class="my-4">

<ul class="nav nav-tabs mb-4">
    <li class="nav-item"><a class="nav-link active"
    href="#dashboard" data-toggle="tab">Dashboard</a></li>
    <li class="nav-item"><a class="nav-link" href="#payments" data-
    toggle="tab">Payments</a></li>
    <li class="nav-item"><a class="nav-link" href="#invoices" data-
    toggle="tab">Invoices</a></li>
    <li class="nav-item"><a class="nav-link" href="#settings" data-
    toggle="tab">Settings</a></li>
</ul>

<div class="tab-content">
    <div id="dashboard" class="tab-pane active">
        <p>
            <strong>Dashboard:</strong> Lorem ipsum dolor sit amet,
            consectetur adipiscing elit, sed do eiusmod tempor
            incididunt ut labore et dolore magna aliqua. Ut enim
            ad minim veniam, quis nostrud exercitation ullamco
            laboris nisi ut aliquip ex ea commodo consequat. Duis
            aute irure dolor in reprehenderit in voluptate velit
            esse cillum dolore eu fugiat nulla pariatur. Excepteur
            sint occaecat cupidatat non proident, sunt in culpa qui
            officia deserunt mollit anim id est laborum.
        </p>
    </div>

    <div id="payments" class="tab-pane">
        <p>
```

```
        <strong>Payments:</strong> Lorem ipsum dolor sit amet,
        consectetur adipiscing elit, sed do eiusmod tempor
        incididunt ut labore et dolore magna aliqua. Ut enim
        ad minim veniam, quis nostrud exercitation ullamco
        laboris nisi ut aliquip ex ea commodo consequat. Duis
        aute irure dolor in reprehenderit in voluptate velit
        esse cillum dolore eu fugiat nulla pariatur. Excepteur
        sint occaecat cupidatat non proident, sunt in culpa qui
        officia deserunt mollit anim id est laborum.
    </p>
</div>

<div id="invoices" class="tab-pane">
    <p>
        <strong>Invoices:</strong> Lorem ipsum dolor sit amet,
        consectetur adipiscing elit, sed do eiusmod tempor
        incididunt ut labore et dolore magna aliqua. Ut enim
        ad minim veniam, quis nostrud exercitation ullamco
        laboris nisi ut aliquip ex ea commodo consequat. Duis
        aute irure dolor in reprehenderit in voluptate velit
        esse cillum dolore eu fugiat nulla pariatur. Excepteur
        sint occaecat cupidatat non proident, sunt in culpa qui
        officia deserunt mollit anim id est laborum.
    </p>
</div>

<div id="settings" class="tab-pane">
    <p>
        <strong>Settings:</strong> Lorem ipsum dolor sit amet,
        consectetur adipiscing elit, sed do eiusmod tempor
        incididunt ut labore et dolore magna aliqua. Ut enim
        ad minim veniam, quis nostrud exercitation ullamco
        laboris nisi ut aliquip ex ea commodo consequat. Duis
        aute irure dolor in reprehenderit in voluptate velit
```

```
                        esse cillum dolore eu fugiat nulla pariatur. Excepteur
                        sint occaecat cupidatat non proident, sunt in culpa qui
                        officia deserunt mollit anim id est laborum.
            </p>
        </div>
    </div>

    <h1>Alerts</h1>
    <hr class="my-4">

    <div class="alert alert-primary">
        A simple primary alert.
    </div>
    <div class="alert alert-secondary">
        A simple secondary alert.
    </div>
    <div class="alert alert-success">
        A simple success alert.
    </div>
    <div class="alert alert-danger">
        A simple danger alert.
    </div>
    <div class="alert alert-warning">
        A simple warning alert.
    </div>
    <div class="alert alert-info">
        A simple info alert.
    </div>
    <div class="alert alert-light">
        A simple light alert.
    </div>
    <div class="alert alert-dark">
        A simple dark alert.
    </div>
    <div class="alert alert-info">
```

```
    <strong>London</strong> Read more about London from <a
    class="alert-link" href="https://en.wikipedia.org/wiki/
    London">Wikipedia London Link</a>.
</div>

<h1>Progress Bars</h1>
<hr class="my-4">

<div class="progress mb-1 h-4">
    <div class="progress-bar bg-primary" style="width: 60%;">60%
    Complete - primary</div>
</div>
<div class="progress mb-1 h-4">
    <div class="progress-bar bg-secondary" style="width: 60%;">60%
    Complete - secondary</div>
</div>
 <div class="progress mb-1 h-4">
    <div class="progress-bar bg-success" style="width: 60%;">60%
    Complete - success</div>
 </div>
 <div class="progress mb-1 h-4">
     <div class="progress-bar bg-danger" style="width: 60%;">60%
     Complete - danger</div>
 </div>
<div class="progress mb-1 h-4">
    <div class="progress-bar bg-warning" style="width: 60%;">60%
    Complete - warning</div>
</div>
<div class="progress mb-1 h-4">
    <div class="progress-bar bg-info" style="width: 60%;">60%
    Complete - info</div>
</div>
<div class="progress mb-1 h-4">
    <div class="progress-bar bg-light" style="width: 60%;">60%
    Complete - light</div>
</div>
```

```
<div class="progress mb-1 h-4">
    <div class="progress-bar bg-dark" style="width: 60%;">60%
    Complete - dark</div>
</div>
<div class="progress mb-1 h-4">
    <div class="progress-bar bg-primary" style="width: 30%;">30%
    primary</div>
    <div class="progress-bar bg-success" style="width: 50%;">50%
    success</div>
    <div class="progress-bar bg-warning" style="width: 10%;">10%
    warning</div>
</div>

<h1>Cards</h1>
<hr class="my-4">

<div class="row row-cols-1 row-cols-md-2 row-cols-lg-3">
    <div class="col">
        <div class="card">
            <h5 class="card-header">Voted #1</h5>
            <img src="https://live.staticflickr.com/3869/14437071
            224_43fb23705b_h.jpg" class="card-img-top" alt="lion
            sitting and looking around" style="height: 220px"/>
            <div class="card-body">
                <h5 class="card-title">Lions</h5>
                <h6 class="card-subtitle">Lions Are Amazing</h6>
                <p class="card-text">
                    The lion (Panthera leo) is a large mammal of
                    the Felidae (cat) family. Some large males
                    weigh over 250 kg (550 lb).
                    Today, wild lions live in sub-Saharan Africa
                    and in Asia. Lions are adapted for life in
                    grasslands and mixed areas
                    with trees and grass. The relatively small
                    females are fast runners over short distances,
                    and coordinate their hunting of herd animals.
                </p>
```

```
        <a href="https://simple.wikipedia.org/wiki/Lion"
           class="btn btn-primary">Learn more</a>
    </div>
    <div class="card-footer">
        from Wikipedia
    </div>
  </div>
</div>
<div class="col">
  <div class="card">
      <h5 class="card-header">Voted #2</h5>
      <img src="http://www.felineworlds.com/wp-content/
      uploads/Cheetah_Looking_Around_600.jpg" class="card-
      img-top" alt="cheetah looking around" style="height:
      220px"/>
      <div class="card-body">
          <h5 class="card-title">Cheetahs</h5>
          <h6 class="card-subtitle">Cheetahs Are Really
          Fast</h6>
          <p class="card-text">
              The cheetah (Acinonyx jubatus; /ˈtʃiːtə/) is a
              large cat of the subfamily Felinae that occurs
              in North, Southern and East Africa, and a few
              localities in Iran. It inhabits a variety of
              mostly arid habitats like dry forests, scrub
              forests, and savannahs. The species is IUCN
              Red Listed as Vulnerable, as it suffered
              a substantial decline in its historic range in
              the 20th century...
          </p>
          <a href="https://en.wikipedia.org/wiki/Cheetah"
          class="btn btn-primary">Learn more</a>
      </div>
```

```
                <div class="card-footer">
                    from Wikipedia
                </div>
            </div>
        </div>
        <div class="col">
            <div class="card">
                <h5 class="card-header">Voted #3</h5>
                <img src="https://cdn.thinglink.me/api/
                image/601481335449583616/1240/10/scaletowidth"
                class="card-img-top" alt="panther looking around"
                style="height: 220px"/>
                <div class="card-body">
                    <h5 class="card-title">Black Panthers</h5>
                    <h6 class="card-subtitle">Black Panthers Are Really
                    Scary</h6>
                    <p class="card-text">
                        A black panther is the melanistic colour
                        variant of any Panthera, particularly of the
                        leopard (P. pardus) in Asia and Africa, and the
                        jaguar (P. onca) in the Americas.
                    </p>
                    <a href="https://en.wikipedia.org/wiki/Black_
                    panther" class="btn btn-primary">Learn more</a>
                </div>
                <div class="card-footer">
                    from Wikipedia
                </div>
            </div>
        </div>
    </div>

    <div class="page-header">
        <h1>Carousels</h1>
    </div>
```

```
<div id="carousel-example-generic" class="carousel slide carousel-
fade" data-ride="carousel">
    <!-- Indicators -->
    <ol class="carousel-indicators">
        <li data-target="#carousel-example-generic" data-slide-
        to="0" class="active"></li>
        <li data-target="#carousel-example-generic" data-slide-
        to="1"></li>
        <li data-target="#carousel-example-generic" data-slide-
        to="2"></li>
    </ol>

    <!-- Wrapper for slides -->
    <div class="carousel-inner" role="listbox">

        <div class="carousel-item active">
            <img src="https://tclf.org/sites/default/files/styles/
            crop_2000x700/public/thumbnails/image/GovernorsIsland_
            hero_CharlesABirnbaum_2016_0.jpg"
                alt="New York Landscape Image"
                class="d-block w-100"
                style="height: 500px;">
            <div class="carousel-caption d-none d-md-block">
                New York
            </div>
        </div>

        <div class="carousel-item">
            <img src="https://1920x1080hdwallpapers.com/
            image/201502/city/338/tokyo-night-landscape-top-view.
            jpg"
                alt="Tokyo Landscape Image"
                class="d-block w-100"
                style="height: 500px;">
            <div class="carousel-caption d-none d-md-block">
                Tokyo
            </div>
```

```
            </div>

            <div class="carousel-item">
                <img src="https://thumbor.forbes.com/thumbor/960x0/
                https%3A%2F%2Fspecials-images.forbesimg.com%2Fdam%2Fimage
                serve%2F1154977741%2F960x0.jpg"
                    alt="Athens Landscape Image"
                    class="d-block w-100"
                    style="height: 500px;">
                <div class="carousel-caption d-none d-md-block">
                    Athens
                </div>
            </div>

        </div>

        <!-- Controls -->
        <a class="carousel-control-prev" href="#carousel-example-
        generic" role="button" data-slide="prev">
            <span class="carousel-control-prev-icon" aria-
            hidden="true"></span>
            <span class="sr-only">Previous</span>
        </a>
        <a class="carousel-control-next" href="#carousel-example-
        generic" role="button" data-slide="next">
            <span class="carousel-control-next-icon" aria-
            hidden="true"></span>
            <span class="sr-only">Next</span>
        </a>
    </div>
</div>
<!-- end of main content container -->

<!-- Optional JavaScript -->
<!-- jQuery first, then Popper.js, then Bootstrap JS -->
```

```
<script src="https://code.jquery.com/jquery-3.4.1.slim.min.js"
integrity="sha384-J6qa4849blE2+poT4WnyKhv5vZF5SrPoOiEjwBvKU7imGFAVOwwj1
yYfoRSJoZ+n" crossorigin="anonymous"></script>
<script src="https://cdn.jsdelivr.net/npm/popper.js@1.16.0/dist/umd/
popper.min.js" integrity="sha384-Q6E9RHvbIyZFJoft+2mJbHaEWldlvI9IOYy5n3
zV9zzTtmI3UksdQRVvoxMfooAo" crossorigin="anonymous"></script>
<script src="https://stackpath.bootstrapcdn.com/bootstrap/4.4.1/js/
bootstrap.min.js" integrity="sha384-wfSDF2E50Y2D1uUdjOO3uMBJnjuUD4Ih7
YwaYd1iqfktjOUod8GCExl3Og8ifwB6" crossorigin="anonymous"></script>
</body>
</html>
```

Closing Note

This closes a long encounter with Twitter Bootstrap. You have created a page with a big list of Twitter Bootstrap features that can be used as a reference to the most commonly used features.

However, there is a lot more to cover on Twitter Bootstrap. This will be done in the next chapters.

Tasks and Quizzes

TASK DETAILS

---

1. Create a web page like the following (Figure 5-21).

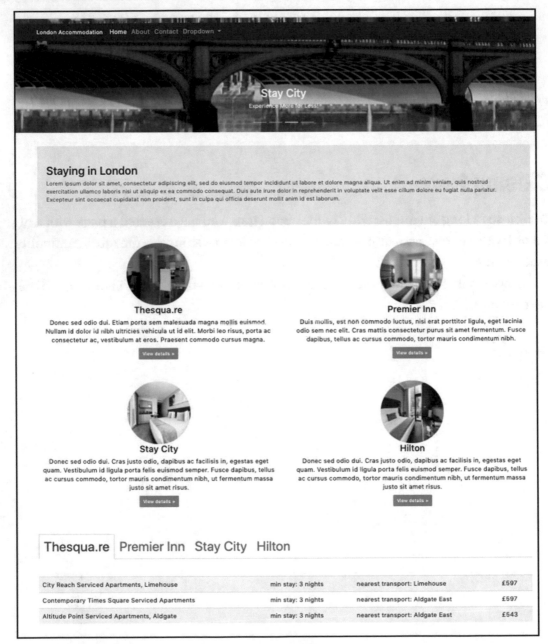

Figure 5-21. *Task Page*

2. It is a page with the following elements (Figure 5-22).

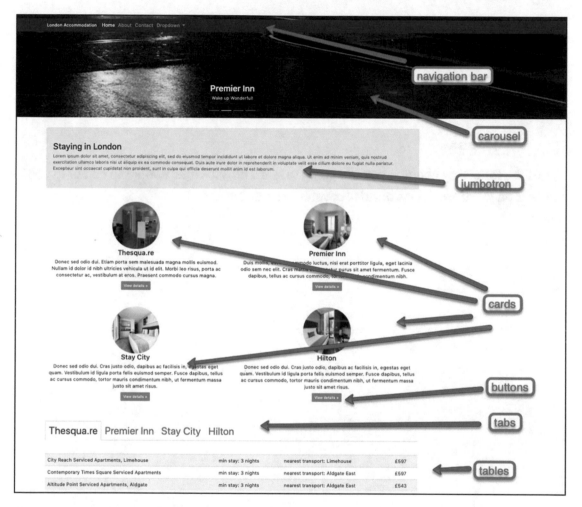

Figure 5-22. *Elements of the Task Page*

Key Takeaways

- Tabs

- Alerts

- Progress bars

- Cards

- Carousels

In the following chapter, you are going to learn how Twitter Bootstrap can help you create a page whose background is covered with an image.

CHAPTER 6

Cover Page Project

This chapter teaches you how to style the navigation bar and how to have a background image to cover the whole page of your site. Also, it teaches you a technique to vertically align content irrespective of its height.

You will create a page like the following (Figure 6-1).

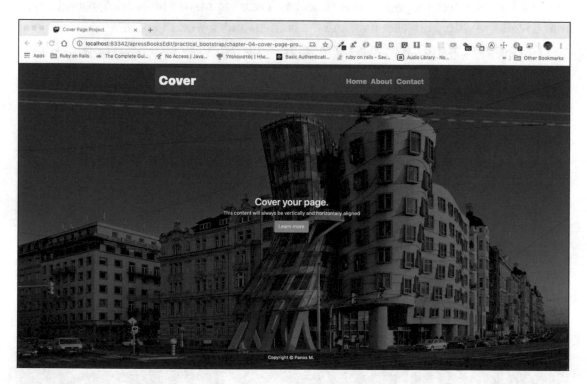

Figure 6-1. *Cover Page Project*

© Panos Matsinopoulos 2020
P. Matsinopoulos, *Practical Bootstrap*, https://doi.org/10.1007/978-1-4842-6071-5_6

Learning Goals

1. Learn how to pull the non-brand options of a navigation bar to the right.

2. Learn how to center content both vertically and horizontally using the `table`/`table-cell` technique.

Introduction

This is a chapter that will teach you how to create another nice-looking Twitter Bootstrap project. I call this a cover page project because it encompasses a large background image that covers the whole browser page. All the content appears on top of this page.

The purpose of this exercise is to combine some Twitter Bootstrap knowledge with some techniques that you have learned in the book *Master HTML & CSS* and that are not Twitter Bootstrap specific.

Here is the page that you will build (Figure 6-2).

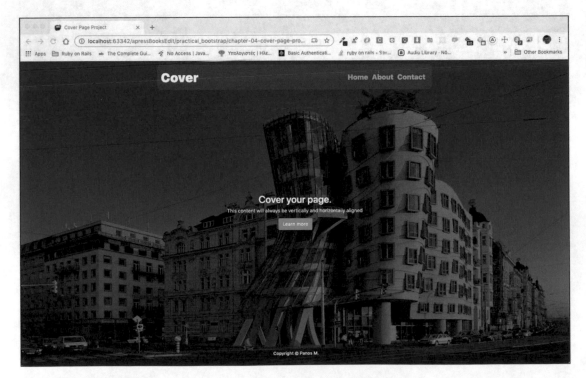

Figure 6-2. *Page That You Will Build*

Notable Things of This Page

1. There is a background image that covers the whole page.

2. The image covers the page no matter what the size of the page is.

3. Although the original image is bright, the image displayed on the page has reduced brightness. This helps the text that overlays the image to have a better contrast and be easier to read.

4. The top navigation bar is similar to the navigation bars that we have built earlier. However, the non-brand part of the options is aligned to the right.

5. The main content of this page is vertically and horizontally centered.

6. There is a footer fixed at the bottom of the page, with text horizontally aligned at the center.

Empty Twitter Bootstrap Page

Let's start with the empty Twitter Bootstrap page (Listing 6-1).

Listing 6-1. Empty Twitter Bootstrap Page

```
<!DOCTYPE html>
<html lang="en">
<head>
  <!-- Required meta tags -->
  <meta charset="utf-8">
  <meta name="viewport" content="width=device-width, initial-scale=1,
  shrink-to-fit=no">

  <!-- Bootstrap CSS -->
  <link rel="stylesheet" href="https://stackpath.bootstrapcdn.
  com/bootstrap/4.4.1/css/bootstrap.min.css" integrity="sha384-
  Vkoo8x4CGsO3+Hhxv8T/Q5PaXtkKtu6ug5TOeNV6gBiFeWPGFN9MuhOf23Q9Ifjh"
  crossorigin="anonymous">
```

```
  <!-- Custom CSS -->
  <link rel="stylesheet" href="stylesheets/main.css" type="text/css">

  <title>Cover Page Project</title>
</head>
<body>

  <!-- Optional JavaScript -->
  <!-- jQuery first, then Popper.js, then Bootstrap JS -->
  <script src="https://code.jquery.com/jquery-3.4.1.slim.min.js"
  integrity="sha384-J6qa4849blE2+poT4WnyKhv5vZF5SrPo0iEjwBvKU7imGFAVOwwj1yY
  foRSJoZ+n" crossorigin="anonymous"></script>
  <script src="https://cdn.jsdelivr.net/npm/popper.js@1.16.0/dist/umd/
  popper.min.js" integrity="sha384-Q6E9RHvbIyZFJoft+2mJbHaEWldlvI9IOYy5n3zV
  9zzTtmI3UksdQRVvoxMfooAo" crossorigin="anonymous"></script>
  <script src="https://stackpath.bootstrapcdn.com/bootstrap/4.4.1/js/
  bootstrap.min.js" integrity="sha384-wfSDF2E50Y2D1uUdj0O3uMBJnjuUD4Ih7YwaY
  d1iqfktj0Uod8GCExl3Og8ifwB6" crossorigin="anonymous"></script>
</body>
</html>
```

Save the preceding file as index.html and also create an empty file stylesheets/main.css. If you load this page on your browser, you will see an empty page, but with Twitter Bootstrap loaded.

The Background Image

You should already know how to apply background images (if not, see my previous book *Master HTML & CSS*, which has Chapter 22 titled "Image Backgrounds"). We are going to do that on the body element of this page. Add the following rules to your stylesheets/main.css file (Listing 6-2).

Listing 6-2. CSS File Contents

```
html {
    height: 100%;
    background-color: White;
}
```

```
body {
    min-height: 100%;
    background-color: #2b542c;
    background-image: url("../images/prague-czech-republic.jpg");
    background-repeat: no-repeat;
    background-attachment: fixed;
    background-position: left top;
    background-size: 100% 100%;
}
```

This is pretty standard.

If you save that and reload the page, you will see the following (Figure 6-3).

Figure 6-3. *Background Image Applied to the Body Element*

As you can see in Figure 6-3, the image is clearly displayed. It covers the whole browser window, and if you try to resize the window, you will see that it is being automatically adjusted to cover the new window size.

The Image Brightness

Let's see how we can reduce the brightness of the image. We can definitely change the brightness of the image using an image editing software like GIMP or Adobe Photoshop. But, if you do not know how to do that or if you do not want to change the original image, you can always do the following trick.

You define a div element, as a child of the body element. This div will be positioned absolutely at the top-left corner of the page and will cover the whole width and height of its parent body element. Let's call this div cover div. The cover div needs to have a black background color, but with some transparency so that some of the image colors behind it will be visible. You can try rgba(0, 0, 0, 0.5) for that.

Let's do that.

Add the cover div:

```
<body>

    <div id="cover"></div>

</body>
```

Then add the following CSS rules:

```
body {
    position: relative;
}
#cover {
    position: absolute;
    width: 100%;
    height: 100%;
    top: 0;
    left: 0;
    background-color: rgba(0, 0, 0, 0.5);
}
```

As you can see in the preceding code, it is a prerequisite for the position: absolute; on #cover to work correctly for its parent element, body, to have a non-static positioning. That's why we set the position: relative; to the body element.

If you save the preceding code and reload the page on your browser, you will see Figure 6-4.

Figure 6-4. *Black Cover with Transparency Applied*

This is exactly the result that you want to achieve. The background image is, now, a little bit dark, so any text that you will overlay on top of the background image will be easy to read.

The Navigation Bar

We are now going to attach a navigation bar, like we did in the previous chapters.

Add the following content (Listing 6-3) after the cover div.

Listing 6-3. HTML Fragment for the Navigation Bar

```
<nav id="navigation-bar-container" class="navbar navbar-expand-lg navbar-
dark bg-dark fixed-top">
    <a class="navbar-brand" href="#">Cover</a>
    <button type="button" class="navbar-toggler" data-toggle="collapse"
    data-target="#navbar" aria-expanded="false" aria-controls="navbar">
```

```
        <span class="navbar-toggler-icon"></span>
    </button>

    <div id="navbar" class="collapse navbar-collapse">
        <ul class="nav navbar-nav">
            <li class="nav-item"><a class="nav-link" href="#">Home</a></li>
            <li class="nav-item"><a class="nav-link" href="#about">
            About</a></li>
            <li class="nav-item"><a class="nav-link"
            href="#contact">Contact</a></li>
        </ul>
    </div>

</nav>
```

If you save the HTML content of your page and reload it on your browser, you will see the following (Figure 6-5).

Figure 6-5. *Added Standard Bootstrap Navigation Bar*

If you pay attention to the code in Listing 6-3, you will see that the brand link is defined before the toggler button (see Figure 6-6).

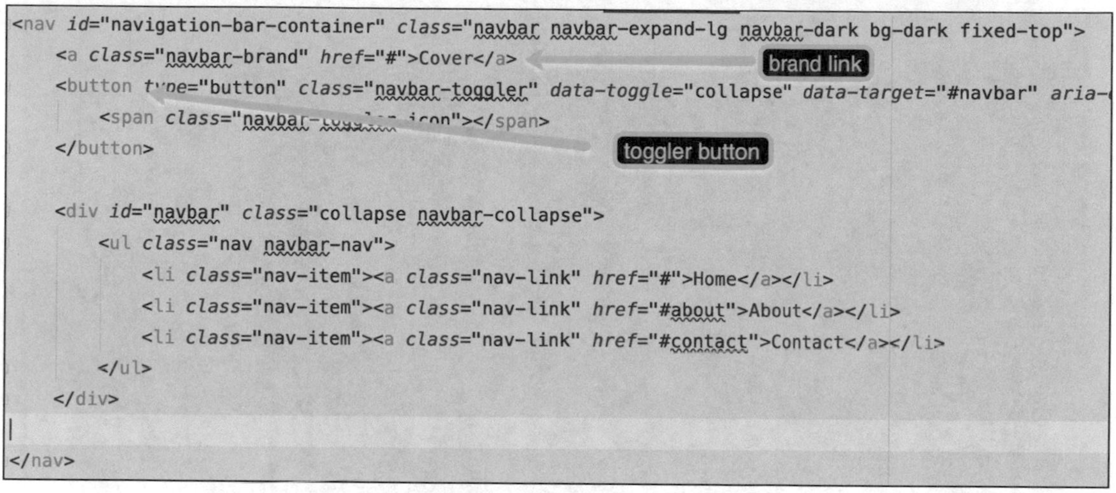

```
<nav id="navigation-bar-container" class="navbar navbar-expand-lg navbar-dark bg-dark fixed-top">
    <a class="navbar-brand" href="#">Cover</a>              ◀━━━━━━  brand link
    <button type="button" class="navbar-toggler" data-toggle="collapse" data-target="#navbar" aria-
        <span class="navbar-toggler-icon"></span>
    </button>                                                         toggler button

    <div id="navbar" class="collapse navbar-collapse">
        <ul class="nav navbar-nav">
            <li class="nav-item"><a class="nav-link" href="#">Home</a></li>
            <li class="nav-item"><a class="nav-link" href="#about">About</a></li>
            <li class="nav-item"><a class="nav-link" href="#contact">Contact</a></li>
        </ul>
    </div>

</nav>
```

Figure 6-6. *Brand Link Before the Toggler Button*

This will make the toggler button appear on the far right. Try to shorten the width of the display, and you will see the following (Figure 6-7).

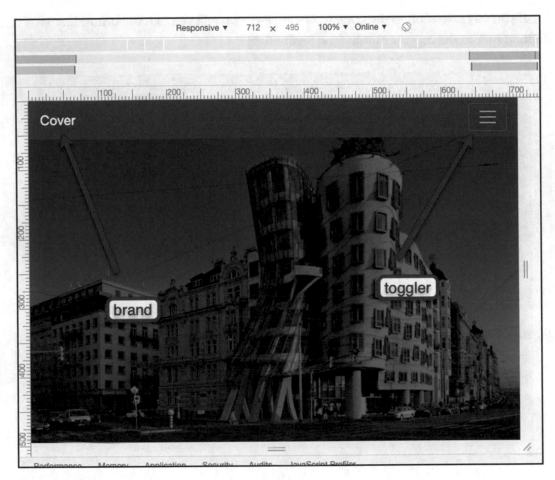

Figure 6-7. *Toggler Appears on the Far Right*

Try switching the position of the HTML fragments, first the button and then the brand link, like in Listing 6-4.

Listing 6-4. First, the Toggler Button and Then the Brand Link

```
<button type="button" class="navbar-toggler" data-toggle="collapse" data-
target="#navbar" aria-expanded="false" aria-controls="navbar">
    <span class="navbar-toggler-icon"></span>
</button>
<a class="navbar-brand" href="#">Cover</a>
```

This will make the brand link appear on the far right and the toggler on the far left of the navigation bar. See Figure 6-8.

Figure 6-8. *Toggler Left, Brand Link Right*

So far, so good, but if you look carefully at the page you want to achieve, you will notice that

- The navigation bar has some margins, left and right. It does not occupy the whole width of the page.

- Also, it has some margin above it.

- Finally, its border has rounded corners.

Before you actually implement the preceding requirements, you will also set one more. You want the navigation bar to be full width for extrasmall and small devices, but only 50% of the page width for all other cases.

The following CSS rules will satisfy these requirements (Listing 6-5).

Listing 6-5. CSS Rules for Navigation Bar Requirements

```
#navigation-bar-container {
    margin: 10px auto;
    border-radius: 10px;
}

@media (min-width: 768px) {
    #navigation-bar-container {
        width: 50%;
    }
}
```

As you can read from the preceding code, the default width of the navigation bar is 100%, since it is a div. You are using a @media query rule in order to turn that to 50% for larger devices.

Add the preceding rules inside your stylesheets/main.css and reload the page on your browser. You will see what is depicted in Figure 6-9 (assuming that you have a display with width >=768px).

Figure 6-9. *Navigation Bar as Displayed on Large Devices*

If you reduce the size of your browser window to less than 768px, you will see that the navigation bar occupies the whole width (Figure 6-10).

Figure 6-10. *Navigation Bar Occupies the Whole Page Width on <768px Devices*

Further working on the navigation bar, what you want to achieve now is to pull the non-brand options of the menu to the right. This can be easily done with the `ml-auto` Twitter Bootstrap utility class that needs to be applied to `ul` holding these options.

Let's add the `ml-auto`. Instead of just

```
<ul class="nav navbar-nav">
```

write

```
<ul class="nav navbar-nav ml-auto">
```

The `ml-auto` is translated to *margin left auto*. In other words, the left margin of the `ul` element will automatically be set to the maximum available.

If you save the preceding code and reload the page on your browser, you will see the following (Figure 6-11).

Figure 6-11. *Options Moved to the Right*

You have not finished with the navigation bar yet. If you compare the current version to the original one, you will see that the font size and colors are different.

Let's do the following amendments to the CSS rules with regard to this (Listing 6-6).

Listing 6-6. CSS Amendments for Font and Color of the Nav Bar

```
#navigation-bar-container a.navbar-brand,
#navbar ul a {
    font-weight: 900;
}
```

```
#navigation-bar-container a.navbar-brand {
    font-size: 3.2rem;
}

#navbar ul a {
    font-size: 1.8rem;
}
```

If you save the preceding code and reload the page on your browser, you will see the following (Figure 6-12).

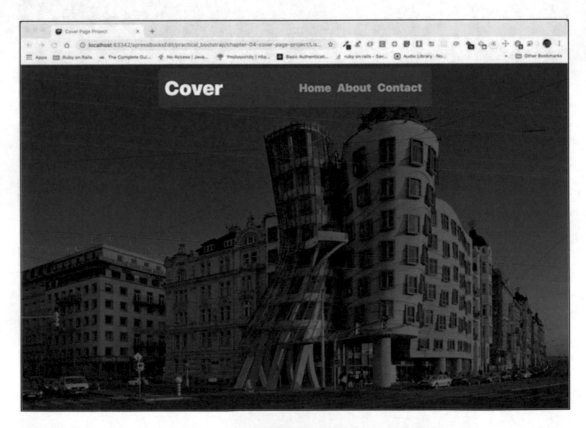

Figure 6-12. *Navigation Bar with Required Font Size and Color*

These are the required font size and color properties. And with this, you finished the work on the navigation bar.

Content on the Center of the Page

You continue by trying to implement the following (Figure 6-13).

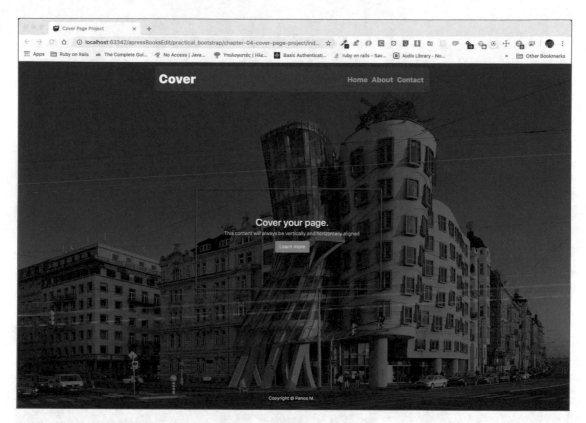

Figure 6-13. *Content on the Center of the Page*

There is some piece of HTML content that appears on the center of the page, both horizontally and vertically. Let's add, first, the HTML content (Listing 6-7).

Listing 6-7. Content on the Center of the Page

```
<div id="center-content">
  <h1>Cover your page.</h1>
  <p class="lead">This content will always be vertically and horizontally
  aligned</p>
```

```
<p class="lead">
  <a href="#" class="btn btn-lg btn-success">Learn more</a>
</p>
</div>
```

Add the preceding code below the nav element, before the end of the body element. This is all pretty simple HTML code. You have already learned about this in the previous chapters.

Let's save that and reload the page on your browser. You will see the following (Figure 6-14).

Figure 6-14. *Content Placed on the Top Left—Cannot Be Easily Read*

As you can see, the content has been placed on the top left. And it is not easy to read. This is where we have to introduce our z-index skills, because it seems that the #cover div is being drawn after the content we just put earlier.

But wait! Why don't we have the same problem with the navigation bar? This is because the navigation bar already has `position: fixed` with `z-index` a positive integer (equal to 1030—you only have to inspect with the developer tools to confirm that), whereas our `#center-content` div has `position static`. So the `#center-content` is the first non-positioned element:

1. `body` is positioned, because it has `position relative`.

2. `#cover` is positioned, because it has `position absolute`.

3. `#navigation-bar-container` is positioned, because it has `position fixed`.

If you read Chapter 23, "Element Positioning," of my previous book *Master HTML & CSS*, you will know that positioned elements and non-positioned elements will play well if you control the stack context they belong to. And a new stack context starts whenever you use the `z-index` property with value different from `auto`.

In other words, you are going to start a new stack context by setting `z-index: 0` to the body element. Then, the `#cover` is going to have a z-index equal to `-1`, because you want it to be behind every non-positioned element inside the body element. Again, make sure you read the last part of Chapter 23, "Positioning," in my previous book *Master HTML & CSS*, in which I explained the order in which things are drawn by the browser.

Having said that, please, go ahead and make the following amendments to body and #cover CSS rules:

```
body {
  ...
  z-index: 0;
}

#cover {
  ...
  z-index: -1;
}
```

If you save and load the page on your browser, you will see the following (Figure 6-15).

Figure 6-15. *Content on Foreground but It Is Still Difficult to Read Text*

You can tell from the colors of the button that the content is now drawn on the foreground. But still, you cannot easily read the text, although this is only a problem of the color of the text.

Let's change the color first. You will make sure that the color of any text element is white. Add `color: white;` to the body element in your CSS file.

If you do that and reload the page, you will see the following (Figure 6-16).

Figure 6-16. *Content Now with Correct Color*

That's good. The content color is looking good. Now, you need to fix the position.
In order to fix the position, you will use the `table/table-cell` technique:

1. You will tell the browser to assume that the `div` that contains the
   main content is a table cell. You will do that by setting `display:
   table-cell;` for this element.

2. You will tell the browser to assume that the parent element, a.k.a.
   the body, is a table. You will do that by setting `display: table;`
   for the body element.

3. You want the table (`body`) to occupy all the available space defined
   by its parent (`html`). For that reason, you will define `width:100%;`
   `height: 100%;` for the body element.

4. You want the document root to occupy all the available space
   given by the browser window. Hence, you will set `width: 100%;`
   `height: 100%;` for the `html` element too.

5. You will tell the table cell (center-content div) to center its
content both horizontally (text-align: center;) and vertically
(vertical-align: middle;).

The following are the rules (Listing 6-8).

Listing 6-8. CSS Rules to Make Content Vertically and Horizontally Centered

```
html {
    width: 100%;
    height: 100%;
}

body {
    display: table;
    width: 100%;
    height: 100%;
}

#center-content {
    display: table-cell;
    text-align: center;
    vertical-align: middle;
}
```

If you save the preceding rules in your CSS file and reload the page on your browser,
you will see the following (Figure 6-17).

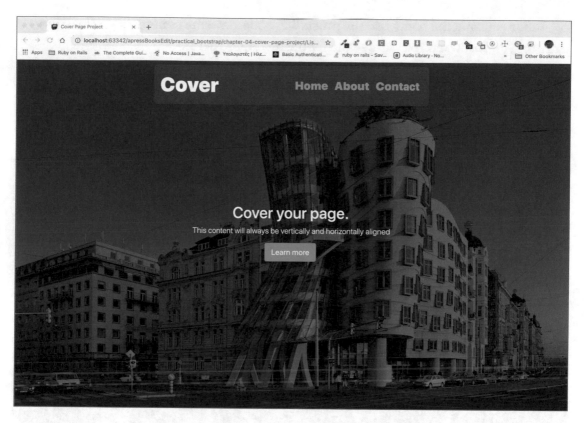

Figure 6-17. *Content Correctly Placed on the Center of the Page*

Note   There are other techniques that one can use to center content vertically. This technique, with `table/table-cell`, makes sure that even if you change the actual content, the margins, top and bottom, will be adjusted automatically.

Footer

You are now left with creating the footer. This is pretty much easy. Let's add the `footer` element first:

```
<footer id="footer-content">
  <small>Copyright &copy; Panos M.</small>
</footer>
```

Before closing the body, add the preceding code. Save the content and reload the page on your browser. You will see the following (Figure 6-18).

Figure 6-18. *Footer Added but Layout Destroyed*

The layout has been destroyed. But it is easy to fix. You need to specify the position attributes of the footer:

```
#footer-content {
    position: absolute;
    bottom: 20px;
    left: 0;
    width: 100%;
    text-align: center;
}
```

You need to add the preceding code to the CSS rules. The footer needs to have position absolute. Save your CSS file and reload the page on your browser. You will see the following (Figure 6-19).

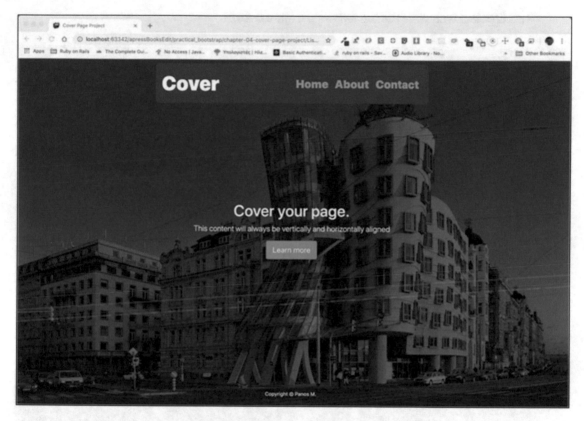

Figure 6-19. *After Correcting the Footer Position, the Page Is Ready*

After correcting the footer position, the page is now ready.

Closing Note

You have seen how you can have the navigation bar options be on the right side of the bar. You have also learned about a technique to center content vertically and horizontally.

Tasks and Quizzes

TASK DETAILS
---

1. Create a web page like the following (Figure 6-20).

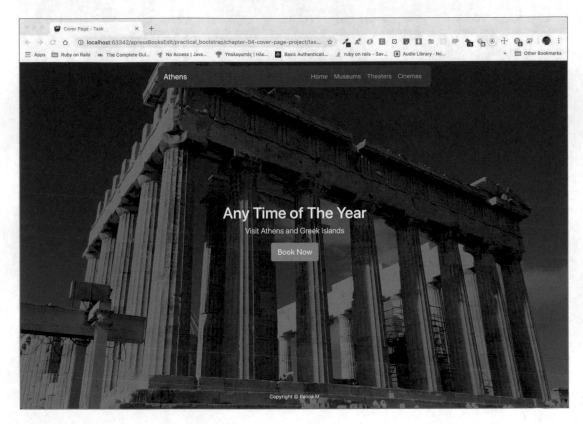

Figure 6-20. *Task, Cover Page—Visit Athens*

2. It is similar to the page you have built in the chapter. There is a difference though—on the navigation bar. Can you see that?

Key Takeaways

- How to style the navigation bar and bring the links to the right

- How to display a background image

- How to display content on the center of the page

- How to position the footer at the bottom of the page

In the following chapter, you are going to learn how to create an admin dashboard page.

CHAPTER 7

Admin Dashboard

In this chapter, we will work to build a Twitter Bootstrap admin dashboard, like the
following (Figure 7-1).

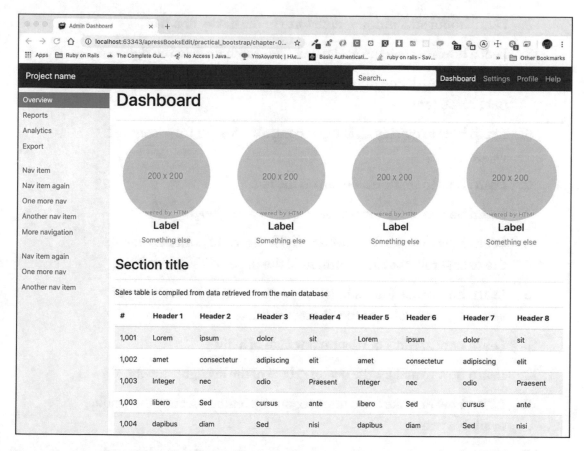

Figure 7-1. *Basic Admin Dashboard*

A site like the one in Figure 7-1 has the sidebar on a fixed position. The sidebar
disappears on extrasmall devices, and the dashboard changes its layout according to the
device display width.

© Panos Matsinopoulos 2020
P. Matsinopoulos, *Practical Bootstrap*, https://doi.org/10.1007/978-1-4842-6071-5_7

Also, the table is responsive and can be displayed equally well on both large and small displays.

You will also learn various other new concepts like how to display an image in a circle shape or how to alter the text color using text color–specific classes.

Learning Goals

1. Learn how to use a `container` or `container-fluid` element inside a navigation bar.

2. Learn about attaching a search form in the navigation bar.

3. Learn how to move the navigation bar search form to the right.

4. Learn how to define the correct vertical position of the navigation bar search form.

5. Learn how to quickly style input controls with the `form-control` class.

6. Learn how to create a sidebar, on the left.

7. Learn how to make the sidebar extend on full height.

8. Learn how to make the sidebar stay in the same position even if the user scrolls the main content of the page.

9. Learn how to use the visibility classes to show and hide parts of your page according to the display width.

10. Learn how to add a border on one side of a div.

11. Learn how to make a div occupy 100% of the available height.

12. Learn how to make the content of an `ul` element occupy the whole available width.

13. Learn how to create nice page headers with a horizontal line at the bottom.

14.   Learn how to display images in a circle shape.

15.   Learn about the text alignment classes.

16.   Learn how to use responsive images.

17.   Learn about the classes that affect the text color.

18.   Learn how to create responsive tables.

19.   Learn how to apply multiple Twitter Bootstrap techniques in order to create an admin-like layout.

Introduction

In this chapter, you will create a basic admin dashboard page, using Twitter Bootstrap facilities.

Note   This is a long chapter with many new things for you to learn. But, after you do some little extra work, you will be rewarded by the final result.

You can see the final page in Figure 7-2.

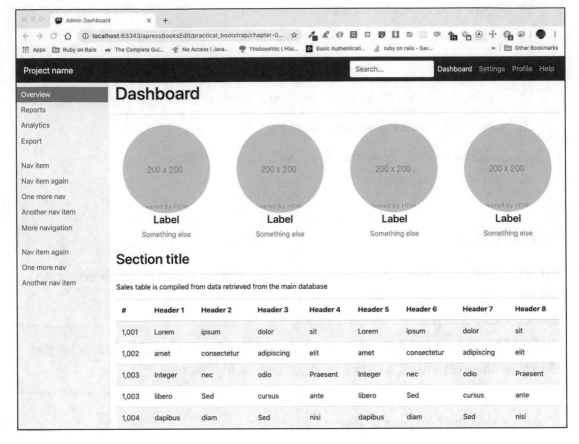

Figure 7-2. *Basic Admin Dashboard*

The characteristics of this page are as follows:

1. It has a navigation bar, the content of which extends the whole page width.

2. The navigation bar non-brand options are aligned to the right.

3. The navigation bar has a search form inside.

4. There is a left sidebar with navigation options. Let's call it a left-side navigation bar.

5. The left-side navigation bar is not displayed on extrasmall devices (Figure 7-3).

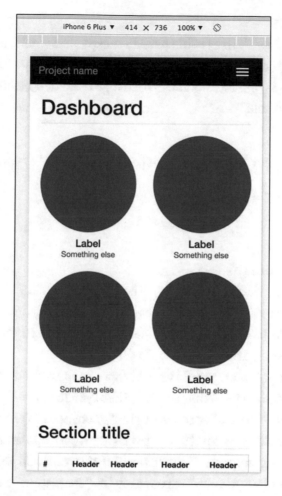

Figure 7-3. *Admin Dashboard on Extrasmall Devices*

Empty Twitter Bootstrap Page

Let's start with the empty Twitter Bootstrap page (Listing 7-1).

Listing 7-1. Empty Twitter Bootstrap Page

```
<!DOCTYPE html>
<html lang="en">
<head>
  <!-- Required meta tags -->
  <meta charset="utf-8">
  <meta name="viewport" content="width=device-width, initial-scale=1,
  shrink-to-fit=no">
```

```
<!-- Bootstrap CSS -->
<link rel="stylesheet" href="https://stackpath.bootstrapcdn.
com/bootstrap/4.4.1/css/bootstrap.min.css" integrity="sha384-
Vkoo8x4CGsO3+Hhxv8T/Q5PaXtkKtu6ug5TOeNV6gBiFeWPGFN9MuhOf23Q9Ifjh"
crossorigin="anonymous">

<!-- Custom CSS -->
<link rel="stylesheet" href="stylesheets/main.css" type="text/css">

<title>Admin Dashboard</title>
</head>
<body>

<!-- Optional JavaScript -->
<!-- jQuery first, then Popper.js, then Bootstrap JS -->
<script src="https://code.jquery.com/jquery-3.4.1.slim.min.js"
integrity="sha384-J6qa4849blE2+poT4WnyKhv5vZF5SrPo0iEjwBvKU7imGFAVOwwj1y
YfoRSJoZ+n" crossorigin="anonymous"></script>
<script src="https://cdn.jsdelivr.net/npm/popper.js@1.16.0/dist/umd/
popper.min.js" integrity="sha384-Q6E9RHvbIyZFJoft+2mJbHaEWldlvI9IOYy5n3z
V9zzTtmI3UksdQRVvoxMfooAo" crossorigin="anonymous"></script>
<script src="https://stackpath.bootstrapcdn.com/bootstrap/4.4.1/js/
bootstrap.min.js" integrity="sha384-wfSDF2E50Y2D1uUdjOO3uMBJnjuUD4Ih7Ywa
Yd1iqfktj0Uod8GCExl3Og8ifwB6" crossorigin="anonymous"></script>
</body>
</html>
```

Navigation Bar

The first thing that you will add and work with is the navigation bar.

Standard Navigation Bar Content

Let's add the standard navigation bar. Listing 7-2 contains the HTML fragment for the navigation bar that you have to add as the first child of the body element.

Listing 7-2. Navigation Bar

```
<nav class="navbar navbar-expand-lg navbar-dark bg-dark fixed-top">
    <button type="button" class="navbar-toggler" data-toggle="collapse"
    data-target="#navbar"
            aria-controls="navbar"
            aria-expanded="false"
            aria-label="Toggle navigation">
        <span class="navbar-toggler-icon"></span>
    </button>

    <a class="navbar-brand" href="#">Project name</a>

    <div class="collapse navbar-collapse" id="navbar">
        <ul class="nav navbar-nav">
            <li class="nav-item">
                <a class="nav-link active" href="#">Dashboard <span
                class="sr-only">(current)</span></a>
            </li>
            <li class="nav-item">
                <a class="nav-link" href="#settings">Settings</a>
            </li>
            <li class="nav-item">
                <a class="nav-link" href="#profile">Profile</a>
            </li>
            <li class="nav-item">
                <a class="nav-link" href="#help">Help</a>
            </li>
        </ul>
    </div>
</nav>
```

If you save that and reload your page, you will see the following (Figure 7-4).

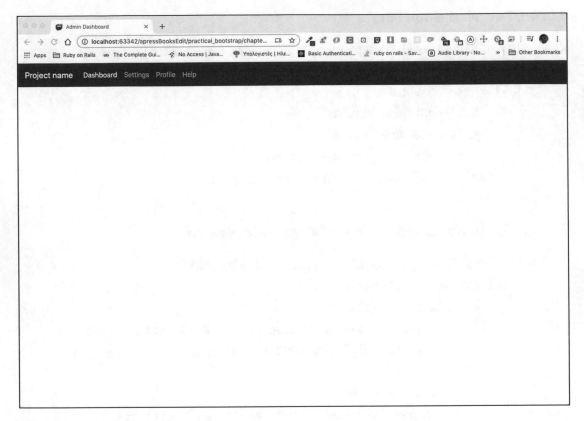

Figure 7-4. *Adding the Navigation Bar*

Aligning to the Right

The navigation bar has its main options aligned to the left. You need to bring them to the right. You have already learned how to do that, with the use of the ml-auto class. Let's add the ml-auto class to the ul holding the main navigation options (Listing 7-3).

Listing 7-3. Adding the ml-auto Class to the ul Element

```
<nav class="navbar navbar-expand-lg navbar-dark bg-dark fixed-top">
    <button type="button" class="navbar-toggler" data-toggle="collapse"
    data-target="#navbar"
            aria-controls="navbar"
            aria-expanded="false"
            aria-label="Toggle navigation">
        <span class="navbar-toggler-icon"></span>
    </button>
```

```html
<a class="navbar-brand" href="#">Project name</a>

<div class="collapse navbar-collapse" id="navbar">
    <ul class="nav navbar-nav ml-auto">
        <li class="nav-item">
            <a class="nav-link active" href="#">Dashboard <span
            class="sr-only">(current)</span></a>
        </li>
        <li class="nav-item">
            <a class="nav-link" href="#settings">Settings</a>
        </li>
        <li class="nav-item">
            <a class="nav-link" href="#profile">Profile</a>
        </li>
        <li class="nav-item">
            <a class="nav-link" href="#help">Help</a>
        </li>
    </ul>
</div>
</nav>
```

Save the changes and reload the page on your browser. You will see the following (Figure 7-5).

Figure 7-5. *Navigation Options Pulled Right*

Adding the Search Form

You want to add a search form inside the top navigation bar. This will not be part of the list of options, but it needs to be part of the div that collapses when you switch to small devices, that is, part of the #navbar div.

Let's put the following code inside the #navbar div, but before the ul with the nav options:

```
<form>
    <input type="text" placeholder="Search...">
</form>
```

Hence, the nav element needs to be like the following (Listing 7-4).

Listing 7-4. Navigation Bar with Search Form

```
<nav class="navbar navbar-expand-lg navbar-dark bg-dark fixed-top">
    <button type="button" class="navbar-toggler" data-toggle="collapse"
    data-target="#navbar"
            aria-controls="navbar"
            aria-expanded="false"
            aria-label="Toggle navigation">
        <span class="navbar-toggler-icon"></span>
    </button>

    <a class="navbar-brand" href="#">Project name</a>

    <div class="collapse navbar-collapse" id="navbar">
        <form>
            <input type="text" placeholder="Search...">
        </form>

        <ul class="nav navbar-nav ml-auto">
            <li class="nav-item">
                <a class="nav-link active" href="#">Dashboard <span
                class="sr-only">(current)</span></a>
            </li>
            <li class="nav-item">
                <a class="nav-link" href="#settings">Settings</a>
            </li>
            <li class="nav-item">
                <a class="nav-link" href="#profile">Profile</a>
            </li>
            <li class="nav-item">
                <a class="nav-link" href="#help">Help</a>
            </li>
        </ul>

    </div>
</nav>
```

If you save the preceding code and reload the page, you will see the following (Figure 7-6).

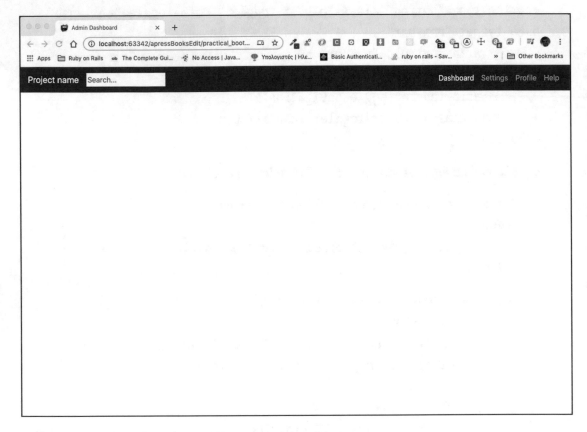

Figure 7-6. *Search Form in the Navigation Bar*

The search form has been put inside the navigation bar. But we want to move it to the right. If you add the `ml-auto` class on the form, you will get the following (Figure 7-7).

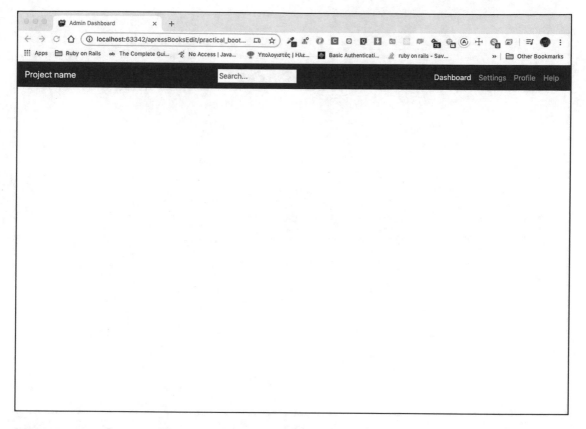

Figure 7-7. *ml-auto Class on the Search Form*

The search form is not positioned at the far right, but to the left of the options, because you need to remove the ml-auto class from the ul. You can't have both on the search form and on the ul element.

Go ahead and remove the ml-auto from the ul element. If you save and reload the page, you will see the following (Figure 7-8).

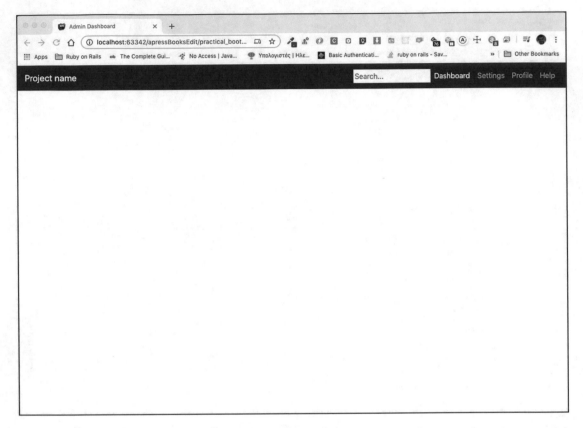

Figure 7-8. *Search Form Positioned on the Right*

There are two classes that you can apply to the search form and that will make it look much better. I will talk about these classes in the next chapter, but nothing prevents you from using them right now to style the search form:

- Use the class `form-inline` on the form HTML element.

- Use the class `form-control` on the input HTML element.

Hence, the form markup should be like this:

```
<form class="form-inline ml-auto">
    <input type="text" placeholder="Search..." class="form-control">
</form>
```

If you save and reload the page on your browser, you will see the following (Figure 7-9).

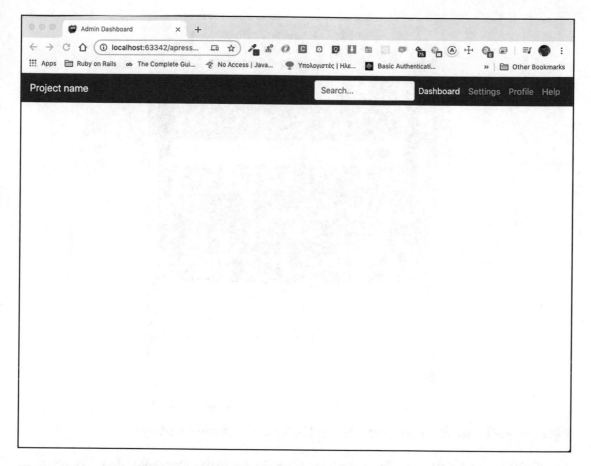

Figure 7-9. *Search Form with Styling Classes*

You have finished with the top navigation bar. Now that you have introduced the search form inside it, it might be a good idea to check how this search form appears when the page is displayed on small devices (Figure 7-10).

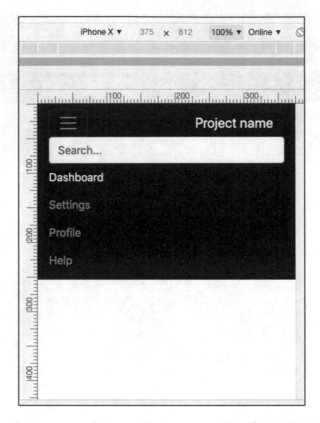

Figure 7-10. *Search Form and Menu Options on Small Devices*

There is a problem with the search form on the preceding layout. It does not have some margin on top of it. It would have been better if it had some top margin like the following (Figure 7-11).

Figure 7-11. *Search Form with Top Margin*

In order to achieve this, you can use a sizing Bootstrap utility class, for example, mt-3, which adds a top margin of size 3. Change the form markup to be like this:

```
<form class="form-inline ml-auto mt-3">
    <input type="text" placeholder="Search..." class="form-control">
</form>
```

And reload the page on your browser. Switch to the small-display (e.g., iPhone X) devices. When you unfold the menu, you will see the search form with the top margin looking much better, like what is depicted in Figure 7-11.

However, if you switch back to large-display devices, you will see the following (Figure 7-12).

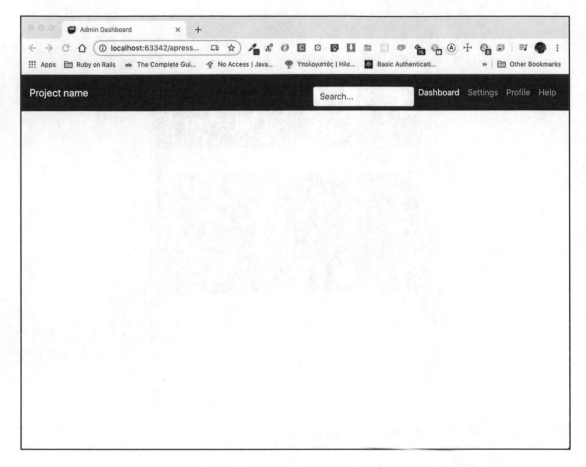

Figure 7-12. *Search Form Top Margin on Large Displays*

As you can see, the layout of the navigation bar has been destroyed, because of the mt-3 presence. In other words

- You want the mt-3 only on small devices when the menu options collapse.

- You don't want the mt-3 when the menu options are expanded.

You know that your menu expands on the lg breakpoint (thanks to the navbar-expand-lg class). Hence, in order to negate the effect of the mt-3 class when you are above the lg breakpoint, you will add the class mt-lg-0. Hence, the form markup should be

```
<form class="form-inline ml-auto mt-3 mt-lg-0">
    <input type="text" placeholder="Search..." class="form-control">
</form>
```

Again, the preceding markup preserves the mt-3 on devices with display less than the lg breakpoint and uses the class mt-lg-0 on displays above the lg breakpoint.

If you save the preceding code and reload the page on your browser, you will see that the navigation bar is back to its correct style. And shrinking to a small display, it still works as expected.

Aligning Using Flex Utility Classes

You have used margin utility classes to align the items of the navigation bar to the right. But Twitter Bootstrap heavily relies on flexbox. It provides classes that can be used to align content accordingly.

For example, you can use the class flex-row-reverse and have your HTML markup in reverse order. Doing so, you don't need to use ml-auto on the form element. See in the following what I mean (Listing 7-5).

Listing 7-5. Using flex-row-reverse

```
<div class="collapse navbar-collapse flex-row-reverse" id="navbar">
    <ul class="nav navbar-nav">
        <li class="nav-item">
            <a class="nav-link active" href="#">Dashboard <span class="sr-
            only">(current)</span></a>
        </li>
        <li class="nav-item">
            <a class="nav-link" href="#settings">Settings</a>
        </li>
        <li class="nav-item">
            <a class="nav-link" href="#profile">Profile</a>
        </li>
        <li class="nav-item">
            <a class="nav-link" href="#help">Help</a>
        </li>
    </ul>
```

```
<form class="form-inline">
    <input type="text" placeholder="Search..." class="form-control">
</form>
</div>
```

1. You have written the form markup after the ul markup.

2. You have added the class flex-row-reverse on the div that contains both the menu options and the search form.

3. You have removed the margin classes from the form markup.

If you save the preceding code and load the page on your browser, you will see the following (Figure 7-13).

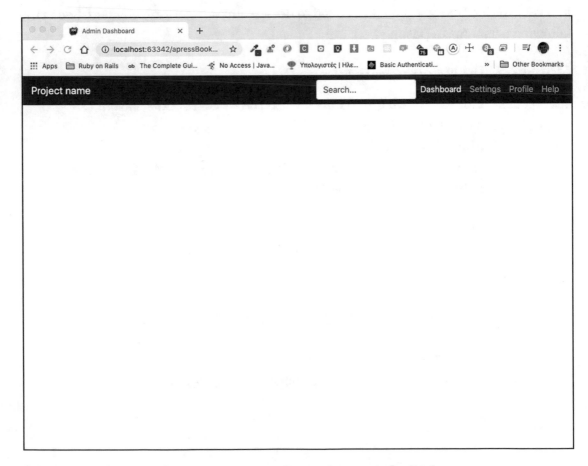

Figure 7-13. *Using flex-row-reverse to Draw Items on the Right*

As you can see, the direct children of the `flex-row-reverse` div have been drawn in reverse order, that is, first the search `form` and then the `ul` element.

Note that the fact that we have moved the `form` to the bottom of the `div` makes things look better on small devices too. The search form is displayed at the bottom. The `flex-row-reverse` does not have any effect on these devices because the menu options are displayed top to bottom (Figure 7-14).

Figure 7-14. *Search Form Appears at the Bottom*

All good! Now, let's move to the left-side navigation bar.

Left-Side Navigation Bar

We proceed now to build the left-side navigation bar (Figure 7-15).

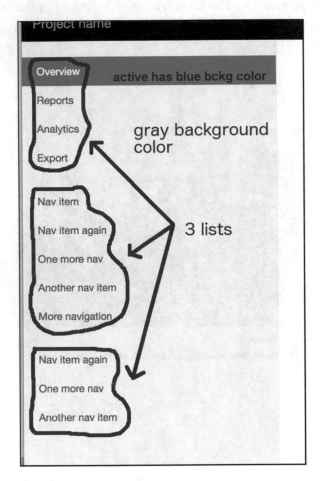

Figure 7-15. *Left-Side Navigation Bar Properties*

As you can see in Figure 7-15, the left-side navigation bar should have some properties:

1. Its background color is not white; it is more like a gray.

2. The active menu item has white color and blue background color.

3. There are three groups of menu items, a.k.a. three different lists.

4. It occupies a specific width of the page. Let's assume one-sixth
    of the width for medium, large, and extralarge devices (a.k.a. two
    columns out of 12) and one-fourth of the width for small devices
    (a.k.a. three columns out of 12). On extrasmall devices, the sidebar
    will not be visible.

Layout

Let's start with the fourth property. Since we want the sidebar to occupy part of the width
of the page, we will use the correct grid classes. Add the following content below the nav
element (Listing 7-6).

Listing 7-6. Layout Markup

```
<div id="main-container" class="container-fluid">
    <div class="row">
        <div class="col-sm-3 col-md-2">
            <!-- Left Sidebar Content will go here -->

        </div>

        <div id="main-content-container" class="col-sm-9 col-md-10">
            <!-- Main Content will go here -->

        </div>
    </div>
</div>
```

As you can see in the preceding code, we have a div for the sidebar that uses the grid
class col-sm-3 for small devices, hence occupying three columns out of 12, and the class
col-md-2 for medium, large, and extralarge devices, hence occupying two columns out
of 12.

The main content will go inside the second div, which also uses grid classes col-
sm-9 and col-md-10 so that it occupies the rest of the available width. For small devices,
it will occupy nine out of 12 columns; and for medium, large, and extralarge devices, it
will occupy ten out of 12 columns.

Save the preceding content. If you load the page again on your browser, you will not see any difference, because the sidebar and main content do not have any actual content inside.

Lists Inside the Sidebar

You have identified three lists inside the left-side navigation bar. Let's create them, as you usually do, with ul elements (Listing 7-7).

Listing 7-7. HTML with ul Elements for the Lists

```
<div id="main-container" class="container-fluid">
    <div class="row">
        <div class="col-sm-3 col-md-2">
            <!-- Left Sidebar Content will go here -->

            <ul>
                <li class="active"><a href="#">Overview</a></li>
                <li><a href="#">Reports</a></li>
                <li><a href="#">Analytics</a></li>
                <li><a href="#">Export</a></li>
            </ul>

            <ul>
                <li><a href="#">Nav item</a></li>
                <li><a href="#">Nav item again</a></li>
                <li><a href="#">One more nav</a></li>
                <li><a href="#">Another nav item</a></li>
                <li><a href="#">More navigation</a></li>
            </ul>

            <ul>
                <li><a href="#">Nav item again</a></li>
                <li><a href="#">One more nav</a></li>
                <li><a href="#">Another nav item</a></li>
            </ul>

        </div>
```

```
    <div id="main-content-container" class="col-sm-9 col-md-10">
        <!-- Main Content will go here -->

    </div>
  </div>
</div>
```

If you save the preceding code and reload the page on your browser, you will see the following (Figure 7-16).

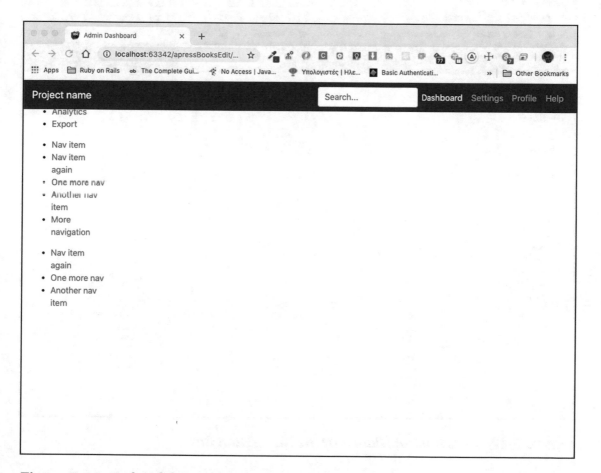

Figure 7-16. *Left Sidebar—Lists Added*

One problem that you see now is that the top list is hidden by the navigation bar. This is a problem that you have faced in the past. You need to give some top padding to the body content, at least equal to the height of the navigation bar. You will give 56px.

Inside the stylesheets/main.css file, add the following rule:

```
body {
    padding-top: 56px;
}
```

Save and reload the page on your browser. You will see the following (Figure 7-17).

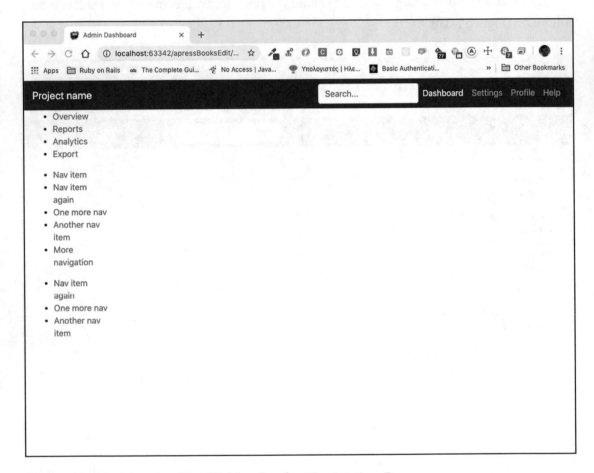

Figure 7-17. *Lists Are Not Hidden by the Navigation Bar*

That's an improvement. Now, you will apply the class nav on the lists. As you remember from previous chapters, the nav class on ul elements removes the default bullets displayed on the list items.

Go ahead and add the class nav to all ul elements of the left-side navigation bar. Then load the page on your browser. You will see the following (Figure 7-18).

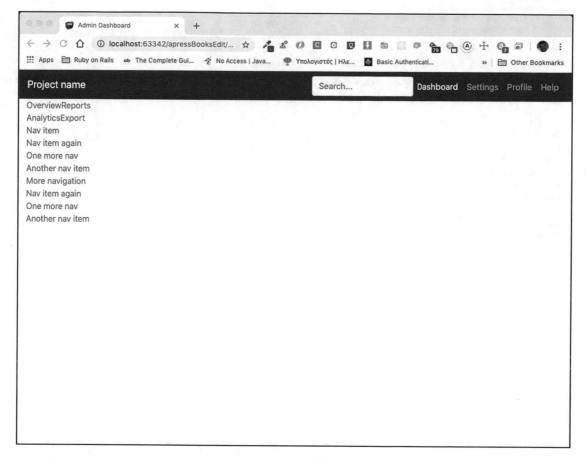

Figure 7-18. *Class nav Applied to ul Elements*

The class nav has removed the bullets from the elements of the lists. But it has also done something else. It has turned the ul elements to display flex, with flex-wrap equal to wrap. That's why you see the li elements one next to the other.

Since you want your lists to be enlisted top to bottom, you can add the class flex-column that will make all the direct children to be drawn in a column.

Go ahead, and next to the nav class, add the flex-column class too. Save and load the page on your browser. You will see the following (Figure 7-19).

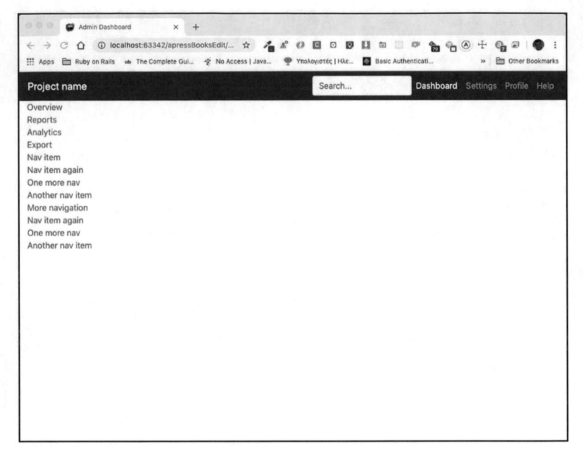

Figure 7-19. `flex-column` *Class Applied*

The left sidebar starts to look much better. Yet, it is not finished.

Hide the Sidebar on Extrasmall Devices

You want to hide the sidebar on extrasmall devices and display it only for small, medium, large, and extralarge devices. You can achieve this with the display utility classes:

- Class d-none will hide the element.

- Class d-sm-block will display the element for any display above the sm breakpoint.

Let's apply that to the container div that holds the left-side navigation bar lists. Listing 7-8 gives the HTML markup fragment.

Listing 7-8. HTML Fragment for the Container of the Left-Side Navigation Bar

```
<div class="col-sm-3 col-md-2 d-none d-sm-block">
    <!-- Left Sidebar Content will go here -->

    <ul class="nav flex-column">
        <li class="active"><a href="#">Overview</a></li>
        <li><a href="#">Reports</a></li>
        <li><a href="#">Analytics</a></li>
        <li><a href="#">Export</a></li>
    </ul>

    <ul class="nav flex-column">
        <li><a href="#">Nav item</a></li>
        <li><a href="#">Nav item again</a></li>
        <li><a href="#">One more nav</a></li>
        <li><a href="#">Another nav item</a></li>
        <li><a href="#">More navigation</a></li>
    </ul>

    <ul class="nav flex-column">
        <li><a href="#">Nav item again</a></li>
        <li><a href="#">One more nav</a></li>
        <li><a href="#">Another nav item</a></li>
    </ul>

</div>
```

If you save and reload the page on your browser, you will see that the left-side navigation bar is hidden on a display with width 575px (Figure 7-20).

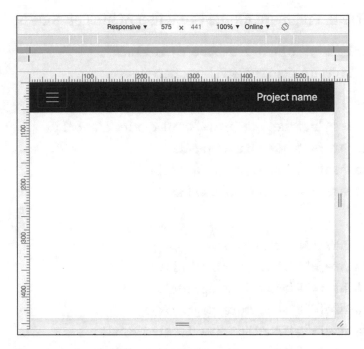

Figure 7-20. *Left Sidebar Hidden on 575px Displays*

However, it is visible on a 576px display (Figure 7-21).

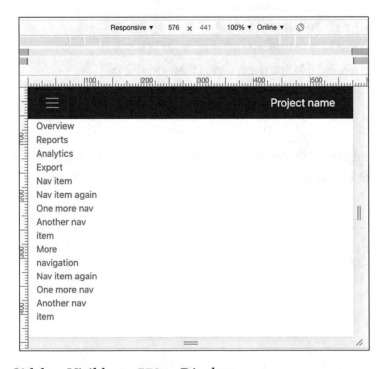

Figure 7-21. *Sidebar Visible on 576px Displays*

Further Styling of the Sidebar

You will proceed now to further style the sidebar. In order to do that, you will apply the class sidebar on the div container that holds the three lists, and then you will write some CSS rules for this particular class. The following are the rules (Listing 7-9).

Listing 7-9. First Styling Rules for the Left Sidebar

```
.sidebar {
    padding-top: 10px;
    padding-bottom: 10px;
    background-color: #f5f5f5;
    border-right: 1px solid #eee;
}
```

Don't forget to add the class sidebar to the div that contains the three ul elements with the left-side navigation bar options.

Then, save, and reload the page on your browser. You will see the following (Figure 7-22).

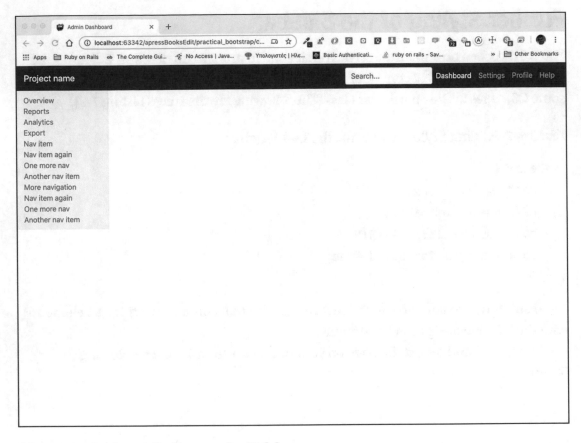

Figure 7-22. *Some Styling on the Sidebar*

The preceding styling sets the background color and border on the right side of the sidebar and also some padding on the top and bottom.

You now want to make sure that the sidebar height occupies the whole available height. In order to do that, you need to specify `height: 100%` both on `row div` and on all of its ancestor elements.

Make sure that the `stylesheets/main.css` file has the following content (Listing 7-10).

Listing 7-10. stylesheets/main.css File Content

```
html {
    height: 100%;
}
```

```css
body {
    padding-top: 56px;
    height: 100%;
}

#main-container,
#main-container .row{
    height: 100%;
}

.sidebar {
    padding-top: 10px;
    padding-bottom: 10px;
    background-color: #f5f5f5;
    border-right: 1px solid #eee;
}
```

Note that with #main-container, you are referring to the id of the container that holds the main content of the page, exactly after the nav element. For your help, the HTML fragment of the #main-container should be as in Listing 7-11.

Listing 7-11. #main-container HTML Content

```html
<div id="main-container" class="container-fluid">
  <div class="row">
    <div class="col-sm-3 col-md-2 d-none d-sm-block sidebar">
      <!-- Left Sidebar Content will go here -->

      <ul class="nav flex-column">
        <li class="active"><a href="#">Overview</a></li>
        <li><a href="#">Reports</a></li>
        <li><a href="#">Analytics</a></li>
        <li><a href="#">Export</a></li>
      </ul>

      <ul class="nav flex-column">
        <li><a href="#">Nav item</a></li>
        <li><a href="#">Nav item again</a></li>
        <li><a href="#">One more nav</a></li>
```

```
      <li><a href="#">Another nav item</a></li>
      <li><a href="#">More navigation</a></li>
    </ul>

    <ul class="nav flex-column">
      <li><a href="#">Nav item again</a></li>
      <li><a href="#">One more nav</a></li>
      <li><a href="#">Another nav item</a></li>
    </ul>

  </div>

  <div id="main-content-container" class="col-sm-9 col-md-10">
    <!-- Main Content will go here -->

  </div>
 </div>
</div>
```

If you save the preceding code and reload the page on your browser, you will see the following (Figure 7-23).

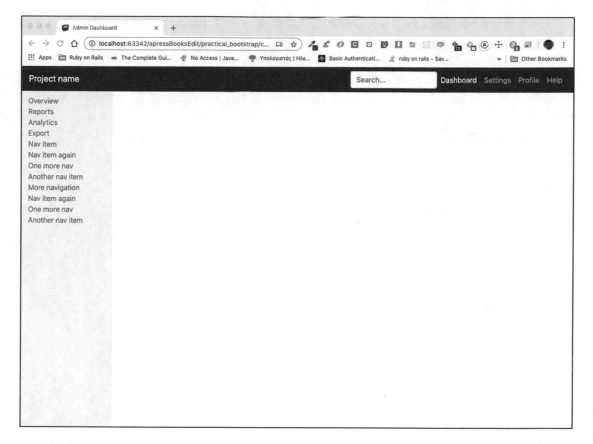

Figure 7-23. *Sidebar Occupies the Full Height*

You continue with the styling of the sidebar:

1. You will make sure that the user can tell one group of options from the next. You will apply a bottom margin on the ul elements of the sidebar.

2. You will increase the height of the elements in the list so that the options are quite distinct and there is some vertical space from one to the next.

3. You want the lists to occupy all the available width. So that when one moves the mouse pointer over any of the elements, the highlight goes from left to right. In order to achieve that, you will remove the left and right padding from the sidebar container.

4. However, you want each list item to have some padding so that the text does not start at the left edge of the bar.

Here is the content of the `stylesheets/main.css` with blue color on the changes that you have to apply (Listing 7-12).

Listing 7-12. Further Styling of the Sidebar

```css
html {
    height: 100%;
}

body {
    padding-top: 56px;
    height: 100%;
}

#main-container,
#main-container .row{
    height: 100%;
}

.sidebar {
    padding: 10px 0;
    background-color: #f5f5f5;
    border-right: 1px solid #eee;
}

.sidebar ul {
    margin-bottom: 20px;
}

.sidebar ul li {
    padding-left: 10px;
    min-height: 2.2rem;
}
```

If you save and reload the page on your browser, you will see the following (Figure 7-24).

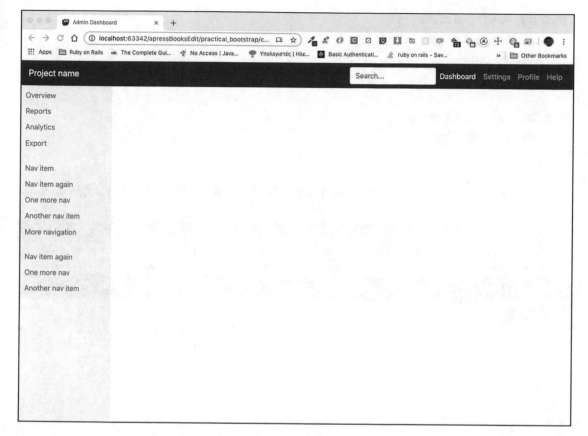

Figure 7-24. *Further Styling of the Left Sidebar*

You proceed with applying some background and foreground colors on options of the sidebar menu. Here are the extra CSS rules that you need to apply (Listing 7-13).

Listing 7-13. Extra CSS Rules for Left Sidebar Options

```
.sidebar ul li a {
    text-decoration: none;
}

/* Active <li> and <a>, and for hover over NON-active <li> and <a> */
.sidebar ul li.active,
.sidebar ul li.active a,

.sidebar ul li:hover,
.sidebar ul li:hover a,
```

```
.sidebar ul li a:hover {
    background-color: #428BCA;
    color: White;
}

.sidebar ul li:hover {
    cursor: pointer;
}
```

If you save and load the page on your browser, you will see the following (Figure 7-25).

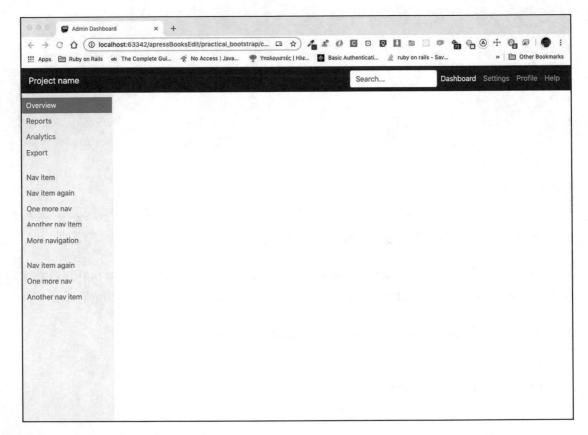

Figure 7-25. *Options with Colors*

If you move your mouse over the options of the left-side navigation bar, you will see that they get a different background color and text color. Also, the cursor is becoming a mouse pointer (Figure 7-26).

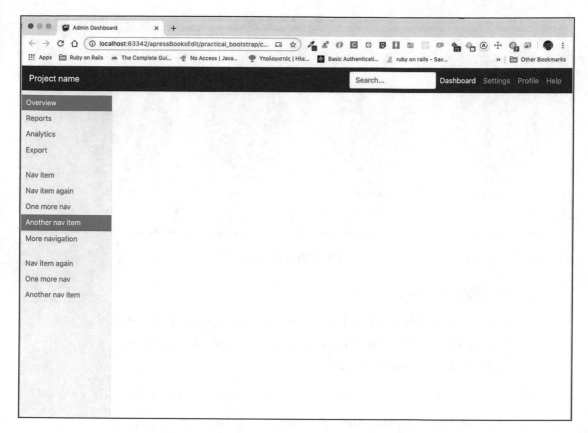

Figure 7-26. *Hover Over a Nonactive Option*

Main Content Area

You stop styling the sidebar, and you proceed to constructing the main content area. You will start with the dashboard top area, in which you are supposed to be presenting a series of graphs (Figure 7-27).

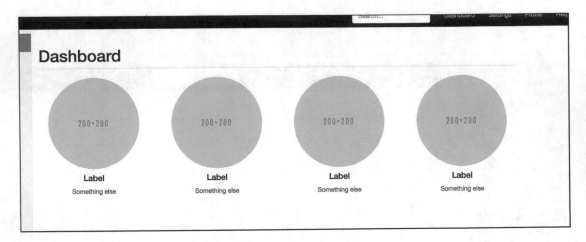

Figure 7-27. *Dashboard—Top Area with Graphs*

Note the following about the objective:

1. There is a Dashboard header with horizontal lines at the bottom. You can create this effect with an hr and the class my-4 that you have seen in previous chapters.

2. You can see four information containers (graph image + text).

3. On extralarge displays, the information containers displayed on one row are four. Same goes for large and medium devices. On small and extrasmall devices, we display two information containers per row (Figure 7-28).

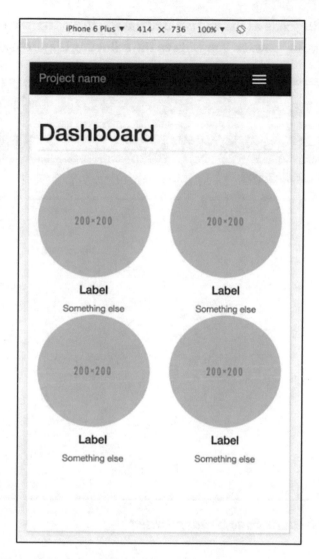

Figure 7-28. *On Extrasmall Devices—Two Information Containers per Row*

4. You will use some placeholder images for the graph images.

Let's start.

Dashboard Header

First, add the Dashboard header:

```
<h1>Dashboard</h1>
<hr class=my-4>
```

317

Add the preceding code as the first child of the `#main-content-container`. Save and reload the page on your browser. You will see the following (Figure 7-29).

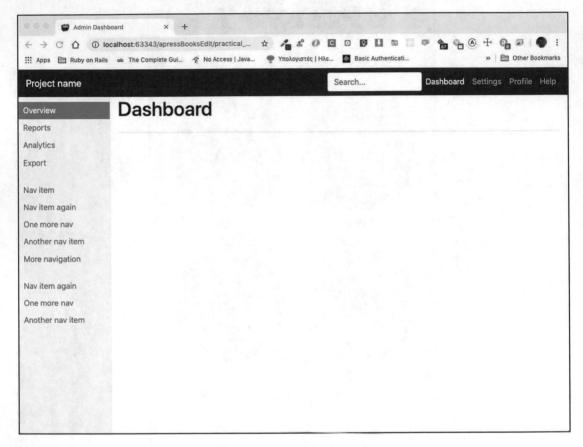

Figure 7-29. *Dashboard Page Header Added*

That was pretty easy, and you have done that in the past. You can now see the `Dashboard` styled as a page header with the help of the `hr` element and the class `my-4`.

Information Containers

The information containers are blocks of HTML code that contain

1. An image, an `img` element

2. A small label, inside an `h4` element

3.   A span with some text displayed below the label

```
<img src="https://via.placeholder.com/200" width="200" height="200"
    alt="Generic placeholder thumbnail">
<h4>Label</h4>
<span>Something else</span>
```

Each one of the containers—we have four of them—we need to enclose inside a div with the correct Twitter Bootstrap grid classes:

```
<div class="col-6 col-md-3">
    <img src="https://via.placeholder.com/200" width="200" height="200"
        alt="Generic placeholder thumbnail">
    <h4>Label</h4>
    <span>Something else</span>
</div>
```

The div has grid classes col-6 and col-md-3. On extrasmall and small devices, each information container block will occupy half of the available width (six out of 12 columns). Hence, you are going to have two such columns on each row. On larger devices, it will occupy a quarter of the available width (three out of 12 columns). Hence, you are going to have four such columns on each row.

You need to repeat this three more times and enclose the whole set of div columns to a div with class row (Listing 7-14).

Listing 7-14. HTML Fragment with Information Blocks

```
<div class="row">
  <div class="col-6 col-md-3">
      <img src="https://via.placeholder.com/200" width="200" height="200"
          alt="Generic placeholder thumbnail">
      <h4>Label</h4>
      <span>Something else</span>
  </div>
```

```
<div class="col-6 col-md-3">
    <img src="https://via.placeholder.com/200" width="200" height="200"
        alt="Generic placeholder thumbnail">
    <h4>Label</h4>
    <span>Something else</span>
</div>

<div class="col-6 col-md-3">
    <img src="https://via.placeholder.com/200" width="200" height="200"
        alt="Generic placeholder thumbnail">
    <h4>Label</h4>
    <span>Something else</span>
</div>

<div class="col-6 col-md-3">
    <img src="https://via.placeholder.com/200" width="200" height="200"
        alt="Generic placeholder thumbnail">
    <h4>Label</h4>
    <span>Something else</span>
</div>
</div>
```

Place the preceding code exactly below the Dashboard div container. Save the file and reload the page on your browser. You will see the following (Figure 7-30).

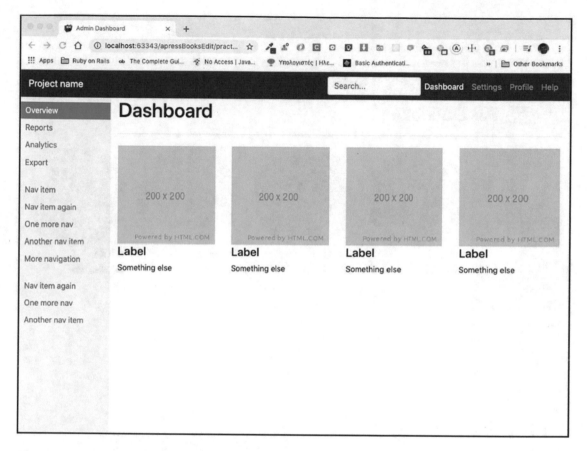

Figure 7-30. *Dashboard—Information Containers Put on the Page*

Now, information containers have successfully been put on the page, below the page header. But you need to do some style tuning in order to achieve the desired result.

Let's first make sure that the images are displayed with a circle shape. This is very easy to do. You only have to add the class `rounded-circle` on the `img` elements.

If you do that, save, and reload the page on your browser, you will see the following (Figure 7-31).

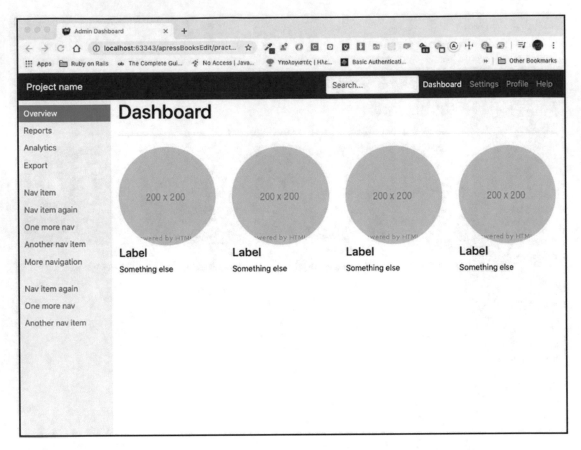

Figure 7-31. *Information Containers Have Images with Circle Shape*

Next thing that you want to do is to make sure that both the image and the text of the information container are center aligned. You will use the class `text-center` to all the `div` elements that wrap the image and the text.

`text-center` is a class provided by Twitter Bootstrap. It essentially applies the CSS style `text-align: center;` on the element that it is attached to. There are more alignment-related classes provided by Twitter Bootstrap. The full list is here:

1. `text-left`: Corresponds to `text-align: left;`

2. `text-right`: Corresponds to `text-align: right;`

3. `text-center`: Corresponds to `text-align: center;`

4. `text-justify`: Corresponds to `text-align: justify;`

Also, you can use these classes with their breakpoint-specific variation. For example, you can use the class text-md-center, which will center the content but only for medium or wider displays.

Go ahead and apply the class text-center on all information containers, and then reload the page on your browser. You will see the following (Figure 7-32).

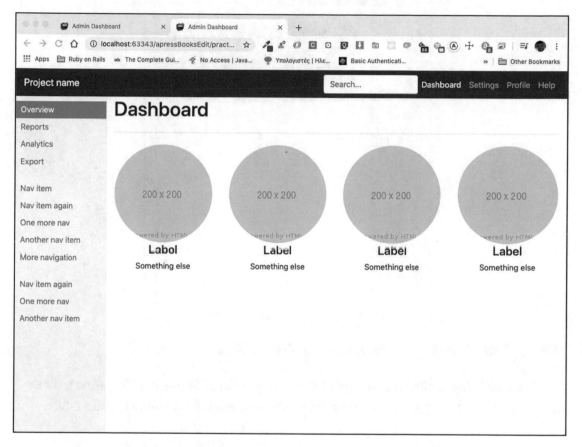

Figure 7-32. *Content Aligned on the Center*

Although the Figure 7-32 looks as if you have finished with the information containers, there is a small problem that becomes obvious if you see your page on a device with shorter width. For example, try iPad simulation with your developer tools. You will see the following (Figure 7-33).

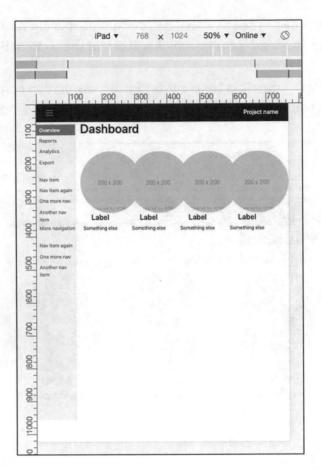

Figure 7-33. *Images Are Not Displayed OK on iPad*

This can be remedied if you apply the class img-fluid to the img elements. Let's do that. Then reload the page on your browser. You will see the following (Figure 7-34).

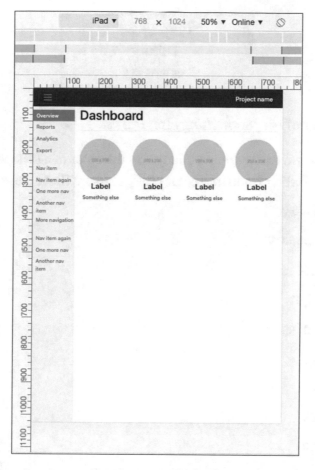

Figure 7-34. *Images Are Displayed OK with the Class* `img-fluid`

The `img-fluid` class does two things:

1. It sets the `max-width` to `100%`. This means that the image width cannot be wider than the parent block the image is in.

2. It sets the `height` to `auto`. This means that the height will automatically be calculated based on the width, so that the image has the correct aspect ratio.

With these restrictions in place, the images end up drawn correctly on any display size.

What remains to be done is to change the color of the text `Something else`. It needs to be a light-gray color (see Figure 7-35).

Figure 7-35. *Color of the "Something else" Phrase*

You can quickly and easily apply a change on the color of a text element by only applying one of the Twitter Bootstrap color utility classes. These classes are

1. `text-primary`

2. `text-secondary`

3. `text-success`

4. `text-danger`

5. `text-warning`

6. `text-info`

7. `text-light`

8. `text-dark`

9. `text-body`

10. `text-muted`

11. `text-white`

12. `text-black-50`

13. `text-white-50`

You can see their color equivalent in Figure 7-36.

Figure 7-36. *Bootstrap Text Color Utility Classes*

Let's apply the class text-black-50 on the span that holds the Something else text. Save and load the page on your browser. You will see the following (Figure 7-37).

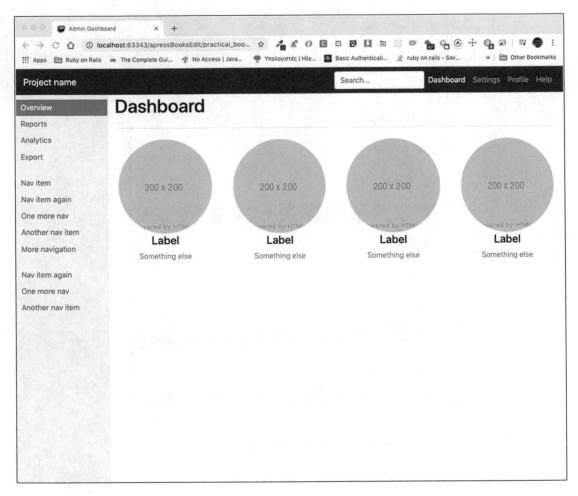

Figure 7-37. *"Something else" Phrase with the text-black-50 Class Applied*

Before we close this section on information containers, I will give you here the HTML fragment that should exist inside the #main-content-container div, as it has been composed until now, that is, with the Dashboard header and the information blocks. See Listing 7-15.

Listing 7-15. Main Container Content

```
<div id="main-content-container" class="col-sm-9 col-md-10">
    <!-- Main Content will go here -->
    <h1>Dashboard</h1>
    <hr class="my-4">
```

```
<div class="row">
    <div class="col-6 col-md-3 text-center">
        <img src="https://via.placeholder.com/200" width="200"
        height="200"
            class="rounded-circle img-fluid"
            alt="Generic placeholder thumbnail">
        <h4>Label</h4>
        <span class="text-black-50">Something else</span>
    </div>

    <div class="col-6 col-md-3 text-center">
        <img src="https://via.placeholder.com/200" width="200"
        height="200"
            class="rounded-circle img-fluid"
            alt="Generic placeholder thumbnail">
        <h4>Label</h4>
        <span class="text-black-50">Something else</span>
    </div>

    <div class="col-6 col-md-3 text-center">
        <img src="https://via.placeholder.com/200" width="200"
        height="200"
            class="rounded-circle img-fluid"
            alt="Generic placeholder thumbnail">
        <h4>Label</h4>
        <span class="text-black-50">Something else</span>
    </div>

    <div class="col-6 col-md-3 text-center">
        <img src="https://via.placeholder.com/200" width="200"
        height="200"
            class="rounded-circle img-fluid"
            alt="Generic placeholder thumbnail">
        <h4>Label</h4>
        <span class="text-black-50">Something else</span>
    </div>
</div>
</div>
```

Dashboard Table

The next part on the admin page is the dashboard table. You have already learned how to design tables using Twitter Bootstrap. So this will not be a difficult exercise.

Section Header

You add the section header with the following piece of HTML code:

```
<h2>Section title</h2>
<hr class="my-4">
```

Put that exactly after the closing row div that contains the information containers you implemented earlier. If you save the code and reload the page on your browser, you will see the following (Figure 7-38).

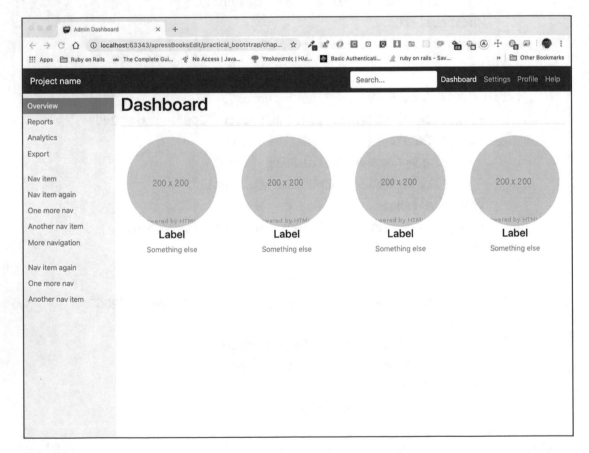

Figure 7-38. *Section Title Is Not Displayed*

As you can see, the section title is not displayed. Why is that? In fact, you can see the section title if you scroll down. It is at the bottom of the page as in Figure 7-39.

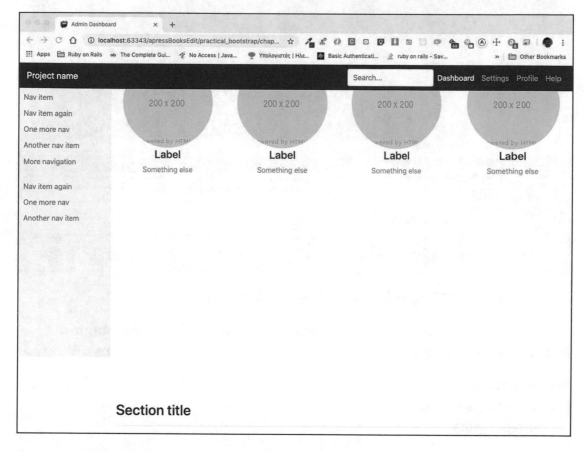

Figure 7-39. *Section Title at the Bottom of the Page*

Why does this happen? This happens because of the 100% `height` that you have applied to the `#main-container .row` CSS selector (see your `stylesheets/main.css` file). That rule was there to make the sidebar occupy the whole height. But, from the moment we added an extra `row div` element, the one that holds the information blocks, then this rule was applied to that `div` too. This last application pushed the section title at the position that you see (Figure 7-40).

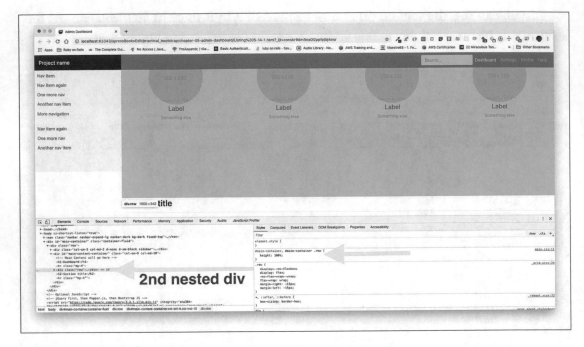

Figure 7-40. *How Nested Div 100% Height Affects Layout*

What you really want is this 100% height CSS statement to be applied only to the first-level nested `div` inside the `#main-container` div. In order to do that, the rule

```
#main-container,
#main-container .row {
    height: 100%
}
```

needs to be changed to

```
#main-container,
#main-container > .row {
    height: 100%
}
```

The `>` is the direct child selector. The preceding CSS rule selects the `#main-container` as well as its first-level direct child element with class `.row`.

In order to make sure that your code is aligned, I give you here the whole `stylesheets/main.css` file that your page should be using (Listing 7-16).

Listing 7-16. stylesheets/main.css Content

```
html {
    height: 100%;
}

body {
    padding-top: 56px;
    height: 100%;
}

#main-container,
#main-container > .row {
    height: 100%
}

.sidebar {
    padding: 10px 0;
    background-color: #f5f5f5;
    border-right: 1px solid #eee;
}

.sidebar ul {
    margin-bottom: 20px;
}

.sidebar ul li {
    padding-left: 10px;
    padding-top: 5px;
    min-height: 2.2rem;
}

.sidebar ul li a {
    text-decoration: none;
}

/* Active <li> and <a>, and for hover over NON-active <li> and <a> */
.sidebar ul li.active,
.sidebar ul li.active a,
```

```css
.sidebar ul li:hover,
.sidebar ul li:hover a,
.sidebar ul li a:hover {
    background-color: #428BCA;
    color: White;
}

.sidebar ul li:hover {
    cursor: pointer;
}
```

If you save the preceding code and reload the page on your browser, you will see the following (Figure 7-41).

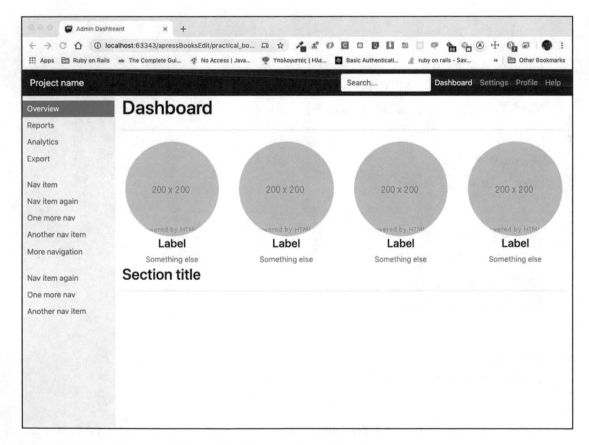

Figure 7-41. *Section Title at the Correct Position*

A problem I see on this layout is that the section header needs some room at the top side. You can add some top margin by adding the class mt-4 to the h2 of the section:

```
<h2 class="mt-4">Section title</h2>
```

If you save this change and reload the page on your browser, you will see the following (Figure 7-42), which is much better.

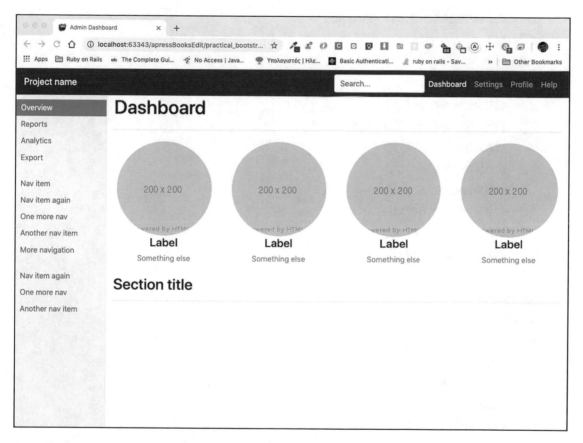

Figure 7-42. *Section with Some Top Margin*

The Table

Let's now add the table below the section header (Listing 7-17).

Listing 7-17. Table HTML Fragment

```
<p>Sales table is compiled from data retrieved from the main database</p>

<table class="table table-striped">
    <thead>
    <tr>
        <th>#</th>
        <th>Header 1</th>
        <th>Header 2</th>
        <th>Header 3</th>
        <th>Header 4</th>
        <th>Header 5</th>
        <th>Header 6</th>
        <th>Header 7</th>
        <th>Header 8</th>
    </tr>
    </thead>
    <tbody>
    <tr>
        <td>1,001</td>
        <td>Lorem</td>
        <td>ipsum</td>
        <td>dolor</td>
        <td>sit</td>
        <td>Lorem</td>
        <td>ipsum</td>
        <td>dolor</td>
        <td>sit</td>
    </tr>
```

```
<tr>
    <td>1,002</td>
    <td>amet</td>
    <td>consectetur</td>
    <td>adipiscing</td>
    <td>elit</td>
    <td>amet</td>
    <td>consectetur</td>
    <td>adipiscing</td>
    <td>elit</td>
</tr>
<tr>
    <td>1,003</td>
    <td>Integer</td>
    <td>nec</td>
    <td>odio</td>
    <td>Praesent</td>
    <td>Integer</td>
    <td>nec</td>
    <td>odio</td>
    <td>Praesent</td>
</tr>
<tr>
    <td>1,003</td>
    <td>libero</td>
    <td>Sed</td>
    <td>cursus</td>
    <td>ante</td>
    <td>libero</td>
    <td>Sed</td>
    <td>cursus</td>
    <td>ante</td>
</tr>
```

```
    <tr>
        <td>1,004</td>
        <td>dapibus</td>
        <td>diam</td>
        <td>Sed</td>
        <td>nisi</td>
        <td>dapibus</td>
        <td>diam</td>
        <td>Sed</td>
        <td>nisi</td>
    </tr>
    <tr>
        <td>1,005</td>
        <td>Nulla</td>
        <td>quis</td>
        <td>sem</td>
        <td>at</td>
        <td>Nulla</td>
        <td>quis</td>
        <td>sem</td>
        <td>at</td>
    </tr>
    <tr>
        <td>1,006</td>
        <td>nibh</td>
        <td>elementum</td>
        <td>imperdiet</td>
        <td>Duis</td>
        <td>nibh</td>
        <td>elementum</td>
        <td>imperdiet</td>
        <td>Duis</td>
    </tr>
```

```
<tr>
    <td>1,007</td>
    <td>sagittis</td>
    <td>ipsum</td>
    <td>Praesent</td>
    <td>mauris</td>
    <td>sagittis</td>
    <td>ipsum</td>
    <td>Praesent</td>
    <td>mauris</td>
</tr>
<tr>
    <td>1,008</td>
    <td>Fusce</td>
    <td>nec</td>
    <td>tellus</td>
    <td>sed</td>
    <td>Fusce</td>
    <td>nec</td>
    <td>tellus</td>
    <td>sed</td>
</tr>
<tr>
    <td>1,009</td>
    <td>augue</td>
    <td>semper</td>
    <td>porta</td>
    <td>Mauris</td>
    <td>augue</td>
    <td>semper</td>
    <td>porta</td>
    <td>Mauris</td>
</tr>
```

```
    <tr>
        <td>1,010</td>
        <td>massa</td>
        <td>Vestibulum</td>
        <td>lacinia</td>
        <td>arcu</td>
        <td>massa</td>
        <td>Vestibulum</td>
        <td>lacinia</td>
        <td>arcu</td>
    </tr>
    <tr>
        <td>1,011</td>
        <td>eget</td>
        <td>nulla</td>
        <td>Class</td>
        <td>aptent</td>
        <td>eget</td>
        <td>nulla</td>
        <td>Class</td>
        <td>aptent</td>
    </tr>
    <tr>
        <td>1,012</td>
        <td>taciti</td>
        <td>sociosqu</td>
        <td>ad</td>
        <td>litora</td>
        <td>taciti</td>
        <td>sociosqu</td>
        <td>ad</td>
        <td>litora</td>
    </tr>
```

```
    <tr>
        <td>1,013</td>
        <td>torquent</td>
        <td>per</td>
        <td>conubia</td>
        <td>nostra</td>
        <td>torquent</td>
        <td>per</td>
        <td>conubia</td>
        <td>nostra</td>
    </tr>
    <tr>
        <td>1,014</td>
        <td>per</td>
        <td>inceptos</td>
        <td>himenaeos</td>
        <td>Curabitur</td>
        <td>per</td>
        <td>inceptos</td>
        <td>himenaeos</td>
        <td>Curabitur</td>
    </tr>
    <tr>
        <td>1,015</td>
        <td>sodales</td>
        <td>ligula</td>
        <td>in</td>
        <td>libero</td>
        <td>sodales</td>
        <td>ligula</td>
        <td>in</td>
        <td>libero</td>
    </tr>
    </tbody>
</table>
```

If you save the preceding code and reload the page on your browser, you will see the following (Figure 7-43).

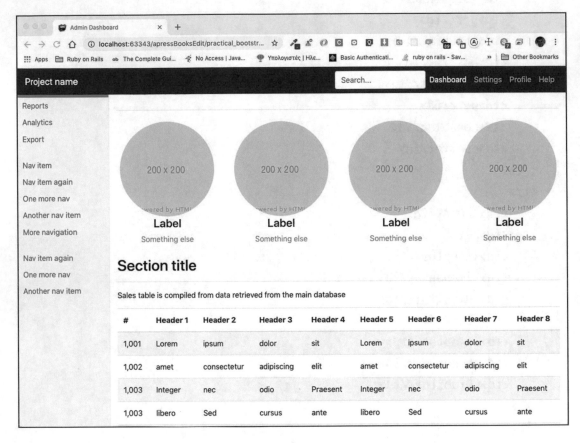

Figure 7-43. *Table Is Correctly Displayed*

However, there is a small problem when viewing the page on small devices. Try with the iPhone X emulation. You will see that the table is truncated. Actually, the page is horizontally expanded in order to display the whole table data. If the user scrolls in order to reveal the rest of the table data hidden, then the image graphs are scrolled to the left too, and the final experience is very bad. See a screenshot of the problem in Figure 7-44.

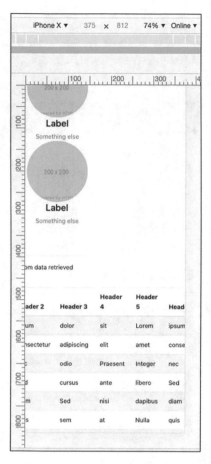

Figure 7-44. *Table Is Badly Styled on Mobile Devices*

There is a very easy way you can fix this problem. You can use the Twitter Bootstrap class `table-responsive`. You need to give this class to the `table` element. In fact, it may be a better idea to set it only for the extrasmall, small, and medium devices. For large and extralarge devices, you can have the table behave as default.

Hence, go ahead and attach the class `table-responsive-lg` to the table. This class does the following: From the `lg` breakpoint and up, the table will behave as normal. But below this breakpoint, that is, for displays <992px, it will get, automatically, without you having to add it in your CSS rules, an `overflow-x: auto;`, which will allow the user to scroll horizontally in order to see the whole content of the table.

Save and reload the page on your browser, for the iPhone X simulator. You will see the following (Figure 7-45).

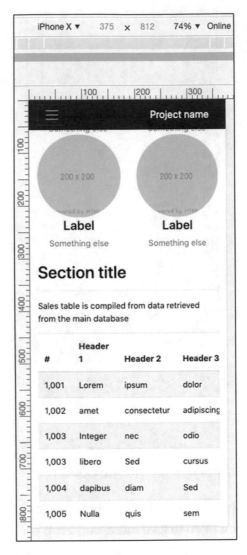

Figure 7-45. *Table Displayed Correctly on iPhone X*

If you scroll horizontally, you will see how the rest of the page is still being displayed correctly.

Some Final Tuning

You have managed to bring the page to look exactly like the page you initially had as a target. There is a small improvement that I would like to work with you on.

When the browser height is short, the user scrolls on the main dashboard area, in order to access/see the content of the table that is not visible. For example, in the following, you can see what the user sees when they scroll to the bottom of the page in order to reveal the bottom of the table (Figure 7-46).

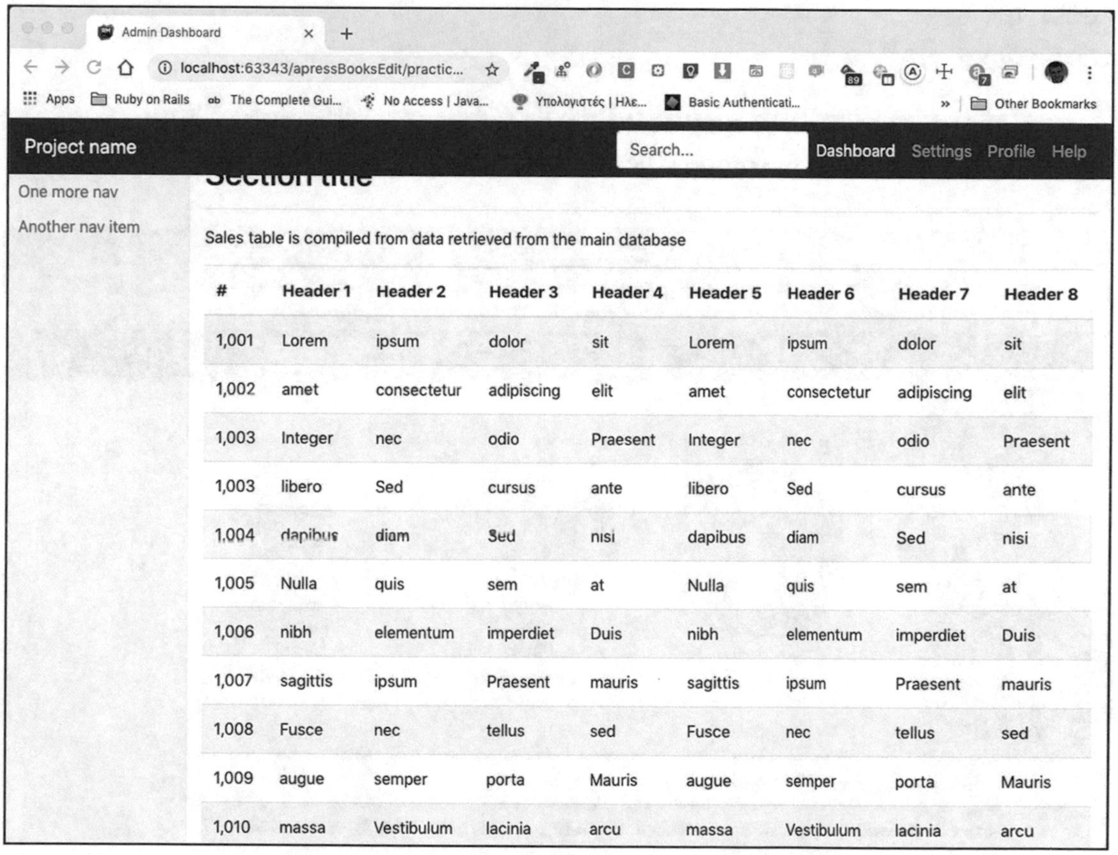

Figure 7-46. *Problem with the Left-Side Navigation Bar*

As you can see, there is a problem with the left-side navigation bar. The options disappear, as the sidebar content scrolls along with the rest of the main content. You want all the sidebar options to be accessible and visible all the time, so that the user is able to click them irrespective of the actual scroll position of the main content.

In order to have a `div always` visible, irrespective of the scrolling position of the browser window, then you need to fix its position. Let's add the following in our CSS file:

```
/* fix the position of the sidebar */
position: fixed;
left: 0;
top: 56px;
```

Add the preceding CSS properties inside the `sidebar` CSS selector block. Save the preceding code and load the page on your browser. You will see something like Figure 7-47.

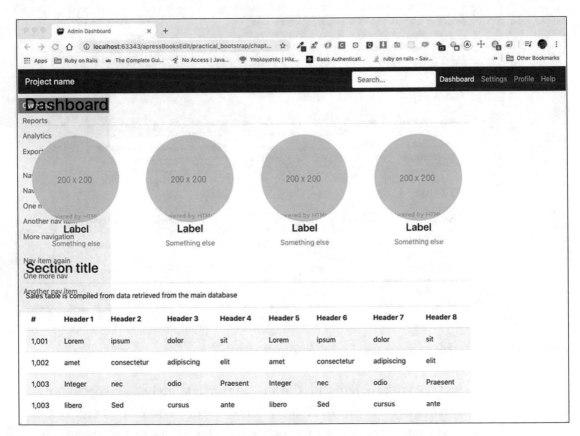

Figure 7-47. *Sidebar with Fixed Position—Problem on Main Content*

This is an improvement with regard to the sidebar being on a fixed position. Try to scroll the main content; and you will see that the options on the sidebar, all of them, remain visible.

On the other hand, it has brought the main content part far to the left, overlapping with the sidebar content. This is because the sidebar `div` is not part of the normal page element flow. You have specified the width of the sidebar `div`, with the grid classes `col-sm-3` and `col-md-2`, but the actual position has been fixed, and, hence, this element is not taken into account when the browser positions the `#main-content-container div`.

How can you solve this problem? There is a very easy solution. All you have to say to Bootstrap is to align the contents of the row of the container to the right. You have learned how to do that with the help of the `justify-content-*` classes and, in particular, with the class `justify-content-end`.

Add the class justify-content-end to the row that is the parent of all the content:

```
<div id="main-container" class="container-fluid">
    <div class="row justify-content-end">
        <div class="col-sm-3 col-md-2 d-none d-sm-block sidebar">
            <!-- Left Sidebar Content will go here -->
        ...
```

If you save the HTML content and load the page on your browser, you will see the following (Figure 7-48).

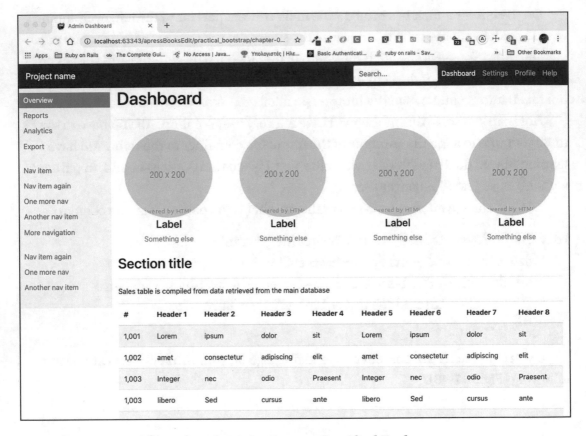

Figure 7-48. *Dashboard with Main Content Justified End*

The last problem that remains to be sorted out is the fact that the left-side navigation bar does not extend to the bottom of the window. This is expected because you have turned the `sidebar div` into a positioned element with position fixed. Positioned elements extend up to the necessary width and height according to the content they contain.

You can easily change this for the height of the `sidebar div` by setting its `min-height` property to 100%. Go ahead and add this CSS property inside your `stylesheets/main. css` file. Then reload the page on your browser. You will see Figure 7-49.

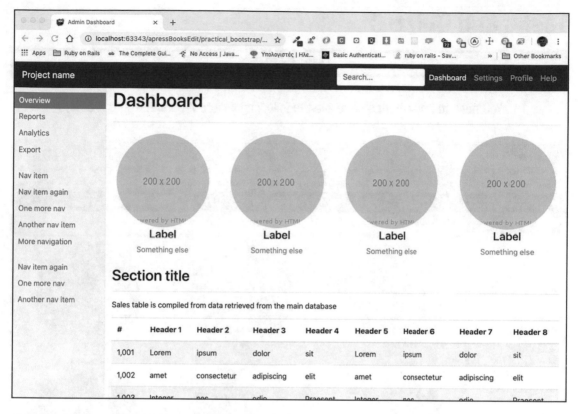

Figure 7-49. *Left Sidebar with Full Height*

Perfect! The left sidebar now occupies the whole height. Try scrolling and changing display widths. You will see that everything works as expected.

Tasks and Quizzes

TASK DETAILS

---

1. You need to implement a page like the following (Figure 7-50 and Figure 7-51).

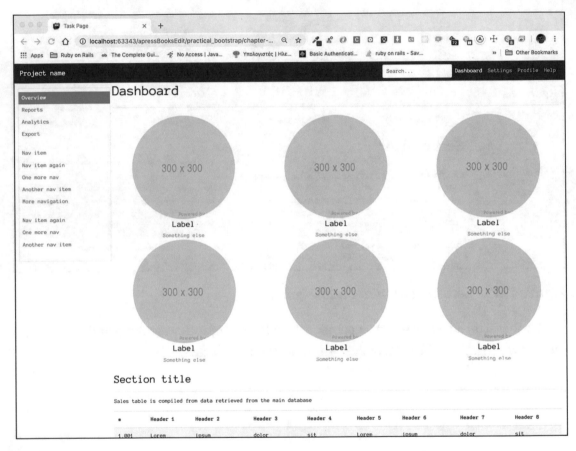

Figure 7-50. *Task—Admin Dashboard (Top Part of the Page)*

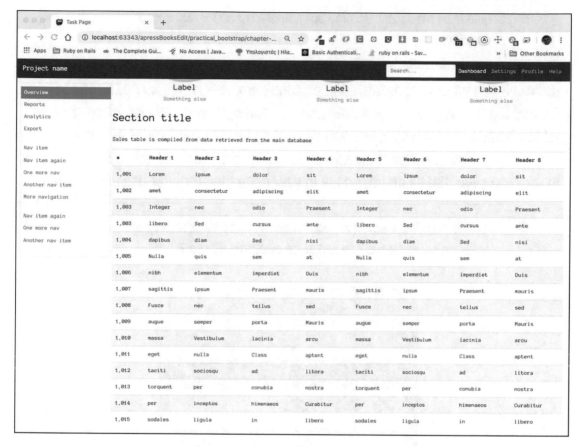

Figure 7-51. *Task—Admin Dashboard (Bottom Part of the Page)*

2. Things you need to take care of are as follows:

    - You need to use the font family Anonymous Pro. Look at Google Fonts for that.

    - The sidebar

1. Should not extend its height to be equal to the maximum height available

2. Should have transparent background color

3. Should have a color #eee border, solid and 1px all around it

4. Should have its border radius be 2px

5. Should have its position be fixed even if we scroll the main content area

6. Should have the position be left 10px and top 70px

7. Should have the dashboard area be composed of 300 × 300 image placeholders

---

Note   If you want to generate such placeholders, visit `https://placehold.it` and learn how you can generate one. For example, you can visit `https://placehold.it/450x450`, and you will get an image placeholder with the requested 450px × 450px dimensions. You can right-click and select `Save Image` in order to save that as an image file in your computer, for later use in your site.

---

8. When the page is displayed on extrasmall and small devices, only one information container per row should be displayed (Figure 7-52).

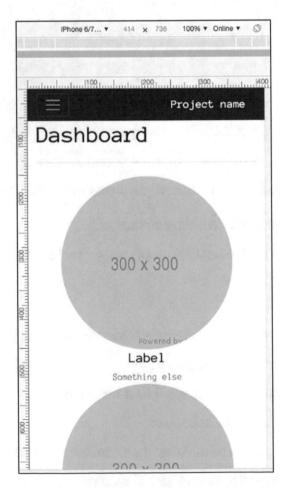

Figure 7-52. *One Information Container per Row on Extrasmall Devices*

9. When the page is displayed on medium devices, two information containers per row should be displayed (Figure 7-53).

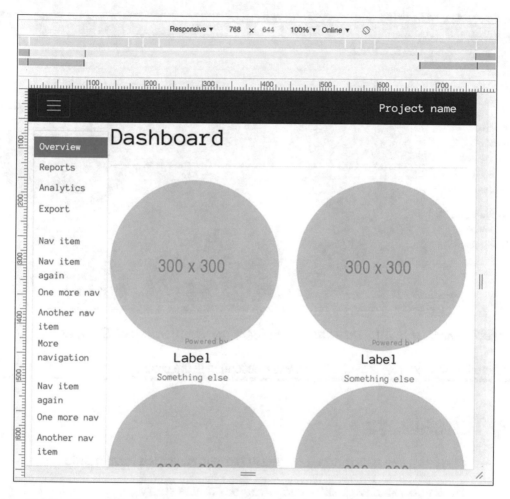

Figure 7-53. *Two Information Containers per Row on Medium Devices*

10. When the page is displayed on large and extralarge devices, three information containers per row should be displayed (Figure 7-54).

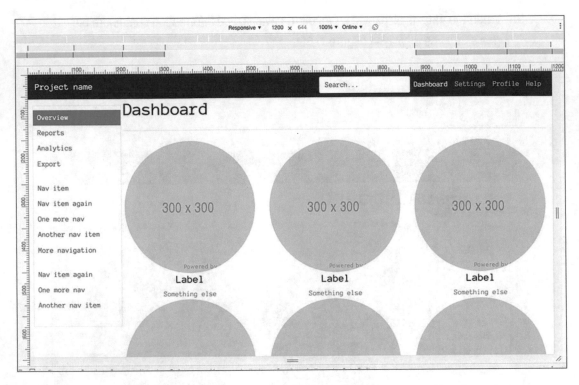

Figure 7-54. *Three Information Containers per Row on Large Devices*

Otherwise, the exercise is similar to the work described in the chapter.

Key Takeaways

- How you can have a top navigation bar with a search form inside

- How you can have a side navigation bar that is sticky

- How to hide parts of a page on small devices

- How to create circle-shaped images

- How to align content and make an admin dashboard

- How to create responsive tables

- Lots of other details and techniques to tune the layout of your page

In the following chapter, you will build stunning forms with Twitter Bootstrap.

CHAPTER 8

Forms

You have already learned about the HTML forms and each one of the form controls. Twitter Bootstrap gives you some extra tools in your hands, in the form of classes, that will allow you to style your forms very easily.

You will be able to build a basic form as in Figure 8-1

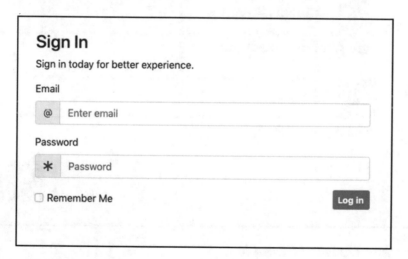

Figure 8-1. *Sign In Form Example*

or a form like the one in Figure 8-2.

© Panos Matsinopoulos 2020

P. Matsinopoulos, *Practical Bootstrap*, https://doi.org/10.1007/978-1-4842-6071-5_8

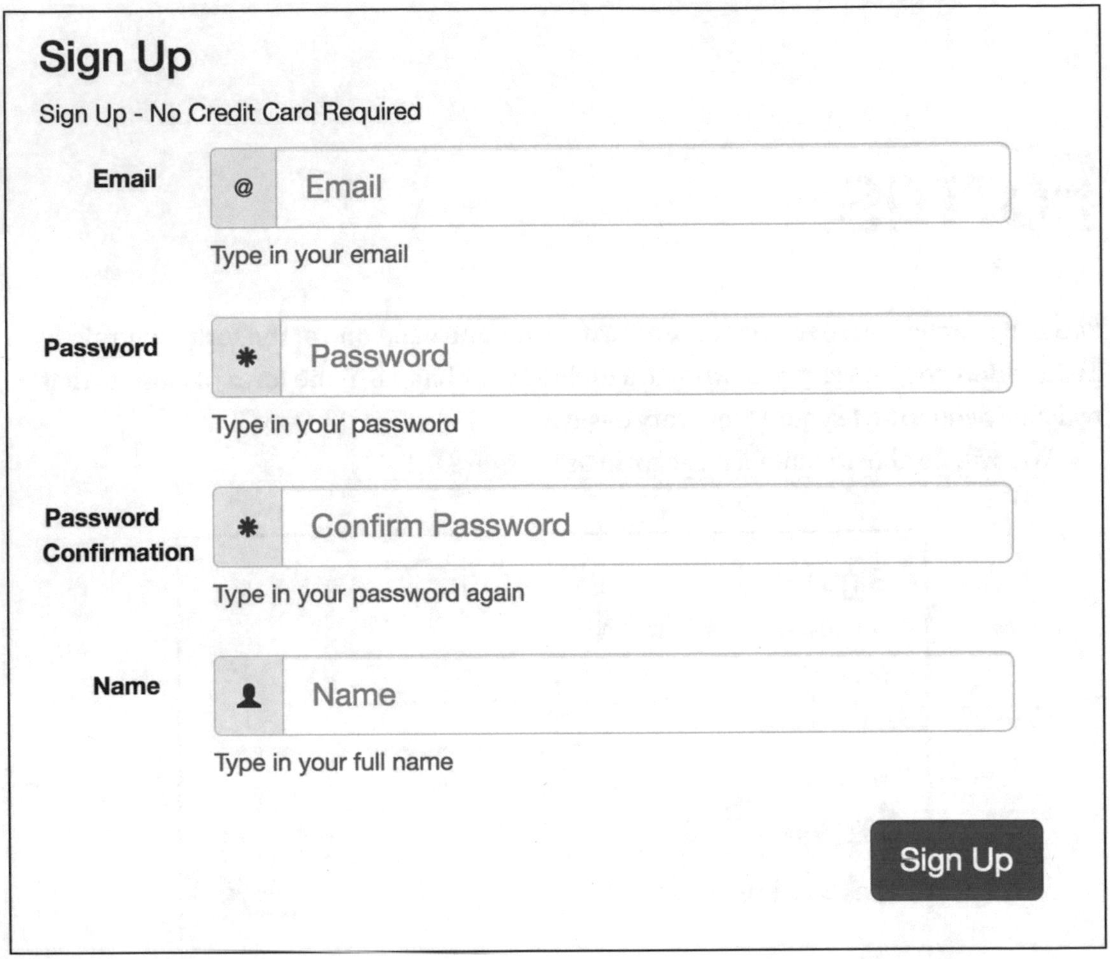

Sign Up

Sign Up - No Credit Card Required

| Email | @ | Email |

Type in your email

| Password | ✳ | Password |

Type in your password

| Password Confirmation | ✳ | Confirm Password |

Type in your password again

| Name | 👤 | Name |

Type in your full name

Sign Up

Figure 8-2. *Sign Up Form Example*

You will also be able to display, very intuitively, which fields have been filled in successfully and which ones not (Figure 8-3).

Figure 8-3. *Sign Up Form with an Error*

Learning Goals

1. Learn how to implement Twitter Bootstrap basic forms.

2. Learn about the Twitter Bootstrap horizontal forms.

3. Learn how the horizontal form uses the grid classes to lay out the labels and the input controls to different columns but on the same row.

4. Learn about Twitter Bootstrap inline forms.

5. Learn how you can display help text below an input control.

6. Learn about read-only controls.

7. Learn how you can display select boxes using Twitter Bootstrap.

8. Learn about the validations.

9. Learn how you can change the size of input controls.

10. Learn how you can group two controls together and create an input group.

Introduction

Twitter Bootstrap offers a series of classes that affect how forms and form controls are styled. In this chapter, you will design a Twitter Bootstrap Forms Reference page, in which you will lay out all the major facilities Twitter Bootstrap offers you with regard to this subject.

Let's start.

Empty Twitter Bootstrap Page

You will start with the standard empty Twitter Bootstrap page (Listing 8-1).

Listing 8-1. Empty Bootstrap Page

```
<!DOCTYPE html>
<html lang="en">
<head>
  <!-- Required meta tags -->
  <meta charset="utf-8">
  <meta name="viewport" content="width=device-width, initial-scale=1,
  shrink-to-fit=no">

  <!-- Bootstrap CSS -->
  <link rel="stylesheet" href="https://stackpath.bootstrapcdn.
  com/bootstrap/4.4.1/css/bootstrap.min.css" integrity="sha384-
  Vkoo8x4CGsO3+Hhxv8T/Q5PaXtkKtu6ug5TOeNV6gBiFeWPGFN9MuhOf23Q9Ifjh"
  crossorigin="anonymous">

  <!-- Custom CSS -->
  <link rel="stylesheet" href="stylesheets/main.css" type="text/css">

  <title>Twitter Bootstrap Forms Reference Page</title>
  <link rel="stylesheet" href="stylesheets/main.css">
</head>
```

```
<body>
  <div id="main-container" class="container">
    <!-- Content will be inserted here -->

  </div>

  <!-- Optional JavaScript -->
  <!-- jQuery first, then Popper.js, then Bootstrap JS -->
  <script src="https://code.jquery.com/jquery-3.4.1.slim.min.js"
  integrity="sha384-J6qa4849blE2+poT4WnyKhv5vZF5SrPoOiEjwBvKU7imGFAV0wwj1yY
  foRSJoZ+n" crossorigin="anonymous"></script>
  <script src="https://cdn.jsdelivr.net/npm/popper.js@1.16.0/dist/umd/
  popper.min.js" integrity="sha384-Q6E9RHvbIyZFJoft+2mJbHaEWldlvI9IOYy5n3zV
  9zzTtmI3UksdQRVvoxMfooAo" crossorigin="anonymous"></script>
  <script src="https://stackpath.bootstrapcdn.com/bootstrap/4.4.1/js/
  bootstrap.min.js" integrity="sha384-wfSDF2E50Y2D1uUdjOO3uMBJnjuUD4Ih7YwaY
  d1iqfktjOUod8GCExl3Og8ifwB6" crossorigin="anonymous"></script>
</body>
</html>
```

Save the preceding HTML content in the index.html file. Also, prepare an empty stylesheets/main.css file that will store your CSS rules. If you save those files and load the page on your browser, you will not see anything, because the body does not contain any content.

The intention is to add the whole content of your page inside a container div. That's why you can see inside the body the div with the class container.

Basic Form

You will start with the basic Twitter Bootstrap form. Add the following content inside the main-container element (Listing 8-2).

Listing 8-2. Basic Form

```
<div class="row">
    <div class="col-12 col-lg-6">
        <h3>Sign In</h3>
        <p>Sign in today for better experience.</p>

        <form>
            <div class="form-group">
                <label for="email">Email</label>
                <input type="email" id="email" placeholder="Enter email"
                class="form-control">
            </div>

            <div class="form-group">
                <label for="password">Password</label>
                <input type="password" id="password" placeholder="Password"
                class="form-control">
            </div>

            <div class="d-flex justify-content-between align-items-center">
                <div class="form-check">
                    <input type="checkbox" class="form-check-input"
                    id="remember-me-checkbox">
                    <label class="form-check-label" for="remember-me-
                    checkbox">Remember Me</label>
                </div>

                <button class="btn btn-sm btn-primary" type="submit">
                    <strong>Log in</strong>
                </button>
            </div>

        </form>
    </div> <!-- left column -->

    <div class="col-12 col-lg-6">

    </div> <!-- right column -->
</div> <!-- row inside main container -->
```

As you can read in the preceding code, you are going to create, initially, a two-column layout. The right column is empty, for the time being. The left column contains a header h3 and a small paragraph p. But the important stuff here is the form element.

This is a simple form element without any class attached to it. This is the basic form style that Twitter Bootstrap offers.

Things to point out here are the following:

1. Labels and inputs are grouped together in div. Each div has the class form-group. However, there is an exception for the checkbox-related div. It does not have this class. I will explain why in a while.

2. Each input control has the class form-control, except for the checkbox input, which has the class form-check-input.

3. You use the flexbox-related classes justify-content-between and align-items-center in order to position the checkbox and the login button on the same row. More explanation will be provided in the following.

4. The class form-check is used on a div that includes a checkbox.

5. The class form-check-label is used on the label that accompanies a checkbox.

Otherwise, anything else on the preceding code is pretty straightforward and does not use anything new.

If you save the preceding code and load the page on your browser, you will see the following (Figure 8-4).

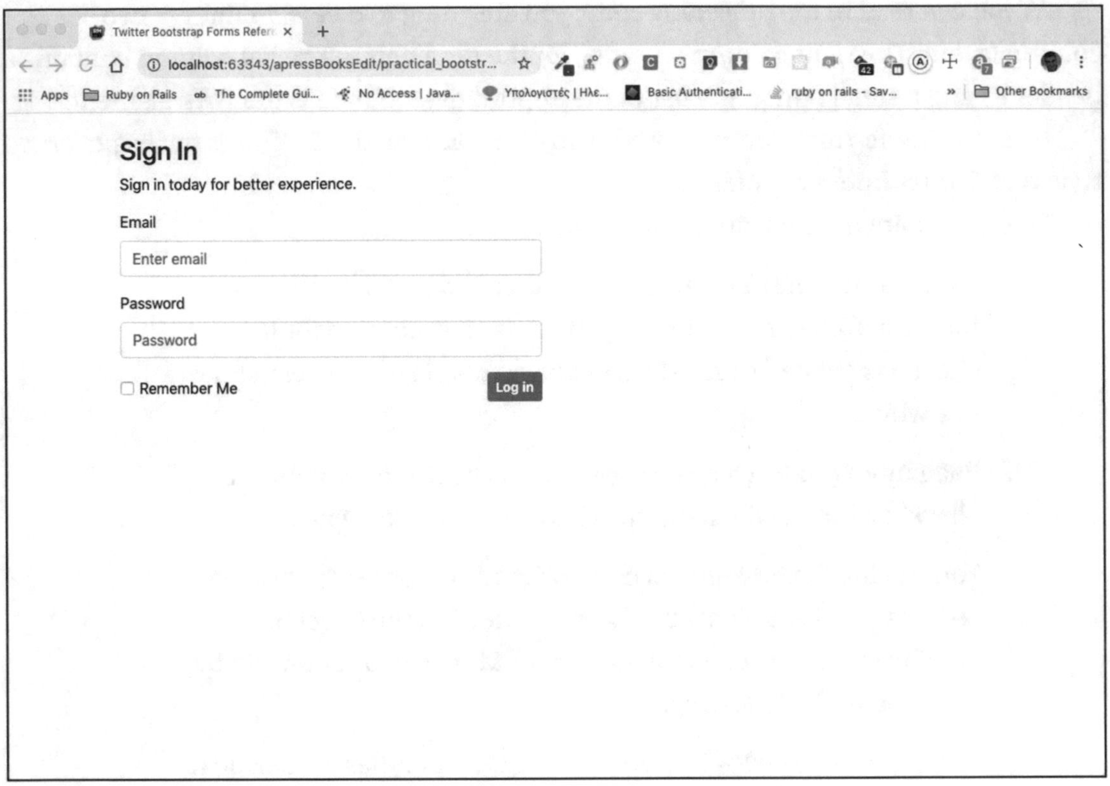

Figure 8-4. *Sign In Form*

As you can see, with a little more HTML on a standard form, you are getting a lot of things. See how input is highlighted when it gets the focus. Look how easy it was to move things left and right with the flexbox utility classes (Figure 8-5).

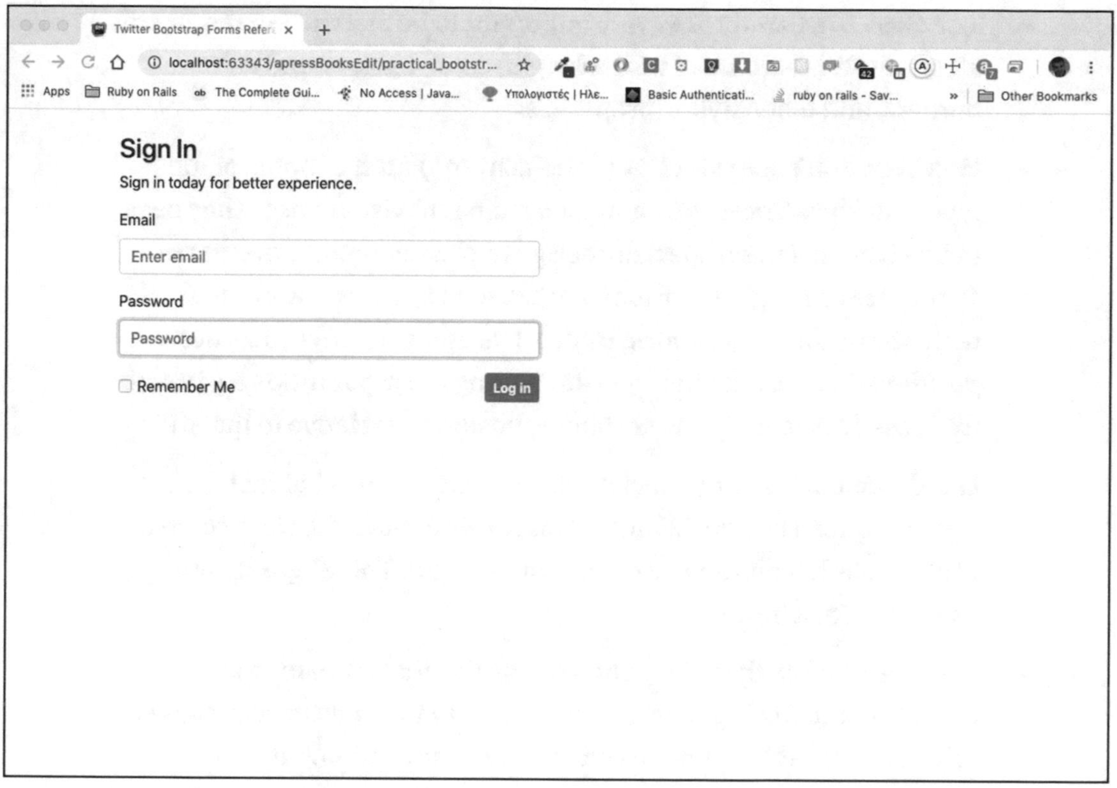

Figure 8-5. *Input highlighted when it gets the focus*

I will now give some more explanation about some of the classes you used in the previous code fragment:

- The class form-group does something very simple. It adds a bottom margin of value 1rem. Hence, it is useful if you have a vertical form, like in the example, in which the input and their labels flow in the vertical direction.

- The class form-check has been used for the input and label that have to do with the checkbox. The most important rule this class applies is a left padding of value 1.25rem. This makes the checkbox align left nicely with the other elements of the form in the vertical direction. You can, if you want, apply the form-group class too, especially if other controls follow below your first checkbox.

- The class form-control is very important to be attached to the input elements. It takes care of width, height, color, background color, borders, and other styling properties.

- However, don't use this class (form-control) for the inputs of the type checkbox. These are completely different visual-wise. They need to be given their own specially designed class named form-check-input. This class gives position absolute to the checkbox input, with no specific coordinates. Hence, it is drawn relative to its nearest *positioned*[1] ancestor. Since you are putting the input inside a div with the class form-check, it is absolutely positioned relative to that div.

- Labels do not take any special class, except for the label that accompanies a checkbox input. This needs to have the class form-check-label. It eliminates the bottom margin. This aligns it better with the actual input.

- The class d-flex that is attached on the div that contains the checkbox and the login button turns the div into a flexbox container. This means that it lays out its elements in a row direction. If you temporarily remove it, you will see the login button appearing below the checkbox input.

- The class justify-content-between takes the two child elements of the flexbox div and aligns them in the row direction so that they have blank space in between. Hence, one child is aligned left, and the other is aligned right.

- The class align-items-center aligns the children of a flex div but on the non-main axis direction. The default main axis is row (x, horizontal). Hence, the align-items-* class aligns the children in the column (y, vertical) axis direction. This particular one aligns them centrally.

---

[1]A positioned element is any element that does not have position static.

Horizontal Forms

The previous form had one row for the label and a separate row, below the label, for the input control. You have the alternative here to implement a horizontal form. This form has the label and the input control on the same row, occupying adjacent columns. The HTML markup is more complex and uses grid-related classes. Let's see how.

Add the following content inside the right column div (Listing 8-3).

Listing 8-3. Right Column div with Horizontal Form

```
<div class="col-12 col-lg-6">
    <h3>Sign In</h3>
    <p>Sign in today for better experience.</p>

    <form>
      <div class="form-group row">
        <label class="col-lg-2 col-form-label" for="email2">Email</label>
        <div class="col-lg-10">
          <input type="email" placeholder="Email" class="form-control"
          id="email2">
          <small class="form-text text-muted">Example block-level help text
          here.</small>
        </div>
      </div>

      <div class="form-group row">
        <label class="col-lg-2 col-form-label" for="password2">
        Password</label>
        <div class="col-lg-10">
          <input type="password" placeholder="Password" class="form-
          control" id="password2">
        </div>
      </div>
```

```
    <div class="form-group row justify-content-end">
      <div class="col-lg-10">
        <div class="form-check">
          <input type="checkbox" class="form-check-input" id="remember-
          me-checkbox-2">
          <label class="form-check-label" for="remember-me-checkbox-
          2">Remember Me</label>
        </div>
      </div>
    </div>

    <div class="form-group row justify-content-end">
      <div class="col-lg-10">
        <button class="btn btn-sm btn-secondary" type="submit">Sign in
        </button>
      </div>
    </div>
  </form>
</div> <!-- right column -->
```

Before I explain the HTML markup of Listing 8-3, let's save the HTML page and load it on your browser. You should see the following (Figure 8-6).

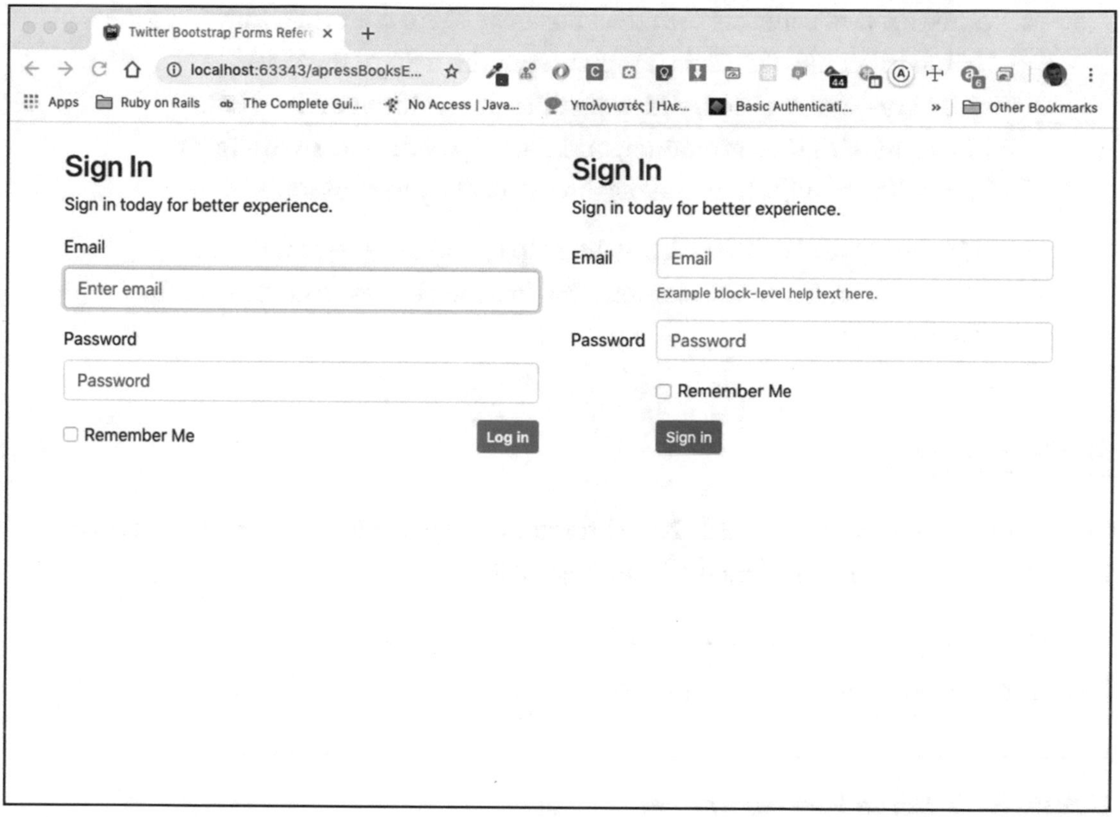

Figure 8-6. *Horizontal Form on the Right Column*

As you can see in Figure 8-6, the horizontal form divides each row into two columns, one for the label and one for the input control itself. Here are the things that you need to be aware of from the code:

1. Each form group (`div` with class `form-group`) now has an additional class `row`. This will allow us to use the grid feature of Bootstrap to lay out the children within each group.

2. The two labels, for email and password, occupy a two-column width. That's why they have `col-lg-2`. Note that they also need to have the class `col-form-label`. This class is specially designed to align the label vertically.

3. The two inputs, for email and password, are wrapped into a `div` with class `col-lg-10`, which makes them occupy the rest of the available horizontal space.

4. The row that contains the checkbox occupies a column width of ten, right aligned. This happens with the help of the class `justify-content-end`, which justifies the children of the `div` to the right of the flex container, and the help of the class `col-lg-10` at the inner `div`, which makes the `div` occupy ten columns.

5. Finally, notice how we create the help text below the email input. It is done with a `small` element that has the classes `form-text` and `text-muted`.

Inline Form

There are cases in which you only have one row to display all the input controls of a form. Here is an example of such a form (Figure 8-7).

Figure 8-7. *Inline Form Example*

You will create such a form below the two forms. Use Listing 8-4, and add it as the last child of the `div` with id `#main-container`.

Listing 8-4. Inline Form HTML Fragment

```
<div id="inline-form-container">
    <hr class="m-4">
    <form class="form-inline">
        <div class="form-group mr-sm-2">
            <label for="email3" class="mr-sm-2">Email address</label>
            <input type="email" placeholder="Enter email" id="email3"
            class="form-control">
        </div>
```

```
    <div class="form-group mr-sm-2">
        <label for="password3" class="mr-sm-2">Password</label>
        <input type="password" placeholder="Password" id="password3"
        class="form-control">
    </div>

    <div class="form-check mr-sm-2">
        <input type="checkbox" id="checkbox1" class="form-check-input">
        <label for="checkbox1" class="form-check-label">
            Remember me
        </label>
    </div>

    <button class="btn btn-primary" type="submit">Sign in</button>
    </form>
</div>
```

If you save the preceding code and reload the page on your browser, you will see the following (Figure 8-8).

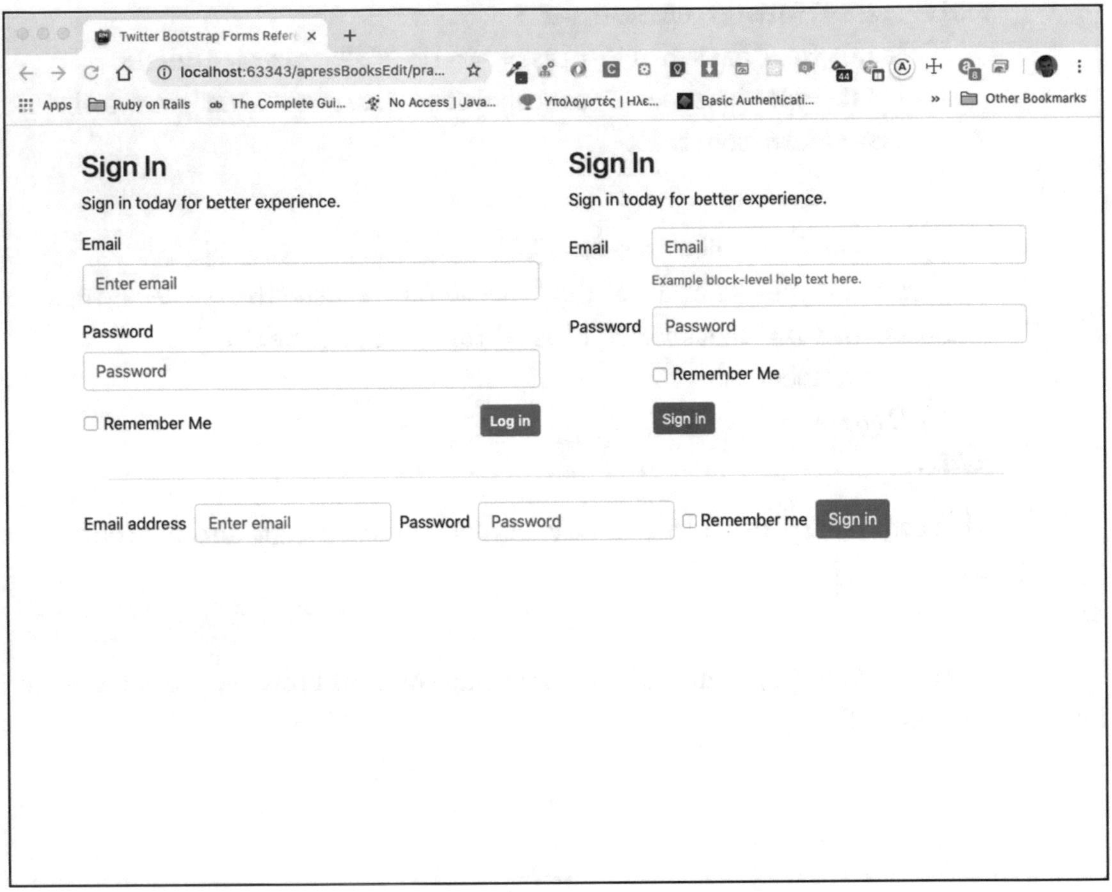

Figure 8-8. *Bootstrap Inline Form, at the Bottom*

The `form` tag needs to have the class `form-inline`. And this makes the whole difference. Otherwise, no form-related classes have been added other than the ones you already know. You have only used some margin utility classes, such as the class `mr-sm-2`. The only thing that these classes do is to add some margin in order to make the elements of the form have some free space around them.

Help Text

There are many times that an input control requires the user to enter a piece of information that is not very common. The UI needs to make sure that the user understands what they have to key in. The label helps. The placeholder helps too. But there are times that an extra hand of help is needed, in order to offer a more detailed explanation. In that case, you might want to use the tool that is called `Help Text`.

The help text, usually, appears below the input control; and it is a phrase explaining to the user what they have to key in.

Let's add the following piece of HTML code as the last elements inside the main container div (Listing 8-5).

Listing 8-5. Page with Help Text

```
<h3 class="mt-4">Other Form Elements</h3>
<hr class="my-4">

<form>
    <div>
        <em>Help Text</em>
        <hr class="my-3">
    </div>

    <div class="form-group row">
        <label for="help-text" class="col-lg-2 col-form-label">VAT number
        </label>
        <div class="col-lg-10">
            <input type="text" class="form-control" id="help-text"
            placeholder="Key in your VAT number"/>
            <small class="form-text text-muted">Give your company VAT
            number. Enter the VIES VAT number with the two char prefix
            indicating your country.</small>
        </div>
    </div>
</form>
```

Here is an explanation of the preceding HTML fragment:

1. You add a page header with title Other Form Elements. This is pretty much done with an h3 element with some top margin (class mt-4) and an hr element with some vertical margin (class my-4).

2. You are introducing a new form on your page. This will be a horizontal form and will be used to enclose a series of form elements that I would like to talk to you about.

3. Start with the Help Text. This is implemented with a simple
    small element that has the classes form-text and text-muted. It
    is positioned exactly after the input control that it accompanies.
    Other than that, there is nothing special to the preceding piece of
    code.

If you save the preceding code and load the page on your browser, you will see the
following (Figure 8-9).

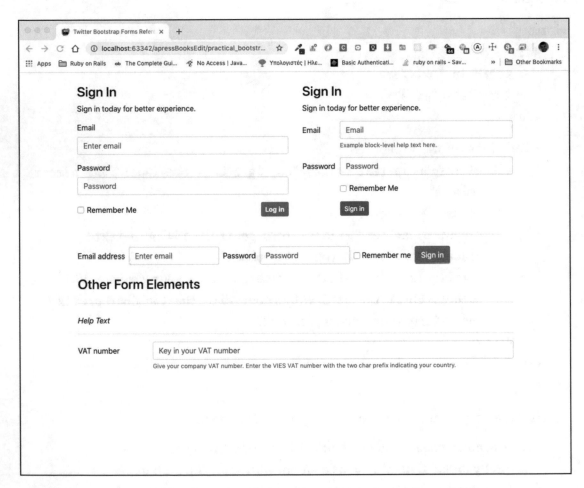

Figure 8-9.   *Start of the Other Form Elements Part of the Page*

Read-Only Plain Text

The plain text input control is used to represent a read-only piece of information, next to a label. Let's add the following HTML fragment as part of our last form (Listing 8-6).

Listing 8-6. Input Control as Read-Only Plain Text

```
<div>
    <em>Readonly Plain Text</em>
    <hr class="my-3">
</div>

<div class="form-group row">
    <label class="col-sm-2 col-form-label" for="readonly-email">Email:</label>
    <div class="col-sm-10">
        <input type="text" readonly class="form-control-plaintext"
        id="readonly-email" value="foo@bar.com">
    </div>
</div>
```

If you save the preceding code and load the page on your browser, you will see Figure 8-10.

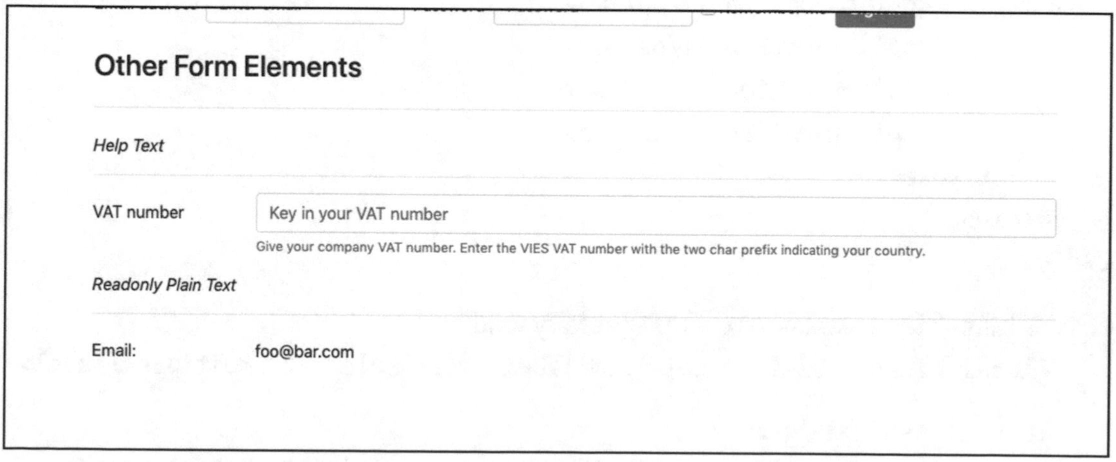

Other Form Elements

Help Text

VAT number   Key in your VAT number

Give your company VAT number. Enter the VIES VAT number with the two char prefix indicating your country.

Readonly Plain Text

Email: foo@bar.com

Figure 8-10. *Input Control as Read-Only Plain Text*

Do you see? The email input with value foo@bar.com has been styled so that it does not look like a normal input control. This is done with the help of the class form-control-plaintext. Otherwise, all the rest of the HTML markup is as you know it.

Select Boxes

There is nothing special with select boxes and Twitter Bootstrap. The only thing that you have to do is to attach the class form-control to the select element. Let's add the following HTML code as part of our last form (Listing 8-7).

Listing 8-7. Single and Multiple Select Box

```
<div>
    <em>Select Boxes</em>
    <hr class="my-3">
</div>

<div class="form-group row">
    <label class="col-lg-2 col-form-label" for="select-1">Single</label>

    <div class="col-lg-10">
        <select class="form-control" name="account" id="select-1">
            <option>option 1</option>
            <option>option 2</option>
            <option>option 3</option>
            <option>option 4</option>
        </select>
    </div>
</div>

<div class="form-group row flex-justify-end">
    <label class="col-lg-2 col-form-label" for="select-2">Multiple</label>

    <div class="col-lg-10">
        <select class="form-control" multiple="multiple" id="select-2">
            <option>option 1</option>
            <option>option 2</option>
            <option>option 3</option>
```

```
        <option>option 4</option>
      </select>
    </div>
</div>
```

That's pretty straightforward. There is nothing new here except for the fact that the select elements have the class form-control attached. If you save the page and reload it on your browser, you will see the following (Figure 8-11).

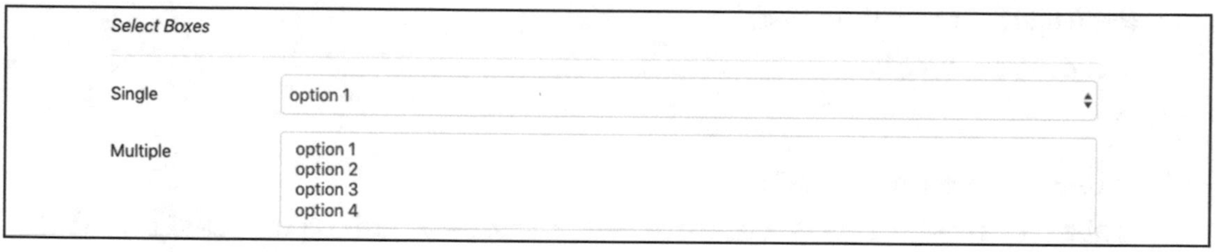

Select Boxes	
Single	option 1
Multiple	option 1 option 2 option 3 option 4

Figure 8-11. *Page Part with Select Boxes*

The class form-control styles the select boxes, similarly to the styling that other input controls get with this class.

Input Validation

There are many times that one wants to highlight the input controls that have been given erroneous input by the user. Or one may want to highlight the ones that had correct input. One way to do that is by coloring the input controls accordingly, for example, the erroneous inputs with red color.

Twitter Bootstrap offers a set of classes that are specially designed to deal with this. The classes are

1. is-valid

2. is-invalid

3. valid-feedback

4. invalid-feedback

You attach the class is-valid or is-invalid to the input you want to style as valid or invalid, respectively.

You attach the valid-feedback and invalid-feedback classes onto a div that holds a feedback message, for valid and invalid cases, respectively. This div needs to exist exactly below the input element, as the first direct sibling.

Let's add the following HTML code at the end of the form you are working on (Listing 8-8).

Listing 8-8. Input Validation

```
<div>
    <em>Input Validation</em>
    <hr class="my-4">
</div>

<div class="form-group row">
    <label class="col-lg-2 col-form-label" for="valid-input">Email</label>
    <div class="col-lg-10">
        <input type="email" class="form-control is-valid" id="valid-input"
        placeholder="Your username" value="foo@bar.com" required/>
        <div class="valid-feedback">
            Nice!
        </div>
    </div>
</div>

<div class="form-group row">
    <label class="col-lg-2 col-form-label" for="invalid-input">Password
    </label>
    <div class="col-lg-10">
        <input type="password" class="form-control is-invalid" id="invalid-
        input" placeholder="Your password" required>
        <div class="invalid-feedback">
            You have to give your password
        </div>
    </div>
</div>
```

If you save the preceding code and load the page on your browser, you will see the following (Figure 8-12).

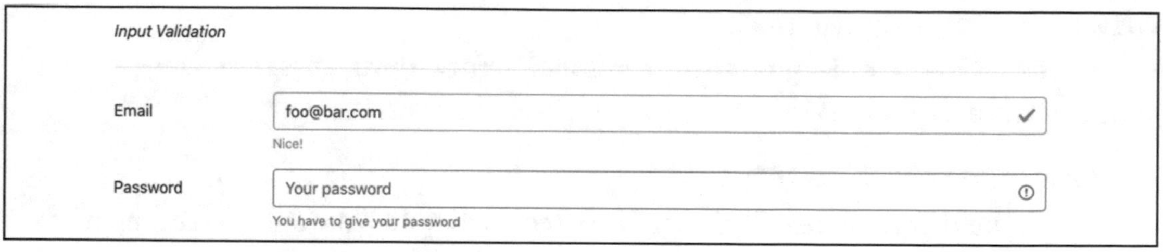

Input Validation		
Email	foo@bar.com	✓
	Nice!	
Password	Your password	ⓘ
	You have to give your password	

Figure 8-12. *Input Validation*

Do you see how valid and invalid inputs are styled? With the help of a small bunch of classes, Bootstrap allows you to do amazing work on styling.

Size of Input Controls

Twitter Bootstrap offers some very handy classes that relate to the size of input controls. You can use large controls, with the class `form-control-lg` attached to the input control. Or you can use small controls, with the class `form-control-sm` attached instead. Let's add the following piece of HTML code at the end of your form (Listing 8-9).

Listing 8-9. Different Input Control Sizes

```
<div>
    <em>Size of Input Controls</em>
    <hr class="my-4">
</div>

<div class="form-group row">
    <label class="col-lg-2 col-form-label" for="large-size-input">Large
    </label>

    <div class="col-lg-10">
        <input type="text" class="form-control form-control-lg" id="large-
        size-input"/>
    </div>
</div>
```

```
<div class="form-group row">
    <label class="col-lg-2 col-form-label" for="default-size-
input">Default</label>

    <div class="col-lg-10">
        <input type="text" class="form-control" id="default-size-input"/>
    </div>
</div>

<div class="form-group row">
    <label class="col-lg-2 col-form-label" for="small-size-input">Small
    </label>

    <div class="col-lg-10">
        <input type="text" class="form-control form-control-sm" id="small-
        size-input"/>
    </div>
</div>
```

If you save this and reload the page on your browser, you will see the following (Figure 8-13).

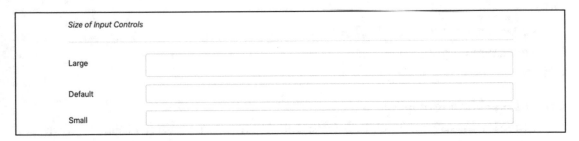

Figure 8-13. *Different Input Control Sizes*

The differences in sizes become more obvious if you try to add some input too (Figure 8-14).

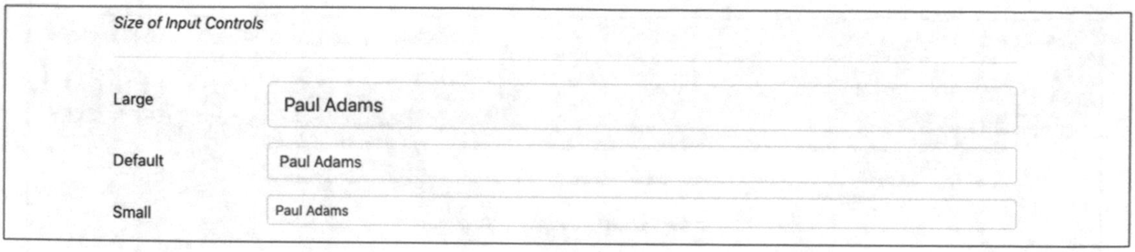
Size of Input Controls
Large
Paul Adams
Default
Paul Adams
Small
Paul Adams

Figure 8-14. Different Input Control Sizes with Some Input

Input Groups

Sometimes you want to create the following effect (Figure 8-15).

@
Username

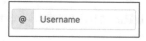

Figure 8-15. Input Group Example

This is an input group example. Other examples are the following two (Figure 8-16 and Figure 8-17).

.00

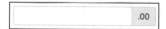

Figure 8-16. Decimals Input Group Example

$
.00

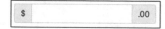

Figure 8-17. Dollars and Decimals Input Group Example

What you have here is a combination of a small label and a text input control (Figure 8-18).

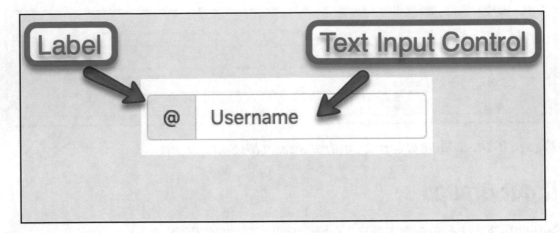

Figure 8-18. *Label and Input Control Grouped Together*

Combining these two (and, on the third example, three) controls into one is called input grouping.

Let's add the following code in your form (Listing 8-10).

Listing 8-10. Examples of Input Groups

```
<div>
    <em>Input Groups</em>
    <hr class="my-4">
</div>

<div class="row justify-content-end" id="input-groups-container">
    <div class="col-lg-10">

        <div class="input-group">
            <div class="input-group-prepend">
                <span class="input-group-text">@</span>
            </div>
            <input type="text" placeholder="Username" class="form-
            control"/>
        </div>

        <div class="input-group">
            <input type="text" class="form-control"/>
            <div class="input-group-append">
```

```
            <span class="input-group-text">.00</span>
        </div>
    </div>

    <div class="input-group">
        <div class="input-group-prepend">
            <span class="input-group-text">$</span>
        </div>
        <input type="text" class="form-control">
        <div class="input-group-append">
            <span class="input-group-text">.00</span>
        </div>
    </div>

    <div class="input-group">
        <div class="input-group-prepend">
            <div class="input-group-text">
                <input type="checkbox">
            </div>
        </div>
        <input type="text" class="form-control">
    </div>

    <div class="input-group">
        <div class="input-group-prepend">
            <div class="input-group-text">
                <input type="radio">
            </div>
        </div>
        <input type="text" class="form-control">
    </div>
    </div>
</div>
```

Also add the following CSS rule inside the stylesheets/main.css file:

```
#input-groups-container .input-group {
    margin-bottom: 1.2rem;
}
```

Save all the preceding code and reload the page on your browser. You will see the following (Figure 8-19).

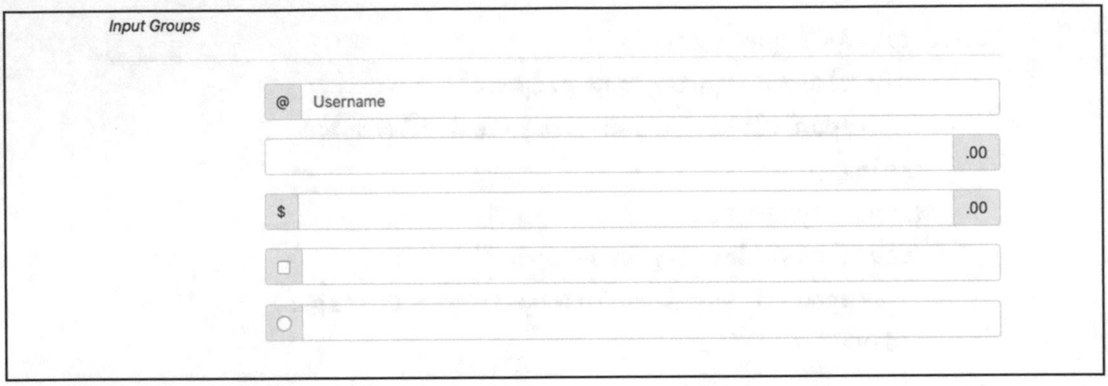

Figure 8-19. *Input Groups*

Let's see what makes the input group in the HTML code. I analyze the first input group which is this:

```
<div class="input-group">

  <div class="input-group-prepend">

    <span class="input-group-text">@</span>

  </div>

  <input type="text" placeholder="Username" class="form-control"/>

</div>
```

1. The input-group needs to be a div with class input-group.

2. The div needs to contain the input element. It is the place where the user will input their username, in our example.

3. The visual adornment is before the actual input. Hence, the input needs to be prepended with a div that has the class input-group-prepend.

4. This div, with class input-group-prepend, needs to have the adornment inside a span with class input-group-text.

Very easy!

Then you need to be watching of the following:

1. If the visual adornment needs to go after the input element, then its div class needs to be written after the input element, and its class needs to be input-group-append (instead of input-group-prepend).

2. You can have two visual adornments—one before and one after the main input control. You just use one div with class input-group-prepend before the main input control and another one with class input-group-append after it.

3. Make special provision for checkboxes and radio buttons inside the prepend or append part of the group. They should not be wrapped in a span, but they should be wrapped in a div.

Another variation of the preceding grouping is the grouping of an input control with a button. Add the following HTML code at the end of your form (Listing 8-11).

Listing 8-11. Input Group with a Button

```
<div>
    <em>Input & Button Groups</em>
    <hr class="my-4">
</div>

<div class="row justify-content-end">
    <div class="col-lg-10">
        <div class="input-group">
            <input type="text" class="form-control"/>
            <div class="input-group-append">
                <button type="button" class="btn btn-primary">Go!</button>
            </div>
        </div>
    </div>
</div>
```

If you save the preceding code and reload the page on your browser, you will see the following (Figure 8-20).

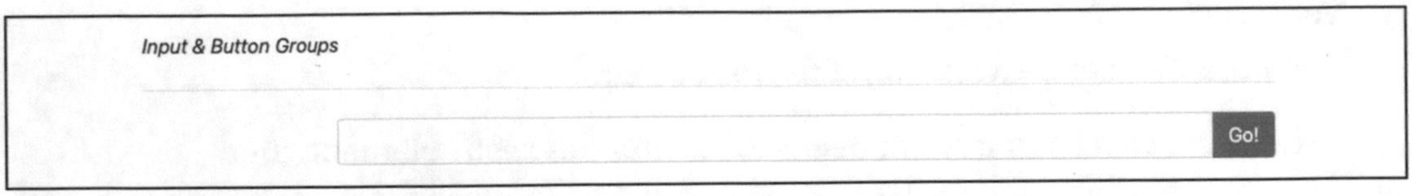

Figure 8-20. *Input and Button Group*

As you can see in the HTML code, the implementation is quite similar to the previous cases. The only difference is that you don't wrap the button inside any span or div with class input-group-text. You have the button as a direct and only child of the div with class input-group-prepend (or input-group-append).

Tasks and Quizzes

TASK DETAILS

1. You need to create one Twitter Bootstrap page with three forms on it.

2. The first form needs to be a sign in form like the following (Figure 8-21).

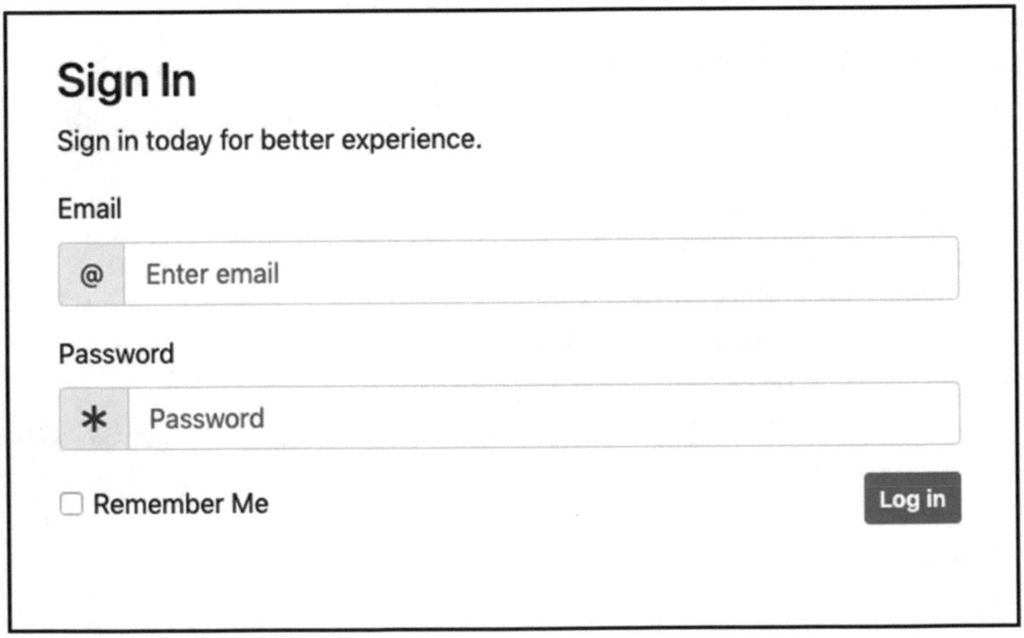

Figure 8-21. *Task: Sign In Form*

3. This is a basic Twitter Bootstrap form. The only difficulty that you may have is the symbol in the password input group. In order to add that, you will need to

   a. Import/reference the FontAwesome library with fonts in your project. The FontAwesome project explains exactly how you can do that.

   b. Add the HTML fragment that will represent the icon. It can be something like this:

   ```
   <i class="fas fa-asterisk"></i>
   ```

4. This needs to be followed by a second form, the sign up form, like the following (Figure 8-22).

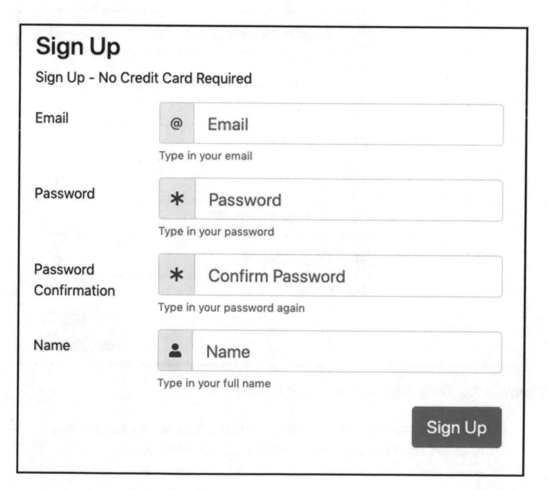

Figure 8-22. *Task: Sign Up Form*

5. Nothing is new here. Make sure that you use the correct FontAwesome icons for the passwords and the name fields.

6. Pay attention that the input controls are large.

7. The third form is the same as the second one, but all the input fields have been marked as valid or invalid. In fact, all are valid except for the password confirmation which is invalid (Figure 8-23).

Figure 8-23. *Task: Sign Up Form with Validations*

8. Note that on this third form, all input fields are populated with a value. You have to do that. Hint: Set the `value` attribute of the `input` HTML element.

9. Also, the red message "It does not match your password" is an invalid feedback. This needs to be a `div` element exactly next to the input control it accompanies, that is, the password confirmation input control.

Key Takeaways

- How to create stunning forms

- How to lay out the form inputs horizontally and vertically

- How to group the label and the input field and style them together

- How to group input with other visual adornments

- How to make small and large input controls

- How to display help text below the input controls

- How to show validation success and error inputs

- How to give validation feedback

- How to style read-only input controls

In the next chapter, I proceed to more dynamic pages. You will learn how to create modal dialogs.

CHAPTER 9

Modal Dialogs

In this chapter, you start to apply JavaScript to Twitter Bootstrap. You will see how Bootstrap provides very useful JavaScript libraries to help you add dynamic behavior to your web application, with as little effort as possible.

You start with modals, which are dialog windows that try to attract the user's attention and focus, like the one in Figure 9-1.

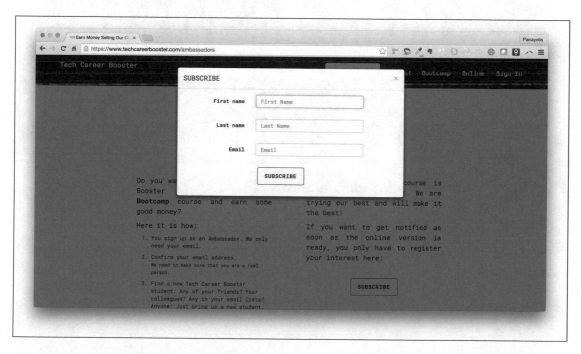

Figure 9-1. *Modal Dialog Example*

Then I explain how you integrate Twitter Bootstrap JavaScript libraries with your own HTML page.

You learn about the modal HTML markup and its main parts and how to create impressive modals with pictures, like the following (Figure 9-2).

© Panos Matsinopoulos 2020
P. Matsinopoulos, *Practical Bootstrap*, https://doi.org/10.1007/978-1-4842-6071-5_9

Figure 9-2. *Example Modal with Pictures*

Finally, you learn all about events related to modals, and you are asked to build a modal that handles related events. You will build a modal like the following (Figure 9-3).

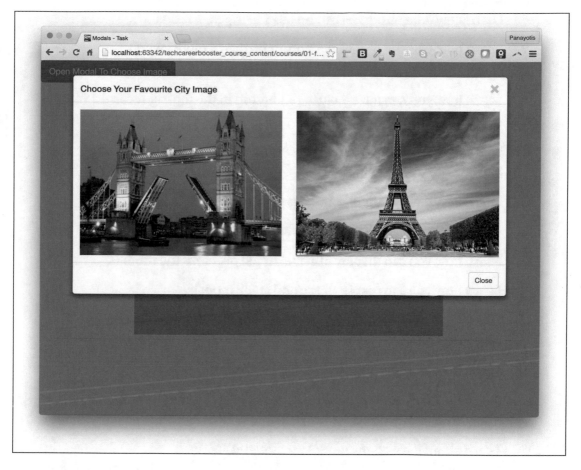

Figure 9-3. *Modal with Two Cities to Choose from*

Learning Goals

1. Learn about modals.

2. Learn how to reference the Twitter Bootstrap JavaScript files.

3. Learn about the bare-minimum HTML markup that introduces the modal functionality.

4. Learn which Twitter Bootstrap classes have to do with the modal functionality.

5. Learn about the main parts of the Twitter Bootstrap HTML markup.

6.   Learn how data attributes can be used to trigger a modal.

7.   Learn how you can program a button to open a modal when clicked.

8.   Learn how you can have a close [X] button in the top-right corner of the modal.

9.   Learn how you can use FontAwesome as an icon for the close button.

10.   Learn how you can display images on the modals.

11.   Learn how you can display YouTube videos on the modals.

12.   Learn how you can display other/external pages on the modals.

13.   Learn how you can display large and small modals.

14.   Learn how you can use the Twitter Bootstrap grid system inside the modal body.

15.   Learn how to activate modals using JavaScript.

16.   Learn how you can customize modal behavior by setting various options using JavaScript.

17.   Learn about the various modal methods available.

18.   Learn about the various modal events that you can hook event handlers on.

Introduction

Modals are a very user-friendly way to present information to the user or ask for information to be given. Modals are windows that overlay your page and do not allow the user to interact with other parts of your page. In other words, the user has to close the modal before returning back to the main page:

1.   Users can read the information and then close the modal. A modal can have a Close button or a [X] button in the top-right corner that closes it.

2. Users can fill in some form and then click the submit button of the form. This usually closes the modal and returns the user back to the main page.

Let's see a modal in action (Figure 9-4).

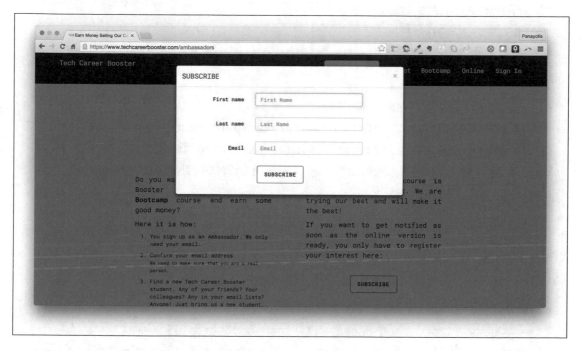

Figure 9-4. *Modal Example*

Twitter Bootstrap offers modals for free, as part of the JavaScript integration. Let's see how.

Bootstrap JavaScript Files

In order to be able to use modals, you will need to reference the Twitter Bootstrap JavaScript files. These need to be referenced **after** the jQuery JavaScript files.

The following is a bare-minimum HTML page that references Twitter Bootstrap and jQuery (Listing 9-1).

Listing 9-1. Empty Twitter Bootstrap Page with JavaScript

```html
<!DOCTYPE html>
<html lang="en">
<head>
  <!-- Required meta tags -->
  <meta charset="utf-8">
  <meta name="viewport" content="width=device-width, initial-scale=1,
  shrink-to-fit=no">

  <!-- Bootstrap CSS -->
  <link rel="stylesheet" href="https://stackpath.bootstrapcdn.
  com/bootstrap/4.4.1/css/bootstrap.min.css" integrity="sha384-
  Vkoo8x4CGsO3+Hhxv8T/Q5PaXtkKtu6ug5TOeNV6gBiFeWPGFN9MuhOf23Q9Ifjh"
  crossorigin="anonymous">

  <title>Modal Dialogs</title>

</head>
<body>

  <!-- Optional JavaScript -->
  <!-- jQuery first, then Popper.js, then Bootstrap JS -->
  <script src="https://code.jquery.com/jquery-3.4.1.slim.min.js"
  integrity="sha384-J6qa4849blE2+poT4WnyKhv5vZF5SrPo0iEjwBvKU7imGFAVOwwj1yY
  foRSJoZ+n" crossorigin="anonymous"></script>
  <script src="https://cdn.jsdelivr.net/npm/popper.js@1.16.0/dist/umd/
  popper.min.js" integrity="sha384-Q6E9RHvbIyZFJoft+2mJbHaEWldlvI9IOYy5n3zV
  9zzTtmI3UksdQRVvoxMfooAo" crossorigin="anonymous"></script>
  <script src="https://stackpath.bootstrapcdn.com/bootstrap/4.4.1/js/
  bootstrap.min.js" integrity="sha384-wfSDF2E50Y2D1uUdjOO3uMBJnjuUD4Ih7YwaY
  d1iqfktjOUod8GCExl3Og8ifwB6" crossorigin="anonymous"></script>
</body>
</html>
```

As you can read from the preceding code, you have to load three external files in order to use Twitter Bootstrap JavaScript libraries and components. See the correct order of loading them in Figure 9-5.

Figure 9-5. *Correct Order of Loading External JavaScript Libraries*

As you can see in Figure 9-5, I am using a reference to a CDN version of the Twitter Bootstrap JavaScript file. And I load it after the jQuery and Popper files, because Twitter Bootstrap JavaScript relies on jQuery and Popper.

Note that if you want to add custom, that is, your own, JavaScript files, you will have to put them at the correct position. Your own custom JavaScript file needs to be put after the third-party JavaScript files, hence after the Twitter Bootstrap JavaScript reference (Figure 9-6).

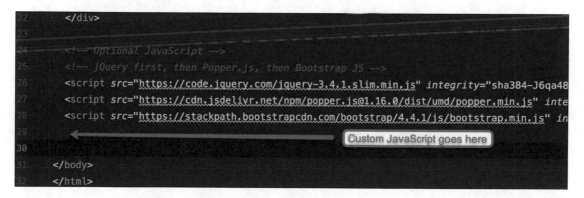

Figure 9-6. *Custom JavaScript File Correct Position*

Modal Markup

Having prepared the bare-minimum HTML page, let's add some modal functionality on it. Add the content of Listing 9-2 inside the body of the page, as the first child of the body element.

Listing 9-2. HTML Markup for a Modal

```
<div class="modal fade" tabindex="-1" role="dialog">
    <div class="modal-dialog">
        <div class="modal-content">
            <div class="modal-header">

                <h4 class="modal-title">This is an h4 inside Modal Header
                </h4>
                <button type="button" class="close" data-dismiss="modal"
                aria-label="Close"><span aria-hidden="true">&times;
                </span></button>
            </div>

            <div class="modal-body">

                <p>This is a paragraph inside Modal Body</p>

            </div>
            <div class="modal-footer">

                <button type="button" class="btn btn-default" data-
                dismiss="modal">Close</button>
                <button type="button" class="btn btn-primary">Save
                changes</button>

            </div>
        </div>
    </div>
</div>
```

If you save and load the page on your browser, you will see a blank page. This is because the modal is not meant to be displayed, unless the user chooses to do so or they carry out an action that triggers the display of the modal.

The classes that make the modal content invisible are the classes modal and fade. The modal adds a display:none; and the fade adds an opacity: 0.

See in the following picture how disabling these two properties makes the modal appear on the page (Figure 9-7).

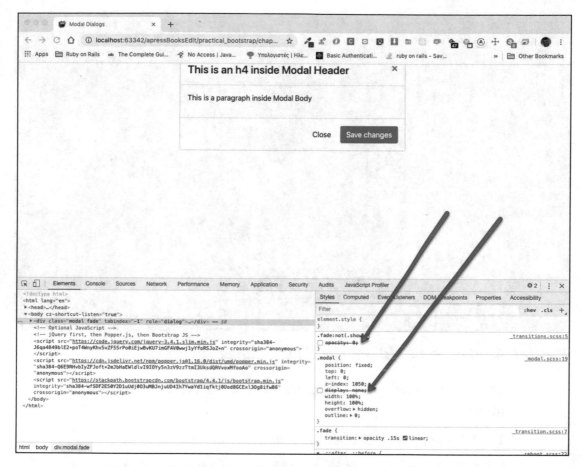

Figure 9-7. *Disabling Properties to Reveal the Modal*

All the modals have the same HTML markup. Its main parts are shown in Figure 9-8.

```
17    <body>
18
19    <div class="modal fade" tabindex="-1" role="dialog">
20      <div class="modal-dialog">
21        <div class="modal-content">
22          <div class="modal-header">
23
24            <button type="button" class="close" data-dismiss="modal" aria-label="Close"><span aria-hidden="true">&times;</sp
25            <h4 class="modal-title">This is an h4 inside Modal Header</h4>
26
27          </div>
28
29          <div class="modal-body">
30
31            <p>This is a paragraph inside Modal Body</p>
32
33          </div>
34          <div class="modal-footer">
35
36            <button type="button" class="btn btn-default" data-dismiss="modal">Close</button>
37            <button type="button" class="btn btn-primary">Save changes</button>
38
39          </div>
40        </div>
41      </div>
42    </div>
```

Figure 9-8. *Main Parts of the Modal HTML Markup*

- Three divs cascade each other, and they contain the actual content of
  the modal:

  1. A div with classes modal and fade

  2. A div inside the previous one (the one with class modal fade)
     with class modal-dialog

  3. A div inside the previous one (the one with class modal-
     dialog) with class modal-content

- There are three sibling divs, all children of the div with class modal-
  content, in the same nested level:

  1. A div for the modal header with class modal-header

  2. A div for the modal body with class modal-body

  3. A div for the modal footer with class modal-footer

Note that these last three parts are optional. Also, inside them, you can put (almost)
any HTML markup that you like.

Triggering the Modal

Modals are hidden until the user takes an action that would display them or until the web application decides that it has to display them. How does this trigger take place?

You will continue this example by introducing a button that would allow the user to open the modal dialog. Let's amend the HTML body content as follows:

```
<button class="btn btn-lg btn-success" data-toggle="modal" data-target=".
modal">Open Modal</button>
```

Add the preceding markup exactly before the modal starting div, below the <body> opening tag.

Save the HTML page and reload it on your browser. You will see the following (Figure 9-9).

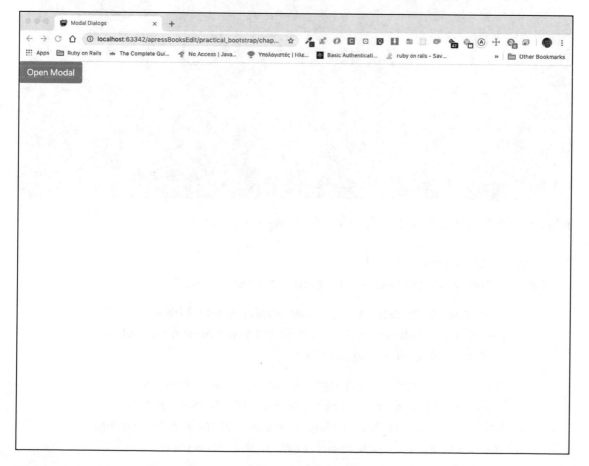

Figure 9-9. *Page with a Button to Open the Modal*

If you click the button Open Modal, you will see the following (Figure 9-10).

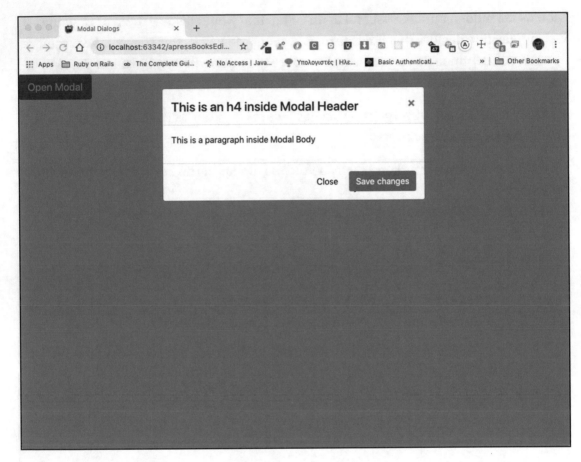

Figure 9-10. *Modal Displayed After Clicking the Button*

Perfect! This is what a modal is.

Let's explain some important details about the button markup:

1. It has the attribute data-toggle with value modal. This is
    necessary to indicate to Bootstrap that this is a button that, when
    clicked, will open a modal dialog.

2. It has the attribute data-target which has a value being a CSS
    selector and needs to uniquely select the HTML element that
    holds the modal HTML markup. In the modal you are developing,
    you have used the value modal, because this is the class that

uniquely matches the div holding your modal markup. Usually, here, you use a CSS selector that represents an id, rather than a class, in order to make the identification unique and avoid ambiguities.

Note that with this little HTML markup and using the data attributes that are identified by Twitter Bootstrap, you have managed to add dynamic behavior to your page. You didn't have to write any JavaScript. All this modal JavaScript functionality has been provided by the Twitter Bootstrap JavaScript library.

More on Modal Markup

Besides the standard HTML modal markup that I have talked about before, there are some other elements on the previous example that deserve your attention (Figure 9-11).

The Close [x] Button on the Top Right

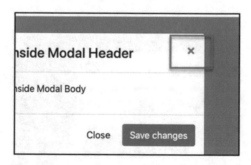

Figure 9-11. *The [x] Button*

The [x] button that you see in the top-right corner can be clicked by the user to close the modal dialog. Its markup has been put inside the modal-header div as follows:

```
<button type="button" class="close" data-dismiss="modal" aria-
label="Close">
  <span aria-hidden="true">&times;</span>
</button>
```

It is a button of class close with the data attribute data-dismiss equal to modal, instructing Twitter Bootstrap to close the modal if clicked. The actual icon appearing there is the <span aria-hidden="true">×</span>. The × entity element is a special character displayed as the cross [x].

Inside the button, you can use any HTML that can suit there and that can indicate to the user the ability to close the modal. For example, you can use a FontAwesome icon. Let's try to use one of them. Replace the HTML markup <span aria-hidden="true">×</span> with

<i aria-hidden="true" class="fas fa-window-close"></i>.

Also, at the bottom of your page, before the Bootstrap JavaScript file is referenced, add a reference to the FontAwesome special kit designed for your account. It should be a line like this:

<script src="https://kit.fontawesome.com/**your-account-kid-id**>.js" crossorigin="anonymous"></script>

Save, reload the page, and open the modal. You will see the following (Figure 9-12).

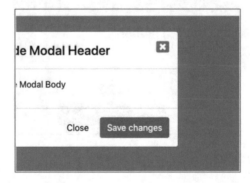

Figure 9-12. *A FontAwesome Icon Is Used as the Modal Close Button*

Note   Creating an account on FontAwesome is quite easy. You visit the page https://fontawesome.com, and you sign up. Then you need to create a kit. The site will give you directions on how to get your kit identifier in order to reference/ use it in your HTML page.

The Close [Close] Button at the Bottom

There is a button inside the modal-footer div that works like the one in the top-right corner. It closes the modal dialog. Its markup is

```
<button type="button" class="btn btn-default" data-dismiss="modal">Close
</button>
```

Again, the important thing is that it has the data attribute data-dismiss equal to modal which makes it function as a modal close button.

Note   The Save changes is a button that does nothing. I have not attached a functionality to it.

Adding an Image

As I have said earlier, you can add (almost) any HTML content inside the modal. Let's see the following HTML page (Listing 9-3).

Listing 9-3. HTML for a Modal with Image

```
<!DOCTYPE html>
<html lang="en">
<head>
  <!-- Required meta tags -->
  <meta charset="utf-8">
  <meta name="viewport" content="width=device-width, initial-scale=1,
  shrink-to-fit=no">

  <!-- Bootstrap CSS -->
  <link rel="stylesheet" href="https://stackpath.bootstrapcdn.
  com/bootstrap/4.4.1/css/bootstrap.min.css" integrity="sha384-
  Vkoo8x4CGsO3+Hhxv8T/Q5PaXtkKtu6ug5TOeNV6gBiFeWPGFN9MuhOf23Q9Ifjh"
  crossorigin="anonymous">
```

```
  <!-- Custom CSS -->
  <link rel="stylesheet" href="stylesheets/main.css" type="text/css">

  <title>Modal Dialogs</title>
</head>
<body>

  <button class="btn btn-lg btn-success" data-toggle="modal" data-target=".
  modal">Open Modal</button>

  <div class="modal fade" tabindex="-1" role="dialog">
    <div class="modal-dialog">
      <div class="modal-content">
        <div class="modal-header">

          <h4 class="modal-title">Zakynthos - Shipwreck</h4>
          <button type="button" class="close" data-dismiss="modal" aria-
          label="Close">
            <span>&times;</span>
          </button>

        </div>

        <div class="modal-body">

          <img src="images/zakynthos-shipwreck.jpg" alt="Zakynthos
          Shipwreck"/>

        </div>
        <div class="modal-footer">

          <button type="button" class="btn btn-default" data-
          dismiss="modal">Close</button>
          <button type="button" class="btn btn-primary">Save changes
          </button>

        </div>
      </div>
    </div>
  </div>
```

```
<!-- jQuery first, then Popper.js, then Bootstrap JS -->
<script src="https://code.jquery.com/jquery-3.4.1.slim.min.js"
integrity="sha384-J6qa4849blE2+poT4WnyKhv5vZF5SrPo0iEjwBvKU7imGFAVOwwj1yY
foRSJoZ+n" crossorigin="anonymous"></script>
<script src="https://cdn.jsdelivr.net/npm/popper.js@1.16.0/dist/umd/
popper.min.js" integrity="sha384-Q6E9RHvbIyZFJoft+2mJbHaEWldlvI9IOYy5n3zV
9zzTtmI3UksdQRVvoxMfooAo" crossorigin="anonymous"></script>
<script src="https://stackpath.bootstrapcdn.com/bootstrap/4.4.1/js/
bootstrap.min.js" integrity="sha384-wfSDF2E50Y2D1uUdj0O3uMBJnjuUD4Ih7YwaY
d1iqfktj0Uod8GCExl3Og8ifwB6" crossorigin="anonymous"></script>
</body>
</html>
```

If you read the HTML, you will see that the modal-body div contains only an img element.

Also, note that there is a reference to an external custom stylesheets file named stylesheets/main.css. Please, add the following CSS rule inside. It will add a border around the image:

```
img {
    border: 1px solid Darkblue;
}
```

If you save and load this page on your browser, you will see the following (Figure 9-13).

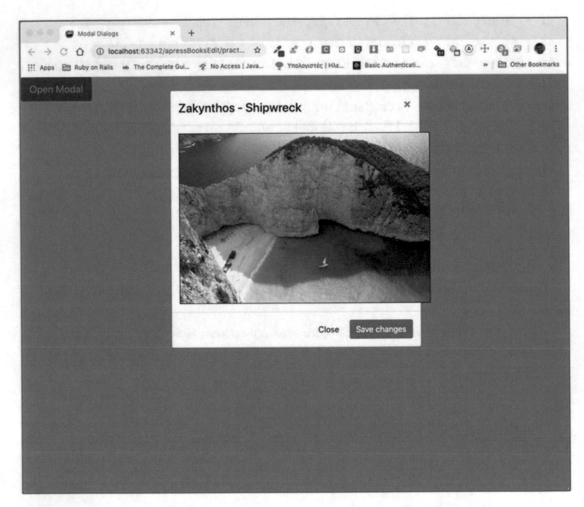

Figure 9-13. *Modal with the img Element—Problem with Wide Images*

As you can see, there is a problem with the image. It expands beyond the boundaries of the modal. In order to fix that, you have to attach the class img-fluid on the img element. Do that and reload the page. You will see the following (Figure 9-14).

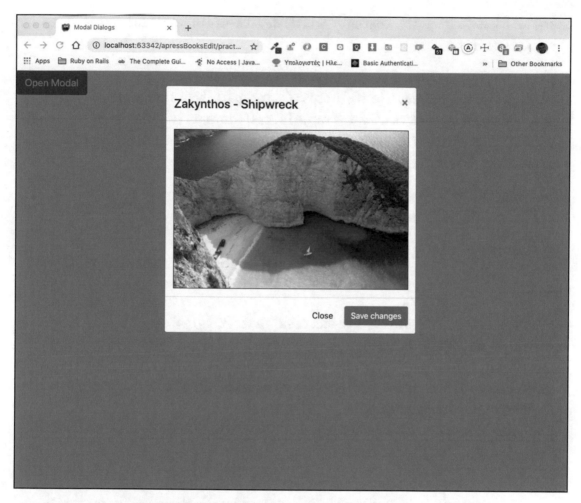

Figure 9-14. *Image Displayed Correctly Inside the Modal*

Adding a YouTube Video

Like you did for the image, you can similarly add a YouTube embedded video reference.
Try the following HTML (Listing 9-4).

Listing 9-4. Embedding a YouTube Video

```
<!DOCTYPE html>
<html lang="en">
<head>
  <!-- Required meta tags -->
  <meta charset="utf-8">
```

```
  <meta name="viewport" content="width=device-width, initial-scale=1,
  shrink-to-fit=no">

  <!-- Bootstrap CSS -->
  <link rel="stylesheet" href="https://stackpath.bootstrapcdn.
  com/bootstrap/4.4.1/css/bootstrap.min.css" integrity="sha384-
  Vkoo8x4CGsO3+Hhxv8T/Q5PaXtkKtu6ug5TOeNV6gBiFeWPGFN9MuhOf23Q9Ifjh"
  crossorigin="anonymous">

  <!-- Custom CSS -->
  <link rel="stylesheet" href="stylesheets/main.css" type="text/css">

  <title>Modal Dialogs</title>
</head>
<body>

  <button class="btn btn-lg btn-success" data-toggle="modal" data-target=".
  modal">Open Modal</button>

  <div class="modal fade" tabindex="-1" role="dialog">
    <div class="modal-dialog">
      <div class="modal-content">
        <div class="modal-header">

          <h4 class="modal-title">Zakynthos - Shipwreck</h4>
          <button type="button" class="close" data-dismiss="modal" aria-
          label="Close">
            <span>&times;</span>
          </button>

        </div>

        <div class="modal-body">

          <iframe width="100%" height="315" src="https://www.youtube.com/
          embed/tqy0Uvw_bFU" frameborder="0" allowfullscreen></iframe>

        </div>
```

```
    <div class="modal-footer">

        <button type="button" class="btn btn-default" data-
        dismiss="modal">Close</button>
        <button type="button" class="btn btn-primary">Save changes
        </button>

    </div>
   </div>
  </div>
</div>

<!-- jQuery first, then Popper.js, then Bootstrap JS -->
<script src="https://code.jquery.com/jquery-3.4.1.slim.min.js"
integrity="sha384-J6qa4849blE2+poT4WnyKhv5vZF5SrPo0iEjwBvKU7imGFAVOwwj1yY
foRSJoZ+n" crossorigin="anonymous"></script>
<script src="https://cdn.jsdelivr.net/npm/popper.js@1.16.0/dist/umd/
popper.min.js" integrity="sha384-Q6E9RHvbIyZFJoft+2mJbHaEWldlvI9IOYy5n3zV
9zzTtmI3UksdQRVvoxMfooAo" crossorigin="anonymous"></script>
<script src="https://stackpath.bootstrapcdn.com/bootstrap/4.4.1/js/
bootstrap.min.js" integrity="sha384-wfSDF2E50Y2D1uUdj0O3uMBJnjuUD4Ih7YwaY
d1iqfktj0Uod8GCExl3Og8ifwB6" crossorigin="anonymous"></script>
</body>
</html>
```

As you can read in the preceding code, you can embed a YouTube video with the use of an `iframe` element. Make sure that `width` is set to 100% and `height` to reasonable height that will keep your video displaying with the correct aspect ratio. Note that YouTube gives you the code for the `iframe` element, when you choose to share a video via embedding. You only have to tune the width and height attributes so that the video is displayed nicely inside your modal.

If you save the preceding HTML and load the page on your browser, you will see the following (Figure 9-15).

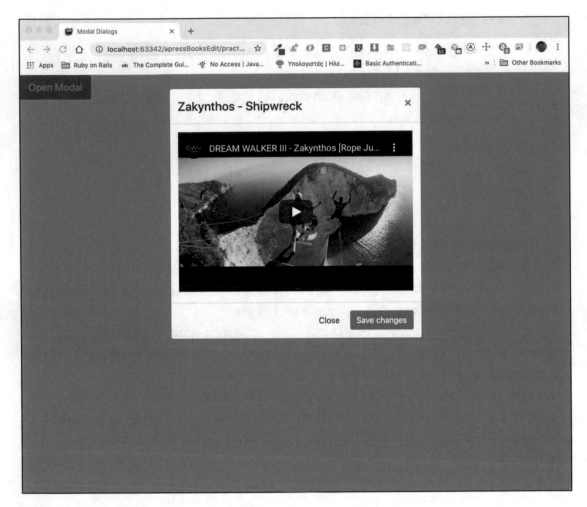

Figure 9-15. *Modal with a YouTube Video*

Optional Sizes

Twitter Bootstrap offers three optional sizes for your modals:

1. Extralarge modals: You need to append the class modal-xl next to the modal-dialog class. It basically sets the modal max-width to 1140px.

2. Large modals: You need to append the class modal-lg next to the modal-dialog class. It sets the max-width to 800px.

3. Small modals: You need to append the class modal-sm next to the modal-dialog class. It sets the max-width to 300px.

If you don't specify any of the preceding size classes, then the default sets the max-width to 500px.

The next one is a modal demo for a large size (Listing 9-5).

Listing 9-5. Large Modal Demo

```
<!DOCTYPE html>
<html lang="en">
<head>
  <!-- Required meta tags -->
  <meta charset="utf-8">
  <meta name="viewport" content="width=device-width, initial-scale=1,
  shrink-to-fit=no">

  <!-- Bootstrap CSS -->
  <link rel="stylesheet" href="https://stackpath.bootstrapcdn.
  com/bootstrap/4.4.1/css/bootstrap.min.css" integrity="sha384-
  Vkoo8x4CGsO3+Hhxv8T/Q5PaXtkKtu6ug5TOeNV6gBiFeWPGFN9MuhOf23Q9Ifjh"
  crossorigin="anonymous">

  <!-- Custom CSS -->
  <link rel="stylesheet" href="stylesheets/main.css" type="text/css">

  <title>Modal Dialogs</title>
</head>
<body>

  <button class="btn btn-lg btn-success" data-toggle="modal" data-target=".
  modal">Open Modal</button>

  <div class="modal fade" tabindex="-1" role="dialog">
    <div class="modal-dialog modal-lg">
      <div class="modal-content">
        <div class="modal-header">

          <h4 class="modal-title">Zakynthos from Wikipedia</h4>
          <button type="button" class="close" data-dismiss="modal" aria-
          label="Close">
            <span>&times;</span>
```

```
        </button>

      </div>

      <div class="modal-body">

        <iframe width="100%" height="400" src="https://en.wikipedia.org/
        wiki/Zakynthos" id="frame-in-modal"></iframe>

      </div>
      <div class="modal-footer">

        <button type="button" class="btn btn-default" data-
        dismiss="modal">Close</button>
        <button type="button" class="btn btn-primary">Save changes
        </button>

      </div>
    </div>
  </div>
</div>

<!-- jQuery first, then Popper.js, then Bootstrap JS -->
<script src="https://code.jquery.com/jquery-3.4.1.slim.min.js"
integrity="sha384-J6qa4849blE2+poT4WnyKhv5vZF5SrPo0iEjwBvKU7imGFAVOwwj1yY
foRSJoZ+n" crossorigin="anonymous"></script>
<script src="https://cdn.jsdelivr.net/npm/popper.js@1.16.0/dist/umd/
popper.min.js" integrity="sha384-Q6E9RHvbIyZFJoft+2mJbHaEWldlvI9IOYy5n3zV
9zzTtmI3UksdQRVvoxMfooAo" crossorigin="anonymous"></script>
<script src="https://stackpath.bootstrapcdn.com/bootstrap/4.4.1/js/
bootstrap.min.js" integrity="sha384-wfSDF2E50Y2D1uUdj0O3uMBJnjuUD4Ih7YwaY
d1iqfktj0Uod8GCExl3Og8ifwB6" crossorigin="anonymous"></script>
</body>
</html>
```

If you save the files of this page and load it on your browser, you will see the following (Figure 9-16).

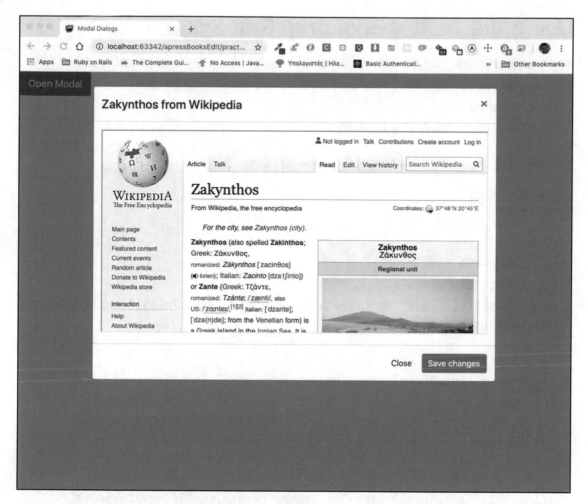

Figure 9-16. *Large Modal Demo*

Remove Animation

If you have noticed, when you open the modal, it animates from top to bottom. You can remove this animation and make the modal appear at once, by removing the class fade from the top-level div container.

Try that by removing the fade class from the previous example. You will see the modal appearing without top fade in animation.

Using the Twitter Bootstrap Grid System

You can use the Twitter Bootstrap grid system inside the body of the modal. Use
`container-fluid` and then `row` and `column-xx-x` classes appropriately inside the `modal-body` div container.

Let's see an example (Listing 9-6).

Listing 9-6. Grid System Inside the Modal Body

```
<!DOCTYPE html>
<html lang="en">
<head>
  <!-- Required meta tags -->
  <meta charset="utf-8">
  <meta name="viewport" content="width=device-width, initial-scale=1,
  shrink-to-fit=no">

  <!-- Bootstrap CSS -->
  <link rel="stylesheet" href="https://stackpath.bootstrapcdn.
  com/bootstrap/4.4.1/css/bootstrap.min.css" integrity="sha384-
  Vkoo8x4CGsO3+Hhxv8T/Q5PaXtkKtu6ug5TOeNV6gBiFeWPGFN9MuhOf23Q9Ifjh"
  crossorigin="anonymous">

  <!-- Custom CSS -->
  <link rel="stylesheet" href="stylesheets/main.css" type="text/css">

  <title>Modal Dialogs</title>
</head>
<body>

  <button class="btn btn-lg btn-success" data-toggle="modal" data-target=".
  modal">Open Modal</button>

  <div class="modal fade" tabindex="-1" role="dialog">
    <div class="modal-dialog modal-lg">
      <div class="modal-content">
        <div class="modal-header">

          <h4 class="modal-title">Zakynthos from Wikipedia</h4>
```

```
  <button type="button" class="close" data-dismiss="modal" aria-
  label="Close">
    <span>&times;</span>
  </button>

</div>

<div class="modal-body">

  <div class="container-fluid">
    <div class="row">
      <div class="col-md-6">
        <img src="images/ithaki-1.jpg" alt="Ithaki"/>
      </div>
      <div class="col-md-6">
        <img src="images/elafonisos-2.jpg" alt="Elafonisos"/>
      </div>
    </div>

    <div class="row">
      <div class="col-md-6">
        <img src="images/karpathos-3.jpg" alt="Karpathos"/>
      </div>
      <div class="col-md-6">
        <img src="images/chios-4.jpg" alt="Chios"/>
      </div>
    </div>
  </div>

</div> <!-- modal body -->

<div class="modal-footer">

  <button type="button" class="btn btn-default" data-
  dismiss="modal">Close</button>
  <button type="button" class="btn btn-primary">Save change
  s</button>

</div>
```

```
      </div>
    </div>
  </div>

  <!-- jQuery first, then Popper.js, then Bootstrap JS -->
  <script src="https://code.jquery.com/jquery-3.4.1.slim.min.js"
  integrity="sha384-J6qa4849blE2+poT4WnyKhv5vZF5SrPo0iEjwBvKU7imGFAVOwwj1yY
  foRSJoZ+n" crossorigin="anonymous"></script>
  <script src="https://cdn.jsdelivr.net/npm/popper.js@1.16.0/dist/umd/
  popper.min.js" integrity="sha384-Q6E9RHvbIyZFJoft+2mJbHaEWldlvI9IOYy5n3zV
  9zzTtmI3UksdQRVvoxMfooAo" crossorigin="anonymous"></script>
  <script src="https://stackpath.bootstrapcdn.com/bootstrap/4.4.1/js/
  bootstrap.min.js" integrity="sha384-wfSDF2E50Y2D1uUdj0O3uMBJnjuUD4Ih7YwaY
  d1iqfktj0Uod8GCExl3Og8ifwB6" crossorigin="anonymous"></script>
</body>
</html>
```

Here's the CSS:

```
img {
    padding: 10px 10px;
    width: 100%;
    height: 250px;
}
```

If you save the preceding code and load the page on your browser, when you open the modal, you will see the following (Figure 9-17).

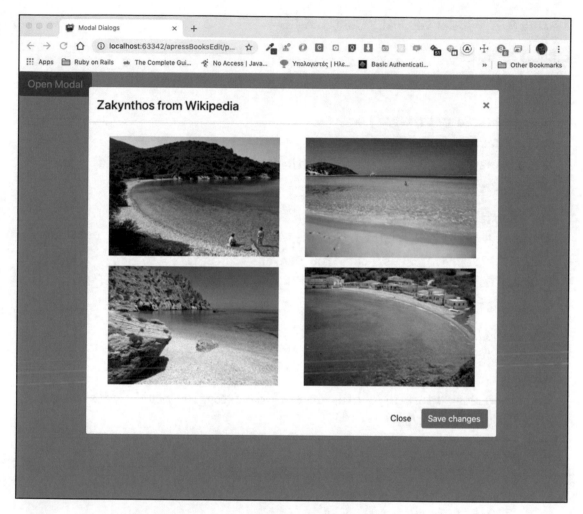

Figure 9-17. *Grid System Used Inside the Modal Body*

Vertically Centered

The default behavior of the modal is to appear at the top side of the page. If you want to make the modal appear in the middle, that is, vertically aligned, then you have to attach the class `modal-dialog-centered` next to the `modal-dialog` class.

Listing 9-7 demonstrates that.

Listing 9-7. Modal Vertically Centered

```
<!DOCTYPE html>
<html lang="en">
<head>
  <!-- Required meta tags -->
  <meta charset="utf-8">
  <meta name="viewport" content="width=device-width, initial-scale=1,
  shrink-to-fit=no">

  <!-- Bootstrap CSS -->
  <link rel="stylesheet" href="https://stackpath.bootstrapcdn.
  com/bootstrap/4.4.1/css/bootstrap.min.css" integrity="sha384-
  Vkoo8x4CGsO3+Hhxv8T/Q5PaXtkKtu6ug5TOeNV6gBiFeWPGFN9MuhOf23Q9Ifjh"
  crossorigin="anonymous">

  <title>Modal Dialogs</title>
</head>
<body>
  <button class="btn btn-lg btn-success" data-toggle="modal" data-target=".
  modal">Open Modal</button>

  <div class="modal fade" tabindex="-1" role="dialog">
    <div class="modal-dialog modal-dialog-centered">
      <div class="modal-content">
        <div class="modal-header">

          <h4 class="modal-title">This is an h4 inside Modal Header</h4>
          <button type="button" class="close" data-dismiss="modal" aria-
          label="Close"><span aria-hidden="true">&times;</span></button>

        </div>

        <div class="modal-body">

          <p>This is a paragraph inside Modal Body</p>

        </div>
        <div class="modal-footer">
```

```
        <button type="button" class="btn btn-default" data-
        dismiss="modal">Close</button>
        <button type="button" class="btn btn-primary">Save changes
        </button>

      </div>
    </div>
  </div>
</div>

<!-- Optional JavaScript -->
<!-- jQuery first, then Popper.js, then Bootstrap JS -->
<script src="https://code.jquery.com/jquery-3.4.1.slim.min.js"
integrity="sha384-J6qa4849blE2+poT4WnyKhv5vZF5SrPoOiEjwBvKU7imGFAVOwwj1yY
foRSJoZ+n" crossorigin="anonymous"></script>
<script src="https://cdn.jsdelivr.net/npm/popper.js@1.16.0/dist/umd/
popper.min.js" integrity="sha384-Q6E9RHvbIyZFJoft+2mJbHaEWldlvI9IOYy5n3zV
9zzTtmI3UksdQRVvoxMfooAo" crossorigin="anonymous"></script>
<script src="https://stackpath.bootstrapcdn.com/bootstrap/4.4.1/js/
bootstrap.min.js" integrity="sha384-wfSDF2E50Y2D1uUdjOO3uMBJnjuUD4Ih7YwaY
d1iqfktjOUod8GCExl3Og8ifwB6" crossorigin="anonymous"></script>

</body>
</html>
```

If you save this page, load it on your browser, and open the modal, you will see the following (Figure 9-18).

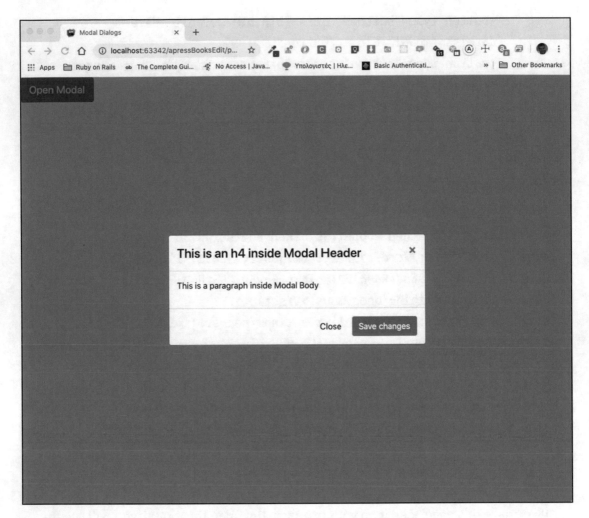

Figure 9-18. *Modal Vertically Centered*

As you can see, the modal appears vertically centered.

Modal Activation with JavaScript

You have seen that you can activate a modal without actually using any JavaScript code. The button example that you used was something like this:

```
<button class="btn btn-lg btn-success" data-toggle="modal" data-target=".
modal">Open Modal</button>
```

The important bits here are data-toggle="modal" and data-target=".modal".

You can also open a modal dialog using JavaScript instead. Let's see (Listing 9-8) the Greek Islands example again, but this time, you will not use a button as in the previous example.

Listing 9-8. Greek Islands with JavaScript to Open the Modal

```html
<!DOCTYPE html>
<html lang="en">
<head>
  <!-- Required meta tags -->
  <meta charset="utf-8">
  <meta name="viewport" content="width=device-width, initial-scale=1,
  shrink-to-fit=no">

  <!-- Bootstrap CSS -->
  <link rel="stylesheet" href="https://stackpath.bootstrapcdn.
  com/bootstrap/4.4.1/css/bootstrap.min.css" integrity="sha384-
  Vkoo8x4CGsO3+Hhxv8T/Q5PaXtkKtu6ug5TOeNV6gBiFeWPGFN9MuhOf23Q9Ifjh"
  crossorigin="anonymous">

  <!-- Custom CSS -->
  <link rel="stylesheet" href="stylesheets/main.css" type="text/css">

  <title>Modal Dialogs</title>
</head>
<body>

  <button class="btn btn-lg btn-success" id="open-modal-button">Open
  Modal</button>

  <div class="modal fade" tabindex="-1" role="dialog">
    <div class="modal-dialog modal-lg">
      <div class="modal-content">
        <div class="modal-header">

          <h4 class="modal-title">Zakynthos from Wikipedia</h4>
          <button type="button" class="close" data-dismiss="modal" aria-
          label="Close">
```

```
          <span>&times;</span>
        </button>

      </div>

      <div class="modal-body">

        <div class="container-fluid">
          <div class="row">
            <div class="col-md-6">
              <img src="images/ithaki-1.jpg" alt="Ithaki"/>
            </div>
            <div class="col-md-6">
              <img src="images/elafonisos-2.jpg" alt="Elafonisos"/>
            </div>
          </div>

          <div class="row">
            <div class="col-md-6">
              <img src="images/karpathos-3.jpg" alt="Karpathos"/>
            </div>
            <div class="col-md-6">
              <img src="images/chios-4.jpg" alt="Chios"/>
            </div>
          </div>
        </div>

      </div> <!-- modal body -->

      <div class="modal-footer">

        <button type="button" class="btn btn-default" data-
        dismiss="modal">Close</button>
        <button type="button" class="btn btn-primary">Save changes
        </button>

      </div>
    </div>
  </div>
</div>
```

```
<!-- jQuery first, then Popper.js, then Bootstrap JS -->
<script src="https://code.jquery.com/jquery-3.4.1.slim.min.js"
integrity="sha384-J6qa4849blE2+poT4WnyKhv5vZF5SrPoOiEjwBvKU7imGFAVOwwj1yY
foRSJoZ+n" crossorigin="anonymous"></script>
<script src="https://cdn.jsdelivr.net/npm/popper.js@1.16.0/dist/umd/
popper.min.js" integrity="sha384-Q6E9RHvbIyZFJoft+2mJbHaEWldlvI9IOYy5n3zV
9zzTtmI3UksdQRVvoxMfooAo" crossorigin="anonymous"></script>
<script src="https://stackpath.bootstrapcdn.com/bootstrap/4.4.1/js/
bootstrap.min.js" integrity="sha384-wfSDF2E50Y2D1uUdj0O3uMBJnjuUD4Ih7YwaY
d1iqfktj0Uod8GCExl3Og8ifwB6" crossorigin="anonymous"></script>

<!-- Custom JavaScript -->
<script src="javascripts/open-dialog.js"></script>
</body>
</html>
```

The preceding file has two differences from the previous version:

1. It references a JavaScript file with custom JavaScript code. The file
    is javascripts/open-dialog.js. See this reference at the bottom
    of the file, before the closing body tag.

2. The other one is that the button to open the modal does not have
    the modal-related data- attributes anymore.

Without giving you the open-dialog.js contents yet, if you save the preceding code, load the page on your browser, and try to open the dialog by clicking the button, nothing will happen.

In order for the dialog to open, you now need to provide the corresponding JavaScript commands:

```
$(document).ready(function() {
   $('#open-modal-button').on('click', function() {
      $('.modal').modal();
      return false;
   });
});
```

If you save the preceding code inside the `javascripts/open-dialog.js` file and reload the page, then the modal dialog will open when you click the `Open Modal` button.

The new stuff here is this:

```
$('.modal').modal();
```

It is inside the implementation of the click handler for the button `#open-modal-button`. So, when you click this button, you call the `modal()` method of the Twitter Bootstrap JavaScript library. This is called on the selection of elements that match the `$('.modal');`, hence on the modal `div` container.

Modal and Options

When calling the `$(...).modal()` method, then you can give a JavaScript object with options for the modal function. The options that you can give are the following:

1. `backdrop`: Boolean with default value `true`. It can also be a string with the value `static`. If you set the value to `false`, then the modal will open without a backdrop, and you will not be able to click outside of the modal in order to close it (Figure 9-19).

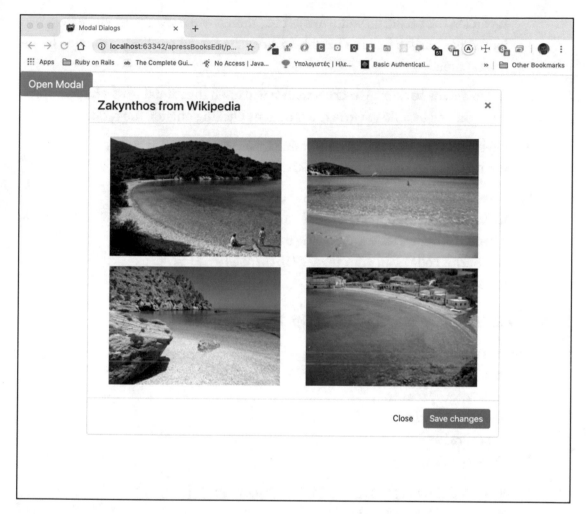

Figure 9-19. *Modal Without Backdrop*

The code to open the modal without backdrop is this:

```
$(document).ready(function() {
    $('#open-modal-button').on('click', function() {
        $('.modal').modal({
            backdrop: false
        });
        return false;
    });
});
```

If you set the backdrop value to static, then it will open the modal with a backdrop, but you will not be able to close the modal by clicking outside of the modal area.

If you set the backdrop to true, then it will open the modal with a backdrop, and you will be able to close the modal by clicking outside the modal area.

2. keyboard: Boolean with default value true. When true, it closes the modal if you click the key <ESC>.

3. show: Boolean with default value true. It shows the modal when initialized. This is useful because you might want to initialize a modal without actually showing that until later. Change the JavaScript code inside the javascripts/open-dialog.js as follows (Listing 9-9).

Listing 9-9. Initialize Modal Without Opening

```
$(document).ready(function() {
    $('.modal').modal({
        backdrop: 'static',
        keyboard: false,
        show: false
    });

    $('#open-modal-button').on('click', function() {
        $('.modal').modal('show');
        return false;
    });
});
```

This is not much different from the original version. But it is better because it splits the functionality in two. First, it initializes the modal; and then, when the button is clicked, it just shows it.

The initialization of a modal with modal({....}); and the show of an already initialized modal with the call modal('show'); fall into the category of modal methods. Let's see some more details about them.

Modal Methods

Here is the list of modal methods:

1. `.modal('show');`

   `$('modal-selector').modal('show');`

   It is used to show an initialized modal.

2. `.modal('hide');`

   `$('modal-selector').modal('hide');`

   It is used to hide an initialized modal.

3. `.modal('toggle');`

   `$('modal-selector').modal('toggle');`

It is used to hide an open modal or show a hidden modal.

Modal Events

You may already know that JavaScript programming involves a lot of event programming. Lots of JavaScript plugins out there define their custom events. Same goes for the Twitter Bootstrap modal.

The following are the events that are fired against the modal itself:

1. `show.bs.modal`: This event fires immediately when the `show` method is called. If caused by a click, the clicked element is available as the `relatedTarget` property of the event.

   Let's do an example (Listing 9-10).

Listing 9-10. Demo of the `show.bs.modal` Event

```
<!DOCTYPE html>
<html lang="en">
<head>
  <!-- Required meta tags -->
  <meta charset="utf-8">
```

```
<meta name="viewport" content="width=device-width, initial-scale=1,
shrink-to-fit=no">

<!-- Bootstrap CSS -->
<link rel="stylesheet" href="https://stackpath.bootstrapcdn.
com/bootstrap/4.4.1/css/bootstrap.min.css" integrity="sha384-
Vkoo8x4CGsO3+Hhxv8T/Q5PaXtkKtu6ug5TOeNV6gBiFeWPGFN9MuhOf23Q9Ifjh"
crossorigin="anonymous">

<!-- Custom CSS -->
<link rel="stylesheet" href="stylesheets/main.css" type="text/css">

<title>Modal Dialogs</title>
</head>
<body>

<button class="btn btn-lg btn-success" data-toggle="modal" data-target=".
modal">Open Modal 1</button>
<button class="btn btn-lg btn-success" data-toggle="modal" data-target=".
modal">Open Modal 2</button>
<button class="btn btn-lg btn-success" data-toggle="modal" data-target=".
modal">Open Modal 3</button>

<div class="modal fade" tabindex="-1" role="dialog">
  <div class="modal-dialog">
    <div class="modal-content">
      <div class="modal-header">

        <h4 class="modal-title">Modal Demo of relatedTarget</h4>
        <button type="button" class="close" data-dismiss="modal"
        aria-label="Close"><span aria-hidden="true" class="glyphicon
        glyphicon-remove"></span></button>

      </div>

      <div class="modal-body text-center">

      </div>
      <div class="modal-footer">
```

```
        <button type="button" class="btn btn-default" data-
        dismiss="modal">Close</button>

      </div>
    </div>
  </div>
</div>

<!-- jQuery first, then Popper.js, then Bootstrap JS -->
<script src="https://code.jquery.com/jquery-3.4.1.slim.min.js"
integrity="sha384-J6qa4849blE2+poT4WnyKhv5vZF5SrPo0iEjwBvKU7imGFAVOwwj1yY
foRSJoZ+n" crossorigin="anonymous"></script>
<script src="https://cdn.jsdelivr.net/npm/popper.js@1.16.0/dist/umd/
popper.min.js" integrity="sha384-Q6E9RHvbIyZFJoft+2mJbHaEWldlvI9IOYy5n3zV
9zzTtmI3UksdQRVvoxMfooAo" crossorigin="anonymous"></script>
<script src="https://stackpath.bootstrapcdn.com/bootstrap/4.4.1/js/
bootstrap.min.js" integrity="sha384-wfSDF2E50Y2D1uUdjOO3uMBJnjuUD4Ih7YwaY
d1iqfktjOUod8GCExl3Og8ifwB6" crossorigin="anonymous"></script>

<!-- Custom JavaScript -->
<script src="javascripts/related-target.js"></script>
</body>
</html>
```

The preceding HTML page is using the JavaScript file javascripts/related-target.js. This is given in Listing 9-11.

Listing 9-11. JavaScript File for Listing 9-10

```
$(document).ready(function(){
    $('.modal').on('show.bs.modal', function(event){
      var $buttonClicked = $(event.relatedTarget);

      $(this).find('.modal-body').html("<h1>" + $buttonClicked.html() + "
      Clicked!</h1>");
    });
});
```

As you can see from the HTML markup, the modal-body of the modal dialog is empty. You are going to add content dynamically, using JavaScript, reacting to the show. bs.modal event. Also, the content that you will add will be related to the button that has triggered the opening of the modal. As you can see, there are three buttons that all open the modal dialog.

With regard to the JavaScript file content, I attach a handler on the show.bs.modal event for the modal (.modal) target. I also declare the argument event which will be holding the relatedTarget when the handler is called. I save the relatedTarget to $buttonClicked, and then I just use the .html() jQuery function to set the HTML content of the modal-body div. The modal-body div is selected using the jQuery method .find().

This is going to be the final result depicted in the following 3 figures, Figure 9-20, Figure 9-21, Figure 9-22:

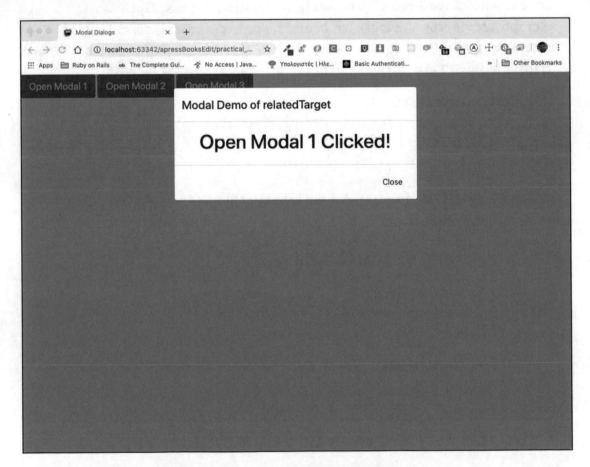

Figure 9-20. *Page Modal When Clicking the First Button*

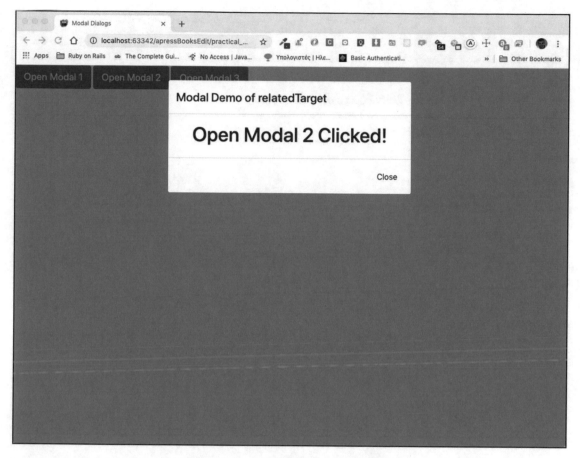

Figure 9-21. *Page Modal When Clicking the Second Button*

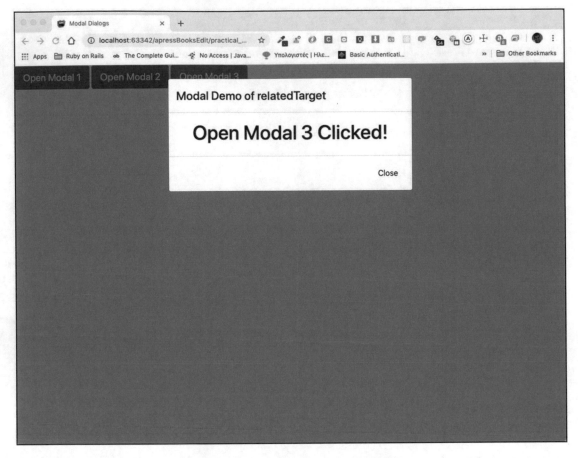

Figure 9-22. *Page Modal When Clicking the Third Button*

2. `shown.bs.modal`: This event is fired when the modal has been made visible to the user and after all the `fade` transitions have been completed. If caused by a click, the clicked element is available as the `relatedTarget` property of the event.

3. `hide.bs.modal`: This event is fired immediately when the `hide` instance method has been called. This might be useful when you want to program some actions that need to be executed when the modal is being hidden.

4. `hidden.bs.modal`: This event is fired when the modal has finished being hidden from the user (will wait for CSS transitions to complete).

5. `hidden.Prevented.bs.modal`: This event is fired when

   a. The modal is shown.

   b. Its backdrop is `static`.

   c. A click outside the modal is performed or clicking an <ESC> key.

Tasks and Quizzes

TASK DETAILS

You need to implement a page in which the user picks up one of two favorite cities. In fact

1. When the page loads, it has the button to open the modal and an image placeholder, like this (Figure 9-23):

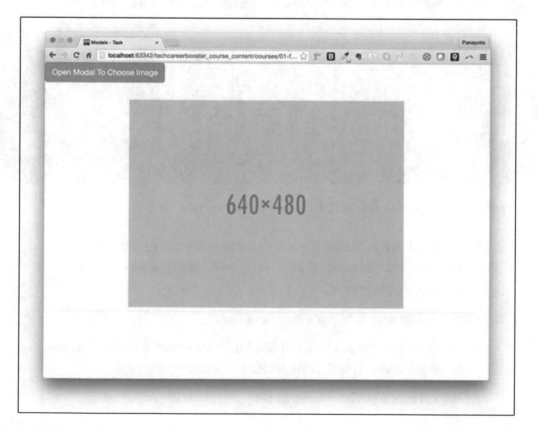

Figure 9-23. *Task—Page with a Button to Open the Modal and an Image Placeholder*

2. When the user clicks the button to open the modal, the modal should appear as follows (Figure 9-24):

Figure 9-24. *Task—Modal with Cities to Choose from*

3. Users should be able to click one of the images. When clicked, the modal should close, and the image selected should be displayed on the main page in the place of the placeholder.

4. Here are some hints to help you finish your task:

    1. You might want to have a custom CSS file. This will need to style the images inside the modal, as well as the central image on the main page.

    2. You will need a custom JavaScript file:

1. Its responsibility will be to respond to the click performed on any of the two images in the modal dialog.

2. The click handler on the images needs to

    1. Close the modal.

    2. Replace the `src` of the central image with the `src` attribute of the clicked image.

Key Takeaways

- How to implement a modal dialog

- The modal dialog parts, header, body, and footer

- The backdrop of a modal

- How to vertically center a modal

- How to use the grid system inside the modal body

- How to remove the fade effect on open

- How to show an image inside the body of the modal

- How to show a YouTube video inside the body of the modal

- How to open small and large modals

- How to customize the modal with its options

- How to use the methods of the modal

- How to attach to different modal events

In the following chapter, you will learn how to build a page with very long content, alongside a navigation bar whose active menu changes according to the content position on the window.

CHAPTER 10

ScrollSpy

Long-content pages usually have top navigation bars that allow the user to quickly navigate to sections within the pages. This feature is accompanied by the fact that the menu item highlighted as active is automatically updated/changed according to the visible section of the page. ScrollSpy is a Twitter Bootstrap JavaScript plugin that, when used, automatically changes the highlighted menu item according to the position in the document.

In this chapter, you will learn how Twitter Bootstrap allows you to quickly incorporate such a feature in your long-content pages.

Learning Goals

1. Learn how to add scrollspying functionality to your long-content pages.

2. Learn how you should set up your HTML markup to support scrollspying.

3. Learn how you can adjust the offset and activation point of the scroll sections.

A Long Page with a Menu

Let's start with a long HTML page with a menu (Listing 10-1).

© Panos Matsinopoulos 2020
P. Matsinopoulos, *Practical Bootstrap*, https://doi.org/10.1007/978-1-4842-6071-5_10

Listing 10-1. Long Page with a Menu

```
<!DOCTYPE html>
<html lang="en">
<head>
    <!-- Required meta tags -->
    <meta charset="utf-8">
    <meta name="viewport" content="width=device-width, initial-scale=1,
    shrink-to-fit=no">

    <!-- Bootstrap CSS -->
    <link rel="stylesheet" href="https://stackpath.bootstrapcdn.com/bootstrap/
    4.4.1/css/bootstrap.min.css" integrity="sha384-Vkoo8x4CGsO3+Hhxv8T/
    Q5PaXtkKtu6ug5TOeNV6gBiFeWPGFN9MuhOf23Q9Ifjh" crossorigin="anonymous">

    <!-- Custom CSS -->
    <link rel="stylesheet" href="stylesheets/main.css" type="text/css">

    <title>ScrollSpy</title>
</head>
<body>
    <nav class="navbar navbar-expand-lg navbar-dark bg-dark fixed-top">
        <div class="container">
            <a class="navbar-brand" href="main.html">Home</a>

            <button type="button" class="navbar-toggler" data-
            toggle="collapse" data-target="#navbar"
                    aria-controls="navbar"
                    aria-expanded="false"
                    aria-label="Toggle navigation">
                <span class="navbar-toggler-icon"></span>
            </button>

            <div class="collapse navbar-collapse" id="navbar">
                <ul class="nav navbar-nav">
                    <li class="nav-item">
                        <a class="nav-link active" href="#introduction">
                        Introduction<span class="sr-only">(current)</span></a>
                    </li>
```

```
                <li class="nav-item">
                    <a class="nav-link" href="#origins">Origins</a>
                </li>
                <li class="nav-item">
                    <a class="nav-link" href="#creating-new-state-
                    constitutions">State Constitutions</a>
                </li>
                <li class="nav-item">
                    <a class="nav-link" href="#military-hostilities-
                    begin">Military Hostilities</a>
                </li>
                <li class="nav-item">
                    <a class="nav-link" href="#independence-and-
                    union">Independence And Union</a>
                </li>
                <li class="nav-item">
                    <a class="nav-link" href="#more">More</a>
                </li>
            </ul>
        </div>
    </div>
</nav>

<div class="container">
    <h1 id="introduction">American Revolution History</h1>

    <h2>Introduction</h2>

    <p>
        The American Revolution was a political upheaval that took
        place between 1765 and 1783 during which colonists in the
        Thirteen American Colonies rejected the British monarchy and
        aristocracy, overthrew the authority of Great Britain, and
        founded the United States of America.
    </p>
```

```
<p>
```

Starting in 1765, members of American colonial society rejected the authority of the British Parliament to tax them and create other laws affecting them, without colonial representatives in the government. During the following decade, protests by colonists—known as Patriots—continued to escalate, as in the Boston Tea Party in 1773 during which patriots destroyed a consignment of taxed tea from the Parliament-controlled and favored East India Company.[1] The British responded by imposing punitive laws—the Coercive Acts—on Massachusetts in 1774, following which Patriots in the other colonies rallied behind Massachusetts. In late 1774 the Patriots set up their own alternative government to better coordinate their resistance efforts against Great Britain, while other colonists, known as Loyalists, preferred to remain aligned to the British Crown.

```
</p>
<p>
```

Tensions escalated to the outbreak of fighting between Patriot militia and British regulars at Lexington and Concord in April 1775. The conflict then evolved into a global war, during which the Patriots (and later their French, Spanish, and Dutch allies) fought the British and Loyalists in what became known as the American Revolutionary War (1775-1783). Patriots in each of the thirteen colonies formed Provincial Congresses that assumed power from the old colonial governments and suppressed Loyalism, and from there built a Continental Army under the leadership of General George Washington. Claiming King George III's rule to be tyrannical and infringing the colonists' "rights as Englishmen", the Continental Congress declared the colonies free and independent states in July 1776. The Patriot leadership professed the political philosophies of liberalism and republicanism to reject monarchy and aristocracy, and proclaimed that all men are created equal. Congress rejected British proposals requiring allegiance to the monarchy and abandonment of independence.

```
</p>
```

```
<p>
```

The British were forced out of Boston in 1776, but then captured and held New York City for the duration of the war. The British blockaded the ports and captured other cities for brief periods, but failed to defeat Washington's forces. In early 1778, following a failed patriot invasion of Canada, a British army was captured at the Battle of Saratoga, following which the French openly entered the war as allies of the United States. The war later turned to the American South, where the British captured an army at South Carolina, but failed to enlist enough volunteers from Loyalist civilians to take effective control. A combined American-French force captured a second British army at Yorktown in 1781, effectively ending the war in the United States. The Treaty of Paris in 1783 formally ended the conflict, confirming the new nation's complete separation from the British Empire. The United States took possession of nearly all the territory east of the Mississippi River and south of the Great Lakes, with the British retaining control of Canada and Spain taking Florida.[2][3]

```
</p>
```

```
<p>
```

Among the significant results of the revolution was the creation of a new Constitution of the United States. The 'Three-Fifths Compromise' allowed the southern slaveholders to consolidate power and maintain slavery in America for another eighty years,[4] but through the expansion of voting rights and liberties over subsequent decades the elected government became responsible to the will of the people.[5] The new Constitution established a relatively strong federal national government that included an executive, a national judiciary, and a bicameral Congress that represented both states in the Senate and population in the House of Representatives.[6][7]

```
</p>
```

```
<p>
    Among the significant results of the revolution was the
    creation of a new Constitution of the United States. The
    'Three-Fifths Compromise' allowed the southern slaveholders to
    consolidate power and maintain slavery in America for another
    eighty years,[4] but through the expansion of voting rights and
    liberties over subsequent decades the elected government became
    responsible to the will of the people.[5] The new Constitution
    established a relatively strong federal national government
    that included an executive, a national judiciary, and a
    bicameral Congress that represented both states in the Senate
    and population in the House of Representatives.[6][7]
</p>

<h2 id="origins">Origins</h2>

<p>
    Historians typically begin their histories of the American
    Revolution with the British victory in the French and Indian
    War in 1763, which removed France as a major player in North
    American affairs. Lawrence Henry Gipson, the historian of the
    British Empire, states:
</p>

<p>
    It may be said as truly that the American Revolution was an
    aftermath of the Anglo-French conflict in the New World carried
    on between 1754 and 1763.[8]
</p>

<p>
    The Royal Proclamation of 1763 may have played a role in the
    separation of the United States from Great Britain as colonists
    at the time wanted to continue in the economically beneficial
    cultural practice of taking land for one's own livelihood as
    part of the drive west. The lands west of Quebec and west of a
    line running along the crest of the Allegheny mountains became
```

Indian territory, temporarily barred from settlement (to the great disappointment of the land speculators of Virginia and Pennsylvania, who had started the Seven Years' War to gain those territories).
</p>

<p>

For the prior history see Thirteen Colonies.
</p>

<h3>1764-1766: Taxes imposed and withdrawn</h3>

<p>

In 1764 Parliament passed the Currency Act to restrain the use of paper money that British merchants saw as a means to evade debt payments.[original research?] Parliament also passed the Sugar Act imposing customs duties on a number of articles. That same year Prime Minister George Grenville proposed to impose direct taxes on the colonies to raise revenue, but delayed action to see if the colonies would propose some way to raise the revenue themselves.[citation needed] None did, and in March 1765 Parliament passed the Stamp Act which imposed direct taxes on the colonies for the first time. All official documents, newspapers, almanacs and pamphlets—even decks of playing cards— were required to have the stamps.
</p>

<p>

The colonists objected chiefly on the grounds not that the taxes were high (they were low),[9] but because they had no representation in the Parliament. Benjamin Franklin testified in Parliament in 1766 that Americans already contributed heavily to the defense of the Empire. He said local governments had raised, outfitted and paid 25,000 soldiers to fight France— as many as Britain itself sent—and spent many millions from American treasuries doing so in the French and Indian War alone.[10][11] Stationing a standing army in Great Britain

during peacetime was politically unacceptable. London had to
deal with 1,500 politically well-connected British officers who
became redundant; it would have to discharge them or station
them in North America.[12]

</p>

<p>

In 1765 the Sons of Liberty formed. They used public
demonstrations, boycotts, violence and threats of violence
to ensure that the British tax laws were unenforceable. While
openly hostile to what they considered an oppressive Parliament
acting illegally, colonists persisted in sending numerous
petitions and pleas for intervention from a monarch to whom
they still claimed loyalty. In Boston, the Sons of Liberty
burned the records of the vice admiralty court and looted
the home of the chief justice, Thomas Hutchinson. Several
legislatures called for united action, and nine colonies sent
delegates to the Stamp Act Congress in New York City in October
1765. Moderates led by John Dickinson drew up a "Declaration
of Rights and Grievances" stating that taxes passed without
representation violated their rights as Englishmen. Colonists
emphasized their determination by boycotting imports of British
merchandise.[13]

</p>

<p>

The Parliament at Westminster saw itself as the supreme law
making authority throughout all British possessions and thus
entitled to levy any tax without colonial approval.[14] They
argued that the colonies were legally British corporations
that were completely subordinate to the British parliament
and pointed to numerous instances where Parliament had made
laws binding on the colonies in the past.[15] They did not see
anything in the unwritten British constitution that made taxes
special[16] and noted that Parliament had taxed American trade
for decades. Parliament insisted that the colonies effectively

enjoyed a "virtual representation" like most British people did, as only a small minority of the British population elected representatives to Parliament.[17] Americans such as James Otis maintained the Americans were not in fact virtually represented.[18]
</p>

<p>

In London, the Rockingham government came to power (July 1765) and Parliament debated whether to repeal the stamp tax or to send an army to enforce it. Benjamin Franklin made the case for repeal, explaining the colonies had spent heavily in manpower, money, and blood in defense of the empire in a series of wars against the French and Indians, and that further taxes to pay for those wars were unjust and might bring about a rebellion. Parliament agreed and repealed the tax (February 21, 1766), but in the Declaratory Act of March 1766 insisted that parliament retained full power to make laws for the colonies "in all cases whatsoever".[19] The repeal nonetheless caused widespread celebrations in the colonies.
</p>

<p>

Briggs says unnamed modern American economic historians have challenged the view that Great Britain was placing a heavy burden on the North American colonies and have suggested the cost of defending them from the possibility of invasion by France or Spain was £400,000 - five times the maximum income from them. Briggs rejects the analysis, saying that issue was not invoked at the time.[20]
</p>

<h3>1767-1773: Townshend Acts and the Tea Act</h3>

```
<p>
```

In 1767 the Parliament passed the Townshend Acts, which
placed duties on a number of essential goods including paper,
glass, and tea and established a Board of Customs in Boston
to more rigorously execute trade regulations. The new taxes
were enacted on the belief that Americans only objected to
internal taxes and not external taxes like custom duties. The
Americans, however, argued against the constitutionality of the
act because its purpose was to raise revenue and not regulate
trade. Colonists responded by organizing new boycotts of
British goods. These boycotts were less effective, however, as
the Townshend goods were widely used.

```
</p>

<p>
```

In February 1768 the Assembly of Massachusetts Bay issued a
circular letter to the other colonies urging them to coordinate
resistance. The governor dissolved the assembly when it refused
to rescind the letter. Meanwhile, in June 1768 a riot broke
out in Boston over the seizure of the sloop Liberty, owned
by John Hancock, for alleged smuggling. Custom officials
were forced to flee, prompting the British to deploy troops
to Boston. A Boston town meeting declared no obedience was
due to parliamentary laws and called for the convening of a
convention. A convention assembled but only issued a mild
protest before dissolving itself. In January 1769 Parliament
responded to the unrest by reactivating the Treason Act 1543
which permitted subjects outside the realm to face trials
for treason in England. The governor of Massachusetts was
instructed to collect evidence of said treason, and although
the threat was not carried out it caused widespread outrage.

```
</p>
```

```
<p>
```
On March 5, 1770 a large mob gathered around a group of British soldiers. The mob grew more and more threatening, throwing snowballs, rocks and debris at the soldiers. One soldier was clubbed and fell.[21] There was no order to fire but the soldiers fired into the crowd anyway. They hit 11 people; three civilians died at the scene of the shooting, and two died after the incident. The event quickly came to be called the Boston Massacre. Although the soldiers were tried and acquitted (defended by John Adams), the widespread descriptions soon became propaganda to turn colonial sentiment against the British. This in turn began a downward spiral in the relationship between Britain and the Province of Massachusetts. [21]
```
</p>

<p>
```
A new ministry under Lord North came to power in 1770 and Parliament withdrew all taxes except the tax on tea, giving up its efforts to raise revenue while maintaining the right to tax. This temporarily resolved the crisis and the boycott of British goods largely ceased, with only the more radical patriots such as Samuel Adams continuing to agitate.
```
</p>

<p>
```
Two ships in a harbor, one in the distance. On board, men stripped to the waist and wearing feathers in their hair are throwing crates into the water. A large crowd, mostly men, is standing on the dock, waving hats and cheering. A few people wave their hats from windows in a nearby building.
This 1846 lithograph by Nathaniel Currier was entitled "The Destruction of Tea at Boston Harbor"; the phrase "Boston Tea Party" had not yet become standard.[22]
```
</p>
```

```
<p>
```

In June 1772, in what became known as the Gaspee Affair, American patriots including John Brown burned a British warship that had been vigorously enforcing unpopular trade regulations. The affair was investigated for possible treason, but no action was taken.

```
</p>

<p>
```

In 1772 it became known that the Crown intended to pay fixed salaries to the governors and judges in Massachusetts. Samuel Adams in Boston set about creating new Committees of Correspondence, which linked Patriots in all 13 colonies and eventually provided the framework for a rebel government. In early 1773 Virginia, the largest colony, set up its Committee of Correspondence, on which Patrick Henry and Thomas Jefferson served.[23]

```
</p>

<p>
```

A total of about 7000 to 8000 Patriots served on "Committees of Correspondence" at the colonial and local levels, comprising most of the leadership in their communities — Loyalists were excluded. The committees became the leaders of the American resistance to British actions, and largely determined the war effort at the state and local level. When the First Continental Congress decided to boycott British products, the colonial and local Committees took charge, examining merchant records and publishing the names of merchants who attempted to defy the boycott by importing British goods.[24]

```
</p>

<p>
```

In 1773 private letters were published where Massachusetts Governor Thomas Hutchinson claimed the colonists could not enjoy all English liberties, and Lieutenant Governor Andrew Oliver called for the direct payment of colonial officials. The

letters, whose contents were used as evidence of a systematic plot against American rights, discredited Hutchinson in the eyes of the people the Assembly petitioned for his recall. Benjamin Franklin, postmaster general for the colonies, acknowledged that he leaked the letters which led to him being berated by British officials and fired from his job.
</p>

<p>

Meanwhile, Parliament passed the Tea Act to lower the price of taxed tea exported to the colonies in order to help the East India Company undersell smuggled Dutch tea. Special consignees were appointed to sell the tea in order to bypass colonial merchants. The act was opposed not only by those who resisted the taxes but also by smugglers who stood to lose business. In most instances the consignees were forced to resign and the tea was turned back, but Massachusetts governor Hutchinson refused to allow Boston merchants to give into pressure. A town meeting in Boston determined that the tea would not be landed, and ignored a demand from the governor to disperse. On December 16, 1773 a group of men, led by Samuel Adams and dressed to evoke the appearance of American Indians, boarded the ships of the British East India Company and dumped £10,000 worth of tea from their holds (approximately £636,000 in 2008) into Boston Harbor. Decades later this event became known as the Boston Tea Party and remains a significant part of American patriotic lore.[25]
</p>

<h3>1774-1775: Intolerable Acts and the Quebec Act</h3>

<p>

The British government responded by passing several Acts which came to be known as the Intolerable Acts, which further darkened colonial opinion towards the British. They consisted of four laws enacted by the British parliament. [26] The first, the Massachusetts Government Act, altered

the Massachusetts charter and restricted town meetings. The
second Act, the Administration of Justice Act, ordered that all
British soldiers to be tried were to be arraigned in Britain,
not in the colonies. The third Act was the Boston Port Act,
which closed the port of Boston until the British had been
compensated for the tea lost in the Boston Tea Party. The
fourth Act was the Quartering Act of 1774, which allowed royal
governors to house British troops in the homes of citizens
without requiring permission of the owner.[27]

</p>

<p>

In response, Massachusetts patriots issued the Suffolk
Resolves and formed an alternative shadow government known
as the "Provincial Congress" which began training militia
outside British-occupied Boston.[28] In September 1774,
the First Continental Congress convened, consisting of
representatives from each of the colonies, to serve as a
vehicle for deliberation and collective action. During secret
debates conservative Joseph Galloway proposed the creation
of a colonial Parliament that would be able to approve or
disapprove of acts of the British Parliament but his idea was
not accepted. The Congress instead endorsed the proposal of
John Adams that Americans would obey Parliament voluntarily
but would resist all taxes in disguise. Congress called for a
boycott beginning on 1 December 1774 of all British goods; it
was enforced by new committees authorized by the Congress.[29]

</p>

<p>

The Quebec Act of 1774 extended Quebec's boundaries to the Ohio
River, shutting out the claims of the 13 colonies. By then,
however, the Americans had little regard for new laws from
London; they were drilling militia and organizing for war.[30]

</p>

```
<p>
```

The British retaliated by confining all trade of the New England colonies to Britain and excluding them from the Newfoundland fisheries. Lord North advanced a compromise proposal in which Parliament would not tax so long as the colonies made fixed contributions for defense and to support civil government. This would also be rejected.

```
</p>

<h2 id="creating-new-state-constitutions">Creating New State
Constitutions</h2>

<p>
```

Following the Battle of Bunker Hill in June 1775, the Patriots had control of Massachusetts outside the Boston city limits; the Loyalists suddenly found themselves on the defensive with no protection from the British army. In all 13 colonies, Patriots had overthrown their existing governments, closing courts and driving British officials away. They had elected conventions and "legislatures" that existed outside any legal framework; new constitutions were drawn up in each state to supersede royal charters. They declared that they were states now, not colonies.[31]

```
</p>

<p>
```

On January 5, 1776, New Hampshire ratified the first state constitution. In May 1776, Congress voted to suppress all forms of crown authority, to be replaced by locally created authority. Virginia, South Carolina, and New Jersey created their constitutions before July 4. Rhode Island and Connecticut simply took their existing royal charters and deleted all references to the crown.[32] The new states were all committed to republicanism, with no inherited offices. They decided not only what form of government to create, and also how to select those who would craft the constitutions and how the resulting document would be ratified. But there would be no universal suffrage and real power, including the right to elect the future President would still lay in the hands of a few selected elites for many years. On 26 May 1776 John Adams wrote James Sullivan from Philadelphia;

</p>

<p>

"Depend upon it, sir, it is dangerous to open so fruitful a source of controversy and altercation, as would be opened by attempting to alter the qualifications of voters. There will be no end of it. New claims will arise. Women will demand a vote. Lads from twelve to twenty one will think their rights not enough attended to, and every man, who has not a farthing, will demand an equal voice with any other in all acts of state. It tends to confound and destroy all distinctions, and prostrate all ranks, to one common level".[33][34]

</p>

<p>

In states where the wealthy exerted firm control over the process, such as Maryland, Virginia, Delaware, New York and Massachusetts - the last-mentioned of these state's constitutions still being in force in the 21st century, continuously since its ratification on June 15, 1780 - the results were constitutions that featured:

</p>

<p>

Substantial property qualifications for voting and even more substantial requirements for elected positions (though New York and Maryland lowered property qualifications);[31]
Bicameral legislatures, with the upper house as a check on the lower;
Strong governors, with veto power over the legislature and substantial appointment authority;

```
    Few or no restraints on individuals holding multiple positions
    in government;
    The continuation of state-established religion.
</p>

<p>
    In states where the less affluent had organized sufficiently to
    have significant power—especially Pennsylvania, New Jersey, and
    New Hampshire—the resulting constitutions embodied
</p>

<p>
    universal white manhood suffrage, or minimum property
    requirements for voting or holding office (New Jersey
    enfranchised some property owning widows, a step that it
    retracted 25 years later);
    strong, unicameral legislatures;
    relatively weak governors, without veto powers, and little
    appointing authority;
    prohibition against individuals holding multiple government
    posts;
</p>

<p>
    The radical provisions of Pennsylvania's constitution lasted
    only 14 years. In 1790, conservatives gained power in the
    state legislature, called a new constitutional convention, and
    rewrote the constitution. The new constitution substantially
    reduced universal white-male suffrage, gave the governor veto
    power and patronage appointment authority, and added an upper
    house with substantial wealth qualifications to the unicameral
    legislature. Thomas Paine called it a constitution unworthy of
    America.[6]
</p>

<h2 id="military-hostilities-begin">Military hostilities begin</h2>
```

```
<p>
    Massachusetts was declared in a state of rebellion in February
    1775 and the British garrison received orders to disarm the
    rebels and arrest their leaders, leading to the Battles of
    Lexington and Concord on 19 April 1775. The Patriots set siege
    to Boston, expelled royal officials from all the colonies,
    and took control through the establishment of Provincial
    Congresses. The Battle of Bunker Hill followed on June 17,
    1775. While a British victory, it was at a great cost; about
    1,000 British casualties from a garrison of about 6,000, as
    compared to 500 American casualties from a much larger force.
    [35][36] First ostensibly loyal to the king and desiring to
    govern themselves while remaining in the empire, the repeated
    pleas by the First Continental Congress for royal intervention
    on their behalf with Parliament resulted in the declaration by
    the King that the states were "in rebellion", and the members
    of Congress were traitors.
</p>

<p>
    In the winter of 1775, the Americans invaded Canada. General
    Richard Montgomery captured Montreal but a joint attack on
    Quebec was a total failure; many Americans were captured or
    died of smallpox.
</p>

<p>
    In March 1776, with George Washington as the commander of the
    new army, the Continental Army forced the British to evacuate
    Boston. The revolutionaries were now in full control of all 13
    colonies and were ready to declare independence. While there
    still were many Loyalists, they were no longer in control
    anywhere by July 1776, and all of the Royal officials had fled.
    [37]
</p>
```

```
<p>
```

In August 1775, George III declared Americans in arms against royal authority to be traitors to the Crown. Following their surrender at the Battles of Saratoga in October 1777, there were thousands of British and Hessian soldiers in American hands. Although Lord Germain took a hard line, the British generals on the scene never held treason trials; they treated captured enemy soldiers as prisoners of war.[38] The dilemma was that tens of thousands of Loyalists were under American control and American retaliation would have been easy. The British built much of their strategy around using these Loyalists.[39] Therefore, no Americans were put on trial for treason. The British maltreated the prisoners they held, resulting in more deaths to American sailors and soldiers than from combat operations.[39] At the end of the war, both sides released their surviving prisoners.[40]

```
</p>

<h2 id="independence-and-union">Independence And Union</h2>

<p>
```

In April 1776 the North Carolina Provincial Congress issued the Halifax Resolves, explicitly authorizing its delegates to vote for independence.[41] In May Congress called on all the states to write constitutions, and eliminate the last remnants of royal rule.

```
</p>

<p>
```

By June nine colonies were ready for independence; one by one the last four—Pennsylvania, Delaware, Maryland and New York—fell into line. Richard Henry Lee was instructed by the Virginia legislature to propose independence, and he did so on June 7, 1776. On the 11th a committee was created to draft a document explaining the justifications for separation from Britain. After securing enough votes for passage, independence was voted for on July 2. The Declaration of Independence, drafted largely by

```
        Thomas Jefferson and presented by the committee, was slightly
        revised and unanimously adopted by the entire Congress on July
        4, marking the formation of a new sovereign nation, which called
        itself the United States of America.[42]
    </p>

    <p>
        The Second Continental Congress approved a new constitution,
        the "Articles of Confederation," for ratification by the states
        on November 15, 1777, and immediately began operating under
        their terms. The Articles were formally ratified on March 1,
        1781. At that point, the Continental Congress was dissolved and
        on the following day a new government of the United States in
        Congress Assembled took its place, with Samuel Huntington as
        presiding officer.[43][44]
    </p>

    <h2 id="more">More...</h2>

    <a href="https://en.wikipedia.org/wiki/American_
    Revolution">American Revolution on Wikipedia</a>
</div>

<!-- Optional JavaScript -->
<!-- jQuery first, then Popper.js, then Bootstrap JS -->
<script src="https://code.jquery.com/jquery-3.4.1.slim.min.js"
integrity="sha384-J6qa4849blE2+poT4WnyKhv5vZF5SrPo0iEjwBvKU7imGFAVOwwj1
yYfoRSJoZ+n" crossorigin="anonymous"></script>
<script src="https://cdn.jsdelivr.net/npm/popper.js@1.16.0/dist/umd/
popper.min.js" integrity="sha384-Q6E9RHvbIyZFJoft+2mJbHaEWldlvI9IOYy5n3
zV9zzTtmI3UksdQRVvoxMfooAo" crossorigin="anonymous"></script>
<script src="https://stackpath.bootstrapcdn.com/bootstrap/4.4.1/js/
bootstrap.min.js" integrity="sha384-wfSDF2E50Y2D1uUdjOO3uMBJnjuUD4Ih7Yw
aYd1iqfktjOUod8GCExl3Og8ifwB6" crossorigin="anonymous"></script>

    <script src="./javascripts/main.js" type="text/javascript"></script>
</body>
</html>
```

This page refers to a local `javascripts/main.js` file for custom JavaScript. Consider this empty, for the time being. It also refers to a local `stylesheets/main.css` file for custom CSS. Consider that empty too. If you save the content of the preceding page and load it on your browser, you will see the following (Figure 10-1).

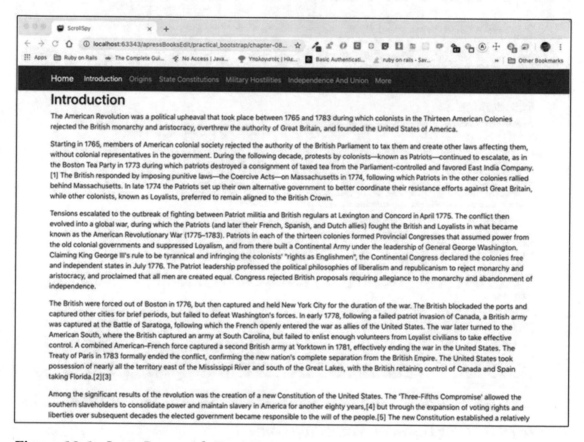

Figure 10-1. *Long Page with Top Navigation*

The navigation bar HTML markup is already known to you from previous chapters. You have also learned how to deal with the problem that it hides the top content of the body. Here is what you have to have in your CSS file:

```
body {
    padding-top: 56px;
}
```

If you save the preceding code and reload the page on your browser, then you will be able to see the top content of your page without that being hidden by the navigation bar (Figure 10-2).

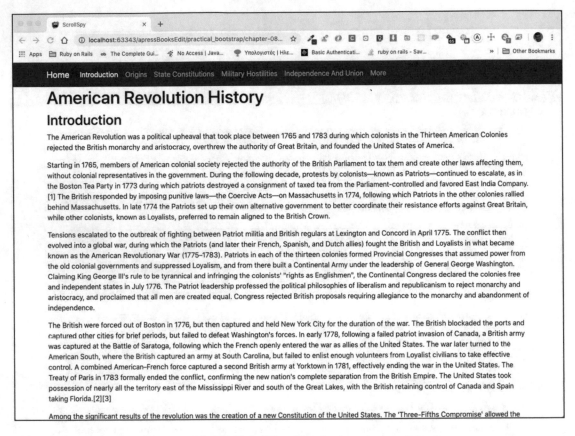

Figure 10-2. *Long Page with Visible Top Content*

Another problem that this page has and that I dealt with in my previous book, *Master HTML & CSS*, in Chapter 23, "Positioning," is the problem with content covered by the navigation bar when you click the menu items. For example, click the menu item `State Constitutions`. You will see the folliwng (Figure 10-3).

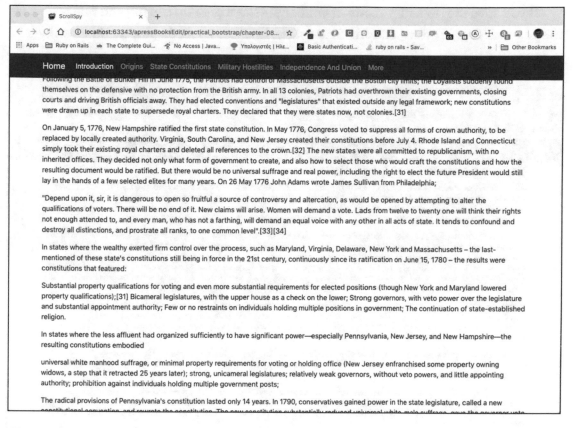

Figure 10-3. *Content Covered by the Navigation Bar*

As you can see, the start of the section that corresponds to the link you linked is covered by the navigation bar.

You will solve this by adding the following `padding-top` and `margin-top` CSS properties to the h1 and h2 elements which are the HTML elements of your page with the anchors that the menu items link to (Listing 10-2).

Listing 10-2. Add to Your CSS File to Fix Hidden Section Content

```
h1, h2 {
    padding-top: 56px;
    margin-top: -56px;
}
```

If you save the preceding code in your `stylesheets/main.css` file and reload the page on your browser, clicking `State Constitutions` will display the foollowing (Figure 10-4).

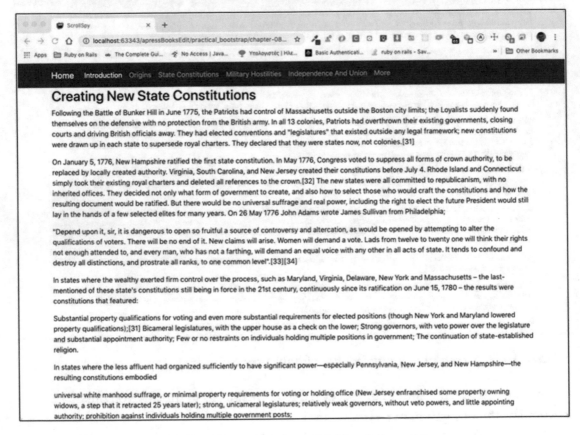

Figure 10-4. *Content Is Not Covered when Clicking Menu Items*

However, you want, when clicking the `More` menu item, the page to bring its content at the top. This does not happen now (Figure 10-5).

In order to fix this, you will add some bottom margin to the `body` of your page.

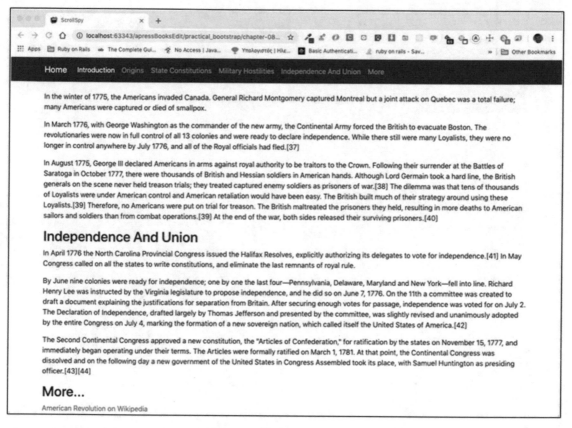

In the winter of 1775, the Americans invaded Canada. General Richard Montgomery captured Montreal but a joint attack on Quebec was a total failure; many Americans were captured or died of smallpox.

In March 1776, with George Washington as the commander of the new army, the Continental Army forced the British to evacuate Boston. The revolutionaries were now in full control of all 13 colonies and were ready to declare independence. While there still were many Loyalists, they were no longer in control anywhere by July 1776, and all of the Royal officials had fled.[37]

In August 1775, George III declared Americans in arms against royal authority to be traitors to the Crown. Following their surrender at the Battles of Saratoga in October 1777, there were thousands of British and Hessian soldiers in American hands. Although Lord Germain took a hard line, the British generals on the scene never held treason trials; they treated captured enemy soldiers as prisoners of war.[38] The dilemma was that tens of thousands of Loyalists were under American control and American retaliation would have been easy. The British built much of their strategy around using these Loyalists.[39] Therefore, no Americans were put on trial for treason. The British maltreated the prisoners they held, resulting in more deaths to American sailors and soldiers than from combat operations.[39] At the end of the war, both sides released their surviving prisoners.[40]

Independence And Union

In April 1776 the North Carolina Provincial Congress issued the Halifax Resolves, explicitly authorizing its delegates to vote for independence.[41] In May Congress called on all the states to write constitutions, and eliminate the last remnants of royal rule.

By June nine colonies were ready for independence; one by one the last four—Pennsylvania, Delaware, Maryland and New York—fell into line. Richard Henry Lee was instructed by the Virginia legislature to propose independence, and he did so on June 7, 1776. On the 11th a committee was created to draft a document explaining the justifications for separation from Britain. After securing enough votes for passage, independence was voted for on July 2. The Declaration of Independence, drafted largely by Thomas Jefferson and presented by the committee, was slightly revised and unanimously adopted by the entire Congress on July 4, marking the formation of a new sovereign nation, which called itself the United States of America.[42]

The Second Continental Congress approved a new constitution, the "Articles of Confederation," for ratification by the states on November 15, 1777, and immediately began operating under their terms. The Articles were formally ratified on March 1, 1781. At that point, the Continental Congress was dissolved and on the following day a new government of the United States in Congress Assembled took its place, with Samuel Huntington as presiding officer.[43][44]

More...

American Revolution on Wikipedia

Figure 10-5. *Clicking More Does Not Bring Content at the Top*

Add `margin-bottom: 900px;`. Save the CSS file and reload the page on your browser. Clicking the More menu item, you will get the following (Figure 10-6).

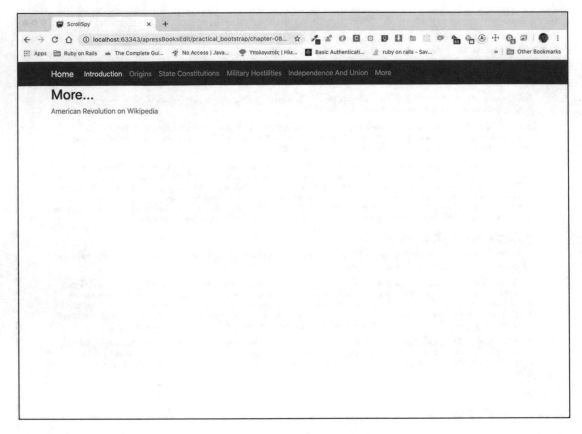

Figure 10-6. *Clicking More Brings Content at the Top*

Showing the Active Section

The problem with the current page is that when you click a menu item and the content is scrolled to that point, the corresponding menu item does not become active. Also, the corresponding menu item does not become active if you just scroll the content from top to bottom, from section to section.

Both of these problems can now be solved with the use of ScrollSpy, which is a Twitter Bootstrap JavaScript plugin:

1. You need to tell ScrollSpy which element contains the content you want to spy. Usually, this is the body. You set the data attribute `data-spy="scroll"`.

2. You need to tell ScrollSpy which is the navigation bar element that contains the list with the menu items. In your case, this is the `div` with id `navbar`. Hence, you have to add the `data-target="#navbar"` attribute to the body element.

3. You also need to set the `position` attribute of the body element to have the value `relative`.

So, first, go to the HTML page and turn

```
<body>
```

to this:

```
<body data-spy="scroll" data-target="#navbar">
```

Add the `position: relative` to the body element inside the `stylesheets/main.css` file.

Save all that stuff and reload the page on your browser. You will see that the first menu item is highlighted and then, when you scroll, according to the visible section of the page, the corresponding menu item is highlighted.

Activating Section Point

Sometimes, you may want the active section to appear highlighted on the menu, when the section start is earlier than the top of the page. For example, you may want to activate a section when the section start is 200px from top of page. You can do that with the data attribute `data-offset` which takes as value the number of pixels you want the section to be activated from.

Change

```
<body data-spy="scroll" data-target="#navbar">
```

to this:

```
<body data-spy="scroll" data-target="#navbar" data-offset="200">
```

Save and reload the page on your browser. Then start scrolling. You will see the sections being activated before the section start reaches the top of the page.

How Does It Work?

Besides the correct data attributes that you need to set as described earlier (data-spy, data-target, and optionally data-offset), you need to make sure that

1. Your menu items point to ids corresponding to the start of the sections. See again the HTML fragment with the menu items in the navigation bar (Figure 10-7):

```
<div class="collapse navbar-collapse" id="navbar">
    <ul class="nav navbar-nav">
        <li class="nav-item">
            <a class="nav-link active" href="#introduction">Introduction<span class="sr-only">(curr
        </li>
        <li class="nav-item">
            <a class="nav-link" href="#origins">Origins</a>
        </li>
        <li class="nav-item">
            <a class="nav-link" href="#creating-new-state-constitutions">State Constitutions</a>
        </li>
        <li class="nav-item">
            <a class="nav-link" href="#military-hostilities-begin">Military Hostilities</a>
        </li>
        <li class="nav-item">
            <a class="nav-link" href="#independence-and-union">Independence And Union</a>
        </li>
        <li class="nav-item">
            <a class="nav-link" href="#more">More</a>
        </li>
    </ul>
```

Figure 10-7. *Menu Items Pointing to the Start Of Sections*

2. The beginnings of the sections need to have the corresponding/ correct ids, for example:

```
<h2 id="military-hostilities-begin">Military hostilities begin</h2>
```

Activating Using JavaScript

You may be in the need to activate ScrollSpy dynamically using JavaScript. So, instead of attaching specific data attributes on the body element, you do not add anything, but you call the following JavaScript code:

```
$('body').scrollspy({ target: '#navbar' });
```

Let's see that in action. Change the HTML body element to be

```
<body>
```

Then update the `javascripts/main.js` file to have the content shown in Listing 10-3.

Listing 10-3. Active ScrollSpy with JavaScript

```
$(document).ready(function() {
    $('body').scrollspy({
        target: '#navbar'
    })
});
```

When you save all files and reload the page on your browser, you will still see ScrollSpy working as before.

Note that you can also give `offset` property in the object that you literally construct and you pass to the `scrollspy()` method.

Tasks and Quizzes

TASK DETAILS

Create a long page to demonstrate the ScrollSpy functionality. Your page needs to have a top navigation menu that would move page content to the start of the corresponding sections. Create two versions—one that is using JavaScript and another that is using data attributes.

Key Takeaways

- How to display a long-content page with a navigation bar
- How to make the content visible and not hidden by the navigation bar
- How to make the last section content appear at the top of the page

- How to automatically change the active menu item as the user scrolls from top to bottom of the page

- How to use either data attributes or JavaScript to activate ScrollSpy

In the last chapter of the book, you will learn about tooltips and popovers, a very appealing feature of a page, because it gives the user extra information about the elements they interact with.

CHAPTER 11

Tooltips and Popovers

Tooltips and popovers are great tools to embed extra, secondary useful information to the content of your page. This chapter teaches you both Twitter Bootstrap tooltips and popovers.

You will create a page likc the following (Figure 11-1).

Figure 11-1. *Example Tooltip Activated*

P. Matsinopoulos, *Practical Bootstrap*, https://doi.org/10.1007/978-1-4842-6071-5_11

You will learn how to embed HTML content like the following (Figure 11-2).

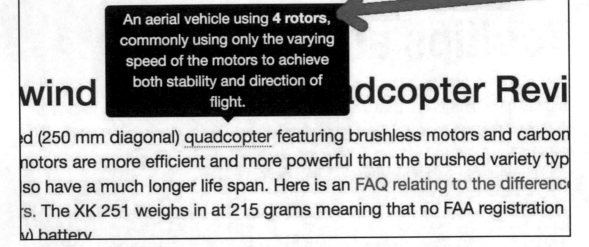

Figure 11-2. *Tooltip HTML Markup Treated As HTML—See Bold Text*

The popovers will enhance the styling of the secondary, helpful information, even more (Figure 11-3).

Figure 11-3. *Popover Example*

Learning Goals

1.   Learn about tooltips.

2.   Learn about activating tooltips and their opt-in feature.

3.   Learn how to wrap a word or phrase into proper HTML in order to attach a tooltip to it.

4.   Learn how to wrap a word or phrase into proper HTML, so that it stands out and a tooltip will appear when the user moves over it.

5.   Learn about the tooltip options that can be used to customize its behavior.

6. Learn about popovers.

7. Learn about the differences and similarities between tooltips and popovers.

8. Learn about the options of the popovers.

Tooltips

Tooltips are a very nice way to display helpful text when a user hovers over a highlighted text. So it is used to give some extra useful information, like a tip or a hint.

Here is an example of a page that uses tooltips (Figure 11-4).

Figure 11-4. *Example Page with Tooltips on Specific Words*

If you mouse over the words that are underlined with a dotted line, then you will see the tooltips. See, for example, Figure 11-5.

Figure 11-5. *Tooltip Activated*

Implementation with Twitter Bootstrap

Let's see how you can implement the preceding example. Here is the HTML page (Listing 11-1).

Listing 11-1. HTML Page with Tooltips

```
<!DOCTYPE html>
<html lang="en">
<head>
    <!-- Required meta tags -->
    <meta charset="utf-8">
    <meta name="viewport" content="width=device-width, initial-scale=1,
    shrink-to-fit=no">

    <!-- Bootstrap CSS -->
    <link rel="stylesheet" href="https://stackpath.bootstrapcdn.
    com/bootstrap/4.4.1/css/bootstrap.min.css" integrity="sha384-
    Vkoo8x4CGsO3+Hhxv8T/Q5PaXtkKtu6ug5TOeNV6gBiFeWPGFN9MuhOf23Q9Ifjh"
    crossorigin="anonymous">

    <!-- Custom CSS -->
    <link rel="stylesheet" href="stylesheets/main.css" type="text/css">

    <title>Tooltips and Popovers</title>
</head>
<body>
    <div class="container">
        <h1>Drones</h1>

        <h2>HK 251 Whirlwind Brushless Quadcopter Review</h2>

        <p>
            The XK 251 is a RTF mid-sized (250 mm diagonal) quadcopter
            featuring brushless motors and carbon fiber arms and landing
            gear.
            Brushless motors are more efficient and more powerful than the
            brushed variety typically found on toy-grade models.
            They also have a much longer life span.

            Here is an <a href="http://droneflyers.com/talk/threads/is-a-
            brushless-motor-better-than-a-brushed-motor.754/">
            FAQ relating to the difference between brushed and brushless
            motors.</a>
```

```
    The XK 251 weighs in at 215 grams meaning that no FAA
    registration is needed. It is powered by a small 2s (7.4v)
    battery.

    </p>

    <div class="text-center">
        <img src="images/drone-image.jpg" alt="Drone Image" id="drone-
        image"/>
    </div>
</div>

<!-- Optional JavaScript -->
<!-- jQuery first, then Popper.js, then Bootstrap JS -->
<script src="https://code.jquery.com/jquery-3.4.1.slim.min.js"
integrity="sha384-J6qa4849blE2+poT4WnyKhv5vZF5SrPo0iEjwBvKU7imGFAVOwwj1
yYfoRSJoZ+n" crossorigin="anonymous"></script>
<script src="https://cdn.jsdelivr.net/npm/popper.js@1.16.0/dist/umd/
popper.min.js" integrity="sha384-Q6E9RHvbIyZFJoft+2mJbHaEWldlvI9IOYy5n3
zV9zzTtmI3UksdQRVvoxMfooAo" crossorigin="anonymous"></script>
<script src="https://stackpath.bootstrapcdn.com/bootstrap/4.4.1/js/
bootstrap.min.js" integrity="sha384-wfSDF2E50Y2D1uUdjOO3uMBJnjuUD4Ih7Yw
aYd1iqfktjOUod8GCExl3Og8ifwB6" crossorigin="anonymous"></script>

    <script src="./javascripts/main.js" type="text/javascript"></script>
</body>
</html>
```

If you save the preceding code and load the page on your browser, you will see the page displayed correctly, but the tooltips will not be functional. If you mouse over the words RTF and quadcopter, you will not see the tooltips bubble up (Figure 11-6).

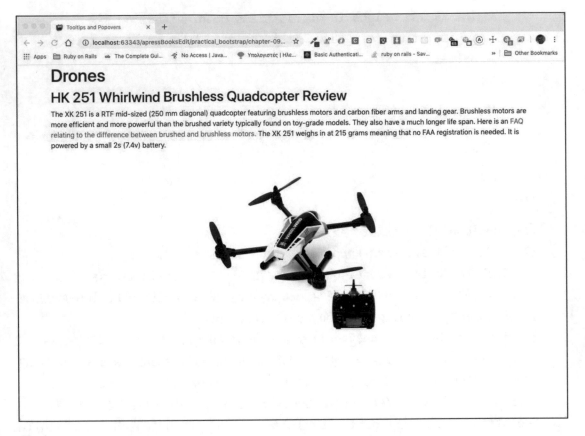

Figure 11-6. *RTF and quadcopter Do Not Have Tooltips Yet*

In order to make a word have a tooltip, you need to do the following:

1. Wrap the word into a span element. Hence, the word will not change its position with regard to the rest of the text.

2. Add the data attribute `data-toggle="tooltip"`. This will tell Bootstrap that the content of the span will be decorated with a tooltip on mouse over.

3. Add the data attribute `data-placement="top"`. This will tell Bootstrap that the tooltip needs to appear on top of the span content. Note that `data-placement` can take the value `left`, `top`, `right`, or `bottom`. Choose any value that best suits your case.

4. Add the attribute `title` having as value the text that you would like to appear on mouse over.

5. Activate the tooltips using JavaScript. This is necessary, because Bootstrap has tooltips not enabled by default. This is done for performance reasons. You have to opt in on each particular case you want tooltips in.

Let's take the preceding steps for the words RTF and quadcopter on your HTML page. Wrap the RTF word as follows:

```
<span data-toggle="tooltip" data-placement="top" title="Ready to Fly">RTF</span>
```

Wrap the quadcopter as follows:

```
<span data-toggle="tooltip" data-placement="bottom"
            title="An aerial vehicle using 4 rotors, commonly using only
            the varying speed of the motors to achieve both stability and
            direction of flight.">quadcopter</span>
```

Next, update the javascripts/main.js file as follows:

```
$(document).ready(function() {
    $('[data-toggle=tooltip]').tooltip();
});
```

This, the preceding code, is the opt-in part of the implementation, which enables tooltips for all the elements that have the data attribute data-toggle="tooltip".

If you save all the preceding code and reload the page on your browser, everything will be ready. When you mouse over the words RTF and quadcopter, you will see the tooltips.

As you can see, the tooltips are displayed on mouse over.

There is a small improvement that we have to introduce. You need to find a way to tell the user that if they mouse over a particular word, a tooltip will appear with further explanation information. If you don't do that, then the user does not know that there is a tooltip hidden behind the word.

In order to achieve that, you usually want the word with the tooltip behind to be underlined with a dotted line. Twitter Bootstrap makes your styling work here easy. Instead of wrapping the text with the tooltip inside a span, you can wrap it inside an abbr element.

Go ahead and change the spans to abbr elements.

For RTF:

```
<abbr data-toggle="tooltip" data-placement="top" title="Ready to Fly">RTF
</abbr>
```

For quadcopter:

```
<abbr data-toggle="tooltip" data-placement="top"
            title="An aerial vehicle using 4 rotors, commonly using only
            the varying speed of the motors to achieve both stability and
            direction of flight.">quadcopter</abbr>
```

When you save these changes and reload the page on your browser, you will see the words RTF and quadcopter underlined with a dotted line (Figure 11-7).

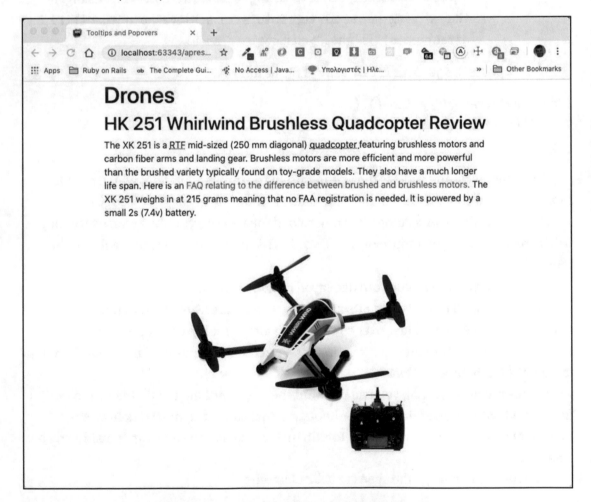

Figure 11-7. *Tooltipped Words Are Displayed Underlined*

Tooltip Options

A tooltip has a lot of different options that can be used for its customization. Let's see the most important ones:

1. `animation`: Has default value `true`. It applies a CSS fade transition when displaying the tooltip.

2. `delay`: This can be either a number or a JavaScript object. If it is a number, then it defines the delay, in milliseconds, to show or hide the tooltip. If it is an object, then it can have the `show` and `hide` properties with integer values representing the delay to show or hide, respectively.

Let's try that. We will set the delay property and see how the tooltip behaves. On the previous page, go ahead and change the `javascripts/main.js` file so that it is like Listing 11-2.

Listing 11-2. Add Delay to Tooltips

```
$(document).ready(function() {
    $('[data-toggle=tooltip]').tooltip({
        delay: {
            show: 3000, // 3 seconds
            hide: 1000  // 1 second
        }
    });
});
```

If you save the preceding code and reload the page on your browser, you will see the tooltip appear 3 seconds after you mouse over the word with the tooltip. You will also see that it disappears after 1 second from the moment you moved your mouse out of the word with the tooltip.

3. `html`: This is a Boolean option that takes the value `true` or `false`. Its default value is `false`. With `false`, the value of the `title` attribute of the tooltip element is inserted using the `.text()` method. This means that even if the title contains HTML markup, this will not actually be used; it will be treated as plain text. On the

other hand, if the html option is set to true, when you have a value on title that includes HTML markup, this will be inserted in the tooltip area using the .html() method, and, hence, the HTML markup will be respected. Let's see an example.

First, add some HTML markup to the title of the quadcopter word:

```
<abbr data-toggle="tooltip" data-placement="top"
    title="An aerial vehicle using <b>4 rotors</b>, commonly using
    only the varying speed of the motors to achieve both stability and
    direction of flight.">quadcopter</abbr>
```

You have added 4 rotors HTML markup inside the title.

Now, make sure that the javascripts/main.js file is as follows:

```
$(document).ready(function() {
    $('[data-toggle=tooltip]').tooltip({
        html: false // default value
    });
});
```

Although it is not necessary when you set the html value to false, you will need the preceding snippet in a while.

Save and load the page on your browser. When you mouse over the quadcopter word, you will see the tooltip, but the 4 rotors part will be printed verbatim, treated as plain text (Figure 11-8).

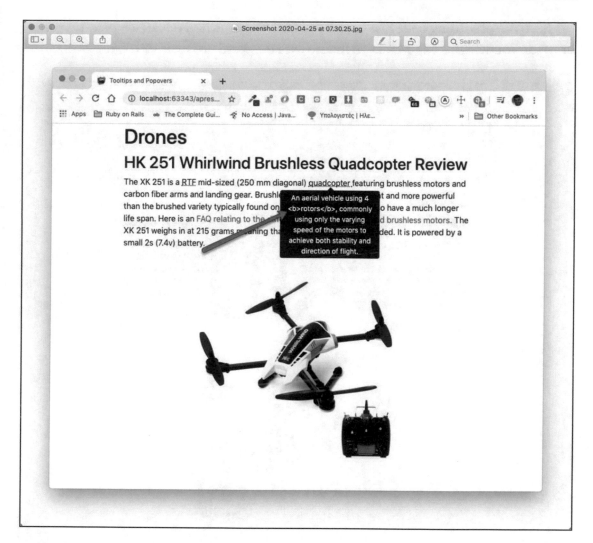

Figure 11-8. *HTML Markup Printed Verbatim*

If you want the HTML markup of the `title` attribute to be treated as HTML and rendered as such, you need to set the value of the option `html` to `true`:

```
$(document).ready(function() {
    $('[data-toggle=tooltip]').tooltip({
        html: true
    });
});
```

Save the preceding code inside `javascripts/main.js` and reload the page on your browser. You will see this when you mouse over the word quadcopter (Figure 11-9).

Figure 11-9. *Tooltip HTML Markup Treated As HTML*

As you can see, the HTML content of the `title` attribute is being displayed as an HTML fragment without problem.

Popovers

Popovers are like tooltips but allow richer and more eye-catching layout and style. Also, the target element needs to be clicked in order for the popover to appear and disappear. Here is an example of a popover (Figure 11-10).

Figure 11-10. *Popover Example*

Let's change the previous page that had tooltips on RTF and quadcopter words. You are going to put popovers.

The HTML page should be like the following (Listing 11-3).

Listing 11-3. HTML Page with Popovers

```
<!DOCTYPE html>
<html lang="en">
<head>
    <!-- Required meta tags -->
    <meta charset="utf-8">
    <meta name="viewport" content="width=device-width, initial-scale=1,
    shrink-to-fit=no">

    <!-- Bootstrap CSS -->
    <link rel="stylesheet" href="https://stackpath.bootstrapcdn.
    com/bootstrap/4.4.1/css/bootstrap.min.css" integrity="sha384-
    Vkoo8x4CGsO3+Hhxv8T/Q5PaXtkKtu6ug5TOeNV6gBiFeWPGFN9MuhOf23Q9Ifjh"
    crossorigin="anonymous">

    <!-- Custom CSS -->
    <link rel="stylesheet" href="stylesheets/main.css" type="text/css">

    <title>Popover Example Page</title>
</head>
<body>
    <div class="container">
        <h1>Drones</h1>

        <h2>HK 251 Whirlwind Brushless Quadcopter Review</h2>

        <p>
            The XK 251 is an RTF
            <a href="#"
                data-toggle="popover"
                data-placement="top"
                title="Ready to Fly"
                data-content="Ready to Fly drones are drones with the key at
                hand. You can start flying them immediately.">
                <i class="fa fa-question-circle"></i>
            </a>
```

```
mid-sized (250 mm diagonal)
quadcopter
<a href="#"
   data-toggle="popover" data-placement="top"
   title="Quadcopter"
   data-content="An aerial vehicle using <b>4 rotors</b>,
   commonly using only the varying speed of the motors to
   achieve both stability and direction of flight.">
     <i class="fa fa-question-circle"></i>
</a>
featuring brushless motors and carbon fiber arms and landing
gear.
Brushless motors are more efficient and more powerful than the
brushed variety typically found on toy-grade models.
They also have a much longer life span.

Here is an <a href="http://droneflyers.com/talk/threads/is-a-
brushless-motor-better-than-a-brushed-motor.754/">
FAQ relating to the difference between brushed and brushless
motors.</a>

The XK 251 weighs in at 215 grams meaning that no FAA
registration is needed. It is powered by a small 2s (7.4v)
battery.
    </p>

    <div class="text-center">
        <img src="images/drone-image.jpg" alt="Drone Image" id="drone-
        image"/>
    </div>
</div>

<!-- Optional JavaScript -->

<script src="https://kit.fontawesome.com/<your-font-awesome-account-
public-key.js" crossorigin="anonymous"></script>
```

```
<!-- jQuery first, then Popper.js, then Bootstrap JS -->
<script src="https://code.jquery.com/jquery-3.4.1.slim.min.js"
integrity="sha384-J6qa4849blE2+poT4WnyKhv5vZF5SrPo0iEjwBvKU7imGFAVOwwj1
yYfoRSJoZ+n" crossorigin="anonymous"></script>
<script src="https://cdn.jsdelivr.net/npm/popper.js@1.16.0/dist/umd/
popper.min.js" integrity="sha384-Q6E9RHvbIyZFJoft+2mJbHaEWldlvI9IOYy5n3
zV9zzTtmI3UksdQRVvoxMfooAo" crossorigin="anonymous"></script>
<script src="https://stackpath.bootstrapcdn.com/bootstrap/4.4.1/js/
bootstrap.min.js" integrity="sha384-wfSDF2E50Y2D1uUdj0O3uMBJnjuUD4Ih7Yw
aYd1iqfktjOUod8GCExl3Og8ifwB6" crossorigin="anonymous"></script>

<script src="./javascripts/main.js" type="text/javascript"></script>
</body>
</html>
```

This should be accompanied by the following stylesheets/main.css (Listing 11-4) and javascripts/main.js files (Listing 11-5).

Listing 11-4. *stylesheets/main.css*

```
a[data-toggle=popover] {
    text-decoration: none;
}
```

Listing 11-5. *javascripts/main.js*

```
$(document).ready(function() {
    $('[data-toggle=popover]').popover({
      html: true
    });
});
```

Note   This page is using FontAwesome again to draw the question mark icons next to the words RTF and quadcopter. In order to use FontAwesome, you have to create an account with them and generate an account-specific reference to their

JavaScript library. You have to use this reference where the preceding code has the line `<script src="https://kit.fontawesome.com/<your-font-awesome-account-public-key.js"crossorigin="anonymous"></script>`.

Here are the differences and similarities of the HTML page with popovers vs. the HTML page with tooltips:

1. For popovers, we use the following data attributes:

   1. `data-toggle="popover"`. For tooltips, we use `data-toggle="tooltip"`.

   2. `data-placement` attribute is used for both to specify the placement of the element.

   3. `title` attribute is used to specify the content of the tooltip. For popovers, this is used to specify the heading of the popover.

   4. `data-content` is used only on popovers and specifies the content of the body of the popover.

See Figure 11-11 for the header and the body of the popover and how they are related to `title` and `data-content`, respectively.

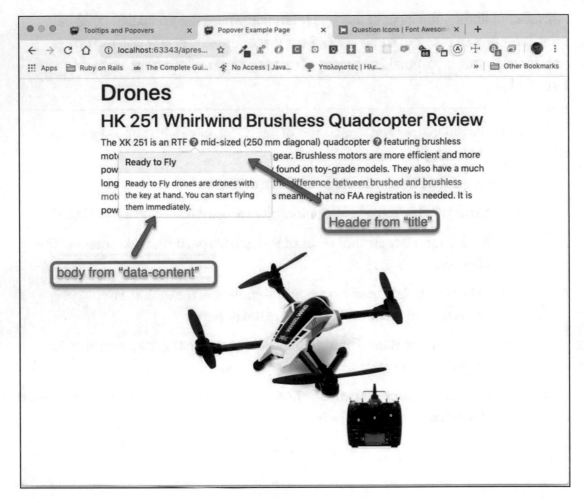

Figure 11-11. *Header and Body of the Popover*

If you save the preceding files and load the page on your browser, you will be able to click the question mark icon in order to see the popover.

As you can experience, the way you have integrated popovers has the problem that the popover can close only if the user clicks the same hot spot it is used to show the popover.

How can you allow the user to click anywhere for the popover to close? In order to achieve that, you need to change a little bit the way popovers are integrated:

1. You need to use the data attribute `data-trigger="focus"`.

2. You need to add the attribute `tabindex="0"` for the first popover, `tabindex="1"` for the second, and so on.

Let's do these updates on the popovers of your page.

For the RTF word:

```
RTF
<a href="#"
    data-toggle="popover"
    data-placement="top"
    title="Ready to Fly"
    tabindex="0"
    data-trigger="focus"
    data-content="Ready to Fly drones are drones with the key at hand. You
    can start flying them immediately.">
    <i class="fa fa-question-circle"></i>
  </a>
```

For the quadcopter word:

```
quadcopter
<a href="#"
    data-toggle="popover" data-placement="top"
    title="Quadcopter"
    tabindex="1"
    data-trigger="focus"
    data-content="An aerial vehicle using <b>4 rotors</b>, commonly using
    only the varying speed of the motors to achieve both stability and
    direction of flight.">
    <i class="fa fa-question-circle"></i>
</a>
```

If you do these changes and you reload the page, then you will be able to close the popover by clicking anywhere on the page.

Tip   When you click to open a popover, you will see a blue border around the question mark icon, while the popover has the focus. You can get rid of it by applying the following CSS rule:

```
a[data-toggle=popover]:focus {outline: transparent;}
```

Options

Like tooltips, popovers have various options. Some of the most useful ones are the following:

1. `animation`: Takes a Boolean value `true` or `false`. The default value is `true`. It applies CSS fade transition to the popover.

2. `delay`: This is either a number or an object. This works exactly like the `delay` option for the tooltips.

3. `html`: Boolean with default value `false`. If `true`, it allows the content to be parsed as HTML rather than plain text.

Tasks and Quizzes

TASK DETAILS

1. You need to develop a web page that demonstrates both the tooltips and the popovers.

2. Try to create a page like the following (for this page, the whole content has been taken from Wikipedia) (Figure 11-12).

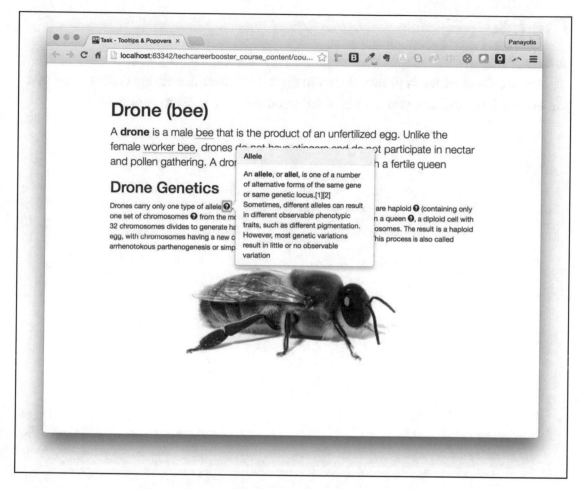

Figure 11-12. *Task Page with Tooltips and Popovers*

Key Takeaways

- How to create tooltips that appear when a user's mouse moves over a special word or phrase

- How to create popovers that appear when a user clicks an icon

The End

Congratulations!

You are done with this practical encounter with Twitter Bootstrap! I really hope that you enjoyed this trip and you learned things that you can apply to your projects.

Index

O

P, Q

R

X

[x] button, 392, 401

Y

YouTube embedded video
 reference, 407–410

Z

z-index property, 267

Printed in the United States
By Bookmasters